An Essay on I

Its Forms, Its Causes, Its Development and Its Value

James Sully

Alpha Editions

This edition published in 2021

ISBN : 9789354943072

Design and Setting By
Alpha Editions
www.alphaedis.com
Email - info@alphaedis.com

As per information held with us this book is in Public Domain.
This book is a reproduction of an important historical work. Alpha Editions
uses the best technology to reproduce historical work in the same manner
it was first published to preserve its original nature. Any marks or number
seen are left intentionally to preserve its true form.

Contents

PREFACE. - 1 -

CHAPTER I.
INTRODUCTORY. - 2 -

CHAPTER II.
THE SMILE AND THE LAUGH. - 17 -

CHAPTER III.
OCCASIONS AND CAUSES OF LAUGHTER. - 32 -

CHAPTER IV.
VARIETIES OF THE LAUGHABLE. - 51 -

CHAPTER V.
THEORIES OF THE LUDICROUS. - 74 -

CHAPTER VI
THE ORIGIN OF LAUGHTER. - 96 -

CHAPTER VII.
DEVELOPMENT OF LAUGHTER DURING THE
FIRST THREE YEARS OF LIFE. - 114 -

CHAPTER VIII.
THE LAUGHTER OF SAVAGES. - 135 -

CHAPTER IX.
LAUGHTER IN SOCIAL EVOLUTION. - 154 -

CHAPTER X.
 LAUGHTER OF THE INDIVIDUAL: HUMOUR. - 180 -

CHAPTER XI.
THE LAUGHABLE IN ART: COMEDY. - 209 -

CHAPTER XII.
ULTIMATE VALUE AND LIMITATIONS OF
LAUGHTER.   - 238 -

NOTES   - 263 -

PREFACE.

The present work is, I believe, the first attempt to treat on a considerable scale the whole subject of Laughter, under its various aspects, and in its connections with our serious activities and interests. As such, it will, I feel sure, lay itself open to the criticism that it lacks completeness, or at least, proportion. A further criticism to which, I feel equally sure, it will expose itself, is that it clearly reflects the peculiarities of the experience of the writer. The anticipation of this objection does not, however, disturb me. It seems to me to be not only inevitable, but desirable—at least at the present stage of our knowledge of the subject—that one who attempts to understand an impulse, of which the intensities and the forms appear to vary greatly among men, of which the workings are often subtle, and of which the significance is by no means obvious, should, while making full use of others' impressions, draw largely on his own experience.

Portions of the volume have already appeared in Reviews. Chapter I. was published (under the title "Prolegomena to a Theory of Laughter") in *The Philosophical Review*, 1900; Chapter V., in the *Revue Philosophique*, 1902; and Chapter VIII., in *The International Monthly*, 1901. The parts of Chapters III. and VI. which treat of the psychology of tickling appeared in the *Compte rendu* of the Fourth International Congress of Psychology (*IVme Congrès International de Psychologie*), Paris, 1901. Some of the ideas in Chapter X. are outlined in an article on "The Uses of Humour," which appeared in *The National Review*, 1897.

Some of my obligations to other writers and workers have been acknowledged in the volume. For friendly assistance in reading the proofs of the work I am greatly indebted to Mr. Carveth Read, Dr. Alexander Hill, Prof. W. P. Ker, Mr. Ling Roth, Dr. W. H. R. Rivers, Miss C. Osborn, and Miss Alice Woods.

CHAPTER I.
INTRODUCTORY.

A writer who undertakes to discourse on laughter has to encounter more than one variety of irritating objection. He finds to his dismay that a considerable part of his species, which has been flatteringly described as the laughing animal, has never exercised its high and distinguishing capacity. Nay, more, he soon learns that a good many oppose themselves to the practice and are laughter-haters. This kind of person (ὁ μισόγελως) is so possessed with the spirit of seriousness that the opposite temper of jocosity appears to him to be something shockingly wrong. All audible laughter is for him an ill-bred display, at once unsightly as a bodily contortion, and, as a lapse from the gravity of reason, a kind of mental degradation. This estimate of laughter as something unseemly is well represented in Lord Chesterfield's *Letters,* in which the writer congratulates himself on the fact that since he has had the full use of his reason nobody has ever heard him laugh. In some cases this feeling of repugnance towards mirth and fun takes on more of an ethical aspect. The laugher is identified with the scoffer at all things worthy and condemned as morally bad—a view illustrated in the saying of Pascal: "Diseur de bons mots, mauvais caractère".

Now it seems evident that one who discourses on laughter is bound to notice this attitude of the laughter-hater. If he believes that the moods of hilarity and the enjoyment of the ludicrous have their rightful place in human experience, he must be ready to challenge the monopoly of wisdom claimed by the out-and-out sticklers for seriousness, and to dispute the proposition that the open, honest laugh connotes either a vulgar taste or a depraved moral nature.

Perhaps, however, our discourser need not distress himself about these rather sour-tempered laughter-haters. In these days we have to confront not so much opposition as indifference. Instead of the denouncer of mirth as vulgar or wicked, we have the refrainer from laughter, the non-laugher pure and simple. As his Greek name "agelast" (ἀγέλαστος) suggests, this rather annoying type was not unknown in ancient times. In merry England, too, Shakespeare had met with the agelasts who would

Not show their teeth in way of smile,

Though Nestor swear the jest be laughable.

Yet it is only of late that the variety has appeared in its full force. To what scanty proportions in these latter days the band of laughers has dwindled is suggested by the name which is now commonly given them, for "humorist" meant not so long ago an odd fellow or "eccentric". Indeed, one of our living writers suggests that "as the world becomes more decorous humour becomes tongue-tied and obsolete".1

Even if we grant that the "gelasts" are getting reduced to the dimensions of a petty sect, the consideration need not deter us from choosing laughter as our theme. Those who have the perfect ear for music are probably but a tiny portion of the human family; yet nobody has suggested that this is an argument against the writing of books on musical form, the science of thorough bass and the rest.

The friends of laughter have, however, always existed, and even in these rather dreary days are perhaps more numerous than is often supposed. In support of this idea one may recall the curious fact that, as the essayist just quoted remarks, we all shrink from the "awful imputation" implied in the words "You have no sense of humour". This recognition of the capacity for appreciating a joke as a human attribute which it is well not to be without is, of course, very far from being proof of a genuine love of fun in the recognisers themselves. Yet it at least attests the existence of this love in a respectable number of their fellows.

Now this true friend of laughter (ὁ φιλόγελως) may urge his own objection to our proposed discussion, an objection less irritating perhaps than that of the zealous laughter-hater and of the indifferent agelast, but on the other hand of a more penetrating thrust. He not unnaturally dislikes the idea of his daily pastime being made the subject of grave inquiry. He feels in its acutest form the resentment of the natural man on seeing his enjoyment brought under the scalpel and lens of the scientific inquirer. He urges with force that the chucklings of humour are the very lightest and flimsiest of human things; and that to try to capture them and subject them to serious investigation looks much like the procedure of the child whose impulsive hand would seize and examine his dainty soap bubbles.

To these objections from the true friends of the mirthful god one owes it to reply courteously and at length. Yet the answer cannot well be given at the outset. A discourse on laughter can remove this kind of objection, if at all, only by showing in its own treatment of the subject that serious thought may touch even the gossamer wing of the merry sprite and not destroy; that all things, and so the lightest, are things to be comprehended, if only we can reach the right points of view; and that the problems which rise above the mental horizon, as soon as we begin to think about man's humorous bent, have a quite peculiar interest, an interest in which all who can both laugh at things and ponder on them may be expected to share.

It seems evident that one who is to probe the spirit of fun in man, and to extract its meaning, should have special qualifications. It is by no means sufficient, as some would seem to suppose, that he should be able to think clearly. He must couple with the gravity of the thinker something of the intellectual lightness and nimbleness of the jester. That is to say, he must be in warm touch with his theme, the jocose mood itself, realising his subject at once vividly and comprehensively by help of a rich personal experience.

Now it cannot be said that those who have offered to teach us the secrets of laughter have commonly exhibited these qualifications in a conspicuous measure. It is a part of the whimsicality which seems to run through human affairs that the spirit of fun should be misunderstood not merely by the avowedly indifferent and the avowedly hostile, but by those who, since they offer to elucidate its ways, might be expected to have some personal acquaintance with it. The combination of a fine feeling for the baffling behaviour of this spirit with a keen scientific analysis, such as is found in Mr. George Meredith's *Essay on Comedy*, seems to be a rarity in literature.

This want of the familiar touch is especially observable in a good deal of the treatment of laughter by philosophic writers. It is not necessary to dwell on the sublime subtleties of the metaphysicians who conceive of the comic as a "moment" in the dialectic process which the æsthetic "Idea" has to pass through. The account of the gyrations which the Idea has to describe, when once it passes out of that state of harmonious union with the sensuous image which we call "the beautiful," reads strangely enough. Having, for reasons that are not made too clear, torn itself away from its peaceful companion (the image), and set itself up as antagonist to this in "the sublime," the august Idea encounters the unpleasant retaliation of the image it has discarded in "the ugly," where we see the determination of the injured party to defy its late companion; though, in the end, it revives from the "swoon" into which this rude behaviour of the image has plunged it, and recovers its legitimate claims—with which it would seem it was at the outset dissatisfied—in what we call "the ludicrous".

I have here tried to put the speculative subtleties of these Hegelian writers, so far as I am able to catch their drift, into intelligible English, and not to caricature them. Even favourable critics of these theories have found it difficult not to treat them with some amount of irony; and, so far as I am aware, no rehabilitator of Hegelian thought in England has as yet been bold enough to introduce to our insular mind a chapter of the sacred mysteries which, as they may well suspect, so easily lends itself to profane jesting.

How remote this kind of conception of the ludicrous is from the homely laughter of mortals may be seen in such attempts as are made by these Hegelian thinkers to connect the two. Hegel himself, in touching on the nature of comedy, asserted that "only that is truly comic in which the persons of the play are comic for themselves as well as for the spectators".

This seems to mean (it is always hazardous to say confidently what a Hegelian pronouncement does mean) that a large part of what the world has foolishly supposed to be comedy, including the plays of Molière, are not so.2

It is, perhaps, too much to expect that the aspiring metaphysician, when, as he fondly thinks, he has gained the altitude from which the dialectic process of the World-idea is seen to unfold itself, should trouble himself about so vulgar a thing as our everyday laughter. But laughter has its mild retaliations for the negligent, and the comedian of to-day, as of old, is more likely to pluck from those who tread the speculative cloud-heights material for his merriment than any further enlightenment on the mysteries of his craft.

It is, however, more to the purpose to refer to those theorists who make some show of explaining what the ordinary man understands by the ludicrous, and of testing their theories by an appeal to recognisable examples. It is instructive to note the cautiousness with which they will sometimes venture on the slippery "empirical" ground. Schopenhauer, for example, in setting out his theory of the ludicrous—a theory which we shall deal with later on—in the first volume of his chief work, thought it "superfluous" to illustrate his theory by example. In the second volume, however, he comes to the help of the "intellectual sluggishness" of his readers and condescends to furnish illustrations. And what does the reader suppose is the first to be selected? The amusing look of the angle formed by the meeting of the tangent and the curve of the circle; which look is due, he tells us, to the reflection that an angle implies the meeting of two lines which, when prolonged, intersect, whereas the straight line of the tangent and the carve of the circle are able merely to graze at one point, where, strictly speaking, they are parallel. In other words, we laugh here because the angle which stares us in the face is irreconcilable with the idea of a meeting of a tangent and a curved line. With a charming candour the writer proceeds: "The ludicrous in this case is, no doubt, extremely weak; on the other hand, it illustrates with exceptional clearness the origin of the ludicrous in the incongruity between what is thought and what is perceived".3

The significance of this invention of his own illustration by Schopenhauer is that he was not a metaphysical recluse, but knew the world and its literatures. Other theorists have not shown the same daring, but have contented themselves with *finding* their instances. Yet in too many cases the arbitrary way in which illustrations have been selected, while instances making against the theory have been ignored, shows clearly enough that there has been no serious effort to build on a large and firm basis of observation. This may be illustrated not only from the works of Germans, but from those of a people which has claimed, and with justice, to be the laughing nation *par excellence*. In a recent volume, marked by great ingenuity, M. Henri Bergson,4 an accomplished thinker, attempts to reduce all forms of the ludicrous to a substitution in our movements, speech and action, of the rigidity (raideur) of a machine for the pliancy and variability of an organism. The writer has no difficulty in finding examples of the stiff mechanical effects which amuse us, say, in gestures and carriage. But the astonishing thing is that he never refers to the complementary group of facts, the instances of excessive spontaneity and freedom of movement where a certain repression and mechanical uniformity are looked for. The exuberant childish boundings of the clown, an excess of emphasis or gesture in social intercourse, these and the like are surely just as comical as the want of the signs of a full play of life may be in other circumstances.

Perhaps an even worse offence than ignoring facts is trying to twist them into a shape that will fit an adopted theory. This occurs, too, and frequently, among writers on our subject. Here is an example among recent theorists. According to a French essayist, when we laugh at a clown pushing hard against an open door, we do not laugh merely at the absurd disproportion between the task to be accomplished and the amount of effort put into it. We only laugh when our minds pass to *a second and reflective stage*, and recognise that the man does not perceive the door to be open, when, consequently, we are able to view the disproportionate and quite needless exertion as natural.5 A more striking instance of inability to understand the swift movement of common men's laughter it would be difficult to find. As we shall see, theories of laughter, like theories of Shakespeare's genius, have frequently come to grief by projecting behind the thing which they seek to account for too much of the author's own habitual reflectiveness.6

Perhaps we shall the better see how theorists have been wont to ignore and to misunderstand the laughing experiences of the plain man if we examine at some length the mode of dealing with the subject adopted by a writer who holds a high place among contemporary psychologists. Prof. Lipps has recently elaborated a theory of the ludicrous, illustrating it at some length.7 This theory may be described as a modification of Kant's, which places the cause of laughter in "the sudden transformation of a tense expectation into nothing". According to Lipps, we have the "comic" when "the little" measures itself with something else and so steps into the daylight. There is a mental movement (Vorstellungsbewegung) from a presentation relatively great or important to one relatively little or unimportant; and the impression of the comic depends on the nullification of the latter through its contrariety to the former and the disappointment which this involves. What may be called the belittling idea—which the reader must bear in mind is the important one—always comes first, the belittled or nullified one, always second.

In order to illustrate his point he takes among other examples that of a hat on the wrong head. A man topped by a child's small cap, and a child covered with a man's big hat are, he tells us, equally comical. But the reason is different in the two cases. In the first, starting with the perception of the worthy man, we expect an adequate head-covering, and this expectation is nullified by the obstinate presence of the tiny cap. Here, then, the funny feature, the belittled thing, is the diminutive cap. In the second case, however, the movement of thought is just the reverse. We here set out with the perception of the headgear, not with that of its wearer. It is the dignified man's hat that now first fixes our attention, and it is the obtrusion of the child beneath when we expect the proper wearer which is the comical feature. In other words, when a man puts on a baby's cap it is the cap which is absurd, when a baby dons his father's cylinder it is the baby which is absurd.

This is ingenious, one must confess, but does it not involve some twisting of facts? Would the unphilosophic humorist recognise this account of the ways of laughter? Has this account the note of familiarity with these ways? Let us see.

At the outset one may enter a modest protest against the quiet assumption that the two incidents here selected are laughable in an equal degree. It may be urged that, to the grown-up spectator at least, the sight of the little one crowned with the whelming headgear of his sire is immeasurably more amusing than the other. Here the author strikes one as proceeding rather hastily, as he seems to do also when he assumes that an exceptionally big and an exceptionally little nose are equally palpable examples of the laughable. This is, to say the least, disputable. One can hardly think of a comedy turning on the smallness of a person's nose, as the *Cyrano de Bergerac* of M. Rostand turns on its bigness. But this objection need not, perhaps, be pressed.

Passing, then, to the explanation of his two examples offered by the author, we are first of all struck by the apparent arbitrariness of the supposition, that the movement of thought which he assumes should in the one case take exactly the reverse direction of that taken in the other. Seeing that both are instances of a grotesquely unsuitable head-covering should one not expect the enjoyment of them to spring out of a similar kind of mental activity?

The author probably means to say that we tend to fix the attention on the more dignified feature in each case, the man beneath the tiny cap, and the man's hat above the tiny head. But that is far from being certain. And in any case there are good reasons against assuming a "contrary motion" of thought here. Dr. Lipps will no doubt allow, as a trained psychologist, that these intellectual movements are subject to well-recognised laws. One deduction from these is that the sight of a hat will suggest the idea of the human figure to which it belongs much more certainly and more powerfully than the sight of the figure will suggest the idea of its appropriate covering. I believe that everybody's experience will confirm this. A hat seen even in a shop-window starts the impulse to think of some wearer; but who would say that seeing a human head, say across the dinner-table or in an adjoining stall at the theatre, prompts us to think of its proper covering? Special circumstances, such as the presence of an exceptional baldness appealing to pity, must be added before our thoughts flit to the out-of-door receptacle. In other words, the whole interest and significance of a hat lie in a reference to a wearer, but not *vice versâ*.

We must, then, reject the idea of a double and opposed movement of thought here. If any movement takes place it must be assumed to be in each case a transition from the perception of the hat to the idea of its customary and proper wearer.

Now, are we aware when we laugh at either of these odd sights of carrying out this movement of thought? Keeping to the indisputable case of the child's head under or in the man's hat, do we, before the agreeable spasm seizes us, first mentally grasp the hat and then pass to the idea of its rightful wearer? I, at least, cannot find this to be true in my own experience. But such inability may be due to the absence of a sufficiently delicate introspection. Let us then try to test the point in another way.

If the smile of amusement with which we greet this spectacle comes from the dissolution of the idea of the adult male figure, we should expect the enjoyment of the ludicrous aspect to be especially conspicuous when the hat appears an instant before the child-wearer, and so thought is compelled to travel in the required direction. Let us suppose that a child in his nursery puts on his father's hat and stands on a chair, and that you enter the room and catch a glimpse of the hat first, say above a piece of furniture, and for a brief moment expect to see an adult beneath. No doubt you will be aware of a definite movement of thought in the required direction and of the dissolution into nothing of the expectant idea. But will the element of clear anticipation and its annihilation intensify your feeling of the funniness of the spectacle, or even make the funniness more patent? You would, no doubt, in such a case, experience a little shock, the full excitement of surprise, and that might add volume to the whole feeling of the moment. You might, too, not improbably, laugh more heartily, for you would have a sense of having been taken in, and there would be a side-current of hilarity directed against yourself. But I venture to affirm that the spectacle as such would not impress you as being one whit more ludicrous when seen in this way, first the hat and then the wearer, than if your eye had lighted on the two together.

What seems to happen when we are amused by this little comic scene in the nursery? Do we not at a glance perceive a grotesque whole, *viz.*, a hat on the wrong head, and is not our amusement too swiftly forthcoming to allow of our singling out a part of what is seen and going through the process of thought described by the ingenious author of this theory? Science seems to bear out what common observation discovers, for the newer psychology teaches that in the first moment of perceiving an object we obtain not a distinct apprehension of parts, but a vague apprehension of a whole into which detail and definiteness only come later and gradually.

An *ensemble*, which can only be described as a whole made up of ill-fitting parts, this seems to be the object on which our attention is focussed when we laugh at the child under the needlessly capacious hat. This intuition involves, no doubt, some rapid seizing of details: but the attention to parts is not to separate objects, as the language of Dr. Lipps suggests, but to related parts, to the hat as worn in relation to the wearer.

This seems to be an adequate account of what takes place so far as it is the palpable unfitness of dimensions which moves us to laughter. But it may be urged, and rightly urged, that the laughable spectacle is more than this, that what tickles us is the uncustomary and topsy-turvy arrangement of things. And here, it may be said, there certainly is implied a movement of thought, namely, to something outside the spectacle, to what is customary and in order.

The supposition is a highly plausible one. Since, moreover, what we perceive is a whole, it is reasonable to assume that if such a movement occurs it must be, not, as Dr. Lipps supposes, from one part of it to another, but from the present whole as oddly and wrongly composed to some other whole as rightly composed. Do we not, it may be asked, here carry out a process fairly well described in Schopenhauer's theory of the ludicrous, that is, conceive of "an incongruity between the real object and its idea," and so, by implication, go back to this idea?

To this I would reply that, so far as I can analyse my own mental state at such a moment, I do not find the presence of any idea of another and normal whole to be a necessary element in a full enjoyment of the grotesque whole before my eyes. Such a second whole would, one supposes, have to be either the same hat on the right head, or the same head under its proper covering, and I find that I am perfectly well able to enjoy the comedy of the child crowned with the tall hat without making present to my mind either of these combinations.

Here, again, I think, a better scientific theory bears out the result of one's individual self-examination. Psychology has made it clear that in recognising an object, say a weasel crossing the road on which we are walking, we do not need to have present to our mind (in addition to the perception of the object) a pictorial idea or image of a weasel as formed from past observations. Owing to the organising of a certain perceptual disposition—a readiness to see an object as a familiar one, as of a particular "sort"—our mind instantly greets it as a weasel. In other words, we recognise things by the help not of images present to the mind at the moment, but of certain ingrained "apperceptive" tendencies or attitudes. All the higher animals seem to share with us this highly useful capability of immediate and instantaneous recognition.

Now I take it that there is another side to these apperceptive tendencies. Not only do they secure for us, without the necessity of calling up distinct ideas, these instant recognitions of a sort of thing, they enable us as well as intelligent animals mentally to reject presentations which do not answer to "the sort of thing". I can say that this wax figure is not a man without having any distinct image of the living man present to my consciousness. This ability to recognise what we see as not of a particular kind of thing, without calling up a definite idea of this kind, extends to combinations and arrangements of parts in a whole. When, after my servant has dusted my books and rearranged them on the shelves, I instantly recognise that they are wrongly placed, I may at the moment be quite unable to say what the right arrangement was.8

According to my view, the perceptions of the laughable which Dr. Lipps illustrates are instantaneous perceptions. As such, they may, and commonly do, arise immediately, that is, without any reversion to the idea of what is the customary or normal arrangement.

But the reader may urge with force that the enjoyment of this charming bit of childish pretence involves more than a perception of the unusual and the irregular. Do we not at least apprehend the fact that the hat is not merely unfitting, and grotesquely wrong, but a usurpation of the prerogative of the superior? Is not the behaviour of the child so deliciously whimsical just because we fix the mental eye on this element of make-believe? And if so, does not this imply that we have present to the mind the proper belongings of the hat, *viz.*, the father's head and figure?

I readily agree that when we make our perceptions reflective, as we may do, this idea is apt to emerge. As has been implied above, the sight of the tall hat does tend to suggest the idea of its usual wearer, and in lingering on this quaint bit of acting we may not improbably catch ourselves imagining the hat on the right head, especially as we see that it is the child's playful aim to personate the privileged owner. And the same thing might occur in laughing at the father topped with the small child's hat; for the laugher, who would in this case more probably be a child, might naturally enough reinstate in imaginative thought the small child's head to which the cap belongs. This combination seems at least to be much more likely to recur to the imagination than the other combination, which retaining the wearer substitutes the idea of the right hat.

How far any distinct image of the hat thus mentally transferred to the right wearer enters into the appreciation of this humorous spectacle, it would be hard to say. Different minds may behave differently here. Judging from my own experience I should say that at most only a vague "schematic" outline of the proper arrangement presents itself to the imagination. This seems to me to be what one might naturally expect. Laughter, as I conceive of it, fastens upon something human. It is the living wearer that is emphasised in the comical juxtaposition; we more naturally describe it as the child wearing his father's hat, than as the father's hat on the child. And for the comic effect it is sufficient that we recognise the hat to be the father's. This we can do without mentally picturing the hat as worn by the father. The hat has become a symbol, and means for us the man's hat and the dignity which belongs to this, though we may have at the time no mental image of it as worn by its rightful possessor.

Our examination seems to show that this apparently simple example of the laughable is very inadequately accounted for by supposing a movement of mind from one presentation or idea to another which contravenes and nullifies the first. It may be added that, with respect to what is certainly present to our consciousness, when we look at this bit of child's play we do not find the relation of part to part to be merely one of contrariety. A curious fact, not as yet fully studied by the psychologist, is what may be called the inter-diffusion of characters between the several parts of a complex presentation. The figure of a finely dressed lady in a gathering of poor people may either throw the shabby look of the latter into greater relief by contrast, or redeem it from its shabbiness by lending it some of its own glory. The latter effect is favoured by a certain contemplative attitude which disposes us to look at the whole as such, and with the least amount of inspection of details and their relations. When we regard the child in the big hat a semblance of the dignity which lies in the meaning of the latter is transferred to the small head; and the mental seizure of this transferred look of dignity by the spectator is essential to a full enjoyment of the show as a bit of make-believe, of innocent hypocrisy. Similarly, if we are disposed to laugh, a little contemptuously, at the man in the child's hat, it is because the hat throws for half a moment over the heavy and lined face something of the fresh sweet look of infancy.9

It has seemed worth while to examine at some length the attempt of Dr. Lipps to deal with a simple instance of the laughable because, in spite of a recognisable effort to connect theory with concrete facts, it illustrates the common tendency to adapt the facts to the theory; and, further, the no less common tendency to overlook the rich variety of experience which our laughter covers, the multiplicity of the sources of our merriment and the way in which these may co-operate in the enjoyable contemplation of a ludicrous object. As we shall see, theories of the ludicrous have again and again broken down from attempting to find one uniform cause in a domain where the operation of "Plurality of Causes" is particularly well marked.

It may be added that such theories, even if they were not one-sided and forced accounts of the sources of our merriment, would still suffer from one fatal defect: as Lotze says of Kant's doctrine,10 they make no attempt to show why the dissolved expectation or the failure to subsume a presentation under an idea should make us *laugh*, rather than, let us say, cough or sigh. Lotze, besides being a psychologist, was a physiologist, and it may be added, a humorist in a quiet way, and the reader of his lines who may have had the privilege of knowing him will see again the ironical little pout and the merry twinkle of the dark eye behind the words.

We have agreed that the discourser on the comic, however gravely philosophic he desires to be, must touch both finely and comprehensively the common experiences of mankind. Yet it may well be thought, in the light of the attempts made in the past, that this is demanding too much. The relish for things which feed our laughter is as we know a very variable endowment. As the Master tells us, "A jest's prosperity lies in the ear of him that hears it more than in the tongue of him that makes it". The facetiæ of earlier ages fall on modern ears with a sound as dull as that of an unstrung drum. It may well be that persons who pass a large number of their hours in abstruse reflection grow incapable of enjoying many of the commoner varieties of laughter. Their capability of lapsing into the jocose vein becomes greatly restricted and may take directions that seem out-of-the-way to the more habitual laugher. Schopenhauer's funny little attempt to extract a joke out of the meeting of the tangent and the circle seems to be a case in point. On reading some of the definitions of the ludicrous contributed by the fertile German mind, one is forced to conclude that the writers had their own peculiar, esoteric modes of laughter. When, for example, Herr St. Schütze, whose "attempt at a theory of the Comic" is pronounced by the renowned Th. Vischer to be "excellent" (vorzüglich), proceeds to define his subject in this way: "The comic is a perception or idea, which after some moments excites the obscure feeling that nature carries on a merry game with man while he thinks himself free to act, in which game the circumscribed liberty of man is mocked (verspottet) by a reference to a higher liberty,"11 one seems to measure the scope of the worthy writer's sense of fun. That the irony of things in their relation to our desires and aims has its amusing aspect is certain: but who that knows anything of the diversified forms of human mirth could ever think of trying to drag all of them under so narrow a rubric?

A vivid perception of the variability of the sense of the laughable in man, of the modification, in the case of individuals and of races, of the range of its play, and of the standards to which it subjects itself, by a thousand unknown influences of temperament and habits of life, may well repel not merely the philosophic recluse who can hardly be expected perhaps to have followed far the many wild excursions of the laughing impulse, but others as well. Have we not, it may be asked, in the appreciation of what is funny or laughable a mode of sensibility pre-eminently erratic, knowing no law, and incapable therefore of being understood? Do not the more grotesque attempts to frame theories of the subject seem to mock the search for law where no law is?

The difficulty may be admitted whilst the practical conclusion drawn is rejected. Certainly no thinker will succeed in throwing light on the dark problem who does not strenuously fight against the narrowing influences of his "subjectivity," who does not make a serious effort to get outside the bounds of his personal preferences, and to compass in large vision the far-ranging play of the mirthful spirit, and the endless differencing of its manifestations. But if a man can only succeed in doing this without losing his head in the somewhat rollicking scene, there is nothing that need repel him from the task; for reason assures us that here too, just as in other domains of human experience where things looked capricious and lawless enough at the outset, order and law will gradually disclose themselves.

A serious inquiry into the subject, such as we propose to make, must, it is evident, start from this scientific presupposition. We take the language of everyday life to imply that human laughter, notwithstanding its variability, its seeming caprices, is subject to law. We speak of an objective region of "the laughable," that is of objects and relations of objects which are fitted and which tend to excite laughter in us all alike. It will be one of our chief problems to determine the characteristics of this field of the laughable, and to define its boundaries.

But a serious inquiry will take us farther than this. While we do well to insist that the lightness and capriciousness of movement, the swift unpredictable coming and going, are of the essence of laughter, it will be one main object of this inquiry to show how our mirthful explosions, our sportive railleries, are attached at their very roots to our serious interests. Laughter, looked at from this point of view, has its significance as a function of the human organism, and as spreading its benefits over all the paths of life. We must probe this value of our laughing moments if we are to treat the subject adequately.

In thus proposing to give to laughter a purpose in the scheme of human life, one must face the risk of offending its friends yet more deeply. To these laughter is so precious and sufficing a good in itself, that to propose to connect it with some extrinsic and serious purpose looks like robbing it of its delicious freeness and enslaving it to its traditional foe, excess of seriousness. To these objectors it may suffice to say at the present stage that their apprehension appears to me to be groundless. To laugh away the spare moments will continue to be to the laughter-loving the same delightful pastime even should we succeed in showing that it brings other blessings in its train. On the other hand, to show that it does bring these blessings may turn out to be a handy *argumentum ad hominem* in meeting the attacks of the laughter-hater. He could not, one supposes, give himself quite so much of the look of flouted virtue if we could convince him that laughter, when perfect freedom is guaranteed it in its own legitimate territory, will unasked, and, indeed, unwittingly, throw refreshing and healing drops on the dry pastures of life. Perhaps some thought of these benefits was present to the Greek philosopher—the very same who was for banishing Homer and other poets from his ideal commonwealth—when he uttered the pretty conceit that the Graces in searching for a temple which would not fall, found the soul of Aristophanes.

Our subject is a large one, and we must endeavour to keep all parts of it steadily in view. To begin with, we will try to avoid the error of those who in their subtle disquisitions on the comic idea forgot that laughter is a bodily act, and not fear to allude to such unmetaphysical entities as lung and diaphragm, where they seem to be a central fact in the situation. A careful examination of the very peculiar behaviour of our respiratory and other organs when the feeling of the comic seizes us, seems to belong to a scientific investigation of the subject. Indeed, it appears to me that in trying to get at the meaning of these gentle and enjoyable shakings of the mind, we shall do well to start, so to speak, with the bodily shakings, which are, to say the least, much more accessible to study.

Further, it seems desirable to study the utterances of the spirit of fun through the whole gamut of its expression. The *gros rire,* the cacophonous guffaw, must not be regarded as too vulgar to be admitted here. The attempts in the past to build up a theory of the ludicrous have commonly failed through a fastidious and highly artificial restriction of the laughable attribute to the field of wit and refined humour which the cultivated man is in the habit of enjoying.

Nor is this all. It may possibly be found that no satisfactory explanation of our enjoyment of the laughable is obtainable without taking a glance at forms of mirth which have preceded it. Among the strange things said about laughter is surely the sentence of Bacon: "In laughing there ever precedeth a conceit of something ridiculous, and therefore it is proper to man". That the father of the inductive philosophy should have approached the subject in this way is one of the ironies that meet us in these discussions; for, allowing that he is right as to his fact that only man laughs, we must surely recognise that his reason is hopelessly weak. The conceit which Bacon here talks about is, we all know, by no means a universal accompaniment of laughter; and, what is more important, even when it occurs it is wont to grow distinct rather in the form of an afterthought than in that of an antecedent. Among all things human, surely laughter ought least of all to be afraid of recognising its humble kinsfolk.

The importance of thus sweeping into our scientific net specimens of all grades of laughter will be seen when it is recognised that the one promising way of dealing with this subject is to trace its development from its earliest and crudest forms. If we begin at the top of the evolutionary scheme, and take no account of the lower grades, we are very likely to fail to penetrate to the core of the laughable, as so many of our predecessors have failed. But if we will only stoop to consider its manifestations at the lowest discoverable levels, and then confine ourselves to the more modest problem: How did the first laughter, mindless as it may well seem to us, get developed and differentiated into the variety of forms which make up the humorous experience of civilised man? we may win a modest success.

It will be evident that any attempt to pursue this line of inquiry will have to take note, not only of facts obtainable from the realm of primitive laughter as represented by infancy and the savage state, but of those social forces which have had so much to do with shaping the manifestations of mirth. The common directions of our laughter attest its social character and illustrate how it has insinuated itself into the many movements of social life.

For a like reason we shall need to discuss to some extent the place of laughter in Art, and the treatment of the sources of merriment by the comedian.

Lastly, this larger consideration of the subject will, we shall probably find, take us to an examination of certain ethical or practical questions, *viz.*, the value which is to be assigned to the laughing propensity, and the proper limits to be set to its indulgence.

The subject so conceived is a large and complex one, and it will be hard to deal with it at once thoughtfully and familiarly, with the genuine ring of laughter ever present to the ear. The present writer will account himself happy if, in a line where so many appear to have missed success, he attain to a moderate measure of it.

CHAPTER II.
THE SMILE AND THE LAUGH.

To treat the facts with proper respect seems to be more than ordinarily incumbent on us in dealing with the nature and the significance of our laughter. This means, as already hinted, that some inquiry be made into the act of laughing itself, the manner of it, and the circumstances which accompany it, and that this inquiry be carried out in the most comprehensive way possible.

We grave elders are wont to think of laughing and smiling as something quite occasional, a momentary lapse once in a while from the persistent attitude of seriousness. This view is apt to be expressed in too unqualified a form. Simple types of humanity, the child and the savage, frequently show us mirthful laughter filling a much larger space in the day's hours than our view would suggest. A jolly boy, the subject of chronic high spirits, which are apt to try the patience of sedate seniors, might perhaps say—if indeed he could be brought to frame a theory of life—that laughing is the proper way to pass the time, and that seriousness is a tiresome necessity which can be tolerated only now and again. And in any case such a view might be said to represent the mental attitude of those happy idiots and imbeciles of whom we read that they "are persistently joyous and benign," and constantly laughing or smiling, and that "their countenances often exhibit a stereotyped smile".12

Yet, attractive as this theory may be for a lover of laughter, it cannot well adjust itself to stern physiological facts. The full process of laughter is, like coughing, sobbing and other actions, a violent interruption of the rhythmic flow of the respiratory movements. As such, its function in the human organism seems to be limited to that of an occasional spurt. Even a perpetual smile, quite apart from its insipidity for others than the smiler, would, strictly speaking, hardly be compatible with the smooth on-flow of the vital processes. What has been named the "everlasting barren simper" does not really amount to this.

The Smile and the Laugh, viewed as physiological events, stand in the closest relation one to the other. A smile is, as we shall see, rightly regarded as an incomplete laugh. Hence we shall do well to study the two together.

Smiling involves a complex group of facial movements. It may suffice to remind the reader of such characteristic changes as the drawing back and slight lifting of the comers of the mouth, the raising of the upper lip, which partially uncovers the teeth, and the curving of the furrows betwixt the comers of the mouth and the nostrils (the naso-labial furrows) which these movements involve. To these must be added the formation of wrinkles under the eyes—a most characteristic part of the expression—which is a further result of the first movements. The increased brightness of the eyes is probably the effect of their tenseness, due to the contraction of the adjacent muscles and the pressure of the raised cheek, though an acceleration of the circulation within the eyeball may have something to do with it.

These facial changes are common to the smile and to the laugh, though in the more violent forms of laughter the eyes are apt to lose under their lachrymal suffusion the sparkle which the smile brings.

As a characteristic group of facial movements the smile is excellently well suited for its purpose—the primitive and most universal expression of a pleasurable or happy state of mind. It forms, in respect of certain of its features at least, a marked contrast to the expression of opposite feelings. Thus it is far removed, and so easily distinguishable, from the facial expression during weeping, *viz.*, the firmly closed eyelids and the wide opening of the mouth in the form of a squarish cavity; as also from the face's betrayal of low spirits and "crossness," in the depressed corners of the mouth, the oblique eyebrows and the furrowed forehead.

I have spoken here of the primitive unsophisticated smile as it may be observed in children and those adults who have not learned to control the primitive, and instinctive movements of the face. Among the cultivated classes of a civilised community, this primitive smile is not only restrained and modified, but serves other uses than the confession of the elemental experiences of pleasure and gladness. With the contemptuous smile, the slightly ironical smile of the superior person, the bitter, sardonic smile, we shall have happily but little to do here. It is enough to remark that these differentiations answer closely to those of laughter, and so further illustrate the organic affinity of the two.

We may now pass to the larger experience of the audible laugh. That this action is physiologically continuous with the smile has already been suggested. The facial expression is approximately the same in the broad smile and the gentle laugh. It is only when laughter grows immoderate that there is a marked addition of other features, *viz.*, the strong contraction of the muscles about the eyes leading to frowning, and the shedding of tears. How closely connected are smiling and moderate laughing may be seen by the tendency we experience when we reach the broad smile and the fully open mouth to start the respiratory movements of laughter. As Darwin and others have pointed out, there is a series of gradations from the faintest and most decorous smile up to the full explosion of the laugh.13

One may, perhaps, go farther and say that the series of gradations here indicated is gone through, more or less rapidly, in an ordinary laugh. Persons who laugh slowly, finding it difficult to "let themselves go," can be seen to pass through these stages. It has been said by an ingenious American inquirer that laughter may begin either with the eyes or with the mouth, the frequency of the former mode, as compared with the latter, in the instances examined being as 7 to 5.14

It may be added that, to this continuity of form in the actions of smiling and laughing, there answers a community of function. As will be shown more fully by-and-by, both are in their primitive forms manifestations of pleasure, laughter being primarily the expression of the fuller measures of the happy or gladsome state, and varying in energy and volume with the degree of this fulness.

The chronological relations of the reign of the smile and the laugh in the life of the individual will occupy us presently. Here it may be enough to say that these relations allow us to think of smiling at once as the precursor and as the successor of her kinsman. The first smiles are a step away from the exceeding gravity of baby-hood towards full hilarity, the last are a step back from this hilarity to the stolid composure of senile infancy.

It would seem to follow that the sharp distinction often drawn between smiling and laughing is artificial. Society, led by its Chesterfield, may emphasise the difference between the incipient and the completed process, allowing the one and forbidding the other; but the natural man is inclined to regard them as one.

The recognition of this identity of the two actions is evidenced by the usages of speech. We see in the classical languages a tendency to employ the same word for the two, laughing like smiling being regarded—primarily and mainly at least—as an object of visual perception. This is particularly dear in the case of the Latin "ridere," which means to smile as well as to laugh, the form "subridere" being rare. This tendency to assimilate the laugh and the smile as facial expressions was naturally supplemented by the employment, both in Greek and in Latin, of a separate word for audible laughter ("καχάζειν", "cachinnare") in cases where it was needful to emphasise the fact of sound. In some modern languages the relation of smiling to laughing is precisely indicated as that of a less full to a fuller action (Italian, "ridere" and "sorridere"; French, "rire" and "sourire"; German, "lachen" and "lächeln"). Possibly the existence of two unrelated words in our own and some other modern languages points to the fact that certain races have been more impressed by the dissimilarity between the audible and the inaudible expression than by the similarity of the visible manifestations.

It is worth noting that even after the two expressions have been distinguished by separate names there is a tendency to use the stronger metaphor "to laugh," rather than the weaker one "to smile," in describing the brighter aspects of nature's beauty, such as meadows when in flower. A painter, whom Dante meets in Purgatory, and recognises as the first in the art of illumination, gracefully transfers this distinction to a brother painter by saying that the leaves which the latter painted "laugh more" (piu ridon) than his own.15

We may now turn to the distinguishing characteristics of laughing, that is, the production of the familiar series of sounds. Like sighing, sobbing and some other actions, it is an interruption of the natural rhythm of the respiratory process, in which inspiration and expiration follow one another at regular intervals. The obvious feature of this interruption in the case of laughter is the series of short, spasmodic, expiratory movements by which the sounds are produced. These are, however, preceded by a less noticed inspiration of exceptional energy and depth. These interruptions of the ordinary respiratory movements involve an unusually energetic action of the large muscles by which the chest is expanded, *viz.,* those which secure the contraction and so the descent of the dome-shaped diaphragm, and those by the action of which the ribs are elevated.

The production of the sounds by the spasmodic expiratory movements shows that the passage from the trachea into the pharynx, *viz.,* the glottis or chink between the vocal cords, is partially closed. The quality of the sounds is explained by the particular arrangements, at the moment of the cachinnation, of the vocal apparatus, and more particularly the shape of the resonance chamber of the mouth.

Familiar though we are with them, we should find it hard to give an accurate description of the sounds of laughter. To begin with, they seem to vary considerably in the case of the same person and still more in that of different persons. Laughter has not yet lent itself to the methods of the experimental psychologist, and so has not been studied with scientific precision. By-and-by, we may hope, the phonograph will capture its sounds, and enable us to observe them at our leisure. Meanwhile, only a very rough account of them is possible.

Taking the laughter of the adult male, which is perhaps more frank and better pronounced, we find the more common forms of iterated sounds to range from the broad vowel sound *aw* (in "law") to the sharp *a* (in "bat"). The long *o* sound (as in "go"), involving the rounded mouth aperture, seems to me to be far less common. The same applies to the long *ee* and *ai* sounds, and those which seem to be most closely allied to them.

These variations appear, so far as I can judge, to go with alterations of pitch. The broader sounds, *e.g., aw,* seem naturally to ally themselves to the hardier deep-pitched explosion, the others to the more cackle-like utterances in the higher parts of the register. This connection shows itself, too, in the change in the vowel-quality when, as frequently happens, the laugh runs through a cadence of pitch from a higher to a lower note.

These considerations will prepare us to find that the vowel-quality of the sound varies in general with sex and with age. According to Haller and Gratiolet the sounds of the laughter of women and children, which correspond with their higher vocal pitch, approach in vowel-quality to the French *i* and *e*.16

Considerable variations from these typical forms would seem to occur now and again. In the American returns already referred to, the mode of laughing described is represented by such odd symbols as "gah! gah!" "iff! iff!" "tse! tse!" etc. These singularities, if, as it seems, they are intended to represent habitual modes of voicing mirth, are, one suspects, hardly referrible to natural differences of vocalisation, but are probably the result of the interfering agencies of nervousness and affectation which, as we know, have much to do with fixing the form of mirthful expression.

The description of laughter here offered applies only to the typical form. It would have to be modified considerably to suit the attenuated forms to which the expression is reduced in "polite society". Of these, more presently. Even where the vocal outburst retains its primitive spontaneity and fulness considerable variations are observable, connected with differences in the whole respiratory and vocal apparatus. The intensity and volume of the sound, the pitch and vowel-quality, the rapidity of the successive expirations, the length of the series, the mode of commencing and of ending, may all exhibit variations which help to make the laughter of one person or of one race different from that of another.

We may now pass to some other accompaniments of the muscular movements of laughter. It is of importance to study these with care if we wish to estimate the precise value of the hilarious explosion in the economy of human life.

Since the movements of laughter are sudden and violent interruptions of the smooth rhythmic flow of the respiratory process, we may expect to find that they have important organic effects, involving not merely the mechanism of respiration, but also that of the circulation of the blood. Here, it seems, we have to do with a double effect First of all (we are told), this series of spasmodic expirations—during which, as we have seen, the glottis is partially closed—increases the pressure within the thorax or chest, and so impedes the entry of blood from the veins into the heart. This effect is seen in the turgidity of the head and neck which appears after prolonged and violent laughing. In the second place, the exceptionally deep inspirations tend to expand the lungs with air, and to drain off the blood from the veins into the heart. The manner in which these two actions, the deepened inspiration and the prolonged expiration, alternate during a fit of laughter, appears to secure a considerable advantage in respect both of accelerated circulation and more complete oxygenation of the blood. The brisker movement of the blood after laughter has recently been observed in some experimental inquiries into the effects of emotional excitement of various kinds on the pulse.17

It is not improbable that this expedited circulation produces more remote effects on the organism. It has been suggested that one of the advantages of a "good laugh" is that it relieves the brain, and this would seem to imply that it quickens the movement of the blood through the fine and readily clogged vessels which permeate the brain-structures.

And here we find ourselves face to face with the question: What truth is there in the saying that laughter has beneficial physiological effects? A curious chapter might be written on the views propounded, both by the light-hearted reveller and the grave and philosophic onlooker, on the wholesomeness of this form of "bodily exercise". Only a bare reference to this aspect of the subject can, however, be given here.

To begin with, the unlearned, who know nothing of diaphragms or of congested veins needing to be relieved, have had a shrewd conviction that laughter sets the current of life moving briskly. Proverbs, such as "laugh and grow fat," attest this common conviction. Those who have catered to the laughter-lovers have not unnaturally made much of this salutary influence. The mediæval writers of the laughable story in verse (the "fabliau" or "Conte à rire en vers") held firmly to the belief in the "sanitary virtue" ("vertu saine") of a burst of laughter.

This popular view has been supported by the weight of learned authority. Vocal exercises, of which laughing is clearly one, have been recommended by experts from the time of Aristotle as a means of strengthening the lungs and of furthering the health of the organism as a whole. By many, moreover, laughter has been specifically inculcated as a hygienic measure. The learned Burton (*b*. 1577) quotes a number of physicians in favour of the ancient custom of enlivening the feast with mirth and jokes.18 The reader may find references to the salutary effects of laughter in the latest text-books of physiology. Both by a vigorous reinforcement of the actions of the large muscles which do the work of respiration, and, still more, by the beneficial effects of these reinforced actions on the functions of the lungs and the circulatory apparatus, laughter properly finds a place among "bodily exercises".19

The beneficial effects of laughter have not been overlooked by the pedagogue. Mulcaster, for example (born about 1530), gives a high place to laughing among his "physical" or health-giving exercises. The physiological reasons adduced are sometimes funny enough: for the author relies on Galen and the doctrine of "spirits". He thinks that laughter will help those who have cold hands and cold chests and are troubled with melancholia, since it "moveth much aire in the breast, and sendeth the warmer spirites outward". Tickling under the armpits may well be added, seeing that these parts have a great store of small veins and little arteries "which being tickled so become warme themselves, and from thence disperse heat throughout the whole bodie".20

How far these benign effects on health, which are recognised by the modern physician as well as by his predecessor, are due to the vigorous reinforcement brought by laughter to the work of respiration and of the circulation of the blood, it is not easy to say. The latter process reminds one of the circulation of pedestrians and vehicles in our London streets. In a general way it manages itself fairly well. Yet now and again a lusty "Move on!" from a policeman seems to be distinctly beneficial. Similar benefits may be extended to the organs of digestion and the rest.

At the same time we must not lose sight of the possibility that laughter may act beneficially on our hard-pressed frames in another way. As has been suggested above, the lusty cachinnation is nature's way of voicing gladness, a sudden increase of pleasure. Now it has been held by psychologists that pleasurable feelings tend to further the whole group of organic functions, by adding to the nervous vigour which keeps them going. Laughter may owe a part of its benign influence on our bodily state to the fact that it produces a considerable increase of vital activity by way of heightened nervous stimulation.21

One feature of the laughing outburst may pretty safely be ascribed to this increase of nervous action under pleasurable excitement. In all genuinely hilarious moods, the laugh is accompanied by a good deal of diffused activity of the voluntary muscles. This is seen most clearly in the unsophisticated laughter of children and savages. The sudden glee which starts the laugh starts also movements of arm, leg and trunk, so that arms flap wing-like, or meet in the joyous clap, and the whole body jumps. In older people matters may not be carried so far, though there are examples of the large shakings of laughter, notably that of Carlyle's Teufelsdröckh, whose great laugh was one "not of the face and diaphragm only, but of the whole man from head to heel"; and it is hard perhaps for any man taken by the "stab" of a good joke to keep his arms down and his body vertical.

It may be added that this supplementing of the energetic respiratory actions by movements of the limbs gives to laughter its clear title to be called a muscular exercise. As such it is vigorous, voluminous and bordering, so to speak, on the violent. Its salutary influence, like that of the surgeon's knife, will consequently depend on the celerity of its operation.

Here we come to the other column in the reckoning. If laughter does good by its occasional irruption into a domain which otherwise would have too much of drowsy monotony, its benefit is rigorously circumscribed. Only too easily can it overdo the "flushing" part, and inundate and destroy when it should merely cleanse. In other words, the mirthful cachinnation, just because it is an irruption, a disorderly proceeding, must not be unduly prolonged.

At what moment in a prolonged fit of laughter the undesirable effects begin to appear, it is not easy to say. It must be remembered that a good part of what remains of modern laughter is by no means pure hilarity. There is in it from the first ejaculation something of a biting sensation, or something of a melancholy pain. Yet, waiving this and looking on what begins as genuine hilarity, we shall find that it is not so simple a matter to determine the moment when further prolongation of the exercise will be weakening rather than strengthening. The excitement of laughter, like that of wine, may in its measurements have to be adjusted to individual constitution. Among the humiliations of life may be reckoned the discovery of an inability to go on laughing at the brilliant descriptions of a caricaturist, and an experience of aching exhaustion, of flabby collapse, while others continue the exhilarating chorus.

It is natural to look on the tears which often accompany boisterous laughter as an unfavourable symptom. Things which do us good should not, we argue, make us cry. Yet we may reflect that men have been known to cry out of sheer happiness. With some laughers, too, the moisture may come at an earlier stage than with others. Was Shakespeare, one wonders, thinking of a violent laughter when he made Iachimo tell Imogen that her lord Leonatus had mocked the French lover's lugubrious despondencies "with his eyes in flood with laughter"? Perhaps in Shakespeare's age, when laughter was held in with looser rein, the tears came more readily.

According to Darwin, who has made a careful study of laughter's tears, their appearance during a violent attack is common to all the races of mankind. He connects them with the contraction of the muscles round the eyes which has for its purpose the compressing of the gorged blood-vessels and so the protection of the eyes. This is the meaning of the tears alike in the case of grief and of extravagant mirth. The paroxysm of excessive laughter thus approaches the other extreme of violent grief; and this fact, Darwin thinks, may help us to understand how it is that hysterical patients and children often laugh and cry alternately.22

However it may be with the tears, there is no doubt that violent and prolonged laughter works mischief in other ways. The sigh that so frequently follows the laugh, and has been supposed to illustrate the wider truth that "all pleasures have a sting in the tail," need not be taken too seriously. It is the sign of restoration of equilibrium after the hilarious upset. The prostrating effects of violent laughter were well known to Shakespeare. Thus he speaks of being "stabbed" with laughter, of laughing oneself "into stitches"—an experience which Milton probably had in mind when he wrote of "laughter holding both his sides"—of the heart being almost broken "with extreme laughing" and of laughing oneself "to death".23 The American returns speak of a whole Iliad of evil after-effects: fatigue, weakness, sadness, giddiness, breathlessness and so forth. It may, however, be urged that these unpleasant experiences hardly justify us in applying to laughter the rather strong epithet of "killing". They are, under normal circumstances, temporary inconveniences only, and to the lover of fun do not seriously count as against its substantial blessings. When laughter kills, as it does sometimes, it is because it has degenerated into something distinctly abnormal, allying itself to hysterical grief or to the unhinging effect of a great mental shock.

As already noted, the laugh, like the smile which is its beginning, is in general an expression of a pleasurable state of feeling. Among unsophisticated children and savage adults it is the common mode of expressing all considerable intensities of pleasure when they involve a sudden brightening of the pleasure-tone of consciousness, as in the overflow of gladness or good spirits. As such it stands in marked dissimilarity to the expression of opposite tones of feeling. To begin with, it presents a striking contrast to states of suffering, sorrow and low spirits in general. It illustrates the broad generalisation laid down by psychologists that a state of pleasure manifests itself in vigorous and expansive movements, whereas a state of pain involves a lowering of muscular energy and a kind of shrinking into oneself. In a more special way it forms an antithesis, in certain of its features at least, to the expression of violent suffering. Darwin remarks that in the production of screams or cries of distress the expirations are prolonged and continuous and the inspirations short and interrupted; whereas in the production of laughter we have, as we have seen, the expirations short and broken and the inspirations prolonged. This is merely one case of the wider generalisation that "the whole expression of a man in good spirits is exactly the opposite of that of one suffering from sorrow".24

The value of this arrangement as helping us to understand one another's feelings is obvious. Among the many mistakes which we are wont to commit in reading our children's minds, that of confusing their joy and grief cannot, fortunately, be a frequent one. It is only in exceptional and abnormal cases, where the extremes of boisterous mirth and grief seem to approach one another, that the language of the one can be mistaken for that of the other.

A curious point, which the ingenuities of some later psychologists compel us to consider, is whether the pleasure, of which laughter is popularly supposed to be the outcome or effect, really stands in this relation to it. According to the theory here referred to, of which Prof. W. James is the best-known advocate in our language, a blush cannot be attributed to an antecedent feeling of modesty or shamefacedness: but for the blush there would be no feeling of modesty: in truth, it is the blush, *i.e.,* the hot sensation of it, that constitutes the feeling. The theory has done much to popularise psychology in these last days. It is, I have found, a plum in a pudding where plums are rare for many who read psychology for examinations. It seems to be particularly dear to young women. It certainly has about it the charm of a lively fancy.

But science has, alas! sometimes to do battle with liveliness of fancy; and it has to do this here. By trying to get all your emotions out of the organic effects, you find yourself in the awkward situation of being unable to say how these organic effects themselves are brought about. You must have something of the emotional thrill and of the nervous thrill which this involves before you get that interference with the routine action of the muscles of the facial capillaries which brings on the blush.

Not only may the presence of an element of feeling at the very beginning of an emotional experience be thus shown to be a necessary assumption, it can, in certain cases at least, be clearly observed. This applies more particularly to such feelings as the admiration of a beautiful landscape or a fine bit of harmonised melody. In these cases it must, one would suppose, be evident to all that the pleasurable emotion is started and sustained by numerous currents of agreeable sensation pouring in by way of eye or ear, and by the agreeable perceptions which grow immediately out of these. To say that all the joyous elevation in these experiences springs out of the secondary, internally excited sensations, those which accompany the altered condition of muscle and gland, the heightened pulse-rate, the bodily thrill and the rest, is surely to inflict an undeserved indignity on "the higher senses," and to exhibit the full depth of ludicrous paradox which lurks in this theory.25

The case of laughter is not quite so clear. It has, indeed, one characteristic which seems to favour the view that the bodily resonance is everything, namely, that it is easily induced in a mechanical or quasi-mechanical manner. It is of all the expressive movements the one most subject to the force of imitation. Children's laughter, and that excited by the popular game, the "laughing chorus," clearly illustrate its contagious character.26 Moreover, as we know, a fit of laughter may be brought on, in part at least, by actions which presumably reinstate some of the physiological elements in the process. Thus my son tells me that he was overtaken by an irresistible impulse to laugh when riding a horse without a saddle, and again when running a race; and my daughter had the same tendency at the end of her first mountain climb. It seems probable that the movements and the changed condition of the breathing function are prime causes of the irresistible tendency in such cases.

It is, however, one thing to allow the indisputable fact that laughter can be excited in this seemingly mechanical way, another thing to claim for the reaction in such cases the value of the full joyous outburst. I believe that a person who watches his mental processes can observe that a merely imitative laughter does not bring the whole delightful psychosis which arises when some agreeable impression initiates the movements.

To this it must be added that in the cases here touched on the imitation is not wholly mechanical. When we laugh because others laugh, do we not accept their laughter as a playful challenge and fall into the gay mood? And are we not, commonly at least, affected by others' voluminous laughter as by a droll sight and sound, which directly stimulates the mirthful muscles? My son's laughter, in the circumstances just referred to, seemed to be directed to the movements of the horse's ears, and to those of the boy running just in front of him. The movements of laughter have, in the case of some adults, come so completely under the initiative control of mental processes, that even when powerful organic forces prompt the movements, it is necessary to make a show of finding some cause of merriment.

Coming now to the ordinary case of the emotional reaction, we note first of all the swift, explosive character of the outburst. If the motor discharge follow the first swell of joyous feeling, which is popularly said to excite it, it seems to do so with such electrical rapidity as to make it impossible to detect this initial swell as distinctly preceding it. Yet this fact need not baffle our inquiry. When for example we laugh at some absurd incongruity in speech or manners, can we not see that the perception which starts the laugh is an emotional perception, one which not only directs itself to something that has emotional interest and value, namely, the incongruous features as such, but is flooded from the very first with the gladness of mirth. To say that my perception of a big woman hanging upon the arm of a small man is a purely intellectual affair, like the perception of the inequality of two lines in a geometrical figure, is, one fears, to confess either to a poverty of humorous experience or to a very scanty faculty of psychological analysis.

But perhaps the clearest disproof of this quaint paradox in the realm of laughter is supplied by the situation already referred to, that of forced abstention from a choral laugh through fatigue. When thus "doubled up" and impotent, we may be quite capable of seizing the funny turns of the good "story," and of feeling all the force of the bugle-call of the others' laughter. In sooth it is just here that the misery of the situation lies, that the joyous sense of fun in the air is now robbed of its sturdy ally and so reduced to a state of limp inefficiency. The comicality still makes full appeal: we feel it, but the feeling is denied its full normal outflow.

This brings us face to face with the kernel, the valuable kernel, of truth which lies in what seems at first an empty paradoxical nutshell. Though the "bodily reverberation" that is, the swiftly returning tidings of a raised or depressed nervous activity in outlying regions of the organism, is not everything in an emotion, it is a part, and an important part. The full experience of the joys of the comic, like other full emotional experiences, implies that the vents are clear, that the nervous swirl started at the centres at the moment when we greet the coming of fun with gladness can find its customary outflow along the familiar channels. Not only so, but as suggested above, this large expansion of the area of nervous commotion throughout the bodily system gives added life and a more distinctive character to the enjoyment of fun.

I have here supposed a perfectly simple instance of laughter in which a sudden increase of pleasure up to the point of gladness brings on the reaction. Even in this case, however, there is some complication, some reciprocal action between the out-pouring mental gladness and the in-pouring somatic resonance. In a good, prolonged laugh the bodily factor does undoubtedly react upon the psycho-physical process which makes up the mental gaiety, and this means that it precedes the later stages of this process. In all cases where this central psycho-physical factor is complex and requires time for its completion, the interactions between it and the bodily factor become vital. As hinted in the preceding chapter, the reflective intuitions which are said by certain theorists to be the cause, and so to precede laughter, are often after-thoughts. This means that when the laughing apparatus is set and ready to discharge, the first joyous perception of something funny, though utterly vague with respect to the particular features and relations wherein lies the funniness, suffices to bring on the reaction, which instantly reinforces the gladsome mood. And the jollity may sustain itself for a while mainly as a fit of laughter; though swift mental glances are all along being shot across the spasms at the provoking "object," glances which make clearer and clearer the ludicrous features, and by so doing raise the force of the mental stimulus.

If, as we have seen to be probable, laughter is within limits a good exercise, bringing a considerable increase of pleasurable activity and furthering the sense of bodily well-being, we can easily understand how essential it is to the full realisation of good spirits and the hilarious mood. Its explosive movements seem, indeed, to belong to the state of exhilaration, of conscious expansion, and to give it much of its piquant flavour: whence the hardship of losing breath through excessive indulgence, or having to stifle the impulse to laugh at its birth when exposed to the shocked look of the agelast. The deep, forcible chest-movements bring a sense of heightened energy, of a high-tide fulness of the life-current. The voluminous mass of sensation which they supply, partly in the stirring sounds which react on the laugher's own ears, and partly in the large, exhilarating effects in the viscera, is in itself a vast expansion of our consciousness. This sudden rise of the tide in our organic life is a part at least of that sense of "sudden glory" which the sight of the ludicrous is said to bring us.

That this organic swell is a large factor, is, I think, shown in more ways than one. To name but one fact; we may begin a laugh with something of bitterness, something of malignity in our hearts; but end it having a freer, serener consciousness, as if the laughter had been a sort of cleansing process, and, like another and widely different κάθαρσις, substituted a happy and peaceful for a disturbed and unhappy state of feeling. It will be seen presently that among the causes of laughter, a moment's relaxation of strain—muscular, intellectual or emotional tension—is one of the most common, if it be not universal. The delicious sense of relief which the collapse of the strained attitude brings us may no doubt be due to a consciousness of the transition, the escape from pressure of the moment before. At the same time, it is not improbable that the physiological processes of laughter themselves, by securing organic relief and refreshment, contribute a large element to the whole mental state.

A like remark applies to the element of disagreeable feeling which frequently, at least, makes our laughter a mixed experience:—

> Our sincerest laughter
>
> With some pain is fraught.

Shelley was hardly the person, one suspects, to judge of the quality of men's laughter: yet his couplet contains an element of truth. This mixture of elements is, no doubt, largely due to the initiating perception itself; for, as we shall see, the laughable spectacle commonly shows us in the background something regrettable. But it seems reasonable to say that the element of sadness in our hilarity has its organic support in the unpleasant feeling-tones which accompany the effects of all violent and prolonged laughter.27

What may be the precise proportions between the initial or "cerebral" joy and the joy reverberated by the organism we have no data for determining. There seems something plausible in the contention that the former, when it lacks the reinforcement of the latter, is but a "thin" and "pale" feeling. This view may be supported by the fact that the response of the body is never wholly silenced. Even when a man controls his laughter, say in church, he is aware of a swift spasm in the throat. But there are facts which tell powerfully in the other direction. We never stifle the organic resonance without introducing other and distinctly adverse influences. When by a forcible effort we hold back our laughter this effort itself, as an artificial and difficult attitude, does much to spoil the whole experience. The conflict between the impulse to laugh and the curbing will is distinctly disagreeable, and may readily grow into an acute suffering. And when the corporeal reverberation fails through sheer fatigue, this fatigue, both in itself and in its antagonism to the appeal to mirth, becomes a large factor in the whole experience. We must consequently wait for this knowledge of the precise shares contributed by the two factors, until some ingenious experimenter can succeed in exciting the mirthful mood and at the same time cutting off the bodily reverberation without inducing a new organic consciousness; or, on the other hand, can devise a method of securing for us in some utterly serious moment the full bodily reverberation of laughter, say by electrically stimulating our respiratory muscles. It may be predicted with some confidence that this waiting will be a long one.

Here again, as in the case of the smile, we have to note various deviations from the typical form of the expression. When laughter no longer springs from pure joy, but has in it something of a sardonic bitterness, or something of a contemptuous defiance, the experience will of course be complicated by a new ingredient of consciousness. Whether this change of experience is due merely to the difference in the initial mental attitude may be doubted. It is not improbable that the physiological processes, that is to say, the respiratory movements, the vocalisation, and the more diffused organic effects, will be altered in such cases. A bitter laugh seems both to taste differently and to sound differently from a perfectly joyous one.

In these deviations from the typical laugh of the joyous mood we see the beginning of the intrusion of a new factor, the will. There is more of intention to be heard in, say, the ironical laughter of one side of the House of Commons than in the laughter of an unsophisticated child.

This intrusion of will serves both to restrain the natural process, reducing it to a degraded and rudimentary form, and to originate various affected counterfeits of the spontaneous outburst. This double action supports the idea that the conventions of polite society aim not merely at suppressing the "vulgar" kind of explosion, but at evoking the signs of amusement when an effort is being made to amuse. Hence the multiplicity of weird utterances which cultivated humanity has adopted. The giggle, the titter, the snicker and the rest appear to be not merely reduced or half-suppressed laughter, but substitutes which can readily be produced when the occasion asks for them.28 Those who confine themselves to this debased laughter are naturally despised by the much-laughing soul. Carlyle—himself a voluminous laugher at times—when writing of Teufelsdröckh's great laugh hurls contempt on these triflers with the big things of mirth in this wise: they "only sniff and titter and sniggle from the throat outwards; or at best produce some whiffling, husky cachinnation, as if they were laughing through wool".29 An accurate scientific record of these strange perversions of laughter, even though it were less picturesque than Carlyle's description, would be of considerable value. The laughter-lover may at least console himself for the injury done him by this kind of imitation with the reflection that it is empty of joy, and even of the refreshing sensations which issue from the genuine laugh. Nay, more, as a forced performance, it presumably has a disagreeable feeling of irksomeness as its accompaniment.

It is sad to reflect that these spurious varieties of laughter are apt to appear early in the life of the individual. Preyer tells us he was able to distinguish, in the third year of his boy's utterances, the genuine laugh of hilarity from that of imitation, which was probably rather more forced. Possibly they all appear among that wondrous gathering of queer sounds for which infancy is famous, and may be permanently selected by a certain number of "highly proper" children in preference to the fuller sounds.

CHAPTER III.
OCCASIONS AND CAUSES OF LAUGHTER.

It seemed desirable to examine the process of laughter itself before taking up the much-discussed question of its causes. In considering this side of our subject, we shall, as already hinted, take a comprehensive view of the occasions and modes of production of the mirthful outburst, and approach the narrower problem of the nature and mode of action of the ludicrous by way of this larger inquiry.

According to the common assumption, laughter, in ordinary cases, is excited by some provocative, to speak more precisely, by some sense-presentation, or its representative idea, such as a "funny" sensation, the sight of a droll human figure, or a quaint fancy. Yet we must not assume that such an initial presentation occurs in all cases. As is implied in what has been said above about the laughter of "good spirits," and as we shall see more clearly presently, there are cases where laughter takes on the appearance of a spontaneous or "automatic" group of movements.

1. It may be well, however, to begin our inquiry by touching on those varieties of laughter in which the action of a sense-stimulus is apparent. And it will be convenient to select a form of distinctly provoked laughter in which the intellectual processes play only a subordinate part. The effect of tickling is clearly of this kind, and as one of the simplest modes of exciting laughter it seems to claim our first attention here. Since, moreover, it is the mode of exciting laughter of which our knowledge has been rendered in a measure precise by means of experiment, I propose to deal with it at some length.

The experience of being tickled is best described in its entirety as a sensational reflex; that is to say, a motor reaction on a process of sensory stimulation which produces a well-marked variety of sensation. To speak of titillation as if it were merely the production of a certain kind of sensation is unscientific. It involves the excitation of certain movements, and where these are not forthcoming we must infer, either that the sensory part of the process is defective, or that the motor impulse is inhibited in some way.

The stimulation in this case is, as we all know, a light tactile one. The agent commonly applied is the finger or a still softer body, such as a feather. The mode of contact is light, or at least does not commonly rise to the point of heavy pressure. The manner of contact is usually intermittent, the finger or fingers giving a series of short and staccato impacts. Movements of the fingers from point to point commonly accompany the series of contacts. In some cases, however, a single light touch, or even a continuous touch with movement from point to point, may suffice to induce the proper effect.

The precise nature of the sensations is not yet fully understood. It is pretty clear that the "minimal stimuli" here employed do not give rise to purely tactile sensations of low intensity. This seems to be established by the fact brought out by Dr. Louis Robinson that the parts of the skin having the most acute tactile sensibility, the tips of the fingers and the tip of the tongue, are "scarcely at all sensitive to titillation".30 It has been pointed out by Wundt that the sensations in this case, as in that of some other skin sensations, tend to spread themselves out, other and even distant parts of the surface being engaged by means of the mechanism of reflex sensation.31 This in itself suggests that the sensations of tickling are more allied to organic than to purely tactile sensations. It is supposed that the light stimuli set up in the skin certain organic changes, more particularly modifications of the circulation of blood in the small vessels.32

It is well known that not all parts of the skin are equally susceptible of the effect of tickling. Certain areas, for example, the sole of the foot and the armpit, are commonly said to be "ticklish places". In the answers to questions sent out by Dr. Stanley Hall we find the order, as determined by most frequent naming of the part, to be as follows: the sole of the foot, the armpit, the neck and part under the chin, the ribs, and so forth. The inquiries brought out the fact that there are considerable differences of experience here, some saying that they were ticklish in all parts, others only in one. The method adopted in this inquiry clearly affords no accurate measurement of comparative sensibility.33

A more scientific attempt to measure this was made by Dr. Louis Robinson, who carried out a large number of experiments on children from two to four years of age with the definite purpose of testing the degree of responsiveness by way of laughter. According to his results the order of decreasing sensibility is as follows: (1) the region in front of the neck; (2) the ribs; (3) axillae; (4) bend of elbow; (5) junction of ribs and abdominal muscles; (6) flanks; (7) region of the hip joint; (8) upper anterior part of the thigh.34

A glance at these statements shows that the determination of the scale of ticklish sensibility over the surface is not yet completed. Dr. L. Robinson, by the way, mentions neither the sole, a highly ticklish spot in the popular creed, nor the palm, which, as we shall see, is decidedly a ticklish region.35 It is highly desirable that more precise experimental inquiries should be directed to these local variations of ticklishness, and that, after the seats of the higher degrees of the sensibility have been ascertained, the question should be considered whether these are marked off by any definite peculiarities of structure.

It is probable that the sensations included under the head of ticklishness are not all of the same quality. It seems safe to say that in all cases the sensation is complex to this extent, that it is composed of a tactile and an organic factor. But we may see that the complexity is often greater than this. An obvious instance is the addition of a peculiarly irritating effect when the orifice of the ear or nostril is tickled, an effect due to the action of the stimulus on the hairs, which are specially abundant here.36 Some surfaces, too, which are free from hair, appear to be endowed with a special modification of the ticklish sensibility. In my own case, at any rate, light touches on the sole, have, as long as I can remember, excited sensations which seem to have almost a character of their own. A further complication probably occurs when the tickling grows rougher and approaches to a digging of the fingers into the soft parts of the armpits; for here the nerve-endings lying deeper are pretty certainly stimulated.

Lastly, it is important to add that prolongation of the tickling seems to introduce changes in the intensity, if not also in the quality of the sensations. Hence it would appear that the sensations falling under the head of ticklishness, though they have certain common characteristics, may vary considerably.

Since we are here concerned with these sensations as provocatives of laughter, it behoves us to look rather closely at their feeling-tones. As largely organic sensations they may be expected to have a strongly marked element of the agreeable or disagreeable; and this is what we find. I, at least, cannot conceive of myself as having the proper sensational experience of tickling, and yet being wholly indifferent.

When, however, we ask what is the precise feeling-tone of one of these sensations, we find no simple answer forthcoming. Some psychologists view them as having, in general, an unpleasant character.37 On the other hand, children are certainly fond of being tickled, ask for it, and make a pastime of it. This at once suggests that we have here to do with a complexity of feeling-tone, as, indeed, our study of the sensations would lead us to suppose.

It is, I think, a plausible supposition that no sensation coming under the head of tickling is merely agreeable or disagreeable. It seems always to be of a mixed feeling-tone: some sensational elements being pleasant, others unpleasant, though analysis may be unable to attribute with exactness their respective tones to the several elements.

Adopting this hypothesis, we should expect that the differences in the composition of the sensations already dealt with would lead to the result that, whereas some are preponderantly agreeable, others are rather disagreeable. And this, I believe, accords with the results of observation. The tickling sensations excited by stimulating the hairy orifices of the ear and the nostril are said by Dr. Louis Robinson to be "distinctly distasteful". The sensations produced by tickling the sole of the foot are commonly held, at least by older children and adults, to be disagreeable in all degrees of their intensity. This certainly accords with my own self-observation. The lightest touch, say from a shampooer's hand, is to me distinctly "nasty," with an uncanny nastiness which I cannot hope to describe.

An example of a distinctly agreeable sensation of tickling is, curiously enough, supplied by another hairless surface, closely analogous to the sole, namely the palm. A lady, who is an excellent observer of children and endowed with an exceptional memory of her early experiences, tells me that when a child she loved to have her hands tickled. Her feeling was a kind of "awful joy," the awfulness coming from a vague suspicion that the pastime was not quite proper. Other preponderantly agreeable varieties appear to be the sensations produced by the lighter stimulation of those parts which seem in a special way to be laughter-provoking areas, *e.g.*, the armpits and ribs. This is, at least, suggested by the fact that younger children love to be tickled in these parts in moderation, and will ask to have the pastime renewed.

An important characteristic of these feeling-tones is their unsteadiness or changefulness. Although at a particular moment we may be able to detect clearly a slight preponderance of the agreeable or of the disagreeable aspect, it is only for a moment. An increase in the degree of pressure, a further prolongation of the stimulation, or even a slight variation in the mode of contact, may suffice to bring up and render prominent the opposed feeling-phase.

We may now pass to the motor reactions, which are of more especial interest in the present connection. Overlooking the less conspicuous elements, such as the contraction of the muscles of the hairs, we find that there are two easily distinguishable groups of movements: (*a*) a number of protective or *defensive* reactions which are adapted to warding off or escaping from the attack of the tickling stimulus; (*b*) movements expressive of pleasure and rollicking enjoyment, from the smile up to uproarious and prolonged laughter.

The defensive movements are such as the following:—retraction of the foot and leg when the sole is tickled; the bending of the head to the shoulder when the neck is tickled; the rendering of the body concave on the side which is attacked; the thrusting away of the hand of the tickler; wriggling and fencing with the arms when a child is tickled lying on his back. These movements appear to introduce important modifications into the sensations excited by tickling. Dr. Louis Robinson tells us that the flexing of the foot when tickled transforms an unpleasant sensation into a rather pleasant one.

We may now pass to the point of chief importance for our present study, the conditions of the laughter-reaction during a process of tickling. This reaction is clearly the typical form of childish risibility.

It has been already more or less clearly implied, that we cannot mark off the laughter in this case as an effect determined by any assignable differences in the characteristics of the sensations involved. Dr. Louis Robinson thinks that the tickling which provokes laughter is a special variety involving the stimulation of the deeper-lying nerves. Dr. Leonard Hill, who has specially tested this point for me, writes, "There is no difference in response to deep and superficial tickling"; and again, "I am sure that the most delicate superficial stimulation can provoke laughter". This certainly seems to agree with ordinary observation. One of the most laughter-provoking forms of tickling consists of a series of pianissimo touches.

Again, in speaking of ticklish areas of the skin, we must be careful not to restrict the titillation which calls forth laughter to any assignable region. It is undeniable that there are areas which more readily respond, in the case of children generally, to the tickling provocation. The armpits perhaps will occur to most readers; and it is noticeable that Darwin speaks of the anthropoid apes giving out "a reiterated sound, corresponding with our laughter, when they are tickled, especially under the armpits".[38] This fact, however, does not imply that the area of sensibility is circumscribed. Dr. Leonard Hill assures me, as a result of his investigations, that laughter under favourable conditions may be excited by tickling *any part* of the body. Dr. L. Robinson in a letter explains to me that he agrees with Dr. L. Hill here. He finds that if a child is in a ticklish mood, the tickling of any part or even the threat of doing so will suffice to provoke laughter. On the other hand, we cannot speak of any part of the surface as one, the tickling of which will uniformly call forth laughter. Here again, as we shall see, the influence of mental agencies modifies the result.

Now these facts suggest that even those varieties of tickling which produce a sensation having a well-marked disagreeable tone may excite the response of laughter. The tickling of the sole of the foot not only provokes laughter in an infant; it tends to do so, I believe, in an adult, who may at the same time express his dislike of the sensation by a grimace.

It seems impossible then to conclude that the laughter which arises from tickling is a mere expression of the pleasure-tone of a sensational process. Even if we supposed that in all cases the sensations were preponderantly agreeable, it would still be impossible to account for the energy of the reaction by the intensity of the sensuous enjoyment experienced.

That we have not to do here merely with the effect of agreeable stimulation is shown by the fact that when a child laughs under, and is said to enjoy, a process of titillation, *the laughter is accompanied by defensive movements.* When, for example, a child is tickled on its back, it will, says Dr. Robinson, "wriggle about, fencing with its arms and dodging the attacks of its playmate . . . *laughing all the time with open mouth and teeth fully displayed*". This surely suggests that the laughter is not merely the result of an agreeable sensation, but rather of a complex mental state, in which the agreeable and disagreeable elements of sensation appear to play only a secondary *rôle*.

Nor again does it seem as if the mere transition from an agreeable to a disagreeable sensation, or the reverse process, would account for the laughter of tickling. A person highly sensitive to the effect of tickling can imitate the process by movements of his own fingers, and produce quite similar sensations of varying feeling-tone *without experiencing the faintest impulse to laugh*. Again we know that other experiences, such as scratching a sore place when it is healing up, involve an alternation of moments of agreeable and disagreeable feeling-tone, and yet are not provocative of laughter.

These and other familiar facts point to the conclusion that the laughter excited by tickling is not a net effect of the sensory stimulation. It is no doubt broadly determined by the characteristics of the sensations. Intensely disagreeable ones would certainly not call forth the laughing response. But the determining conditions include, in addition to a sequence of sensations, *a higher psychical factor,* namely, an apperceptive process or assignment of *meaning* to the sensations. This conclusion is borne out by the fact that the laughter-reaction occurs first of all (to give the earliest date) in the second month—presumably in the second half of this month. The presence of such a psychical factor is more strongly supported by the fact, already referred to, that the reaction does not occur in the first three months save when mental agencies co-operate; and that throughout the ticklish period an exactly similar process of titillative stimulation applied to the same area of the skin will now produce laughter, now fail to do so, according to the varying mood of the child.39

That the interpretation of the sensation is the decisive element in eliciting laughter may, I think, be seen by a simple experiment which any reader who is ticklish may carry out upon himself. The next time he happens to have a subjective, creepy skin sensation, he will find that he can bring on either laughter or a very different state of feeling by adopting one of two ways of mentally envisaging what is happening. The merest suggestion of an invading parasite suffices, I believe, to set up a mental state which completely inhibits the impulse to laugh.

We may now seek to assign with more precision the mental conditions which induce the mode of apperception favourable to laughter.

Beginning with the "objective" characteristics, those which reside in the tickling experience itself, we may observe how much apprehension of meaning has to do with the "funniness" of the experience. It is to be noticed at the outset that when we are tickled there is *an element of the unknown* in the process. This seems to have been recognised by Darwin when he laid emphasis on the fact that the more ticklish parts are those rarely touched, at least on small areas, and, one may add, lightly.40 The familiar fact that one cannot tickle oneself points to the same conclusion. A person who tries to do this knows too much about what is going on. Dr. Ch. Richet observes, however, that one can tickle oneself *by means of a feather;* and he, as I think rightly, explains this apparent exception by saying that in the attempt to tickle oneself with the finger, the double sensation, of the finger and the part tickled, seems to inhibit the effect, whereas, when the feather is interposed this obstacle is eliminated.41

Other facts, too, seem to point to the importance of an element of the unknown. The common way of tickling a child is by running the fingers with discontinuous contact over the skin. Dr. L. Hill describes his mode of tickling in one case as running the fingers up the child's arm *like a mouse*. This evidently brings in an element of *local* uncertainty as well as of change. The effect is increased when, as frequently happens, there are pauses between the attacks of the fingers.

The invasion of the skin-territory, like that of larger territories, is, it would seem, likely to be more effective when it has an element of unpredictableness. The uncertainty is, I believe, sometimes increased by half-voluntary variations in the direction and in the velocity of the tickling movements. Whether the fact communicated by Dr. L. Robinson, that a child is more ticklish when dressed than when undressed, is explained by the increased obscurity of the process in the former case, I am not sure. It is worth noting, however, that some of the areas said to be most ticklish, *e.g.,* the armpits and the neck, are inaccessible to sight. I believe, too, that when a child gives himself up to the full excitement of tickling he makes no attempt to see what is going on.

Now touches of unknown origin at places not closely observable have something of a disturbing character. A touch is always an attack, and has, so to speak, to be condoned. This disturbing element I regard as an essential element in the experience: it goes along with the faintly disagreeable element of sensation, which, as we have assumed, is commonly, if not always, more or less clearly recognisable in the experience.42 Yet it is certain that the disturbing effect (like the disagreeableness of the sensation) is limited. If the unknown bulks too largely and comes near the point of the alarming, the effect of laughter is wholly counteracted. This is a part of the explanation of the refusal of a child to be tickled by a stranger: for he knows here *too little* of what is going to happen, and consequently is disposed to fear. Again, Dr. L. Hill informs me that "tickling a child unexpectedly and from an unseen quarter will not provoke laughter": the element of surprise would seem in this case to be too great. Possibly the comparative difficulty of making a child laugh when naked may be explained by the increased apprehensiveness which goes with the defenceless state of nudity. The familiar fact that the readiness to laugh increases with practice, points to the same need of a certain comfortable assurance lying safely below the slight superficial apprehensions which are excited by the stimuli.

All this suggests, that in order to call forth the glad response of laughter, we must secure a certain adjustment of stimulus to mental attitude. The tickling must fit in with a particular mood, the state of mind which makes enjoyment of fun not only possible but welcome.

Now it is clear that non-adjustment may arise, not only from the presence of unsuitable characteristics in the mode of stimulation, but from some antagonistic force in the child's previous state of mind. The acceptance of the attack in good part depends on the preceding attitude. The dreadfully serious, "on-the-alarm" attitude of the child when nursed by a stranger is an effectual bar to playful overtures. A child when cross will not, says Dr. L. Hill, give genial response, even if the attacker be his familiar tickler, father or nurse; and the same is true, he adds, of a child when suffering from vaccination, or when mentally preoccupied with some hurt for which he is seeking for sympathy, or with a story which he wants you to tell him. As Darwin puts it, the great subjective condition of the laughter of tickling is that the child's mind be in "a pleasurable condition," the state of mind which welcomes fun in all its forms. Possibly the position of lying on the back, which, according to Dr. L. Robinson, makes children more responsive to tickling, may, through a relaxation of the muscles, favour this compliant attitude of self-abandonment to the tickling fingers.

We may perhaps sum up the special conditions of the laughter-process under tickling as follows: when a child is tickled he is thrown into an attitude of indefinite expectancy. He is expecting contact, but cannot be sure of the exact moment or of the locality. This element of uncertainty would in itself develop the attitude into one of uneasiness and apprehensiveness; and this happens save when the child is happy and disposed to take things lightly and as play. In this case we may suppose that the half-developed mild form of fear is each time swiftly dissolved into nothing by a recognition of the unreality of the cause, of the fact that the touches are harmless and come from the good-natured mother or nurse by way of play. This recognition becomes clearer as the process is continued, and so there supervenes a new attitude, that of play, in which all serious interpretation is abandoned and the gentle attacks are accepted as fun or make-believe.

If this is a correct analysis of the experience of the tickling which excites laughter, we seem to have in it at a very early age elements which are to be found, in a more fully developed form, in the later and more complex sorts of mirth, namely, relief from a serious and constrained attitude, a transition from a momentary apprehension induced by the presentation of the partially unknown, to a joyous sense of harmless make-believe. That this is so is further evidenced by the familiar fact that a child, when used to the game, will begin to laugh vigorously when you only threaten with the advancing fingers. As a German writer observes, this is a clear case of Lipps' theory of annihilated expectation;43 only he omits to note that the laughter depends, not on the mere fact of annihilation, but on the peculiar conditions of it in this case, involving a slight shock at the approach of something partially unknown to a specially sensitive region of the organism, and the instant correction of the apprehension by a recognition of its harmlessness.

Much the same kind of stimulative process seems to be present in the other and allied cases of reflex or quasi-reflex laughter. It is well known that certain sense-stimuli which excite sensations of a disagreeable character, but which, though acute, are not violent, such as the application of a cold douche, are apt to provoke laughter. According to the German authority just quoted, the effect depends here, too, on variation in respect of the intensity and the locality of the stimulation. He found further, in carrying out psychological experiments, that whereas the introduction of a stronger stimulus than was expected is apt to excite apprehension in the subject, that of a weaker stimulus will excite laughter.44 Here, too, we seem to have a sensational reflex in which is present a distinctly mental element, *viz.*, a moment of mild shock and apprehension at the sudden coming of something disagreeable and partially unknown, instantly followed by another moment of dissolution of shock in a pleasurable recognition of the harmlessness of the assault.

2. Laughter is not, however, always of this reflex form. It may arise without sensory stimulation in an "automatic" manner as the result of a cerebral rather than of a peripheral process. This is illustrated by the seemingly causeless laughter which breaks out in certain abnormal states and has an "uncanny" aspect for the sane observer. A well-known example of this is the effect of the action on the brain centres of laughing gas and other substances. Such "automatisms" occur, however, within the limits of normal

experience, as when a person laughs during a state of high emotional tension. I propose to speak of such seemingly uncaused reactions as *nervous laughter*.45

A common and simple variety of this nervous laughter is the spasmodic outburst that often succeeds a shock of fear. A child will laugh after being frightened by a dog; a woman often breaks out into a nervous laugh after a short but distinctly shaking experience of fear, *e.g.,* in a carriage behind a runaway horse, or in a boat which has nearly capsized. And it does not seem that such laughter is preceded by a perception of the absurdity of the fear, or of any similar mode of consciousness; it looks like a kind of physiological reaction after the fear.

The same thing will show itself in circumstances which give rise to a prolonged mental attitude, involving a feeling of apprehensiveness and of constraint. Thus a shy man, making his first essay as a public speaker, will sometimes betray his nervousness on the platform by weird little explosions of laughter as well as by awkward gestures. I have noted the same thing in strangers to whom I have spoken at a *table d'hôte* abroad. The way in which little spasms of laughter are apt to intrude themselves into situations which, by making us the object of others' special attention, bring an awkward consciousness of insecurity, is further illustrated in the behaviour of many boys and girls when summoned to an interview with the Head, in the laughter which often follows the going up to take a prize before a large assembly, and the like. The strong tendency to laugh which many persons experience during a solemn ceremony, say a church service, may sometimes illustrate the same effect. When an enforced attitude, difficult to maintain for the required length of time, brings on the impulse, this will gather strength from the growth of a feeling of apprehension lest we should not be equal to the test imposed.

Another variety, coming under the head of nervous laughter, is the sudden outburst which now and again occurs in a state of great emotional strain, having a distinctly painful character, especially when it includes something in the nature of a shock. The news of the death of an acquaintance has been known to excite a paroxysm of laughter in a company of young persons from nineteen to twenty-four years of age.46 One may assume here that the outbreak is not the direct result of the news, but depends on the effect of the shock, with the abnormal cerebral tension which this involves.

A like spasmodic outburst of laughter occasionally occurs during a more prolonged state of painful emotional excitement. It sometimes intrudes itself into a bout of physical suffering. Lange speaks of a young man who, when treated for ulceration of the tongue by a very painful caustic, regularly broke out into violent laughter when the pain reached its maximum.47 Many persons when thrown into a prolonged state of grief, accompanied by weeping, exhibit a tendency to break out into laughter towards the end of the fit. Shakespeare illustrates this tendency when he makes Titus Andronicus, whose hand has been cut off, answer the question why he laughed with the exclamation: "Why I have not another tear to shed".48

Can we find a common element in these different forms of nervous or apparently unmotived laughter? We appear to have in all of them a preceding state of consciousness which is exceptionally intense and concentrated. The situation of fear, of constraint on being made the object of others' unusual observation, of suddenly hearing news of deep import for which the mind is not prepared, of prolonged emotional agitation, these all involve an intensification of the psycho-physical processes which immediately condition our states of consciousness. Looking at these intensified forms of consciousness more closely, we observe that they include something in the nature of psychical pressure, of the presence of forces which make for disorder, whereas the situation calls for severe self-control. This special strain thrown on the volitional process is illustrated in the demand for closer observation and calm reflection during a fit of fear, or other emotional excitement, which tends to bring about a state of wild movement and of disorderly ideas. It is, I believe, *the specially severe strain* belonging to such an attitude which is the essential pre-condition of the laughter. It makes the attitude a highly artificial one, and one which it is exceedingly difficult to maintain for a long period. As such, the attitude is eminently unstable, and tends, so to say, to break down of itself; and will certainly collapse, partially at least, if the demand seems, though only for a moment, to grow less imperative. Hence the readiness with which such a means of temporary relief as laughter undoubtedly supplies is seized at the moment.

It remains to determine the character of this sudden relaxation of the strain of attention more precisely. As a sudden collapse, it is clearly to be distinguished from the gradual breakdown due to "mental fatigue" and nervous exhaustion. The psycho-physical energy concentrated for the special purpose of meeting the strain is by no means used up, but has to find some way of escape. Here, no doubt, we seem to come across Mr. Spencer's ingenious idea that laughter is an escape of nervous energy which has suddenly been set free. It is no less evident that the redundant energy follows the direction of the risible muscles because no other commanding object for the attention presents itself at the moment. The innervation of these muscles is not a mere diversion of attention: it is a *dispersion* of the energies which for the maintenance of attention ought to be concentrated. We are never less attentive during our waking life than at the moment of laughter.

Yet even here, I think, the theory of a convenient waste-pipe arrangement is not adequate. There is, I take it, in the case a relief of sur-charged nerve-centres, which process would seem to be better described by the figure of a safety-valve arrangement.

It is not difficult to surmise why the liberated energy should follow this particular nervous route. There is no doubt that the motor apparatus, by the disturbances of which all such interruptions of the smooth flow of respiration are brought about, is very readily acted on by emotional agencies. Altered respiration, showing itself in altered vocalisation, is one of the first of the commonly recognised signs of emotional agitation; and this effect has been rendered more clear and precise by recent experiments. We should expect, then, that the collapse of strained attitudes, with the great change in feeling-tone which this must carry with it, would deeply affect the respiration. We know, however, more than this. Severe efforts of attention are in general accompanied by a partial checking of respiration, an effect which seems to be alluded to in the French expression, an effort "de longue haleine". On the other hand, the termination of such an effort is apt to be announced by the sigh of relief. Now, though the movements of laughter are not the same as those of sighing, they resemble the latter in their initial stage, that of deepened inspiration. May we not conclude, then, that laughter is likely to occur as another mode of physiological relief from the attitude of mental strain? And supposing, as seems certain, that laughter in its moderate degrees, by bringing a new briskness into the circulation, relieves the congested capillaries of the brain, may we not go farther and say that nature has probably come to our aid by connecting with the mental upheavals and the cruel strains here referred to, which pretty certainly involve a risky condition of the cerebral system of capillaries, a mode of muscular reaction which is peculiarly well fitted to bring the needed relief?

More special conditions may favour the movements of laughter in certain cases. As I have observed above, Darwin suggests that the rapid alternation of crying and laughing which occur among hysterical patients may be favoured by "the close similarity of the spasmodic movements".49 In other words, the motor centres engaged, when in the full swing of one mode of action, may readily pass to the other and partially similar action. This would help to account for the short outbursts of laughter during a prolonged state of painful agitation, and to explain the fact noted by Descartes, that no cause so readily disposes us to laughter as a feeling of sadness.50

Our theory plainly requires that these sudden breakdowns or relaxations of strained mental attitudes should, even when only momentary interruptions, be accompanied by an agreeable sense of relief. I believe that those whose experience best qualifies them to judge will say that this is so.

The dead weight of the fear, the poignancy of the grief, and the constraining effect of the situation of *gêne*, seem to yield at the moment when the "awful laugh" is snatched at. This comforting sense of a lightened load, though in part the direct result of a cessation of cerebral strain, would, as we have seen, pretty certainly derive added volume from the returning sense-reports telling of the ameliorated condition of the bodily organs.

3. We have considered two of the varieties of laughter which lie outside the region of our everyday mirth. We may now pass into this region, and inquire, first of all, into the causes of those varieties which come under the head of joyous laughter.

Here we shall best begin by touching on the simple and early form which may be called the overflow of good spirits. Darwin, as has been mentioned, rightly regards the full reaction of the laugh as the universal expression by our species of good spirits, of a joyous state of mind. We have now to examine the mode of production of this simple type.

It is important to note that all experiences of pleasure do not bring on laughter. There are quiet enjoyments of a soothing character which are far from generating the powerful impulse needed for the movements of diaphragm and rib. To lie on a summer day in a hammock in a wood and indulge in the sweets of *dolce far niente* is to be out of reach of the tickling imp. States of enjoyment, too, which, though exciting, require a measure of close attention, such as those occasioned by a glorious sunset, or stirring music, do not start the spasmodic contractions of muscle.

The enjoyment that moves us to laughter must, it is evident, amount to gladness or joy. And this means, first of all, that the pleasurable consciousness must come in the form of a large accession, and, for a moment at least, be ample, filling soul and body. As the expression "good spirits" suggests, the organic processes during such states of joyousness are voluminous and well marked. As a part of this heightened tide of vital activity, we have the characteristic motor expression of the gladsome mind, the movement of the limbs, the shouting and the laughing.

Not all risings of the vital tide, however, produce laughter. Gentle and gradual augmentations of the sense of well-being and happiness hardly tend to stir the muscles concerned. The joyous outburst marks a *sudden* accession of happy consciousness. It has something of the character of a violent flooding of the spirit and the corresponding bodily conduits.

There is a negative condition, also, to which it may not be superfluous to allude. The flood-like rise of the happy mood which is to produce laughter must not be accompanied by any further demand on the attention. A girl reading a first love letter from the man whom her heart has chosen will be glad, and will grow gladder by leaps and bounds. But the fulness of laughter will not come while unread words still claim the eye.

The laughter of joy is most noticeable, I think, under two sets of conditions. Of these the first is the situation of release from external restraint. The wild jubilant gladness of boys as they rush out of school, provided that they have the requisite reserve fund of animal spirits, is the stock example of this sort of laughter. The explosion seems here to be a way of throwing off the constraint and the dulness of the classroom, and getting a deep breath of the delicious sense of restored liberty. So far as the outflow of good spirits is thus connected with an escape from a serious and difficult attitude—strenuous application of the energies of mind and body in work— it is plainly analogous to the nervous laughter already considered.

But the swift accession of joy may come in another way, from the sudden transformation of one's world, from the arrival of some good thing which is at once unexpected and big enough to lift us to a higher level of happiness. With children and savages the sight of a new and pretty toy is sometimes enough to effect this. The charming bauble will so fill sense and soul that the joy of living leaps to a higher plane and bursts into a peal of mirth. The unexpected sound of the father's voice at the end of a long day devoted to the things of the nursery was, we are told, enough to evoke a shout of laughter in a small American boy: it sufficed to bring back to the little fellow's consciousness another and a glorious world. We older folk have, for the greater part, lost the capacity of simply greeting delightful things in this way, a greeting in which there is no thought either of their meaning or of their interest for us. Yet we may meet the unexpected coming of friends with something of the child's simplicity of attitude. It is hard not to smile on suddenly seeing a friend in a crowded London street: hard to keep the smile from swelling into a laugh, if the friend has been supposed at the moment of encounter to be many miles away. Some of us, indeed, may retain the child's capacity of laughing with a joyous wonder at a brilliant explosion of fireworks.

It remains to account for the persistent fit of laughter which frequently accompanies a prolonged gladness. Does not the fact that the child and the natural man, when taken with the mood of mirth, go on venting their good spirits in renewed peals tell against our theory that the outburst is caused by an accession of joy?

In order to answer this we must look a little more closely at this so-called persistent laughter. The language of observers of unsophisticated human nature is sadly wanting in precision here. When, for example, we are told by travellers that certain savages are always laughing, we know that we are not to take the statement literally. It means only what it means when a mother tells her visitor that her rogue of a boy is for ever laughing and shouting; that under certain favourable conditions the laughing fit comes readily and persists longer than usual. In a lasting mood of jollity we are all strongly inclined to laugh, and need very little to call forth a long outburst.

This preternaturally large output of laughter during a prolonged state of high spirits finds its explanation in part in a kind of physiological inertia, the tendency to go on repeating movements when once these are started. The protracted iteration of laughter in a child is closely analogous to that of his half-unconscious singing to himself. This tendency of movements to perpetuate themselves in a mechanical way probably accounts for the lengthening of the single outburst in the case of a child violently seized with mirth. As mothers know, this reduction of laughter to a mechanical iteration of movement is apt to continue beyond the limits of fatigue and to bring on such unpleasant effects as "hiccup". It is probable, too, that the tendency during a prolonged state of mirth to recommence laughing after a short pause is referrible to a like cause: the physiological springs of the movements being once set going, the explosive fit tends to renew itself.

Discounting this effect of physiological inertia, we seem to find that in these periods of prolonged high spirits laughter retains its fundamental character as a comparatively short process which occurs intermittently. Where the laughing is not merely a trick played off by the bodily mechanism, but holds a germ of mind in the shape of a happy consciousness, it has its large and significant pauses.

If this is so, it seems reasonable to suppose that the mental antecedent which brings on some new explosion is analogous to the sense of "sudden glory" which accounts for the single joyous peal. Owing to the exceptionally strong disposition to laugh during such a period, the antecedent feeling need not be a powerful one, a very slight momentary increase of the joyous tone sufficing to give a fresh start to the muscles.

It is not difficult to suggest possible sources of such slight sudden augmentations of the happy feeling-tone. No prolonged state of consciousness is, strictly speaking, of one uniform colour; in the boisterous merriment of an old-fashioned dinner-party there were alternations of tone, brilliant moments following others of comparative dulness. The course of the bodily sensations in these prolonged states of joy is in itself a series of changes, involving a sequence of exaltations upon relative depressions of the "vital sense". The course of the presentations to eye and to ear in such a festive mood must be subject to like fluctuations in respect of their action upon the feeling-tone; and the same applies to the flow of ideas which can find a place in the mind when thus affected. Lastly, it must not be forgotten that the movements of attention would of themselves always secure a certain rise and fall of enjoyment. We all know how, when we are gladdened by some new and unexpected happiness, the mind after a short digression returns to the delightful theme, and how, as a result of this return, a new wave of joyous feeling seems to inundate the spirit.

There seems much, then, to be said for the hypothesis that all varieties of joyous laughter (when not reduced to a mechanical form) are excited by something in the nature of *a sudden accession of pleasurable consciousness*. Where the laugh is a new thing, unprepared for by a previous mood of hilarity, this rise of the spirits will, as we shall see later, probably involve a transition from a mental state which was relatively depressed. Where, on the other hand, a joyous mood prolongs itself, all that seems needed for re-exciting the movements of laughter (provided that the muscular energies are equal to the explosion) is the sudden increase by an appreciable quantity of the pleasurable tone of the consciousness.

We may further illustrate and verify this generalisation respecting the causes of joyous laughter by an examination of some of the more familiar circumstances in which this is wont to occur. Here we shall of course be dealing with the early and unsophisticated mind. Properly drilled "grown-ups" but rarely exhibit the phenomenon in its full intensity.

(*a*) It is a matter of common observation that joyous laughter is a frequent concomitant of the play-attitude, especially at its first resumption. We have already found this illustrated in the laughter of "happy boys" just liberated from school. Here the conditions indicated, a relief from restraint and a sudden expansion of joyous activity, are patent to all.

Closely related to this situation of released bodily energies is that of relieved mental restraint. During a nursery lesson—if only the teacher is a fond mother or other manageable person—the child is apt to try modes of escape from the irksomeness by diverting the talk, and especially by introducing "funny" topics; and the execution of the bold little manœuvre is frequently announced by a laugh. By such familiar infantile artifices the pressure is lightened for a moment, and the laugh announces a moment's escape into the delicious world of fun and make-believe.

The impulse to be gay and to laugh runs, moreover, through the enjoyment of play. No doubt this in its turn may often grow exceedingly serious, as when the illness of dolly, or the thrilling horrors of a bear's cave, or of an attack by scalping Indians, are realistically lived out. Yet we must remember that this playful tampering with the serious, even on its genuine side, is a part of the enjoyment. The momentary terror is desired by healthy young nerves, because the thrill of it, when the certainty of the nothingness lies securely within mental reach, is delicious excitement. A fuller examination of the relation of laughter to play belongs to a later stage of our inquiry.

(*b*) Another situation which is closely related to play is that of being teased. By "teasing" is here understood those varieties of attack which have in them an element of pretence, and do not cross the boundary line of serious intention to annoy. As thus defined, teasing enters into a good deal of child's play. Tickling is clearly only a special modification of the teasing impulse. In some of the earliest nursery play, the game of bo-peep, for instance, there is an element of teasing in the pretence to alarm by a feigned disappearance, as also in the shock of the sudden reappearance. The teaser of a child, whether he threatens to pinch him or to snatch at his toy, carries out a menace; but it is a make-believe menace—a thing to be a wee bit afraid of for just a moment, yet so light and passing as to bring instantly the delightful rebound of disillusion, if only the subject keeps good tempered. On the teaser's side (when it remains pure teasing) it is prompted by no serious desire to torment, by no motive more serious than the half-scientific curiosity to see how the subject of the experiment will take it.

The explosions of a good-humoured subject under such gentle teasing are closely analogous to those of a tickled child: they spring from a sudden sense of relief, of elastic rebound, after repression. The swift alternations of moments of nascent fear and of joyous recognition of the fun of the thing are eminently fitted to supply the conditions of a sudden rising of the spirits. The child that likes to be teased—in the proper way of course—is perfectly willing to pay for these momentary delights by the momentary trepidations.

On the side of the teaser, the situation is also highly favourable to outbreaks of hilarity. If successful, he reaps the joy of the superior person, and glories in the cleverness of his experiments. The swellings of the sense of power as he watches his victim give just those experiences of "sudden glory" which a philosopher places at the base of all enjoyment of the laughable; and, alas, in the less kindly these risings of the pleasurable consciousness may continue and even increase after the teasing has ceased to be play and becomes indistinguishable from the behaviour of a tormentor.51

(*c*) Much the same kind of remark applies to practical joking, which, when it is not weighted with the serious purposes of punishment and moral correction, is merely an expansion of this playful attack of the tickler and the teaser. When the victim reaches the moral height of being able to enjoy the performance, his enjoyment comes under the head of dissolved apprehension, or disillusion after taking things too seriously. By far the larger share of the pleasure of the practical joke certainly falls, however, to the perpetrator, who in this case, too, realises a "sudden glory," an increased sense of power.

(*d*) Once more, laughter is a common accompaniment of all varieties of contest or sharp encounter, both physical and mental. When, as in the case of the savage, the schoolboy and the civilised soldier, it breaks out after bodily fight, it has some of the characteristics of nervous laughter. It is a concomitant of a sudden remission of physical and mental strain, of a dissolution of the attitude of apprehensive self-protection. In most cases, since it is "they laugh that win," the feeling of relief is reinforced by that of contemptuous exultation at the first taste of victory.

A prolonged combat, if not too unequal, offers on both sides frequent openings for these reliefs of tension and upspringings of the exultant mood. A good fighter in the ring is, I understand, supposed to be able now and again to relieve the grimness of the situation by a sweet smile. This is certainly true of all mental contests. Nothing is more remarkable in the study of popular laughter than the way in which it seems to penetrate those relations and dealings of social life which involve sharp contest and crossing of wits. These will be illustrated more fully by-and-by. It is enough here, to allude to the enormous influence of contests between the sexes on the development of wit and a lively sense of the ludicrous.

(*e*) As a last group of situations favourable to the experience of joyous expansion we have those in which an unusual degree of solemnity is forced upon us. This has already been touched on. Extremes seem to meet here. It might be expected that an impulse born of the play-mood would find its natural dwelling-place in scenes of social gaiety and conviviality. And in the days when society was gay the festive board was doubtless the focus of the activity of the mirthful spirit. In our time it seems almost more natural to associate a laugh with a funeral ceremony than with a dinner-party. Yet the art of extracting fun from solemn things is not of to-day, as may be seen by a glance at the jokes of the church architect and the play writer of the Middle Ages. In such bizarre intrusions of the droll into the domain of the solemn we seem to find the struggling of an irrepressible gladness of spirit against the bonds which threaten to strangle it.

Whether the invasion of the territory of the solemn by the jocose results in a barely mastered impulse to laugh, depends on variable conditions. The frivolous mind, hardly touched by the gravity of the occasion, will, no doubt, often be the first to welcome the delivering hand. Yet it is an error to suppose that a tendency to laugh on a solemn occasion shows want of genuine emotion. The sincerest worshipper in a church may, if he have the requisite sensibility, be moved to laughter by some grotesque incident, such as the *mal à propos* remark of a garrulous child. For the point of our theory is that laughter in such cases is an escape from pressure; and the man who feels deeply at such a moment may experience an emotional pressure which equals, if it does not exceed, that of the external constraint which the non-reverent "worshipper" is experiencing. It is true, of course, that the deeper the feeling the greater the inertia that will have to be overcome before the laughing impulse can make way for itself. Yet here, again, we must remember that emotional temperaments vary, and that with some a genuine awe and even an intense grief may yield now and again for a moment to the challenge of the laughable when its note catches the ear.

The last remarks suggest that in any attempt to deal with the conditions favourable to laughter reference should be made to those physiological characteristics which are supposed to determine the particular temperament of a man: his special bent, say, towards jollity on the one hand, or towards a brooding melancholy on the other. Our forefathers had pretty definite ideas about the sort of bodily constitution which was the foundation of the laughter-loving temper. A full "habit" tending to obesity, as in Falstaff, was, and is, I believe, popularly supposed to be a mainstay of the laughing spirit. The saying "Laugh and grow fat" may imply a vague apprehension of this relation, as well as a recognition of the benefits of laughter. Yet the precise organic substrate of this happy endowment is unknown. Health and all that makes for "good spirits" are no doubt favourable to a voluble laughter of the elemental kind. On the other hand, as we shall see, the laughing capacity frequently co-exists with physiological conditions of quite another kind. Men are to be found of a lean habit, and with a strong bent to grave reflection, who are nevertheless able, not merely to provoke laughter from others, like the "melancholy Jaques," but themselves to contribute a sonorous laughter to the higher intellectual domains of mirth. It is conceivable that the disposition to laugh may have its own restricted physiological conditions in a special instability of the mechanism concerned. This again may presumably include some as yet undefinable property of the nerve-centres which favours rapid change in the mode of brain activity, and those sudden collapses of tension which seem to be the immediate physiological antecedent of the motor discharge in laughter.

CHAPTER IV.
VARIETIES OF THE LAUGHABLE.

In the preceding chapter we have examined those early and elementary forms of laughter which arise from the action of such causes as tickling, the attitude of play, and the sudden uplifting in a feeling of joy. These do not, it is evident, imply the existence of that specific faculty which we call the perception of the laughable in things, or what is commonly spoken of as the sense of the ludicrous. We have now to inquire into the mode of operation of this more intellectual cause of laughter, and to connect it, if possible, with that of the simpler processes of excitation.

The peculiarity in this case is that there is not only an external excitant, such as tickling fingers, but an object of the laughter. A tickled child laughs because of the tickling, but not at this as an object. The same is true of a good deal of the laughter of play: it is only when play represents something funny, or when the play-illusion is interrupted by a moment's critical glance at the poverty of the doll or other plaything, that it gives rise to a proper enjoyment of the laughable; and a like remark holds good of the laughter which springs out of a relief of tension and a sudden transition from grave to gay. In the laughter of educated men and women we see an intellectual element, the perception of a laughable quality in an object, and the justification of the action by a reference to this. The examination of this intellectual type of laughter will bring us to what is undoubtedly at once the most interesting and the most difficult problem in our study.

The objective reference in laughter implied in speaking of the "laughable" may be illustrated by a glance at the contemptuous laughter of the victor surveying his prostrate foe. The boy of ten who danced and screamed and laughed after he had killed his playmate in a street fight[52] was hardly possessed with what we call a sense of the comicality of things. The laughter, though directed *at something*, had not, in the complete sense of the expression, *its object*. The boy himself would not have laughed at the spectacle at another time, but viewed it with quite different feelings. And the object would not have presented itself as laughable to others who chanced to see it. In other words, the laughter was not caused by a mere contemplation of an object, but was conditioned by a particular relation between the laugher and this object.

To say that a thing is laughable, just as to say that a thing is eatable, implies an element of permanence and of universality. This is true even when a person says about a spectacle, *e.g.*, that of a drunken man walking, "It is laughable to me," since he means that for his experience at least it is a general rule that the sight of such movements excites laughter. But the word laughable clearly connotes more than this, a universality which embraces others as well as the individual. A thing is only rightly so called when it is supposed to be fitted to provoke men's laughter in general. Language has been built up by men living the social life, and interested in common forms of experience; and the word laughable and all similar words undoubtedly refer to such common forms.

These common forms of experience may be conceived of narrowly or widely. Much of what is called laughable by a schoolboy, by a savage, or even by an educated Englishman, is made to appear so by the special habits and correlated modes of thought of his community or his class. This clearly holds good of laughter at strange forms of dress, language and the like. Its "universality" is thus strictly conditioned. In dealing with the laughable we shall have constantly to allude to its relativity to particular customs and expectations. It will be a part of our problem to disengage from among the common excitants of laughter what seems to possess a truly universal character.

In speaking of an object of laughter as having universal potency, we do not imply that it will, as a matter of fact, always excite the outburst. The expression means only that a man will be ready to laugh at it, provided that he has certain requisite perceptions with the correlated emotional susceptibilities, and that nothing interferes with the working of these. Hence we shall have to speak of the laughable as answering to a *tendency* only, and to note the circumstances which are apt to counteract it. It is obvious, for example, that the limitations of class-custom, so far as they make laughter relative, will render a man blind to what is "objectively" laughable in his own customs. In truth, the adoption of such relative and accidental standards, which marks all the earlier stages in the growth of intelligence and of æsthetic sentiment, is the great obstacle to a clear recognition of what is laughable in a wider and more strictly universal sense.

Again, when we are considering the question of fact, "What do men really laugh at?" it is important to bear in mind that the tendency to laugh may, on the one hand, be reinforced by a favourable psycho-physical condition at the moment, as well as by previously formed tendencies to apperceive things on their laughable side; while, on the other hand, it may be checked and wholly counteracted by unfavourable conditions, such as a sad mood, or an acquired habit of looking at those aspects of things which excite feelings antagonistic to laughter. Owing to the action of these forces, we find, not only that one man may fail to discern the laughable in an object which moves another to a hearty outburst, but that in many cases in which two men join in laughing at something they may not be touched by the same laughable feature or aspect of the presentation. Nothing, indeed, has more of that appearance of caprice which comes from the influence of uncertain subjective factors than the laughter of men, even of those who have a normal sense of the ludicrous.

A word more is needed on the language here used. The terms laughable and ludicrous may be employed interchangeably up to a certain point without risk of confusion. At the same time it is well to note that the second is used in a stricter sense than the first. The term ludicrous seems to denote particularly what is not only an universal object of laughter, but an object of that more intellectual kind of laughter which implies a clear perception of relations. In everyday language we should speak of incidents and stories, of which the fun is obvious and broad, as "laughable" rather than as "ludicrous". Closely connected with this emphasis on an intellectual element in the meaning of the term ludicrous, is its tendency to take on an ideal connotation, to mark off what we deem to be worthy of laughter. Here, as in the case of other objects of an æsthetic sentiment, there is a half-disguised reference to the regulative principles of art.

This control by an æsthetic principle or standard is more clearly indicated in the use of "comic," a word, by the way, which is used more freely in some European languages than in our own. A comic spectacle means, for one who uses language with precision, a presentation which is choice, which comes up to the requirements of art, and would be excellent material for comedy.

Our problem may now be defined as an analysis of the objects of our common perception and imagination which ordinary men tend to laugh at and to describe as laughable. This inductive inquiry into facts is, as implied above, a necessary preliminary to a discussion of the nature of the "ludicrous" or "comic" as an ideal or regulative conception.

In order to find our way with some degree of certainty to the general characteristics of laughable things, we should do well to take at least a rapid survey of the objects of men's laughter as reflected in popular jests, "*contes pour rire,*" "comic songs" and amusing literature in general; as also in what may be called the standing dishes in the repasts of fun served up in the circus and other places where they laugh. No assemblage of facts of this kind adequate for scientific purposes has, so far as I know, yet been made;[53] so that it must suffice here to indicate some of the leading groups of laughable objects which a brief inspection of the field discloses.

It may be assumed as a matter of common recognition that this field of laughable objects will lie in the main within the limits of the spectacle of human life. It is the situations, appearances and thoughts of men which yield to laughter the larger part of its harvest. At the same time allusion will be made now and again to provocatives lying outside these limits, which are certainly found in simple examples of the laughable.

In attempting to form these groups one must give a warning. It is implied in what has been said above, that the things we laugh at have in many cases, perhaps in most, more than one distinguishably amusing facet. In trying to classify them, therefore, we must be guided by what seems the most massive and impressive feature; and, as already suggested, it is not always easy to say what really is the main determinant of our laughter.

(1) Among the things which are commonly said to be laughable we find many objects distinguished by *novelty*. A presentation which differs widely from those of the ordinary type, and so has a stimulating freshness, may, as we have seen, when agreeable and of sufficient force, excite to laughter by suddenly relieving the dulness of the common and oft-repeated, and raising the feeling-tone of the observer to the level of joyous excitement. The proper effect of a recognised laughable aspect only appears when experience begins to be organised and the mind of the spectator to perceive, dimly at least, a certain contrariety in the new presentation to the usual run of his perceptual experience, in other words, the aspect of "out-of-the-wayness" or *oddity*. Much of the laughter of children, and, as we shall see, of savages, at what is called "funny" illustrates this. A child will laugh vigorously, for example, on first hearing a new and odd-sounding word, or on first seeing a donkey roll on his back, a Highlander in his kilt, his sister's hair done up in curling-papers, and the like. In some of these cases, at least, the appreciation of the new object as odd or singular is aided by the agreeably lively character of the novel impression. This is true also of the amusing effect of two strikingly similar faces seen together; for here the look of oddity, which is explained by the circumstance that our ordinary experience is of dissimilarity between faces, is supported by the stimulative force of the likeness itself.

This expansive effect of the new and the odd on our feeling may come too from the perception of things sub-human. The sight of a crab walking sideways, of an oddly-marked dog, of an eddy of leaves in autumn, and so forth will excite laughter in a child.

A glance at the language employed in describing laughable objects suggests the large scope of the odd. Thus the "whimsical" and the "fantastic" in the realm of ideas and tastes, the "extravagant" in the region of sentiment—these and the like seem to refer directly to what is peculiar, to the point of an amusing remoteness from life's common way.

This enjoyable appreciation of the odd is in a particularly obvious way subject to the condition of relativity. To begin with, the amusing aspect is determined by, and so strictly relative to the manner of the hour; so that, as the word "antic" shows, the old-fashioned begins to take on an amusing aspect as soon as it is so far displaced by a new custom as to be an out-of-the-way thing.

Again, as already hinted, the odd is always relative to the custom of a locality or a class. A savage and a civilised man alike are wont to laugh at much in the appearance and actions of a foreign people; and this because of its sharp contrast to the customary forms of their experience.

The chief counteractive to be noted here is the impulse to distrust and fear the new and unfamiliar. A child may often be noticed oscillating between laughter and fear as some new strange sight bursts upon him. A savage must feel himself secure before he can freely indulge in laughter at all the odd belongings and doings of the white man.

(2) A special variety of the singular or exceptional which is fitted, within certain limits, to excite laughter is *deformity*, or deviation from the typical form. It is certain that, for the unsophisticated palate of the child and the savage, bodily deformity is a large source of mirth. The dwarf, the hunchback, the cripple, the man with the big nose, and the like have been great entertainers of youth. The tendency to regard such deviations from type as amusing extends, as we know, to our perceptions of animals and of plants. A limping quadruped or a tree with a wen-like excrescence seems to reflect a human deformity and to share in its laughable aspect. Even a lifeless object may sometimes entertain us with its appearance of deformity. A house shored up affects us in the same way as a man on crutches, and the back view of a rickety tilted cart, as it wobbles down a street, may gladden the eye much as the sight of a heavy, ill-balanced human figure attempting to run.

While we may view the laughable aspect of bodily deformity as an example of the odd or deviation from the common pattern of our experience, we must not forget that it appeals to the more brutal element in laughter. All ugly things had in them for the Greek mind something contemptible or disgraceful. Much of the point of men's laughter at deformity lies in a recognition of its demeaning effect on the person who is its subject. It is a clear manifestation of the impulse to rejoice in the sight of what is degraded, base, or contemptible. It is not difficult to detect this note of contemptuous rejoicing in the derisive laughter of the coarser sort of boy and savage, the kind of laughter illustrated in Homer's description of the merriment of the Achæan chiefs at the sight of the misshapen Thersites, with his hump, his sugar-loaf head crowned with stubble, and his persecuting squint.54 Here we seem to have an unmistakable ingredient of malignant satisfaction, of rejoicing at another's ills (Aristotle's ἐπιχαιρεκακία).

Roughly speaking, we may say that the laughable force of a deformity varies with its extent. The droll effect of an enlargement of the nose or of a reduction of the chin increases, within certain limits at least, with the amount of the aberration from the normal dimensions. Yet it would be difficult to establish any exact quantitative relation here.

Again, all kinds of deformity are not equally provocative of laughter. In general, perhaps, positive additions or extensions, such as a big nose or big ears, are more conducive to merriment than reductions and losses; they seem to seize perception more aggressively. Then there are varieties of the deformed which probably involve special kinds of droll suggestiveness. Certain squints and twistings of the human face divine may move us as expressions of the roguish; a red nose or a shock of red hair may owe its force to its supposed moral symbolism. Long ears and other deformities affect us through their undignified reminder of affinity to a lower animal species. Much, however, in these preferences of the ruder sort of laughter looks quite capricious, and can only be set down to habit and imitation.

The impulse to laugh at deformity has a narrower and a wider counteractive. The first is pity, the second is the feeling of repugnance at the sight of ugliness.

The inhibition of laughter at deformity by pity and kindly consideration is one of the marks of a refined nature. Where the unsightly feature suggests suffering, whether physical or moral, such consideration may completely counteract the impulse.

Since deformity is a variety of the ugly, and the perception of the ugly as such repels us, we have as a further counteractive a fine æsthetic shrinking from what is unsightly. A person endowed with this repugnance may have his capacity of enjoying the funny aspect of a deformity completely paralysed. At the other extreme, we have a readiness to make fun of all bodily defects, even when they are a revolting spectacle. The area of enjoyment for most men lies between these extremes, when the displeasing element of the ugly is mitigated, so that its effect is lost in the stream of hilarity which its drollery sets flowing.

It may be added that where deformity has been turned into a laughable quality the impulse to "make fun" has commonly been aided by other forces, more particularly a sense of relief from fear and a feeling of retaliation. This is clearly illustrated in the laughter of the people in the Middle Ages at the devil, the demons and the rest. Perhaps children's rather cruel laughter at the hunchback contains an element of retaliative dislike for a person who is viewed as vicious and hurtful.

(3) Another group of laughable objects is closely related to the last. Certain *moral deformities and vices* have always been a special dish in the feast of laughter. We have only to think of popular jokes, the *contes* of the Middle Ages, and the large branches of literature known as comedy and satire, to see how eagerly the spirit of mirth has looked out for this source of gratification.

So far as this laughter directs itself against a vicious disposition, or deformity of character, such as vanity or cowardice, and not against a lighter defect of external manners, it seems to involve a perception of something ugly, like a bodily blemish, and further some appreciation of its disgraceful or degrading aspect.

It is a view commonly held, and as we shall see supported by the practices of art, that all vices are not equally fit subjects for laughter. Some kinds seem to have a specially amusing aspect. There may be peculiar features in the expression of the vicious disposition which give it value for the laughing eye. This is obviously true of drunkenness, for example; and hardly less so of violence of temper, which has a large and impressive drollness in its display. Other vices, such as cowardice and miserliness, have something choice for the eye of laughter in the meanness of their display, the petty, contemptible practices to which they commonly lead. The supreme place given to vanity among laughable moral failings seems to be explicable in part by this consideration. Nothing is more entertaining than the inflation in carriage and speech which comes from an overweening conceit. Hypocrisy, again, together with her kinswomen deceit and lying, seems to have a peculiar value for the mirthful eye by reason of her disguise, and the elemental joy which mortals young and old derive from a good peep behind a mask. As a last example we may take a porcine obstinacy over against the expression of others' wishes, the stupidity against which even "the gods contend in vain," a variety of the amusing which seems to tickle our sensibilities by presenting to us the rigidity of the machine in lieu of the reasonably pliant organism of the man.

This glance at the amusing side of what we call moral deformities suggests that when we laugh at these we are by no means always at the moral point of view, looking at actions and traits of character as immoral. This is seen, first of all, in the fact that, when we are laughing at what we view as vice, we do not, as some say, always recognise its littleness and harmlessness, visiting it, so to speak, with the merely nominal penalty of a laugh. Lying, or a display of brutal appetite, may be turned into a subject of mirth when the least reflection would show that it is decidedly harmful. It is seen, further, in the fact that the laughable in this case extends far beyond the limits of what we commonly call vices. The excessive humility of the friend of our youth, Mr. Toots, is hardly less entertaining a spectacle than excessive vanity.

It seems rather to be want of a certain completeness and proportion of parts in the moral structure which amuses here. This is yet more clearly illustrated by the fact that comedy, as we shall see, holds up to a gentle laughter want of moderation even in qualities which we admire, such as warmth of feeling, refinement of sentiment, and conscientiousness itself.

Here again we may note that the "laughable" will be relative to the special experiences and standards adopted by the particular society. Contrast, for example, the fund of amusement which lies in the spectacle of drunkenness for a people addicted to, and therefore tolerant of, deep drinking, with that available for another people by whom the vice is shunned and judged severely. It is evident, indeed, that our readiness to be entertained by the look of excess or disproportion in a character will vary with the idea of the normal pattern. The old Greek way of scanning character differed, in certain respects, from that habitual, say in England to-day.

In the case of what are palpable vices we have as counteractive tendencies, not merely the finer shrinking from the ugly, but the recoil of the moral sense in the distressed attitude of reprobation. Hence it may be said that the immoral trait must not be of such volume and gravity as to call forth the moral sense within us. Here, too, differences of temperament and habit, and, one may add, of the mood in which the presentation finds us, will affect the result. It is amazing to what an extent even reputable citizens are able to enjoy the presentment of moral failings, when they give themselves up to the mood which seems to belong to a seat before the comic stage.

(4) We may pass to a group of laughable presentations in which the feature specially fixated by the observer's mental eye is some *breach of order and rule*. Laughable displays of vice involve this element, of course, but in the cases now to be considered the violence done to rule is the more conspicuous feature. On the other hand, laughable violations of rule are closely related to the oddities dealt with above. The donkey rolling on his back may be said, for the child's intelligence, to break the rule of the donkey's normal behaviour; yet here the laughableness seems to spring immediately out of the fresh stimulating character of the novelty of the spectacle. In order that an action may impress us as disorderly, we must recognise, vaguely at least, that some custom or rule is disobeyed. The sight of a donkey stepping on to the pavement of a street, or quietly browsing in a garden, would amuse as an exhibition of the disorderly. Perhaps we have the boundary-line between what is merely odd and what is disorderly illustrated by the bizarre aspect of a boy in a class who deviates considerably in height from the approximately uniform height of the rest of the class. It has been pointed out by Dr. Lipps[55] that even a house in a row may assume an amusing appearance under like circumstances. Here the general

uniformity, immediately presented to the eye, seems to supply the spectator with the idea of a rule which the odd-looking individual is violating.56 Under the present head we shall keep to examples of the laughable where the breach of rule is palpable.

To begin with, disorderliness, the upsetting of the usual orderliness of life, is a great source of laughter to the young and even to many adults. All the more extravagant forms of jollity or "high spirits" are wont to pass into the disorderly. This applies not merely to uproar, but to such "jocose" proceedings as smashing windows, the enjoyment of which, as Addison reminds us, is by some laid down as the test of humour.

This being so, we might expect that the appearance of the disorderly would wear an amusing aspect for ordinary men. This is certainly what we find. The crowd loves the spectacle of lawlessness and misrule in the harlequinade and elsewhere. The laughter-moving force of the presentment of a man always in a hurry, or continually changing his purpose, illustrates this effect of the disorderly. The comic value of the man in a rage depends too in part on this circumstance. All appearances of disorder where order is counted on, as in dress, are apt to provoke a smile of amusement. A squad of soldiers marching out of time, or out of line, is a recognised stimulus to laughter. Even the sight of a room turned upside down for a cleaning, or of the confusion of a dinner-table after a meal, takes on something of this amusing aspect of the disorderly.

The droll aspect of the disorderly becomes specialised in the breach of commonly-recognised rules of behaviour. The best marked cases are offences against the code of good manners, and the rules of correct speech. Rude behaviour and *gaucheries*, solecisms, provincialisms, and confusions in the use of language, amuse us as breaches of familiar rule, though they may no doubt entertain us also as manifestations of a naïve ignorance.

It is hardly needful to point out that men's judgments of the laughable element in breach of rule will be relative. The code of manners will vary with the community and with the particular class, and will tend to change with time in the case of the same group. One has only to think of the variations, from period to period, in the fashionable modes of accost, of pronouncing words, and so on.

The great force which tends to counteract this direction of laughter is the respect for order and rule, which has been formed slowly and with much difficulty, at least in the larger part of a community. It follows that if men who are supporters of rule are to laugh at a violation of it, the act of lawlessness must not seem of a gravity sufficient to offend this respect. This condition will be satisfied if it is manifest that the upsetting of rule, so far as it is intentional, is not serious but a sort of make-believe; or that it is confined within the limits of the harmless, as in the case of the angry man vainly threatening denunciation against all and sundry; or, again, that the failure to comply with rule is not intentional but due to ignorance.

(5) We may now pass to a group of presentations where the laughable feature seems to reside in a situation or condition which is distinctly undesirable. *Small misfortunes,* especially those which involve something in the nature of a difficulty or "fix," are for the ordinary onlooker apt to wear an amusing aspect. The loss of one's hat, a fall due to a slip, or a tilting against another pedestrian, are recognised instances of the amusing in the spectacle of the streets. Such sights as Ajax slipping in the foot-race and getting his mouth filled with dirt (*Iliad,* xxiii., 770–85), John Gilpin on his runaway steed, a party in a boat left stranded on a sand-bank, the down in the circus vainly trying to stop a runaway horse by clinging to its tail; these and other illustrations will readily occur to one familiar with the ways of laughter. The older popular entertainments, such as the enjoyment of the performance of grinning through the horse-collar at the country fair, owed something of their value to this delight in seeing a man in a fix—if only that of being compelled to make a fool of oneself—especially when it was due to his lack of foresight.57 A more refined sense of the laughable seizes on the many "awkward" situations of social life, say the unconcealable *gêne* that overtakes a fine lady when she makes a meritorious but ill-judged attempt to get into touch with one of the "lower class".

It is to be noted that many situations involving not only an irritating amount of inconvenience but real suffering may excite this kind of laughter in the vulgar. The spectacle of a cripple dragging his body along has its amusing aspect, not only for jovial mortals but for superior beings. Homer represents the Olympian gods as dissolved in laughter at the sight of the lame blacksmith trying to discharge the dainty office of the cup-bearer Ganymede. We see the same unfeeling rejoicing at mishap in the laughter of the savage and of the coarser product of civilisation at certain forms of punishment, particularly the administration of a good thrashing to a wife, or to some ugly piece of mischief, as Thersites. Even "polite society" seems to have a relish for this form of amusement, if we may judge from the entertainment which the fashionable crowd on one side of the English Channel appears to find in scanning the gloomy figures and wan faces of the passengers as they land after a stormy passage. Here, again, the deep malignity of man peeps out in a rejoicing at the sight of others' hurt (Schadenfreude).

Among these mirth-provoking misadventures, situations and incidents which manifestly involve loss of dignity fill a large space. The spectacle of a flying hat pursued by its owner owes much of its "funniness" to the fact that the loss of a symbol of dignity is involved. Possibly certain bodily deformities, especially a failure of the nose or of the chin, may derive something of their laughableness from our perception of the loss of a dignified feature.58 The laughter which is wont to greet the sight of a man left with a baby on his hands illustrates the same effect. The favourite situations in the lighter popular comedy, as that of the man who is henpecked, and who is subject to a mother-in-law, amuse so much because of the deep descent of the "head" of the house which they involve. The stimulating force of this kind of presentation is the greater where the undignified situation overtakes one who is holding at the time an exalted position, as when a preacher in the pulpit is caught stumbling on too homely an expression, or a judge on the bench giving way to an oppressive somnolence.

As in the other instances, we have here to note the limitations introduced by the variable nature and circumstances of the spectator. Misfortune, the suffering of indignity, clearly appeals to a kind of feeling quite dissimilar to that of mirth. Where pity is strong and alert much of the laughter at mischances, at difficulties, and so forth, is restrained. On the other hand, this pity for men in misadventure comes of knowledge and of insight; and where experience and training have not given these, the restraining influence on laughter will be wanting. Hence the familiar fact that youngsters, though not less capable of pity than their elders, will laugh at sights, such as the old lady slipping and falling, which touch the heart of those who know what they really mean.

(6) We may now touch on a group of laughable objects which has a close kinship with more than one of the groups already illustrated, though it stands apart by right of well-marked peculiarities. I refer to laughter at *the indecent* or obscene, whether in actual presentation or in suggestion.

Any serious attempt to illustrate the variety of the sources of men's ordinary laughter must, I think, find a place for this group. Among men, and one may add the gods, the uncovering of that which decency insists on hiding is a powerful provocative of laughter. In their more direct and potent workings indecent presentations appeal to the loud mirthfulness of the coarse mind, to the *gros rire* of the man tossing the *gros sel*, as Mr. Meredith has it. They bulk among the jocosities of savage tribes—or at least many of these—and of the less refined among civilised societies. Culture is a great restraining influence here. Yet it would be an error to suppose that educated men who are also of the laughter-loving are destitute of this sensibility. The impulse to greet merrily an allusion to the indecent, when it comes unexpectedly, taking us off our guard, so to speak, and when it is neither too pronounced nor enlarged upon, is, I believe, universal among men who laugh.

The laughter at a suggestion of what not only civilised but even savage society seeks to veil from view would seem to be most naturally regarded as a case of the improper, or breach of accepted rule. To make reference to these matters is to break through a well-understood social convention. This breach, moreover, carries with it a plump descent into the depths of the undignified; for since society has willed to throw the veil here any attempt to uplift it implies something shameful. The disgrace falls on the person who is the subject of the allusion—in all cases where there is a definable person concerned. In others, where the allusion is directed to a common "infirmity" of human nature, the indignity done is, of course, more widespread. Not only so, we feel on hearing such an allusion that there is a lapse of dignity all round in speaker and hearers alike. The blush of the refined hearer attests this feeling of shame.

Yet to describe the effect here as due to breach of rule and lapse of dignity is certainly not to give a full account of the *modus operandi* of this variety of the laughable. If to speak of these things is forbidden and branded as an offence to good taste, on the other hand that which is alluded to is a real and an inseparable part of our nature. The enjoyment of these allusions may accordingly be viewed under another aspect as a rejection of the artificial in favour of simple unadorned nature. The casting aside for the moment of the decent veil and the facing of what is customarily hidden away seems, indeed, to be attended by a distinct feeling of liberation from restraint and of joyous expansion. Hence, probably, the fact noted by historians of mediæval manners that the coarseness of the jocosity appeared to increase with the magnitude of the feast. The mood of exuberant hilarity favours the slackening of all artificial restrictions. The same consideration may, perhaps, explain the hold which coarse jokes, if only they have just the right quantum of salt, maintain on the humorous palate of the strong and virile among men of intellect.

In this brief account of the mirthful aspect of the indecent I have confined myself to what discloses itself to consciousness in the moderate forms of laughter, common among civilised men who practise a certain self-restraint. Yet we know that the outbursts which are provoked, in coarser men at least, by the uncovering of sexual matters have a deeper source in the obscure parts of our animal organisation. Our sources of knowledge with respect to the condition of men when they are seized with the sexual orgasm, including the testimony of mythology, suggest that laughter here assumes the function of voicing a state of riotous self-glorification of the animal part of our nature, when fully released for a moment; and, further, that here, as in some forms of nervous laughter, it has an organic connection with a condition of emotional paroxysm.

It is hardly necessary to point out that relativity has a large empire in this branch of the laughable. A man's idea of what is obscene will be relative to the standards of his society, which may vary considerably. The Englishman living abroad is apt to be impressed by the fact that men and women, otherwise as refined as his own people, hesitate less to call a spade a spade and to allude in conversation to subjects which are tabu at home. Similarly, the modern reader of Shakespeare may be shocked by the freedom of speech of the cultivated women of another age.

Further, as implied above, the readiness to laugh here will be modified profoundly by refinement of feeling. If it is true that all men are capable of enjoying an allusion to the indecent, provided that it is delicately executed, it is no less true that only coarse-minded men are able to drink frequently or deeply at this rather muddy spring of laughter.59

(7) Another group of laughable presentations has a certain analogy with the last. Popular mirth has made a prominent target of men's *pretences*. To peep behind the mask and seize the make-believe is a sure means of providing ourselves with laughter. So large, indeed, is the part of affectation and disguise in social life, that not only the ruder popular art, but comedy has made them one chief source of its entertainment. The flavour of the laughter varies greatly according to the moral complexion of the pretence. Seeing through the transparent make-believe of the child sets us laughing in one key; the detection of the half-unconscious humbug, in another; and that of the artful impostor, in yet another.

That the appreciation of this embodiment of the laughable is relative, may not be at once evident. Yet a glance at the numerous little hypocrisies not only allowed, but even exacted by polite society, will suffice to show how the standard may vary. The dulling influence of use is exceptionally apparent here. The shams of life cease to amuse us—save a very few—when they are numerous and ubiquitous. The Englishman who laughs at the little pretences of society abroad, may be quite incapable of discerning the amusing side of quite similar simulations and dissimulations in the ways of his own society.

Here, too, as in the case of moral blemishes generally, the impulse will be restrained by the tendency to judge seriously, and by the higher degrees of moral sensitiveness. Men of easy morals will laugh cynically, perhaps, at forms of imposture which would shock those of a finer moral texture.

(8) We may now pass to a species of the laughable which has a more markedly intellectual character. Among the exhibitions of human quality none appears to have had its ludicrous mark more widely recognised than that of *want of knowledge or of skill*. Here, again, our friend, the clown of the circus, comes to our aid. The spectacle of his futile attempts to imitate the

exploits of the skilled horseman and other experts stirs the risibility of the multitude to one of its *fortissimo* outbursts. Ignorance of locality, especially when it lands a traveller in a mess, is a common source of merriment to the rustic onlooker. Children, savages, and all simple folk delight in such exhibitions of ignorance and incompetence. The more restrained amusement of "society" at the want of *savoir faire* in the uninitiated shows that this enjoyment of the spectacle of ignorance by the well-informed is widespread. The value of the spectacle is evinced by the fact that when in argument a man desires to win the laugh of onlookers to his side, he will do his best to show up a laughable degree of ignorance in his fellow-disputant. The presence of the expert in a gathering of bucolics is a situation pregnant with possibilities of mirthful enjoyment. Let the delightful discussions of Mr. Hardy's Wessex folk suffice as illustration.

These amusing uncoverings of ignorance and inability are a spicy ingredient in the mutual quizzings of men belonging to distinct peoples or classes, such as the savage and the white man, the sailor and the landsman. This will be illustrated later on.

In these cases the spectator may not count on the possession by others of knowledge or skill. The man who laughs has at most a vague expectation that outsiders should be equal to those of his own set. The laugh at ignorance and incompetence takes on another and more ironical ring when knowledge and competence are reasonably to be expected, as for example when an official shows a striking incompetence for the duties of his office.

The spectacle of human ignorance grows particularly entertaining when it has to do with matters supposed to be of common knowledge. M. Bergson gives us an example in the observation of a disappointed traveller on hearing that there was an extinct volcano in the neighbourhood: "They had a volcano and allowed it to go out".[60] It is this element of ignorance of what is generally known which, in part, gives the amusing aspect to many breaches of rule, particularly those of language. So firm is our assumption that everybody, even the foreigner, ought to be able to speak our language that we cannot hear a gross mispronunciation or misapprehension of meaning without feeling it to be naïve. Shakespeare in the same play makes us laugh at the bad English of Dr. Caius and Sir Hugh Evans. Of course the fun is greater if the foreigner stumbles unwittingly into an observation which tells against himself; as when a German visitor to London, being asked how his wife was, answered, "She is generally lying, and when she is not lying she is swindling," meaning to say "lying down" and "feeling giddy" ("hat Schwindel").

The ludicrous side of the paradoxical, of what is violently opposed to common-sense—a matter to be dealt with more fully presently—illustrates the effect of intellectual naïveté. All exaggeration in description and other extravagance of statement are laughed at, in part at least, as showing ignorance of what is credible. On the other hand, insistence on the well known and the obvious, especially when it is accompanied by a laboured argument, amuses us by ignoring the circumstance that the hearer or reader is already quite familiar with the matter.

A delightful exhibition of the naïve intelligence is given by a gross misapprehension of what is happening or of what is being said at the moment. The Londoner may delight his country listener with his misunderstandings of what to the latter seems perfectly self-explanatory. The tickling force of such misapprehension is heightened when it involves an idea which is the very reverse of the truth. The good story of the Yorkshire juryman who remarked that "Lawyer Scarlet gets all the easy cases" turns on the delicious inversion of causal relations. When travelling once in a train I heard a mother say to her little girl, who had been complaining of the heat, "The more you think of it the worse it will be"; upon which the child remarked in a drily humorous tone, "I should say the worse it is the more I shall think of it". The mother's remark had probably seemed an inversion of the true relation.

Other examples of what we call naïveté come, in part at least, under this head. The want of tact, the bringing in of that which has no relevance to the circumstances or the ideas of the moment, is an excitant of laughter for men of all levels of culture. The inappropriate ways in which the kindly savage or child tries to minister to his visitor's comfort are a pretty example of such simplicity. Irrelevances in conversation and discussion, such as *mal à propos,* mistakings of the issue, unfortunate suggestions of reasons, and the like, are among the recognised tributaries of the river of laughter. These irrelevances make a large contribution to the lighter enjoyment of social intercourse. An irrelevance having a peculiarly broad effect is a response to a question which wholly misses its point, as when one reads of a man on a descending balloon who asked a yokel, "Where am I?" and received for answer only the absurdly obvious, "In a balloon".

Children's naïveté—a mine of wealth to the discerning seeker after the laughable—illustrates this tickling property of a perfect simplicity of intelligence, and of those irrelevances of behaviour and of utterance which by their mighty compass seize and occupy for the instant the field of contemplative vision. One of its most valuable manifestations is the habit of quietly substituting the child's point of view for the adult's. A large number of the "funny remarks" of children illustrate this. Here is an example. An improver of occasions asked a child who had seduced her grandfather into a rather alarming romp, "Isn't grandpapa very kind to play with you, dear?" and received the sharp correction, "I'm playing with *him*".

A bare reference may be made to other illustrations of the intellectual simplicity which entertains the mirthful eye. The effect of prejudice and passion in narrowing the mental outlook and setting up erroneous views of things is a favourite subject of comic treatment. As we shall see, the spectacle gains a higher value when the degraded intelligence approaches that of the disordered, and the amusing person, wholly preoccupied with his illusions, utters a string of remarks so widely irrelevant to the actual circumstances of the moment as to upset the gravity even of a serious spectator.

The limiting influence of relativity in the appreciation of this branch of the amusing has been pretty plainly illustrated in what has been said. The lack of skill or of knowledge which excites our merriment is the lack of that which is a familiar possession of our set, which accordingly we, at least, tend to look for in others. Hence, the man of society is amused at your not knowing one kind of thing, say, the history of the British Peerage, the bucolic at your ignorance of another, say, the ways of calves, and so forth. The simplicity of a child's mind only impresses us in relation to our own grown-up and complex ways of thinking. Even the absurdities of paradox are relative, for what we are pleased to regard as the stable, unalterable body of common-sense is, in reality, subject to change.

(9) We will now touch on a group of facts on which writers on the ludicrous are accustomed to lay stress. The spectacle of a child wearing a man's hat, fully considered above, shows us the laughable directly and unmistakably as a juxtaposition of two foreign elements, the semblance of a whole made up of incongruous parts. Here we see the sense of fun fixing its eye on *relations*. It is recognised by all that the perception of certain relations, more particularly the unfitting, the disproportionate, the incongruous and the logically inconsistent, plays a large part in calling forth the more refined sort of laughter.

In dealing with this laughable aspect of relations we must draw a distinction. When a person laughs, say, at the imbecile movements of a skater as he tries to save himself from a fall, or at an outrageous costume, or at the fantastic language of some *précieuse*, he may be aware of half-perceiving a relation; such as want of fitness, extravagant departure from the normal. He knows, however, that his mental eye is not focussed for this relation; on the contrary, he feels as if the presentation in itself, by giving the required jerk to his apperceptive tendencies, were directly provocative of mirth.

On the other hand, he will, I believe, hold that there are cases where the enjoyment of the laughable depends on the mental eye directing itself to a relation. The relation may not be apprehended in a perfectly precise way;

but the point is that it is mentally seized, if only for the fraction of a second; and, further, that a degree of definiteness is given to the apprehension of the relation by a glimpse, at least, of the related terms.

This localising of the laughable in a relation is most evident in the case of those complex presentations where lack of harmony and of mutual fitness—what we call incongruity—appear in the several parts of the whole which are present to the eye, and forces itself on the attention in a thoroughly aggressive fashion. A country woman displaying in her dress or in her speech a bizarre mixture of the peasant and the fine lady, a proposal to climb a mountain in dainty high-heeled shoes, the couching of a vote of thanks in language far below or above the needs of the occasion, these pull at the muscles of laughter because they strike us as a forcing together of things which hurtle and refuse to consort. The same holds true of cases in which the incongruity lies between one presentation and another which has preceded and is still present to the imagination, as in the clown's utter failure to reproduce the model action of the expert which he sets out to equal.

Even in cases where the laughable incongruity holds between things both of which are not present at the same or nearly the same moment, a direct glancing at the relation, involving at least a dim representation of the absent member of the related twain, may be requisite for a full enjoyment. It is probable, for example, that Homer's gods, when they laughed uproariously at the sight of the grimy and lame Vulcan essaying the part of Ganymede, mentally recalled the image of the latter and carried out a comparison between the two. Similarly in many of our nicer judgments of the amusingly excessive in dress, speech and so forth, we may, as suggested above, envisage the relation to a standard of measure in this direct way.61

It may, no doubt, be a question whether the relation made "focal" in consciousness in such cases lies between two parts of a complex presentation, or between the presentation as a whole and a represented standard arrangement. When, for example, we laugh at the intrusion of a too lively gesture into the pulpit, do we mentally fixate the incongruity between the situation and the action, or mentally go back to the idea of the customary and suitable kind and amount of gesture, and view the present performance as disagreeing with these? This point may be reserved for later consideration.

The view that in the cases just illustrated we have to do with another variety of laughter, that of the mind or intelligence, is confirmed by the reflection that much of it is excluded from the popular category. The masses can enjoy a palpable contradiction between profession and performance—witness the enjoyment afforded to the populace of the Middle Ages by the spectacle of the moral inconsistencies of the monks.62 But when it comes to the appreciation of inherent inconsistencies within the character, such as want of stability of purpose, fickleness in the affections and so forth, the need of a certain acuteness in perceiving relations, and of quickness in mentally reinstating what is not present, may greatly restrict the area of the enjoyment. Gross and palpable inconsistencies, such as those represented in the delightful monologue *L'Indécis*, with which M. Coquelin (aîné) rejoices us, are accessible to popular laughter, but most of the self-contradictions with which a Molière, a George Eliot, or a George Meredith refreshes our spirits are "caviare to the general". Much the same is true of the laughter which gladdens the measuring eye when it lights on the unmeasured, the excessive, the disproportionate.

One subdivision of this domain of the laughable is the logically incongruous or *the absurd*. Here, again, we touch on a region into a large part of which culture must give the key of admission. An example of such a laughable absurdity is found in that which conflicts with our deepest and most unalterable convictions. What is logically far-fetched or paradoxical is a familiar provocative of mirth. Since this case, like that of laughing at an extravagant costume, does not imply a direct and clear perception of relation, but only a kind of harmless shock to our firmly rooted apperceptive tendencies, we may expect to find illustrations of it low down in the scale of intelligence. As we shall see later, children will be moved to mirth by the presentation of an idea that directly conflicts with their crude standards of the possible; and savages show the same impulse to laugh at what is manifestly opposed to their fixed traditional standards of truth. So it is with suggestions and proposals which strike the more mature intelligence as paradoxical, that is to say, as a kind of assault on its deeply fixed habits of belief, and what it is pleased to call its "common-sense". Ideas which strike it as revolutionary, whether they appear in the domain of social custom, of political activity, of morals, or of scientific explanation, are greeted by voluminous laughter. Darwin's idea of man's descent from an ape-like ancestor, when first introduced, probably excited almost as much hilarity as indignation.

More restricted is the area for amusement supplied by logical inconsistencies. The spying out of amusing inconsequences in a man's various utterances is the work of an expert. A contradiction must be very palpable, and the contradictory statements must be very near to one another in time, in order that food for laughter may reach the many. The best example of this laughter at contradiction in popular mirth is, I suppose, the "bull," where the incompatibility stares out at you from a single statement, and sets your sides shaking; as in the argument, attributed to an Irish statesman, that, in the prosecution of a certain war, "every man ought to be ready to give his last guinea to protect the remainder".63

One might naturally suppose that in the appreciation of these more intellectual forms of the laughable there would be no room for the restraining action of relativity. An incongruous relation would seem to be one and the same object for all men's intuitions, and the least affected by accidents of temperament and external circumstances. Yet this supposition is not quite correct. Such incongruities as moral and logical inconsistencies have, it must be remembered, their disagreeable and even their painful aspect. When discovered in the character or in the intellect of a person known to be of a high consistency, a contradiction would naturally offend the admiring spectator. Here, too, then, we have to add the qualification, "provided that there is nothing disagreeable and repellant in the manifestation". Not only so, with respect to much that is popularly called paradox it is to be remembered that the standard of truth employed is far from being that of the eternal verities. As the allusion to the ridicule poured on Darwin's theory of natural selection shows, what one generation laughs at as plainly contradictory to fundamental notions may be quietly recognised as a familiar truth by its successor.

(10) A group of laughable presentations making large appeal to the more intellectual kind of laughter meets us in *verbal play and amusing witticism*. A closer examination of the nature of wit will come later.

What seems most manifestly characteristic of verbal forms of the "funny" is the intrusion of the playful impulse. Children's word-play shows this clearly enough. New words are for them sounds to be reduced to familiar ones, and the funnier the results of this reduction the better are they pleased. This leads by a step to punning, where quite intelligible words or phrases are purposely altered so as to bring in a new meaning; or where without any verbal alteration the substitution of a new meaning for the primary and obvious one effects the required change. The playful impulse to get as far away as possible from rule and restriction, to turn things topsy-turvy, to seize on the extravagant and wildly capricious, is clearly enough recognisable here. Much of this word-play, too, has a close kinship with make-believe; a natural and obvious meaning is the pretence in this case, whereas the reality is the half-hidden meaning introduced by the inventive wag. All the same it seems to me that this group of laughable objects has its place close to that of the incongruous and absurd. A pun that claims any intellectual rank must have a point, a bite, and this would appear to be most naturally secured by introducing an element of irony and rendering the primary and obvious meaning of the sentence ludicrously false. When, for example, a preacher whose ponderous dulness had set his congregation genteelly scuttling was said to have delivered "a very *moving* discourse," the point of the witty thrust lay in the complete opposition between the best and the worst result of eloquence brought together in the two meanings of "moving," an opposition which gives the trenchant irony to the description.

In cases, too, where there is no verbal trickery the lighter kind of wit shows the same tendency to a playful capriciousness of fancy. It delights in substituting for our ordinary points of view and standards of reference others which strike the hearer as amusingly fanciful and extravagant. This is illustrated by much of our entertaining talk, which is wont to try to escape for a moment from the leading-strings of sober sense; as when a person *à propos* of a moon looking wan and faint some hours after an eclipse observed that she seemed not yet to have got over the effects of the eclipse.

In this department of contemplative amusement we see once more the limitations introduced by differences of temperament and mental attitude, as well as of experience and knowledge. Nowhere, perhaps, is the habitual inclination of the balance between seriousness and love of fun in a man more clearly indicated than in his readiness to tolerate and enjoy word-play and the entertaining side of nonsense generally. One to whom words and serious points of view are sacred things, will barely suffer any form of this recreation. On the other hand a ready appreciation of these pranks of wit means that the listener's fancy has the requisite speed of wing. It means, too, commonly, that his intelligence is in touch with the wit's standpoint, with his experience and circle of ideas. Bucolic wit is a sealed book to the superior gentleman from the town; the merry verbal sports of the judge, the statesman, the theologian and so forth, reflecting like their dreams daily types of experience and habits of thought, are apt to fall flat on the ears of those who are not in touch with these.

The above may, perhaps, serve as a sufficiently full enumeration of the more prominent of those attributes or aspects of laughable things which, some in some cases, others in others, make direct appeal to our mirth.

That each of these may of itself thus start the currents of laughter will, I believe, be admitted by those who are familiar with the field of human mirth. There is, I hold, ample evidence to show that what is embarrassing, what is contrary to rule, what is demeaning, what is unreal and pretentious, and the rest, do each, under certain limiting conditions, move men's laughter.

It is, no doubt, difficult to supply a perfect demonstration of the fact of the intrinsic laughableness of each of these features. It has already been pointed out that in many of the most agreeable instances of the laughable different stimuli combine their forces. This is so much the case that it is sometimes difficult to decide which of the co-operating attributes is the most prominent. For example, the spectacle of the lackey donning the externals of a fine gentleman—a favourite subject of mirthful treatment by

Molière and others—may amuse us as a transparent pretence, as a fine display of insolent vanity, or, again, as an amusing caricature of the extravagant absurdities of fine manners. Extravagance in dress and the like is frequently found in the company of a deliciously erroneous idea of one's own importance. Intellectual naïveté may peep out at us and a moral naïveté look over its shoulder, as in the remark of a lady whom the astronomer Cassini had invited to see an eclipse, when she found that she had arrived too late: "M. de Cassini will be good enough to begin again for my sake".64 As I have remarked, the unfitting is in a large number of cases an introduction of something unworthy; as when a man at a dinner-party almost suggests something of an animal violence in his mode of eating, or an orator resorts to a "wooden" manner of speech or gesture, or when an unhappy simile hurls the hearer into the lowest region of the commonplace, a proceeding satirised in the well-known lines from Butler's *Hudibras:*—

And like a lobster boil'd, the morn

From black to red began to turn.

As a last example of the many-sidedness of the laughable we may name affectation, particularly when it takes the form of aping another's manners; for this may amuse us as a bit of acting seen through, or as an incongruous intrusion of a foreign element into the natural character of the imitator, or, again, as a weakness, a lack of intellectual or of moral initiative.

Nevertheless, the appearance of cross-division in our scheme is really no objection to it. By collecting a sufficient number of instances, and noting how the presentation of a certain feature affects us when it is plainly the preponderant stimulus, and how it will continue to affect us in much the same way when its concomitants vary, we may satisfy ourselves that each of the aspects here named is effective as a provocative of laughter. It will be for experimental psychology, if ever its methods are competent to grapple with the subject, to make this clearer.

There is another objection, which, though related to the last, is to be carefully distinguished from it. Even in cases where the laughable feature is clearly localised there may seem something arbitrary in our mode of describing it. For example, it may be said, why distinguish the relation of the unfit and kindred relations as a special group, since in all cases they may be regarded as products and expressions of a defective intelligence or taste? To raise this difficulty now is, however, to anticipate our theoretical problem, how far these several varieties of laughable feature lend themselves to reduction to a common principle. In naming each of the above groups I have sought to envisage the laughable aspect as the natural man, innocent of theoretic aims, would envisage it.

What is important here is to emphasise both the frequent combination of entertaining features in the objects which excite our laughter, and the fact that one and the same feature may be envisaged in more than one way. These two circumstances throw an interesting light on the meaning of the long discussions and the want of agreement among theorists.

In drawing up this list of the laughable features in things I have said nothing about the connection between this part of the inquiry and that which preceded it. Yet the connection has not been wholly hidden. In the entertaining effect of new things we have found an element of the laughter which springs from a sudden expansion of joy. In the laughter excited by the indecent we have noted a trace of the laughter of "sudden glory" and of what I have called nervous laughter. Lastly, in dealing with the entertaining quality of the more sportive wit we seem to have got near the laughter of play.

This connection would appear the more clearly if we were to extend our list by adding a pair of groups. These are (11) laughable objects which affect us as expressions of a merry mood; and (12) laughable situations which involve a relation akin to that of victor and vanquished. A word or two on each of these must suffice.

(11) There is little doubt that all presentations which are instantly interpreted as manifestations of a fun-loving disposition tend to excite merriment. This is true of series of sounds, musical as well as non-musical, which have in their rapid staccato movement a resemblance to those of laughter. It holds good also of play-like movements, such as the freakish gambols of a just loosened pony, or of a circus clown. The expression of the mirthful temper in things awakens a sympathetic laughter in the observer. Here, perhaps it would seem to be more correct to say that we laugh not *at* or *over*, but, if one may so say, *to* the playful freak. Nevertheless, we shall find that what we recognise as objectively laughable cannot be understood save by reference to these appearances of playful challenge.

(12) That the sight of a man winning in a struggle or getting the better of another in some way is fitted to furnish amusement, is indisputable. This obviously falls in part under the head of laughter at the spectacle of another's difficulty or scrape; but it certainly deserves a separate place in an enumeration of the larger and popularly distinguished sources of merriment.

There is no need to emphasise the fact that the social spectacle owes much of its interest to combat, competition, all that is understood by men's measuring their powers one against the other. The amusing side of this interest is found in the gleeful satisfaction which the impartial spectator derives from each successful stroke, whether on the one side or on the other. The attraction of all encounters of wit in the market-place, in the political domain, on the stage and so forth, illustrates this. Popular literature will show that the plain man has fed his mirth bounteously from this source.

The situations which minister to this feeling of "sudden glory" in an onlooker are not confined to those of contest. All displays of a capacity to get the better of another seem to be entertaining to the many. Just as the sight of a man chastising his wife is good sport for the savage onlooker, so the spectacle of taking down, of discomfiture and humiliation—especially if it involves an element of deception or befooling, and so takes on the look of outwitting—may yield excellent fun to the civilised spectator.

A more refined variety of the perception of the laughable occurs when we look on Nature or fate as discomfiting man, playing tricks on him or outwitting him. So far as this idea of irony comes into our view of things, any misfortune, especially if it involves disappointment of hopes and frustration of efforts, may excite a note of laughter which has an "over-tone" of triumphant mockery.

The enjoyment of the spectacle of one man triumphing over another or showing superiority to him will in all cases be limited by conditions already sufficiently indicated. Since the laughter excited here is, presumably, in its characteristic ingredient a reflection by way of sympathetic imagination of the victors sudden glory, it must be included in the more brutal variety. If a lively sensibility produces quickly enough a sympathetic apprehension of the feelings of the vanquished, it will effectually check the impulse to laugh.

Finally, a bare allusion may be made to the way in which the laughter of relief from emotional or other strain comes into our appreciation of the laughable in things. The amusing aspect of all lapses from dignity in religious and other ceremonies cannot, I believe, be understood merely as an illustration of an inconsequence and irrelevance, but must be connected with the powerful tendency to throw off a heavy and depressing mental load by a moment's mirth. The laughter at what is lawless, and still more at the indecent and the profane, certainly derives a part of its gusto from a sense of relief from restraint, which is a main ingredient in the enjoyment of all license. But the fuller discussion of the way in which the primal sources of laughter contribute to the impressions we receive from laughable objects belongs to another chapter.

CHAPTER V.
THEORIES OF THE LUDICROUS.

Our survey of laughable things has led us to recognise certain groups which appear to induce the laughing mood: each presenting its special variety of laughable feature. One group may be said, *primâ facie,* to exhibit mischances, another some form of human defect, another, again, something of the misfitting or incongruous, and so forth. We may now advance to the theoretic problem of unifying and explaining these varieties of the laughable.

Here, for the second time, we must touch on the views propounded by authorities on the subject under the name of Theories of the Ludicrous. Happily, it is not necessary to burden the reader with a full account of these. We shall of course pass by all doctrines deduced from *a priori* metaphysical conceptions, and confine ourselves to those which make a show, at least, of grounding themselves on an analysis of facts. Of these I shall select two or three typical theories which come to us with the claims of distinguished authorship. We shall test these by examining how far they succeed in comprehending the diversity of fact now before us.

1. The first of these typical theories localises the secret force of the laughable in something unworthy or degraded in the object. According to this view, the function of laughter is to accompany and give voice to what may be called the derogatory impulse in man, his tendency to look out for and to rejoice over what is mean and undignified. This may be called the Moral Theory, or Theory of Degradation.

Aristotle's brief remarks on comedy in the *Poetics* may be taken as illustrative of this way of envisaging the laughable. Comedy, he tells us, is "an imitation of characters of a lower type—not, however, in the full sense of the word bad"; and, again, the Ludicrous (τὸ γελοῖον) is a subdivision of the ugly (τοῦ αἰσχροῦ), and consists in "some defect or ugliness which is not painful or destructive".65 Of an adequate theory of the subject there is here, of course, hardly a pretence. It seems strange, indeed, that a great thinker with the works of his compatriot Aristophanes before him should have placed the ludicrous wholly in character, altogether overlooking the comic value of situation. Still, the reference of the laughable to the category of ugly and disgraceful things—for τὸ αἰσχρὸν on its moral side connotes the disgraceful (compare the Latin "turpe")—may be said to imply a germ of the principle of degradation.

A more careful attempt to construct a theory of the ludicrous by a reference to something low or degraded in the object is embodied in the famous doctrine of Thomas Hobbes. According to this writer, "the passion of laughter is nothing else but sudden glory arising from sudden conception of some eminency in ourselves, by comparison with the inferiority of others, or with our own formerly". In this theory our laughter is viewed as arising, not immediately from a perception of something low or undignified, but only mediately from this perception, through a recognition of our own superiority and an accompanying emotional movement, namely, an expansion of the "self-feeling," a sudden quickening of the sentiment of pride or power. Nevertheless, the theory may be said to come under the principle of degradation, in so far as it makes the process of laughter start with a perception of some point of inferiority, that is to say of a comparative loss of dignity, in the laughable object.

The main point of this theory, that whenever we enjoy the ludicrous we are consciously realising our superiority to another, will, I think, hardly bear examination. That in this enjoyment there may be, and often is, an element of this agreeable sense of elevation I readily allow, and I shall try to show presently how it gets there. But it is altogether inadequate as an exhaustive account of the several varieties of our laughing satisfaction. Even in the groups of cases to which it seems to be most plainly applicable, for example, those of mischances and awkward situations, it is not a sufficient explanation. Is there any discoverable trace of the uplifting of pride, of the temper of "Schadenfreude"—the malicious satisfaction of watching from the safe shore the tossings of mariners in a storm—in the instantaneous response of our mirth to the spectacle of the skater's wild movements when for a moment he loses equilibrium, or of the hat wind-driven far from its proper seat on the respectable citizen's head? Is there time here for mentally bringing in the contrasting idea of our own immunity? Has the laugh the characteristic taste of the outburst of contempt which is excited by the consciousness of victory, of taking somebody down?

In dealing with this type of theory, it seems only fair to test it in the more mature form given it by a recent writer. Prof. Alexander Bain defines "the occasion of the ludicrous" as "the degradation of some person or interest possessing dignity in circumstances that excite no other strong emotion". The most marked improvements here on Hobbes' statement are (1) that consciousness of our own superiority need not come in, since we may laugh sympathetically with another who scores off his adversary, and so forth; (2) that the object degraded need not be a person, since human affairs in general, *e.g.,* political institutions, a code of manners, a style of poetic composition, may be taken down; and (3) that, as in Aristotle's theory, certain limiting conditions, namely, absence of counteracting emotions, such as pity or disgust, are recognised. These extensions on the one hand and limitations on the other are clearly meant to safeguard the Hobbesian principle against the attacks to which it so dangerously exposes itself.66

Even in this new and more guarded form, however, the theory will not bear the strain put upon it. It will account fairly well for some of the forms of the laughable in our list, such as slight misfortunes or mischances, defects, moral and intellectual, which do not shock or otherwise hurt our feelings, also certain forms of make-believe which are distinctly hypocritical and so capable of being regarded at once as moral defects, and (being seen through) as discomfitures. It *may* apply also, as has been hinted above, to the effect of the obscene; though I, at least, feel that without some forcing the effect cannot be interpreted in this way. There seems to me to lurk in our laughter here something of the joy of the child, of the Naturkind, Walt Whitman, at the sight of what is customarily hidden away.67

Leaving this, however, as a more doubtful case, let us turn to other groups. Is it possible to regard all laughable exhibitions of incongruities as degradations? Is the charming unsuitability of the "grown-up's" coat and hat to the childish form viewed by the laughing spectator as a degradation when he "lets himself go"? Are we laughing at the clothes as degraded by being thus transformed, or at the child's naïveté as a degradation of human intelligence? I confess that such a way of interpreting the spectacle strikes me as grotesquely forced. The look of the whole thing in the complete unfitness of its parts seems to affect one as a delicious absurdity before the sweet simplicity below the surface is detected.

Our author does his best to show that mere incongruity, where nothing is degraded, does not raise the laugh. I readily grant that he has made out his case, so far as to show that in most of the pungent and potently moving examples of the incongruous an element of degradation, of malicious detraction is present. But this is not enough. The question is whether it is always present, and whether in the cases where it is present it is the sole excitant of our mirth. I believe that a finer analysis shows that this is not so. Where, for example, is "the degraded" in a child's laughter at the sight of his nursery all topsy-turvy on a cleaning day? Does he view the nurse as put to shame by the setting of chairs on tables and so forth, instead of observing the proper local congruities? or does he think of the room as something quasi-human which takes on an improper look as he himself does when he makes himself in a glorious mess? Slight movements of fancy of this kind may be present: but do they lie at the sources of his laughter and constitute its main moving force?

As another way of testing the theory, we may glance at those examples of the odd or out of the way in which we find nothing of deformity, and do not seem to focus our mental glance on any loss of dignity, but are content to be amused at the queer spectacle for its own sake. I have seen a child of three or so go into a long fit of laughter at the antics of a skittish pair of horses just turned loose on a common. Did the child see anything of the mean, disgraceful, undignified in these new and lively movements? Were they not immensely, overpoweringly funny, just because they were outrageous deviations from the customary proper behaviour of horses when saddled or harnessed to a carriage? I feel the impulse to laugh at a "guy" in the street who captures my roving nonchalant eye long before I reflect on any loss of dignity which the bizarre costume may signify. In sooth, if, in this first happy moment, any distinct thought of the personality behind the wild, startling figure floats up to the surface of consciousness, it is a friendly one. I am disposed to like and feel grateful to the person who thus for an instant relieves for me the insufferable dulness of the spectacle of London citizens all dressed according to one stupid fashion.

Or let us take another group: the relish for word-play and the lighter kinds of wit. Here, again, I concede to Bain that the taking down of something a good peg-interval intensifies our satisfaction: but it seems impossible to maintain that our mirth depends altogether on the recognition of this. A good pun, a skilful turning of words so as to give a new and startlingly disconnected meaning, can hardly be said to owe its instant capture of our laughing muscles to our perception of a degradation of language and the habits of serious speech. On the contrary, I should say that any focussing of thought on this aspect would considerably weaken and might altogether arrest the laughing impulse. It is to the serious person who keeps his mouth firmly closed that this feature of the case addresses itself. Is there not here, even in the case of mirthful men, some of the delight of the playful child who amuses himself by turning words and expressions into queer nonsense just for the fun of the thing?

2. We may now pass to the second of the main types of theory which have been proposed as explanations of the working of the laughable on our feeling and the correlated muscular mechanism. Its distinctive mark is that, instead of setting behind our enjoyment of the ludicrous an emotion, or a change in our moral attitude, namely, a sense of our own superiority or of something else's degradation, it sets a purely intellectual attitude, a modification of thought-activity. The laughter, according to this second theory, results from a peculiar effect on our intellectual mechanism, such as the nullification of a process of expectation or of an expectant tendency. It is this perfectly disinterested intellectual process which brings about the *feeling* of the ludicrous and its expression in laughter. This may be called the Intellectual Theory, or Theory of Contrariety or Incongruity. Since we have already touched on this mode of conceiving of the effect of the ludicrous in criticising the view of Dr. Lipps, a brief examination of it may content us here.

It may be noted in passing that this way of dealing with the ludicrous is characteristically German. The dominant note in the philosophy of Kant and his successors has been to regard all determinations of experience as fundamentally a rational process. Just as in the domain of ethics these thinkers conceive of what British Ethicists have been wont to call the Moral Sentiment as essentially a process of Reason, so in that branch of Æsthetics which deals with the Comic we find them disposed to regard the effect of the ludicrous, less as the excitation of a concrete and familiar emotion, such as Pride or Power, than as a special modification of the process of thought.

Kant may be taken as the first great representative of this theory. According to him, wit—the only variety of the ludicrous which he touches on—is a kind of play, namely, that of thought. In everything that is to excite a lively laugh there must be something absurd. It is "an affection arising from the sudden transformation of a strained (*gespannte*) expectation into nothing". The transformation is, of course, not directly enjoyable to the understanding: it seems to induce gratification indirectly by means of a furthered *bodily* process. This, by the way, is a noteworthy concession by a German thinker to the claims of the poor body to recognition in these high affairs of the understanding, a concession which his followers quickly struck out. He gives as an example of his theory the story of a Hindoo who, when sitting at an Englishman's table, and seeing a bottle of beer turned into froth, expressed astonishment. Being questioned as to the reason, he remarked: "I am not at all astonished that it should flow out, but I do wonder how you ever got it in".

I have enlarged on Kant's theory mainly because of the authority of the author. German critics themselves recognise how absurdly inadequate is the little he says on the subject as an explanation of the effect of the laughable.68 A few words will perhaps make this plain.

It is evident that what Kant was thinking of under the head of the ludicrous was merely those exchanges of witty words and amusing stories which naturally enough formed a principal pastime of the devoted Königsberg thinker. Yet, even when considered under this narrow aspect, his theory shows itself to be palpably insufficient. It is noteworthy that, in seeking to make it fit the remark of the Hindoo quoted above, Kant feels himself called upon to contradict the suggestion that we laugh "because we deem ourselves cleverer than this ignorant man". This objection, which could not fail to occur to one who remembers Hobbes, cannot, however, be summarily dismissed by a bare assurance such as Kant gives us; and, as a recent writer remarks, "there is good reason to suppose that we laugh at the ignorance (better, 'at the naïveté') of the man who seeks the difficulty in a wrong place".69

One may go farther and venture the assertion that it is impossible to explain any laughable incident, story or remark as due *altogether* to dissolved expectation or surprise.

In examining the adequacy of Kant's theory to this purpose, I set out with the natural presupposition that, when using the word expectation, he does not mean a definite anticipation of some particular concrete sequel to what is presented to the mind at the moment. In the illustration given, he would not have meant that the questioner had a well-defined expectant idea of another explanation of the Hindoo's astonishment. It is only fair to assume that he meant merely what the word "expect" means when, on meeting a friend in a London street whom I had supposed to be out of England, I say "I did not expect to see you". In other words, "expectation" stands here for a general attitude of mind, a mode of apperceptive readiness to assimilate any idea of a certain order, that is to say, standing in a recognisable relation to what is presented. It is the attitude in which we appreciate the evolution of a plot in fiction when this appears natural and does not give a shock to consciousness.

Employing the word in this sense, one may say that, even when we laugh on receiving the solution to a conundrum which has teased and baffled us, it is not because of the dissipation of an expectant attitude. This conclusion is suggested by the familiar fact that, when at the end of our self-puzzling we are told that there is no solution, and when consequently we are unmistakably the subjects of an annulled expectation, we are very likely not to laugh; or, if we are good-natured enough to do so, it is as a result, not of any disappointment, but of a discovery that we have been hoaxed. This laugh at one's befooled self—which we shall not be disposed to repeat if the trick is tried a second time—so far from illustrating the principle of annulled expectation is a particularly clear example of that of lowered dignity.

The best kind of example of the laughable for Kant's purpose would seem to be something odd and fantastic in dress or manners. Here, as I have allowed, a kind of shock is inflicted on our fixed apperceptive tendencies. But to speak of a process of dissipated expectation here seems to be hardly accurate. As I have hinted, the sudden appearance of the unexpected moves us to laughter primarily as a delightful novelty.

It seems to follow that Kant's principle of nullified expectation offers no adequate explanation of those forms of the ludicrous which are most promising for his purpose. I may add that it fails because it makes no serious attempt to mark off the domain of the laughable by certain well-defined characteristics. We have seen that the objects which excite our laughter are things human, or akin to the human. The theory of degradation evidently recognises this: by making the ludicrous consist in a loss of dignity it points at once to the human sphere. But the theory that the effect of the ludicrous comes from an annihilation of a strained expectation suggests that it has nothing specially to do with the spectacle of human life.

As I have not included the capability of dissipating expectation among the laughable features of objects, I may indicate what I hold to be the function of surprise in the effect of the ludicrous. Surprise, the effect of a presentation for which the mind is not perfectly pre-adjusted at the moment, seems to be a common condition of vivid and exciting impressions, certainly of those which induce a state of gladness. Hence we need not wonder that it should be found among the antecedents of that outburst of gladness which we call laughter.

Nevertheless, it seems probable that the part played by surprise in the enjoyment of the laughable has been exaggerated. Does the Londoner who laughs again and again at the rough jocosities of the Punch and Judy show, depend on annihilated expectation for his mirth? Dogberry's love of a mildewy old story is by no means peculiar to him. A really good joke continues to amuse long after the first effect of surprise has worn off. A like conclusion is reached by remembering that even when a definite attitude of expectation for the coming of the ludicrous turn is assumed, laughter's greeting is none the less hearty. When racy stories are circulating and the lips move in anticipation of some new joke it seems an odd way of describing the effect to say that it is due to a dissipation of expectation. There surely seems to be more of realisation than annihilation here, even though the precise form of the impending attack on our laughter is unknown. In certain cases, moreover, as when we are watching with amusement the actions of one on whom a practical joke is being played—actions which we, being in the secret of the plot, are able to forecast with a considerable degree of precision, the element of surprise dwindles to the vanishing point. The essential condition of our laughter would thus appear to be, not the meeting of the amusing presentation with a state of complete unpreparedness of mind at the moment, but such a degree of contrariety between the presentation and our fixed and irrepressible apperceptive tendencies as will, even in spite of a pre-adjustment, secure something of a mild, momentary shock.70

A more carefully developed example of the mode of conceiving of the laughable which finds its essence in the annihilation of a rational attitude is supplied by Schopenhauer. According to this writer, the process which determines our laughter is describable as an intellectual effort and its frustration. "In every instance (he tells us) the phenomenon of laughter indicates the sudden perception of an incongruity between a conception (Begriff) and a real object, which is to be understood or 'thought' through (*i.e.*, by means of) this conception." The incongruity between the perception and the conception under which the understanding necessarily strives to bring it must be of such a degree that the perception strikingly differs from the conception. The greater and the more unexpected the incongruity, the more violent (heftiger) will be our laughter.

The author's example of the absurdity of the presentation of the curve and straight line trying to force itself under the incongruent conception of an angle is intended to illustrate this theory.71 Here is another which has a more promising look. A man who has been arrested by soldiers is allowed to join them in a game of cards. He is found cheating and is kicked out, his playmates quite forgetting that he is their prisoner. Here, according to Schopenhauer, we laugh because the incident, the ejection of a prisoner just arrested, will not fit into the general rule, "cheats at the card-table should be thrust out".

This form of the Intellectual theory clearly avoids the objection to Kant's version, that we frequently laugh at things when there is no discoverable trace of a preceding expectation involving something in the nature of an idea; for we take it as meaning that the conception arises after, and as a result of, the perception. It is further indisputable, as Kant has shown us, that in our explicit judgments, as when we say, "This painting is (or is not) a work of Rubens," a general form of representation or something in the nature of a concept may take part, the percept being (or refusing to be) subsumed under this.

At the same time, as was urged in the first chapter, the distinct calling up of this general representation is occasional only, and, therefore, not a pre-requisite of a perception of conformity or non-conformity to the normal type. When I envisage a person as correctly or as oddly dressed, I do not in either case need to have a schematic representation of the proper typical style of dress. The same holds good of many cases in which a definite rule, say of language or good manners, is felt to be complied with or to be broken: we do not need to call up a distinct representation of the rule. At most we can speak here of a conceptual *tendency*, of an apperceptive acceptance or rejection of a presentation, certain features of which are specially attended to as characteristic of the type or general form; or, on the other hand, as marks of deviation from this.

Even if we adopt this amended form of Schopenhauer's theory, we find that it is not sufficient for explaining his examples. Of the funny tangential angle no more need be said. Nor will his illustration of the self-befooled warders bear close inspection. To begin with, one may note a certain arbitrariness in the use of a mode of interpretation which plainly allows of an alternative. We can say equally well, either (with Schopenhauer) that the extrusion of a cheat who is also a prisoner will not fit into the general rule "cheats have to be ejected," or that the extrusion of a prisoner who is also a cheat will not fit into the rule that prisoners have to be confined.72 It seems to be more fitting here also to regard the incongruity—so far as the perception of this is the direct cause of our laughter—as holding between two aspects of the incident presented. The man is envisaged at once as a cheat and as a prisoner, and as such comes under two *régimes* which directly conflict. The perception of the fun of the story surely begins with a discernment of this mutual interference of two systems of rule.

Yet this is certainly not all or the chief part of the perception. The unstinting laugh comes only when we view the keepers as naïvely "giving themselves away" to their prisoner by consenting to become playmates, and so putting themselves under a rule which wholly destroys their *rôle* as custodians. Here, too, then, the principle of incongruity shows itself to be insufficient.

It only remains to add that if Schopenhauer's theory turns out to be inadequate even when applied to an example chosen by himself, it is pretty certain to fail when applied to other groups of instances of the laughable in our list, in which incongruity does not seem to be a potent ingredient, if indeed it is present at all. To suggest, for example, that our laughter at small and harmless vices, such as Aristotle speaks of, is the outcome of a suddenly conceived incongruity between a "real object" or presentation and a conception sounds sufficiently forced. Would the author of the theory have been prepared to say that in these instances we have present to our mind the concept of a perfectly virtuous man, and that our laughter comes of our failing to bring the perception under this conception? Surely the intrusion of any such exalted "concept" would be fatal to our enjoyment of the laughable aspect of vice.

Facts, moreover, contradict this view on every hand. It may suffice to allude to one of the world's great purveyors of laughter, Sir John Falstaff. According to this theory, we ought to laugh most at his vices when he first reveals them, since this is the moment when we should be most likely to bring to bear on him the "concept" of a proper decent gentleman. But is it not the fact that we laugh more freely when we have quite ceased to think of him as a possible embodiment of sobriety and decency, and when we apperceive his behaviour by help of the conceptual tendency answering, not to the type of virtuous citizen, but to the general manner of behaviour or the character of John Falstaff himself? The same is true in everyday life. We are, I think, most ready to laugh at a man's foibles, say, his vanity or his exaggerations of speech, when we know the man and can say, "Oh, it is only So-and-So!"

Neither the theory of Kant nor of Schopenhauer seems, then, to be competent to do what it undertakes to do, to explain the various forms and impressions of the laughable. These two theories, in spite of their difference, agree in regarding the incongruity which excites our laughter as lying between what we perceive and what our previous experience and our pre-existing ideas and apperceptive habits have prepared us to accept as natural and proper. But our examination of the instance of the ill-matched hat and head supplied by Dr. Lipps, as also our fuller discussion of the relation of incongruity in the preceding chapter, has led us to recognise an amusing contrariety between different parts of a presentation, of what may be called *internal* incongruity in contradistinction to the external dealt with by Kant and Schopenhauer. Hence we have to inquire how these two modes of apprehending incongruity are related.

That, *prima facie,* we have to do in this case with a real difference in the mode of perception, seems indisputable; let the reader compare the effect of the two spectacles, a man wearing an extravagantly tall hat, and a small boy wearing a hat of the height of a man's; or, again, a tiny man alone, and a short man by the side of a tall woman. In some instances, indeed, we may see that there is an intrinsic repugnance between the parts of a presentation, as when two colours in a woman's dress violently clash, or when a statement is palpably self-contradictory. Here there seems to be no reference, however vague, to previous experience or the customary. At the same time we may easily see that this field of the internally incongruent is a very narrow one. Much of what looks like this turns out, on closer inspection, to be, in part at least, externally determined. This is true of what we call a bizarre mixture of incongruent elements in mode of attire or in manners; for it is experience and the habits of social life which dispose our minds to regard them as foreign one to the other. Much of our mirthful gratification at exhibitions of the incongruous arises through a perception of the intrusion of something foreign into a situation. When, for example, we observe a rather sprightly gesture in the pulpit, we mentally view this action against a background which is the situation of the moment. Now this situation is by no means wholly presented: it is a presentation greatly enlarged and profoundly modified by the addition of a general significance. The attitude of the spectator's mind, face to face with the scene, is determined by apperceptive tendencies which imply a readiness to expect *a certain kind* of behaviour. And this, again, evidently means that certain directions of imaginative activity, and something in the nature of a "generic image" and of conceptual thought, are stirring. This effect of experience and apperceptive habits in modifying our perceptions is probably illustrated in all our appreciations of the amusingly incongruous. To revert once more to the spectacle of the man's hat on the child's head, may we not say that in this case, also, we envisage the hat as an interloper in the situation—the sweet sanctum of the nursery?

It seems to follow that Kant and Schopenhauer were wise, when dealing with incongruity, in emphasising the apperceptive factor. Contrariety to what we are accustomed to is undoubtedly the great determining element in the ill-assortments of things which provoke our laughter. Hence, in examining the theories of these two writers, we seem to have dealt with the intellectual principle in its most comprehensive and most favourable form. Nor do I see how any transformation of this principle will make it an adequate theory. The entertaining instances of mischances and awkward situations, of takings down, of moral and intellectual failings, these and other varieties of the laughable dealt with above steadily refuse to yield up their secret at the bidding of this theory.

Let us now sum up the results of our criticism of the theories. We seem to have found that, whereas neither of the two chief types of theory covers the whole field of the laughable, each has its proper, limited domain. It is certain that in many cases we laugh at an incident, a situation, an action, where the provocative is best described as a loss of dignity. It is equally certain that in many other cases our laughter springs directly out of a perception, more or less distinct, of incongruity.

That these principles have each a large sway over our laughter has been sufficiently illustrated in the preceding chapter: also that they frequently co-operate in one and the same amusing presentation. Hence we might expect that the advocate of each theory would be able to find his illustrations, and would sometimes manage to pounce upon one just after it had been carried off by his rival.73

But, it may be urged, even if both principles are shown to be valid they may be unified. If by this is meant that the incongruous and the undignified or unworthy, considered as abstract ideas, are identical, or that logically each involves the other, I am not concerned to discuss the point. It is enough for our present purpose to urge that the modes of perception and the shades of feeling involved are clearly distinguishable.

The same fundamental distinction would nullify the attempt to subsume one of these principles as a special case under the other. If we set out with the Intellectual principle, we may, without doubt, succeed in showing that many, if not all, amusing losses of dignity—such as a slight disgrace, or a bungling into a "fix"—logically involve a contrariety between what is presented and the normal custom or rule. But our question is one not of the logical analysis of meaning but of the psychological analysis of process, and I can find no evidence in favour of the theory that when we laugh at these things we have at the moment any apprehension of such a contrariety.

It is the same if we start with the other or Moral principle. Incongruities which are lapses from standard ideas may certainly, as already conceded, be regarded as degradations. And it may be possible to show that in all cases of incongruity *some* loss of dignity is logically implied. Yet even if it be so, the psychological contention will still stand that in many cases of incongruity, including our old friend the child in the father's hat, we have a full sense of relishing the incongruity and yet none at all of enjoying a degradation. Where is the degradation in the spectacle of a crow on a sheep's back which may flood a child with mirth? In truth, if our theorists had only condescended to take note of so small a matter as children's enjoyment of the world's fun, the hypothesis of degradation could never have stood its ground so long.

Yet another way of evading a glaring dualism may suggest itself. Allowing that the two principles are each valid, we might, at least, be able to combine them in the form of a single generalisation. This is what is done by Hazlitt, for example, who, though he finds the essence of the laughable in the incongruous, defines the ludicrous as involving disappointment of expectation *by something having deformity or (something) inconvenient,* that is *what is contrary to the customary* and desirable.74 Herbert Spencer's expression, a "descending incongruity," is clearly a very similar mode of combining the principles.75 Lipps' theory of incongruity, with its distinction of a little, and a belittling presentation, might also, I think, easily be made to illustrate another mode of such combination. More recently Fouillée and others have urged that the one principle in a manner supplements the other.76

It is evident, however, that this apparent mode of escape will not avail us. The combined theory implies that all cases of the laughable are at once incongruities and degradations, that is to say, perceived and felt to be such. In dealing with the principles separately, however, we have seen that, in the case of each alike, there are well-recognised examples of the laughable to which it does not apply. This conclusion manifestly carries with it the proposition that there are cases to which a combination of the principles does not apply.

A last attempt to escape this theoretic dualism would be to urge that the two principles rule in distinct realms. In that of the *ludicrous* proper, it might be urged, we have to do with the intellectual principle: it is only when the sphere is enlarged to include all that is laughable, and so the region of the *ridiculous,* that the principle of lowered dignity comes in.77 Theorists may insist on such distinctions, but it seems to me that they cannot be maintained as hard and fast boundaries. As has been shown above, laughable things do not all affect us in quite the same way. A spice of malice comes into much of the laughter that greets the spectacle, say of a bit of successful trickery; yet this does not make the experience substantially different from that of enjoying some striking example of incongruity, say a good Irish "bull".

When the note of derision begins to sound clearly, there is of course no longer any suggestion of an effect of the laughable pure and simple.

The attempt to analyse our perceptions of the laughable in the hope of discovering some single uniting principle has proved to be abortive. We find in the end that two causes of laughter remain on our hands.78

The most promising way of bringing the several laughable qualities and aspects of things under one descriptive head would seem to be to say that they all illustrate a presentation of something in the nature of a defect, a failure to satisfy some standard-requirement, as that of law or custom, provided that it is small enough to be viewed as a harmless plaything. Much, at least, of our laughter at the odd as opposed to the customary, at the deformed, at failure in good manners and the other observances of social life, at defects of intelligence and of character, at fixes and misfortunes—so far as the situation implies want of foresight—at the lack of a perception of the fitness of things, and at other laughable features, may undoubtedly be regarded as directed to something *which fails to comply with a social requirement,* yet is so trifling that we do not feel called upon to judge the shortcoming severely.

I am sure that to look at the laughable in this way is an indispensable step in the construction of a theory of the subject. We must, as we shall see presently, supplement the common mode of dealing with laughter as an abstract psychological problem, by bringing into view its *social* function. Yet this does not necessarily mean that the consideration of this function will lead us straightway to a simple theory of the ludicrous. As hinted in the preceding chapter, we may easily exaggerate the more serious function of laughter, and this point will be made clearer in subsequent chapters.

That the effects of the laughable cannot all be brought under the head of means of social correction or improvement, may, even at this stage of our inquiry, be seen by considering another point, to which we will now turn. No analysis of the qualities of things in which the laughable resides will enable us to account for the mirthful effects of these, even while we remain within the limits of what is commonly recognised as the ludicrous. This has been illustrated in the preceding chapter, and a word or two more may suffice to make it clear.

I have tried to show that some at least of the spectacles that shake us with laughter do so by satisfying something within us akin to the child's delight in the gloriously new and extravagant. This, again, means that these spectacles make appeal to that primitive form of laughter, already illustrated, which is called forth by some sudden increase of joy. Our rejoicing at the sight of the clown's droll costume and funny movements has in it something of the laughing joy of the savage when he is shown some mechanical wonder of Europe, something of the laughing joy of the infant at the sudden invasion of his nursery wall by a dancing sunbeam.79

A little more reflection on the groups of laughable things will show that other ingredients of this primitive laughter are present in our appreciation of the ludicrous. Dr. Bain finds himself compelled to eke out the deficiencies of the Hobbesian principle by urging that the spectacle of degradation may move us to laughter, not merely by exciting the feeling of power or superiority (as Hobbes said), but by supplying a sudden release from a state of constraint. The abandonment of the serious attitude in church when some trivial incident occurs is an instance of a lowering of the dignity of a thing, or an occasion, which refreshes us with a sense of liberation.80 This idea carries us much farther than the author thinks. The joyous deliverance from pressure and constraint will, I think, be found to reinforce other mental agencies in many cases of ludicrous presentation in which no degradation is discoverable. Sometimes the constraint is very severe; witness the effect when the narrator of a funny story knows how to wind up the emotion of fear to just the right pitch in order to give us the delicious run down of the mental works when the funny *dénouement* bursts upon us. Here our laughter has a large support in the joyous relief from nervous tension.

In other cases, again, the release comes as an interruption of a solemn occasion by the intrusion of something disconnected, and, by contrast, trifling. The tittering in a church at a small *contretemps* has been our illustration. There is incongruity here between two orders of ideas, if you like; or, as I should prefer to put it, between two levels of interest. For the point is that the interruption must seem ludicrous by exhibiting clearly a trifling character, by powerfully suggesting a non-reverent point of view.

As hinted above, these two sources of laughter, a sudden oncoming of gladness and a relief from restraint, are closely connected. The unexpected presentation which gladdens us seems commonly to bring a kind of relief. This is certainly true of all cases in which the preceding state was one of conscious depression and ennui. The laughter of the young, in response to our often cumbrous attempts to amuse them, may be an escape from a certain strain which belongs to a state of ennui, from the confinement or restraint which the poverty of their surroundings at the moment imposes on them.81

There is another conceivable way of bringing together the effect of sudden gladness and relief from restraint. It has been urged that all laughable things affect us by way of a shock of surprise followed by a sense of relief. Leigh Hunt, for example, thinks that when we laugh at something we receive a shock of surprise which gives *a check to the breath*, a check which is in proportion to the vivacity of the surprise; and that our laughter is a relief from this.82 This theory embodies a sound physiological principle, one which we have already adopted, but it seems to go too far. As I have tried to show, a shock of surprise, as we ordinarily understand the expression, is not an invariable antecedent of our response to laughable things. On the other hand, it may be urged with some reason that even in cases where this full shock of the unexpected is wanting, there is a moment of strain as the presentation affronts the custom-trained eye, and that the laughter is the expression of the condoning of this affront, the acceptance of it as harmless play.

In order to complete our psychological analysis of the tendencies which combine in our enjoyment of ludicrous things, we need to glance at one other variety of primitive laughter, that of contempt. In dealing with this in Chapter III. we drew the line between it and the true enjoyment of the laughable as something "objective". Yet it would be a profound error not to recognise the fact, that there is a real kinship between the two. To begin with, the laugh of contempt, say over a prostrate foe, or over one whom we have succeeded in teasing by playing off on him some practical joke, readily passes into an enjoyment of the laughable proper. It is obviously in part a laugh *at* something. Not only so, as a *laugh* it may be presumed to involve a less serious attitude in the successful spectator than a sneer, say, or the hurling of opprobrious words. It will naturally direct itself to something in the undignified *look* of the discomfited party which would be likely to be recognised by others also as laughter-moving.

Again, though I hold that Hobbes' theory, as he himself formulates it, errs by insisting on the swelling of the spectator's self-consciousness into a feeling of superiority or power, it seems to me to be indisputable that all examples of the laughable which clearly fall into the category of mild degradations do give us a sense of uplifting, something akin to Hobbes' "sudden glory". As we are reminded by Dr. Bain, malevolence or malice has its protean disguises, and one of them is undoubtedly the joy of the laugher. The note of malicious crowing, of Schadenfreude, may, no doubt, be most distinctly heard in some of the laughter of satire and of the more brutal sort of joke. Yet I suspect that a trace of it lurks, like a beaten foe, inexpugnable though greatly reduced in strength, in a large part of our laughter.

There are one or two facts which seem to me to point to the conclusion that superiority is implied in, if not tacitly claimed by, the forms of laughter which have a distinctly personal aim. One of these is the familiar fact that anything in the shape of a feeling of inferiority to, or even of respect for, the laughable person inhibits the laughter of the contemplator. But other facts seem to me to be still more conclusive. Of these the first is that if a person finds himself distinctly involved in the disgrace, the absurd situation, or whatever else provokes laughter, he no longer laughs, or laughs in another key. I see my estimable fellow-pedestrian lose his hat at a street corner where the wind lies in ambush: my soul expands exultingly. The moment after, I, too, may fall a victim to the ambuscade, in which case I probably stop laughing and become the subject of a different emotion. Or, if I am "laughing animal" enough to keep up the hilarity, the laugh will have changed. All the glory, the sense of uplifting, the exultation will have fled, and the new laugh, which embraces myself along with another unfortunate, will have in it something of humiliation, will at most have shrunk into a "chastened joy".

The second fact is still more decisive. If no superiority is implied in our common laughter at others, how does it come about that we all have so very obstinate a dislike to be made its object? The most amiable of men find it hard enough to rise to the level of a bare toleration of others' laughter: the man who can reach the sublime height of finding a real and considerable gratification in it must be a hero, or—as some would say—a craven. There are men of a genuine and most blameless humour who are hardly, if at all, less keenly sensitive to the attack of another laugher than the most serious of prigs. Is this understandable unless we suppose that laughter at a person is instinctively interpreted as an assertion of superiority over him?

It would seem then to be a reasonable view, that if laughter in ordinary cases involves superiority, and is so regarded by its object, the enjoyment of it by its subject will be very apt to bring with it a taste of superiority. This, I conceive, is the element of truth in Hobbes' theory.

The foregoing considerations seem to show clearly that the realm of the ludicrous is not a closed and clearly bounded territory, as the theorists for the most part assume it to be. Our enjoyment of its amusing sights connects itself with, and indeed absorbs into itself, tendencies which we may observe in the laughter of children and uncivilised adults. And, if so, the fact seems to require us to go back upon those primitive tendencies in order to see how far the connection holds, that is to say, how far the effects of the ludicrous can be regarded as due to the play of those tendencies.

An analysis of the primitive forms of laughter, which precede its regulation by a reference to ideas, has disclosed the fact that it is the expression of pleasure, yet not of all pleasure, but only of the sudden oncoming or increase of pleasure, of what we call gladness. It has shown us, further, that this joy of laughter is, in many, if not in all cases, conditioned by a sudden relaxation of mental strain, and may, indeed, be described by reference to this condition as a sense of relief from pressure. This was seen to hold good alike in those graver situations in which nervous laughter is apt to occur, in the lighter ones, such as the escape of schoolboys from the classroom to the playground, and in the still lighter ones in which the strain relaxed is momentary only, of which the laughter induced by tickling is the best representative.

Now it seems evident that we have in all these experiences something analogous to play. The natural alliance of laughter with the play-mood has already been touched on.83 We may now go a step farther and say that these spurts of joyous consciousness which, in simple natures untrammelled by thought of appearances, express themselves in laughter are of the essence of Play. To be glad with the gaiety of laughter, to throw off the stiff and wearing attitude of seriousness and to abandon oneself to mirth and jollity is, in truth, to begin to play.

The deep kinship between laughter and play discloses itself as soon as we begin carefully to compare them. Let us look at some of their common characteristics.

Play contrasts with work, not as rest or inactivity contrasts with it, but as light pleasurable activity contrasts with the more strenuous and partly disagreeable kind. The same holds good of laughter. It is light pleasurable activity in contrast to the more burdensome activity of our serious hours.

Again, play is free activity entered upon for its own sake. That is to say, it is not directed to any end outside itself, to the satisfaction of any want, save that of the play-impulse itself; and so it is free from external restraint, and from the sense of compulsion—of a "must" at the ear, whether embodied in the voice of a master or in that of a higher self—which accompanies the attitude of the worker. Similarly, when we laugh we are released from the strain and pressure of serious concentration, from the compulsion of the practical and other needs which keep men, in the main, serious beings.

It follows at once that play is relative to work, that it is enjoyed as a relief from graver occupations, and cannot be indefinitely prolonged. And, as has been hinted above, the same holds true of laughter and what we appropriately describe as playing the fool.

In saying that play is spontaneous activity, freed from the imperious rule of necessity, I do not mean that it is aimless. The play-impulse provides its own ends; for, without something to aim at, it could not become conscious activity in the full sense. Thus in the case of children, at any rate, and possibly of young animals also, playing at some form of combat implies, as Prof. Groos urges, a keen striving for something akin to conquest. In other words, the instinct which underlies the activity seems to bring with it the setting up of something like an end. Similarly with respect to those varieties of children's play which aim at the realisation of an idea, and so resemble art. In this case, too, an instinct, namely, imitative production, prompts to the semblance of a serious conative process, the striving after an end. The same applies to mirthful activity. In playing off a joke on another we certainly have a definite aim in view. In neither case, however, is the end regarded as a serious or important one. Play ceases to be pure play just as soon as the end, for example conquest, begins to be regarded as a thing of consequence to the player; and, in like manner, laughter ceases to be pure mirth just as soon as the end, say the invention of a witticism, is envisaged as a solid personal advantage, such as heightened reputation.84

A like remark applies to the intrusion of the serious attitude into play when this takes on an elaborate form requiring some concentration of attention. This does not destroy the playful character of the activity so long as the end is not viewed as matter of serious import. In this respect, too, laughter resembles play, for we may take considerable pains in shaping our practical joke without ever losing hold of fun as our end.

This brings us to another point of kinship between play and laughter. Each, though marked off from the things of the real serious world, has to do with these in a manner. The play both of animals and of children is largely pretence, that is to say, the production of a semblance of an action of serious life, involving some consciousness of its illusory character. This seems inferrible, in the case of animal play, *e.g.,* the make-believe combats, from the palpable restriction of the movements within the limits of the harmless.85 And with regard to the play of the nursery, it is probable that all through a play-action there is, in spite of the look of absorbing seriousness, a dim awareness of the make-believe. It is fairly certain that we have to do in this case with a double or "divided" consciousness.86 And, as has been illustrated above, laughter is wont to hover about the domain of the serious. In both cases we find the love of pretence playing pranks with the real world, divesting things of their significance and value for the serious part of our mind, and transmuting them by fancy into mere appearances for our amusement.

Another point of similarity may be just alluded to. Recent discussions on the nature of play have served to bring out its utility or serviceableness. Not only is the sportive activity of children and young animals of physiological benefit as wholesome exercise, it is now seen to be valuable as a preliminary practice of actions which later on become necessary. Thus in play-combats children and young animals begin to learn the arts of skilful attack and defence.87 Much of this benefit of play-activity is due to the circumstance that it is a mode of organised co-operation and supplies a kind of training for the serious social activity of later years. I shall hope to show later that laughter has a like value, not merely as a source of physiological benefit to the individual, but as helping us to become fit members of society. It seems hardly needful to point out that since the fact of this utility is known neither to the player nor to the laugher, it does not in the least affect the truth of our contention, that their activity is not controlled by external ends which have a practical or other serious value.

Our comparison justifies us in identifying play and mirth, so far as to say that when we play and when we laugh our mood is substantially the same. Common language seems to support this view. "Fun," "frolic," "sport," "pastime," these and the like may be said to cover at once all joyous play and all varieties of mirth. We are justified, therefore, in making the principle of play fundamental in our theory of laughter.88 We may now proceed to illustrate rather more fully the presence of the play-attitude in the higher domain of laughter, the enjoyment of ludicrous spectacle.

To begin with, much of the laughable illustrated above may be regarded as an expression in persons or things of the play-mood which seizes the spectator by way of a sympathetic resonance. Examples have been given in the laughter excited by the spectacle of aimless actions which have the look of frolicsomeness. As our name "word-play" clearly suggests, verbal jokes are recognised as an outcome of the play-mood which throws off for the nonce the proper serious treatment of language. Again, the odd when it reaches the height of the extravagant has an unmistakable look of play-license. Much of the amusing effect of disguise, of pretence, including certain kinds of "aping," appears to involve some recognition of the make-believe aspect of play. The disorderly, even when it applies to a room, is, to say the least, powerfully suggestive of the ways of rompish play. Many irregularities of thought and action readily take on the look of a self-abandonment to play; for example, irrelevances and confusions of idea, droll, aimless-looking actions, such as going off the scene and coming back again and again, senseless repetitions of actions by the same person or by others—a common entertainment of the circus and the popular play-house. As a last example, we may instance the effect of the incongruous when it assumes a trifling aspect on a solemn occasion. This is surely amusing because it is so like the interruptions of child's play.

How far can this principle be carried? May not a good deal of the amusingly incongruous in behaviour and in circumstances, of intellectual and of moral collapse, when this wears the aspect of folly, be said to affect us as an expression of the play-mood? And is not our amusement at the sight of certain mischances which have the look of a tripping up, an outwitting or befooling, either by others or by circumstance or "fate," traceable to a perception of something indistinguishable from playful teasing?

Yet we must not rely on this expression of the playful too much. There seem to be many cases of the laughable, for example, amusing vices, absences of mind, and all irrelevances which bring in the solemn where it is out of place, where that which is expressed is a mood the very opposite of the playful. Nor do we need to push this principle to an extreme. Even if the laughable spectacle does not wear the look of a play-challenge, it can bring up the playful mood in the spectator in another way. It may so present its particular feature as to throw us off our serious balance, and by a sweet compulsion force us to play with it rather than to consider it seriously. A brief reference to our store of laughable things may suffice to illustrate this.

To begin with our laughter at novelties, the odd, the extravagant, what is it but the outcome of a play-impulse, a gay caprice which wills for the instant not to take objects seriously, but to disregard their real nature and significance, practical, theoretical, and even æsthetic, for the joy of making them playthings for the eye? Or, if the suggestion of a rule, broken by the newcomer into our field of perception, obtrudes itself, our laughter announces that the infraction does not matter, that the violation of custom's good law itself is passed over and turned into fun by the blithe play-spirit in us.

It is the same with mischances, awkward fixes, and all sorts of moral and intellectual shortcomings. These things obviously have in them what should appeal to our seriousness: they come up for judgment as pitiable, as regrettable, often as distinctly culpable. Yet we laugh and cast aside our judicial responsibilities just because the mood of the moment disposes us to be indulgent, and because the attitude we take up in viewing the offence as a little one instantly brings up the love of play, the impulse to turn the significant into enjoyable nonsense.

Once more, in our laughter at artful allusion to the obscene, it is the same swift transition from the serious attitude to that of play which seems to be at the bottom of our merriment. Here again it is the littleness—a quantity, as pointed out, varying considerably with the quality of the laugher—which disarms the serious attitude and allures it to play.

In pretences, both hypocrisies and less serious kinds, which raise the laugh, we note the same swift lapse into the play-attitude. For, in order to enjoy these vain shows with perfect gaiety, we must be ready to bring a mental "blind spot" to bear on everything in them which has serious moral significance. Here, too, we take a leap into the world of the player, transmuting what has something of seriousness, something even of offending hurtfulness, into a mere plaything.

The more intellectual varieties of the ludicrous disclose the same deep-seated characteristic. The incongruous, the absurd, the tricks of ambiguous speech, these are things which offend us as serious mortals bent on having consistency of ideas and clearness of utterance in our social world. They evoke our laughter when they take such a form as to upset this serious attitude and to win us over to regarding them as nothing but entertaining show.

In all the more intellectual laughter at things we seem to find the perfect form of the mind's play. I say "perfect" because psychologists as well as others are wont to speak of poetic imagination as playful activity, though this, as controlled by the ends of art, is seriousness itself compared with the freer movements of ideas when the sportive temper takes us.

One other illustration of the *rôle* of the playful spirit in the sphere of the laughable must not be overlooked. I have dealt with the intrusion of the trivial into solemn scenes as an expression of the child's playfulness. But, as has been suggested above, it is more than this. Scenes of great formality, where a degree of severe self-control is enforced which is trying to mortals of only a limited gravity, are apt to throw us into a state of highly unstable equilibrium. Hence the welcome we are disposed to give to anything which touches the playful susceptibilities in us. Under such circumstances small occurrences, which at other times would pass wholly unmarked, are grasped at and become laughable things for us, just because of the great necessity of man to escape now and again into the freedom of play.

As already implied, this saturation of laughter with the spirit of playfulness is characteristic only of the gayer kind, that which is purified from all tinge of seriousness. So far as our jocose impulses lend themselves to serious purposes, as for example in the laughter of satire, the playful character tends to become less clearly recognisable. Not that here, too, we are unable to find a resemblance between laughter and play; for, as we know, much of what we call play or sport has its serious interest, and the player, like the laugher, may easily slip across the line which divides the playful from the serious attitude. Nevertheless, we shall need to insist on the point that laughter is a thing of different tones, some more playful than others, and that its nature and its function can only be clearly determined by distinguishing these.

The result of our inquiry is that the impressions of the laughable cannot be reduced to one or two principles. Our laughter at things is of various tones. It gathers up into itself a number of primitive tendencies; it represents the products of widely removed stages of intellectual and moral evolution. This is virtually admitted by all who recognise the Intellectual and the Moral principle; for our laughter at seeing dignity unfrocked is presumably of more ancient origin than the "laughter of the mind," which discoursers on the ludicrous are for the most part thinking of. Our argument takes us farther, namely, to the conclusion that the effect of the laughable, even of what is given by philosophers as a sample of the ludicrous, is a highly complex feeling, containing something of the child's joyous surprise at the new and unheard of; something too of the child's gay responsiveness to a play-challenge; often something also of the glorious sense of expansion after compression which gives the large mobility to freshly freed limbs of young animals and children.

A consequence of this recognition of the relation of the laughable to our laughter as a whole is that we shall need to alter our method of treating the subject. Our problem naturally transforms itself into the question: can we trace out the organic differentiation and integration of the several psychical tendencies which our analysis has disclosed? In other words, we find that we must resort to the genetic method, and try to explain the action of the ludicrous upon us in the modest scientific fashion by retracing the stages of its development. Such explanation may some day be crowned by a distinctly philosophical one, if a finer logical analysis succeeds in discovering the essence of the ludicrous; for the present it seems to be all that is available.

It will at once be evident that a large investigation into the origin and development of the laughing impulse will take us beyond the limits of pure psychology. We shall have to consider how the impulse grew up in the evolution of the race; and this will force us to adopt the biological point of view, and ask how this special group of movements came to be selected and fixed among the characters of our species. On the other hand, laughter is more than a physiological and psychological phenomenon. As hinted above, it has a social significance, and we shall find that the higher stages of its evolution can only be adequately dealt with in their connection with the movement of social progress.

Lastly, it will be by tracing the evolution of laughter in the human community that we shall best approach the problem of the ideal which should regulate this somewhat unruly impulse of man. Such a study would seem to promise us a disclosure of tendencies by which laughter has been lifted and refined in the past, and by the light of which it may consciously direct itself in the future.

CHAPTER VI
THE ORIGIN OF LAUGHTER.

To attempt to get back to the beginnings of human laughter may well seem to be too ambitious a proceeding. Beginnings are small things, and may easily escape detection, even when they lie well-lit not far from the eye. How, then, can we hope to get at them when they are hidden in the darkness of the remote past?

It is evident that our method here can only be the modest one of conjecture, a method which must do its best to make its conjecture look reasonable, while it never loses sight of the fact that it is dealing with the conjectural. Our aim is to get an intelligible supposition, by the help of which we may explain how laughter broke on the earthly scene, adding one more to the many strange sounds of the animal world.

This bit of conjectural inquiry will begin by trying to answer the question: By what process did the laugh, from being a general sign of pleasure, become specialised into an expression of the uprising of the mirthful, fun-loving or jocose spirit? It will then address itself to the problem: What has been the course of development of the spirit of fun and of its characteristic mode of utterance?

It would not, of course, be possible to attempt even a conjectural account of these far-off and unchronicled events, but for the new instruments of hypothetical construction with which the Theory of Evolution has furnished us. In attempting so hazardous a task we have, at least, the example of one of the most modest of men to draw us on. Charles Darwin has taught us how to be at once daring and cautious in trying to penetrate the darkness of the ages behind us; and one can wish nothing better than to be able to walk worthily in his steps.

It will be evident that in essaying an effort which can at best end in only a plausible guess we must use every available clue. This means, not merely that we try to trace back the history of mirthful utterance, alike in the evolution of the individual and of the species, to its rude inchoate forms, but that we search for vestiges of utterances vaguely resembling human laughter in the animal world.

This last suggestion may well seem to the reader like another blow to man's early pride of race. The worthy naturalist who called his species the "laughing animal" did not probably trouble himself about the question of the dignity of the attribute. Since laughing was one of the things that only man could do, it served as a convenient way of describing him. Yet, since the later evolutional psychology has led us to be more generous in recognising in the lower animals something closely similar to our own processes of reasoning, we need not be greatly shocked to hear that it is actually crediting other species than our own with a simple sense of fun, and a characteristic manner of expressing the feeling; that is to say, an utterance answering to our laugh.

Now here, if anywhere, we must be on our guard. In attempting to detect traces of mirthful expression in animals we are exposed to a two-fold danger: that common to all observation of animal ways—a too anthropomorphic kind of interpretation; and that of mistaking in other beings, whether human or sub-human, what we envisage as funny, for their conscious fun. It is eminently natural, when we do not screw ourselves up to the severely scientific attitude, to see signs of chuckling glee in animals. I remember how I watched somewhere in Norway, in the early morning, a magpie as he stood for some time ducking his head and throwing up his long tail, accompanying these movements with chuckle-like sounds; and how I found it exceedingly hard not to believe that he was having a good laugh at something, possibly the absurd ways of the foreign tourists who visit his coast. Yet, judged by the standard of scientific observation, this "natural" interpretation was scarcely satisfactory.

Since our aim compels us to be scientific, we cannot accept common modes of interpreting the "mischievous" performances of animals. Many of a monkey's tricks are "funny" enough; yet we may seriously doubt whether he enjoys them as practical jokes. His solemn mien certainly does not suggest it; but then it may be said that human jokers have a way of keeping up an appearance of gravity. A consideration of greater weight is that what looks to us much like a merry joke may be a display of the *teasing* instinct, when this goes beyond the playful limit, and aims at real annoyance or mischief. The remark probably applies to some of the well-known stories of "animal humour," for example, that of Charles Dickens about the raven. This bird, it may be remembered, had to share the garden with a captive eagle. Having carefully measured the length of this formidable creature's chain, he turned to good account the occasion of the giant's sleep by stealing his dinner; and then, the rightful owner having presumably woke up, made an impudent display of eating the same just safely outside the eagle's "sphere of influence". This doubtless showed some cunning, and something of spite; but it is not clear that it indicated an enjoyment of the fun of the thing.

That this teasing and playing of tricks by animals may now and again approach the human attitude of malicious mirthfulness is not improbable. A cat that "plays" with its captive mouse, half-pretending, as it seems, not to see the small thing's hopeless attempt to "bolt," may, perhaps, be enjoying something of the exultant chuckle of a human victor. So, too, some of the mischievous behaviour of a lively and imperfectly domesticated monkey, which a simple-minded sailor has brought to his mother by way of making her happy, may disclose a germ of the spirit of fun, of a malicious playfulness which is capable of enjoying its jokes as such.

Yet, while we may question the truth of the proposition that these mischievous actions are enjoyed as practical jokes—in the way in which Uncle Remus represents them—we need not hesitate to attribute to animals a simple form of the child's sense of fun. This trait appears most plainly in the pastimes of the young of many familiar species, including our two domestic pets, pastimes which are quite correctly described as animal play. The particular forms of this playful activity, the tusslings, the attacks and retreats on both sides, the chasings and the rest, are pretty certainly determined by special instincts.89 But, as play, these actions are an expression of high spirits and of something analogous to a child's love of "pretending". Is it not a bit of playful make-believe, for example, when a dog, on seeing the approach of a canine stranger, "lies low" wearing the look of an alert foe; yet, as soon as the stranger approaches, "gives away the show" by entering with an almost disgraceful celerity into perfectly friendly relations with him? It is the same when a dog teases another dog by startling him, showing signs of enjoying the trick. H. M. Stanley writes: "My dog took the same delight in coming up quietly behind a small dog and giving a terrifying bark as does the child in jumping out from a corner and crying 'boo'".90

Owing, to no little extent, perhaps, to the fact of its education by man, the dog gives much the clearest indications of a sense of fun. No one can observe a dog during a walk with his child-comrades without noting how readily he falls in with their playful proposals. The infectiousness of an announcement of the playful temper is clearly illustrated here. The dog imitates the gambols, and will even seem to respond to the vocal outbursts of his merry playmates. Darwin has rightly recognised a germ of our "sense of humour" in a dog's joining in the game of stick-throwing. You throw a bit of stick for him to fetch, and having picked it up he proceeds to carry it away some distance and to squat down with it on the ground just before him. You then come quite close as if to take the stick from him, on which he seizes it and bears it off exultingly, repeating the little make-believe with evident enjoyment.91

I have tested a dog again and again when playing with him in this fashion, and have satisfied myself that he is in the play-mood, and knows perfectly well that you are too; so that if you pretend to be serious and to command him in your most magisterial voice to give up the stick he sidles up with a hollow show of obedience which could impose on nobody, as if to say, "I know better: you are not really serious; so I am going on with the game". All the notes of a true sense of fun seem to be present in this case: the gay and festive mood, a firm resolve *desipere in loco,* and a strong inclination to play at "pretending".

Prof. Lloyd Morgan gives an example of what certainly looks like a dog's merry make-believe in which man's lead takes no part. The writer tells us that he used at one time to take an intelligent retriever to a sandy shore, where the dog engaged spontaneously in the following pastime. He buried a number of small crabs in the sand, and then stood waiting till a leg or a claw appeared, "upon which he would run backwards and forwards giving short barks of keen enjoyment".92

I find it hard to doubt that this was a genuine outburst of joyousness and of something indistinguishable from a love of fun, and that it was connected with the "coming off" of a practical joke. The repetitions of the burial when the dog had seen that it was ineffectual, points clearly to a consciousness of the make-believe character of the performance.

Whatever a dog's powers of jocosity when uninstructed by man, it seems safe to set down a good share of his highly developed sense of fun to his profound susceptibility to man's educative influence; which again (as the difference between the educability of the dog and of the cat at once shows) implies an unusual strength of those instincts of attachment to man which have made him almost the type of fidelity.

How far, one wonders, will this educative influence of man be likely to go in the case of the most companionable of our domestic pets? W. Preyer tells us, that the dog is capable of imitating the signs of human gaiety, that an intelligent specimen, when confronted with our laughter will draw back the corners of his mouth and leap into the air with a bright lustre in the eye.93 Here we seem to have a rudiment of a genuine laugh, and may perhaps cease to speak rather confusingly of a dog's "laughing with his tail". G. J. Romanes relates that he had a dog who went some way towards qualifying himself for the office of clown. This animal would perform a number of self-taught tricks which were clearly intended to excite laughter. "For instance, while lying on his side and violently grinning, he would hold one leg in his mouth." Under these circumstances "nothing pleased him so much as having his joke duly appreciated, while, if no notice was taken of him, he would become sulky".94

This animal must, one supposes, have been in an exceptional degree a "funny dog". It seems a pity that the observer did not take a "snapshot" at that grin so that it might be a shade less abstract and "in the air" than the grin of the Cheshire cat, as treated by Mr. Lewis Carroll. What seems clear is, that the physiognomy of a dog manages to execute a weirdly distorted semblance of our smile. With respect to the vocal part of the expression, we must not expect too much. The bark may not be able to adjust itself to our quick explosions of gaiety. It is commonly said that the dog has a special bark for expressing pleasure, and it seems likely that he employs this when he is said to be seized by the sense of the funniness of things.

On the moral side, the possibility of the dog's becoming a humorous beast looks more promising. He certainly exhibits rudiments of feelings and mental attitudes which seem in man to be closely related to a reflective humour. As the inner circle of his human friends know, he can be terribly bored. I saw, not long since, a small dog undergoing the process of chaining by his mistress before she took him into a shop. He drew a long yawn, and his appearance was eminently suggestive of a keen sense of the absurdity of the shopping habits of ladies, a sense which only wanted the appropriate utterance to become a mild, tolerant kind of satire. Yet one must be mindful of one's own warning against a too hasty interpretation of such actions.

We may now turn to animals much nearer ourselves in the zoological scale. Among monkeys we obtain, undoubtedly, something more closely akin to our smile and laugh. Darwin has made a careful inquiry into the similarities between the two. He tells us that some of the essential features of the facial expression during a laugh, the drawing backwards of the corners of the mouth, the formation of wrinkles under the eyes, etc., are "characteristic and expressive of a pleased state of mind in various kinds of monkeys".95

With respect to laughter-like sounds, Darwin gives us several pertinent facts. A young chimpanzee will make a kind of barking noise when he is pleased by the return of any one to whom he is attached, a noise which the keeper interprets as a laugh. The correctness of this interpretation is confirmed by the fact that other monkeys utter a kind of "tittering sound" when they see a beloved person. A young chimpanzee when tickled under the armpits produces a more decided chuckling or laughing sound. "Young ourangs, also, when tickled will make a chuckling sound and put on a grin."

It has been found by Dr. L. Robinson that the young of the anthropoid apes are specially ticklish in the regions of the surface of the body which correspond with the ticklish regions in the case of the child. Not only so, a young chimpanzee will show great pleasure when tickled, rolling over on his back and abandoning himself to the pastime, much as a child does. When the tickling is prolonged he resembles a child further by defending ticklish spots. So, too, does a young ourang. It may be added that young apes, like many children, make a pretence of biting when tickled.

To sum up: the young of the higher apes have something resembling our smile and laugh, and produce the requisite movements when pleased. Their attempt at laughter, as we might be disposed to regard it, appears as a sign of sudden joy in circumstances in which a child will laugh, *e.g.*, on the reappearance of a beloved companion after a considerable interval. It further occurs when the animal is tickled, along with other manifestations which point to the existence of a rudiment of the child's capacity for fun and for the make-believe of play.

One more fact should be added in order to bring out the similarity here to the human attitude towards the laughable. It is probable, from the testimony of several observers, that monkeys dislike being laughed at.96 Now, it is true that the enjoyment of fun and the dislike to being made its object are not the same thing. Nor do they seem to vary together in the case of men; otherwise the agelast would not be so often found among those who keenly resent being the object of others' laughter. Nevertheless, they may be regarded in general as correlative traits; creatures which show a distinct distaste for being made the objects of laughter may be supposed to be capable of the laughing attitude, so far at least as to be able to understand it.

Turning now from sub-human kinds of laughter to the full expression as we know it in ourselves, we may briefly trace the history of the smile and laugh during the first years of life. Here the question of the date of the first appearance of these expressive movements becomes important; and happily we have more than one set of careful observations on the point.

With respect to the smile, which is commonly supposed to be the first to show itself, we have notes made by Darwin and by Preyer. According to the former, the first smile appeared, in the case of two of his children, at the age of forty-five days, and, of a third, at a somewhat earlier date.97 Not only were the corners of the mouth drawn back, but the eyes brightened and the eyelids slightly closed. Darwin adds that the circumstances pointed to a happy state of mind. Preyer is much fuller here.98 He points out the difficulties of noting the first true smile of pleasure. In the case of his own boy, it seems, the movements of the corners of the mouth, accompanied by the formation of dimples in the cheek, occurred in the second week, both in the waking and in the sleeping state. The father thinks, however, that the first smile of pleasure occurred on the twenty-sixth day, when after a good meal the child's eyes lighted on the mother's face. This early smile, he adds, was not an imitation of another's; nor did it imply a joyous recognition of the mother. It was just the instinctive expression of a feeling of bodily satisfaction.

Other observers differ, too, in respect of the date of the first occurrence of the true expressive smile. For example, Dr. Champneys puts it in the sixth, Sigismund in the seventh week, agreeing roughly with Darwin; whereas Miss Shinn gives as the date the latter half of the first month, and so supports Preyer's observations. Another lady, Mrs. K. C. Moore, would go farther than Preyer and say that the first smile occurs on the sixth day of life.99 It may be added that Miss Shinn is more precise than Preyer in her account of the early development of the smile. She tells us that, whereas the first smile of her niece—whom we will henceforth call by her name, Ruth— (latter half of first month) was merely the outcome of general comfort, a smile occurred in the second month which involved an agreeable perception, namely, that of faces bending over the child in which she took great interest. This smile of special pleasure, expressing much gaiety, occurred when she was lying fed, warm, and altogether comfortable.

It is fairly certain that these differences indicate some inequalities of precocity in the children observed. At the same time, it seems probable that the several observers are dealing with different stages in the development of the smile. Preyer shows clearly that it undergoes considerable expansion, involving increased complexity of movement, and the addition of the important feature, the brightening of the eye. Mrs. Moore gives no description of what she saw on the sixth and seventh days, and is presumably referring to a vague resemblance to a rudiment of a smile which had no expressive significance; and some things in Preyer's account lead us to infer that he is speaking of a less highly developed smile than Darwin.100

All that can certainly be said, then, is that the movements of a smile, as an expression of pleasure, undergo a gradual process of development, and that an approach to a perfect smile of pleasure occurs some time in the second month of life.

If we turn to the dates assigned to the first occurrence of a laugh, we find the uncertainties are at least equal to those encountered in the case of the smile. Darwin illustrates how a smile may gradually take on an accompaniment of sound which grows more and more laughter-like. One of his children, who, he thinks, first smiled at the age of forty-five days, developed about eight days later a more distinct and impressive smile, accompanied by a little "bleating" noise, which, he adds, "perhaps represented a laugh". It was not, however, till much later (113th day) that the noises became broken up into the discrete sounds of a laugh. Another child of his, when sixty-five days old, accompanied his smile by "noises very like laughter". A laughter, with all the indications of genuine fun behind it, occurred in the case of one of his children on the 110th day, when the game was tried of throwing a pinafore over the child's face and then suddenly withdrawing it, this being varied by the father's suddenly uncovering his own face and approaching the child's. He adds that, some three or four weeks before this, his boy appeared to enjoy as a good joke a little pinch on his nose and cheeks.

Preyer puts the date of the first laughter-like sounds, as he puts that of the first smile, earlier than Darwin. He says he observed a visible and audible laugh in his boy on the twenty-third day. This was a chuckling at the view of a rose-tinted curtain. The sounds were repeated in the following weeks at the sight of slowly swinging coloured objects and at new sounds, *e.g.,* those of the piano. At the same time he tells us that a prolonged loud laughter, recognisable as such by a person not looking at what was going on, first occurred in the eighth month when the boy was playing with his mother. Among the other observers it may suffice to refer to one of the most careful, Miss Shinn. This lady, who, it will be remembered, puts the date of Ruth's first smile as early as the first month, assigns the child's first genuine laughter to the 118th day. It was excited by the sight of the mother making faces. It is worth adding that Ruth reached her third performance eleven days later.101

In this case, too, it is probable that we have to do, not merely with differences of precocity in the children observed, but with the difficulties of determining what is a clear example of the expression concerned.102 There is no doubt that the full reiteration of our laughter is reached by stages. This is brought out fully by Darwin, and is allowed by Preyer. Yet how much of the series of more or less laughter-like sounds produced by an infant during states of pleasure is to be regarded as entering into the development of laughter, it is not easy to say. Miss Shinn heard Ruth give out curious little chuckling sounds of two syllables on the 105th day, that is thirteen days before she produced her laugh. She adds under the date, 113th day, that is to say, five days before the laugh, that the child had developed new throat sounds, crowing, croaking, etc., and showed a strong disposition to vary sounds in a pleasurable mood. It seems highly improbable that these sounds were not preparatory stages in the development of the laugh.103

It is fairly certain that laughing comes after smiling. Preyer's words may no doubt seem to suggest that the first laugh (twenty-third day) comes before the first smile (twenty-sixth day); but his account of the development of the two shows plainly that this is not his meaning. He distinctly says that laughter is only a strengthened and audible (laut) smile; and remarks, further, that "in all (children) alike the utterance of pleasure begins with a scarcely noticeable smile, which quite gradually passes into laughter in the course of the first three months". He adds that this development depends on that of the higher brain centres, and the capability of having perceptions.104

The first laughter is, like the smile, an expression of pleasure. As Preyer puts it, the laughter is a mere heightening of the look of pleasure. It marks, however, a higher level of agreeable consciousness. Whereas the first clumsy experiments in smiling denote nothing but a comfortable state of repletion, the first attempts at laughter are responses to gladdening sense-presentations, such as swinging coloured objects, and the new sounds of a piano. This laughter at new visual and aural presentations was followed, according to Preyer, between the sixth and the ninth week by a laughter more distinctly joyous or jubilant, as the child regarded his mother's face and appeared to recognise it. This laughter of mental gaiety seems at an early age—about the fourth month—to ally itself with movements of the limbs (raising and lowering of the arms, etc.) as a complex sign of high spirits or gladness.105

How far the provocative of laughter mentioned by Darwin, namely, suddenly uncovering the child's head (or his own) implied a rudiment of fun, I am not sure. It shows, however, the early connection between laughter and agreeable surprise, that is to say, a mild shock, which, though it borders on the alarming, is on the whole gladdening.

One other early form of laughter, which is found also in certain young animals, is that excited by tickling. This has been first observed, in the case of the child, in the second or the third month. Preyer's boy laughed in response to tickling in the second month.106 Dr. Leonard Hill tells me that his little girl, who was by-the-bye specially sensitive to titillation, responded first by laughter in the tenth week.

Since our analysis has led us to regard the effect of tickling as largely mental, and as involving a playful attitude, this fact confirms the conclusion that the specialised laughter which is the accompaniment of play occurs in a well-defined form within the first three months.

To sum up: We find, within the first two or three months, both the smile and the laugh as expressions of pleasure, including sensations of bodily comfort and gladdening sense-presentations. We find, further, in the reflex reaction of laughter under tickling, which is observable about the end of the second month, the germ of a sense of fun, or of mirthful play; and this is indicated too in the laughter excited by little pinches on the cheek at the end of the third month.

It is certain that these tendencies are not learned by imitation. This is proved by the fact, established by Preyer, that imitative movements do not occur in the normal child till considerably later, and by the fact that the child, Laura Bridgman, who was shut out by her blindness and deafness from the lead of companions, developed these expressions. We must conclude, then, that they are inherited tendencies.

Here the psychologist might well stop in his inquiries, if Darwin and others had not opened up the larger vista of the evolution of the species. Can we, by carrying the eye along this vista, conjecture how these instinctive movements came to be acquired in the course of animal evolution?

The first question that arises in this inquiry is whether the smile or the laugh was the earlier to appear in the course of racial development. The expressions of animals below man do not offer any decisive clue here. The anthropoid apes appear both to produce a kind of smile or grin, and to utter sounds analogous to our laughter. It may, however, be contended that this so-called laughter is much less like our laughter than the grin is like our smile. In the absence of better evidence, the fact that the smile appears first in the life of the child must, according to a well-known law of evolution, be taken as favouring the hypothesis that man's remote ancestors learned to smile before they could rise to the achievement of the laugh. This is further supported by the fact that, in the case of the individual, the laugh when it occurs announces a higher form of pleasurable consciousness, the level of perception as distinguished from the level of sensation which is expressed by the first smile. Lastly, I am informed that among imbeciles the smile persists lower down in the scale of degeneration than the laugh. Dr. F. E. Beddard writes to me: "I remember once seeing a defective human monster (with no frontal lobes) whose only sign of intelligence was drawing up the lips when music was played".107

It is commonly held that, since the expression of pain, suffering, or apprehension of danger among animals is a much more pressing necessity for purposes of family and tribal preservation than that of pleasure or contentment, the former is developed considerably earlier than the latter. According to this view, we can understand why the adumbrations of a smile and a laugh which we find in animals closely related to man have been so imperfectly developed and appear only sporadically.

Supposing that the smile was the first of the two expressive movements to appear in the evolution of the human species, can we conjecture how it came to be the common and best-defined expression of pleasurable states? In dealing with this point we may derive more definite aid from Darwin's principles.

The fact that the basis of a smile is a movement of the mouth at once suggests a connection with the primal source of human as of animal enjoyment; and there seems, moreover, to be some evidence of the existence of such a connection. A baby after a good meal will, I believe, go on performing something resembling sucking movements. The first smiles may have arisen as a special modification of these movements when there was a particularly lively feeling of organic contentment or well-being. I believe, further, that an infant is apt to carry out movements of the mouth when food is shown to it. A similar tendency seems to be illustrated by the behaviour of a monkey which, when a choice delicacy was given it at mealtime, slightly raised the corners of the mouth, the movement partaking of the nature of "an incipient smile".108 Again, our hypothesis finds some support in the fact that, according to Preyer and others, the first smiles of infants were noticed during a happy condition of repletion after a good meal.109

Supposing the smile in its origin to have thus been organically connected with the pleasurable experience of sated appetite, we can easily see how it might get generalised into a common sign of pleasure. Darwin and Wundt have made us familiar with the principle that expressive movements may be transferred to states of feeling resembling those of which they were primarily the manifestations. The scratching of the head during a state of mental irritation is a well-known instance of the transference.

There are, I believe, facts which go some way towards verifying the supposition of a transference of eating-signs to states of lively satisfaction and pleasure generally. Savages are wont to express keen pleasure by gestures, *e.g.,* rubbing the belly, which seem to point to the voluminous satisfactions of the primal appetite. The clearest evidence, however, seems to be furnished by the account of a baboon given us by Darwin. This creature, after having been made furiously angry by his keeper, on making friends again, "rapidly moved up and down his jaws and lips and looked pleased". Darwin adds that a similar movement or quiver of the jaws may be observed in a man when he laughs heartily, though with us the muscles of the chest rather than those of the lips and jaws are "spasmodically affected".110

Judging from the interval between the occurrence of the first smile and of the first laugh in the life of the individual, we may conjecture that laughter did not grow into a full reiterated sound in "primitive man," or his unknown immediate predecessor, till much later. We should expect that a considerable development of vocal power would be a condition of man's taking heartily to this mode of emotional utterance. The study of the infant certainly supports this idea. The babble of the second and third months, which is made up of a reiteration of many vocal and consonantal sounds, may prepare for laughter, as it certainly does for speech. The observations of Miss Shinn, quoted above, on the expansion of the range of vocal sound before the occurrence of the first laugh are most significant here. They seem to point to the fact that in the evolution of the species the first laughter was selected from among a great variety of sounds produced in pleasurable states.

Let us now suppose that our immediate animal ancestor has reached the level of clear perceptions, and is given to the utterance of certain reiterated sounds during states of pleasure. Let us further conceive of him as having his sympathies developed up to the point of requiring a medium for expressing not only pains but pleasures, and more particularly for calling others' attention to the presence of cheering and welcome objects, *e.g.,* of a member of the family who has been abroad for a time. Such an animal would need to improve on his primal smiles and grins. He would require vocal utterances of some strength in order to reach distant ears, something answering to the cackle of the hen when she has discovered some choice morsel and desires to bring her brood to her side. How is this improvement to be effected?

One may hazard the guess that the process may have been something of this kind. The position of the open mouth during a broad smile was, we may reason, in itself favourable to the production of vocal sounds. We may, after the analogy of positions of the eyes, speak of it as the "primary position" of the vocal chamber when opened. This primary position would pretty certainly be specially favourable to the utterance of a certain kind of sound, let us say that commonly indicated by "eh,"111 together with something of the guttural or chuckling accompaniment of this in the sound of laughter. We may then infer that, when some of the reiterated babble-like sounds were produced during states of pleasurable satisfaction, the same (primary) position would be taken up. We should thus get, as psycho-physical concomitants of the sensed position of the opened mouth during a broad smile or "grin," not only a disposition to reiterate the "eh" or some similar sound as a completion of the whole action, of which the opening of the mouth is the first stage, but a definite associative co-ordination between the movement of opening the mouth and the reiterated actions of the muscles of the respiratory and vocal apparatus. In this way we may understand how, when the pleasurable state expressed by a smile increased in intensity, as, for example, when the happy feeling excited by the sight of a face passed into the joy of recognising a member of the family, the movements would widen out into those of a laughter-like utterance.

It appears to me that, in this connection, the observed course of development of laughter in the individual is not without its suggestiveness. Miss Shinn remarks that Ruth's mouth was opened wide on the 113th day—five days before the first laugh—while the child was tossed and tumbled. Under date of the 134th day, again, we read of much laughter of an inaudible kind, consisting of broad laughter-like smiles; and these observations certainly show that about the date of the first laughter an expanded smile, indistinguishable from a laugh save by the absence of the respiratory and vocal adjunct, was frequent. In other words, they tell us that about the time when she achieved her first laugh she was freely practising the intermediate facial step between the earlier smile and the true laugh.

This theory would plainly illustrate Mr. Herbert Spencer's principle, that states of feeling affect the voluntary muscles in the order of increasing calibre, the smaller being called into play by feelings of lower intensity, the larger by those of higher intensity. But this theory is not enough. We must take into account also the order of frequency of use, and of consequent liability to discharge in the connected nerve-centres. It seems probable that the muscles engaged in the movements of the mouth and those exercised in phonation would, for these reasons, be specially liable to be acted upon. These wider tendencies would, according to the above hypothesis, be assisted by special associations. These would secure the combination of the two groups of movements, which I have assumed to have been employed independently as utterances of pleasurable feeling: namely, those involved in smiling, and those underlying the first happy reiterated sounds of a quasi-infantile babbling.

One element in the laugh, its explosive vigour, seems unaccounted for on this hypothesis. Here, I think, the effect of relief from strain, which is so common a factor in human laughter, may be called in. The earliest laughter of the child seems to illustrate this element. For example, that which occurs during tickling, in a game of bo-peep, and at the sight of the mother making faces may be said to arise from a serious attitude suddenly dissolved. Perhaps the first great laugh was produced by man or by his proximate progenitor, when relief came after fear or the strain of battle. So far as primitive laughter was the outcome of such concentrated energy seeking relief, this circumstance would help to account for the prolongation as well as for the strength of the sounds.

Our conjecture cannot lay claim to be a hypothesis. It makes no attempt to explain the precise forms of the changes which enter both into the smile and into the laugh. At best, it is only a rough hint as to a possible mode of genesis.

I have here treated of the genesis of laughter under its more general aspect as an expression of pleasurable states of feeling. We have seen, however, that within the first three months of life another and clearly specialised variety of laughter emerges, namely, that called forth by tickling. It follows from our analysis of the effect of tickling that it is one of the earliest manifestations, in a clear form, of the laughter of fun or of play. As such, it demands special attention in any attempt to explain the development of laughter.

As a specialised reaction having a clearly marked reflex form, it is natural to ask whether laughter in response to tickling is not inherited, and, if so, how it arose in the evolution of the race. And we find that suggestions have been made for explaining the genesis of this curious phenomenon. We will first glance again at the facts, and then examine the hypotheses put forward for explaining them.

Here, again, the question how far animals are susceptible of the effect becomes important. I have already alluded to Darwin's remark, that if a young chimpanzee is tickled, more particularly under the armpits, he responds by a kind of laughter. The sound is of a chuckling or laughing kind. The emission of these sounds is accompanied by retraction of the corners of the mouth, and sometimes by a slight amount of wrinkling in the lower eyelids.112 Dr. Louis Robinson publishes other observations of the effect of tickling on the young of anthropoid apes. He tells us that a young chimpanzee when tickled for some time under the armpits would roll over on his back showing all his teeth and accompanying the simian grin by defensive movements, just as a child does. A young ourang at the Zoological Gardens (London) behaved in a very similar way. The young of other animals, too, betray some degree of ticklishness. Stanley Hall remarks that a dog will retract the corners of his mouth and thus go some way towards smiling if tickled over the ribs.113 Dr. Robinson finds that horses and pigs are also ticklish; and he thinks that these animals have specially ticklish regions, which correspond to a considerable extent to those which have been ascertained in the case of the child.

We may now refer to the first appearances of the tickling reflex in the child. As pointed out above, the response by defensive movements appears shortly after birth, whereas the earliest instance of a response by laughter occurs in the second, or in the first half of the third month. It is to be noted that this date is distinctly later than that of the first laughter of pleasure, though it is not far removed from that of the first clear appearance of the laughter of gaiety or jubilation.

These chronological facts bear out the theory that the laughter of a tickled child has a distinct *psychical* antecedent. On this point Dr. L. Robinson writes to me as follows: "I have never been able to succeed in eliciting laughter from young infants under three months old by means of tickling, *unless one also smiled and caught their attention in some such way*". This evidently points to the influence of mental agencies even in the first stages of laughter from tickling.

With respect to the parts in which the tickling first excites laughter, different observers appear to have reached dissimilar results. Preyer distinctly speaks of the tickling of the sole of the foot as provoking laughter in the second month. Whether he tried other parts he does not say. Dr. Leonard Hill tells me that one of his children first responded to tickling when the titillation attacked the palm of the hand, or ran up the arm. Responses to the tickling of the neck and soles of the feet came later.

The fact that the effect of tickling becomes so well defined by, or soon after, the end of the second month, proves pretty conclusively that it is an inherited reflex; and the evolutionist naturally asks what it means, what its significance has been in the life of our ancestors.

Dr. Stanley Hall carries back evolutional speculation very far, and suggests that in tickling we may have the oldest stratum of our psychic life, that it is a survival of a process in remote animal progenitors for which touch was the only sense. He supposes that in these circumstances even light or "minimal" touches, say those coming from the movements of small parasites, being unannounced by sight or other far-reaching sense, would be accompanied by disproportionately strong reactions. He does not attempt to explain how laughter grew out of these reactions. He does indeed call them reactions "of escape," but he does not follow up the idea by hinting that the violent shakings of the body by laughter, when it came, helped to get rid of the little pesterers. In truth, this ingenious thinker hardly appears to make the explanation of the laughter of tickling, as distinguished from the other reactions, the subject of a special inquiry.114

A more serious attempt to explain the evolution of the laughter of tickling has been made by Dr. Louis Robinson. He, too, hints at the vestigial survival of experiences of parasites, but appears to think that these account only for the disagreeable effects which are brought about when the hairy orifices of the nostril and the ear are tickled. This limitation strikes one as a little arbitrary. The reaction of laughter, which Dr. L. Hill called forth when he made his fingers run up the arm of his infant, is surely suggestive of a vestigial reflex handed down from ages of parasitic pestering.115

With regard to the laughing reaction, which, as we have seen, he considers to involve a distinct mode of stimulation, he suggests that it is an inherited form of that common mode of play among young animals, which consists in an exchange of good-natured and make-believe attacks and defences, or a sort of game of sham-fight.

In support of this theory he lays stress on the fact that susceptibility to tickling is shared in by the young of a number of species of animals standing high in point of intelligence, including not only the higher apes, but the dog and the horse. He adds that, in general, there is a concomitance between the degree of playfulness of a young creature and that of its ticklishness, though lambs and kids which are not ticklish are allowed to be an awkward exception.

If tickling is a playing at fighting we may expect it, like other kinds of play, to mimic serious forms of assault. Now we know that the first rude attacks of man, so far as we can gather from the movements of a passionate infant, took the forms of striking, tearing with the nails and biting. Tickling may be said to be a sort of mild pretence at clawing. Dr. Robinson tells us that about 10 per cent. of the children he has examined pretended to bite when they were tickled, just as a puppy will do.

Dr. Robinson goes a step farther and seeks to show that the areas of the bodily surface which are specially ticklish in children are those likely to be attacked in serious warfare. In nearly all of them, he says, some important structure, such as a large artery, is close to the surface and would be liable to injury if the skin were penetrated. They would thus be highly vulnerable regions, and consequently those which would be singled out for attacks by teeth or claws. He argues that the same relation holds in the case of animals which attack one another in the same way as man. The regions of special ticklishness in their case, too, appear to correspond, roughly at least, with vulnerable regions. Indeed, in the young chimpanzee and the young ourang these ticklish areas are approximately the same as in the child.

From all this he concludes that ticklishness, being bound up with the mimic warfare which fills so large a space in the life of many young animals, has its utility. The strong liking to be tickled, which children and, apparently, some other young animals express, serves, in combination with the playful impulse to carry out this gentle mode of attack, to develop mimic attacks and defences which are of high value as training for the later and serious warfare.

These applications of the evolution theory are certainly interesting and promising. I think the idea of relief from parasites might be worked out further. May it not be that the light touches given by the fingers of the parent, or other member of the ancestral family when hunting for parasites on the surface of the young animal, have, by association with the effects of relief from the troublesome visitors, developed an agreeable feeling-tone? As we have seen, the laughter of tickling has a distinctly mental antecedent; it appears in the child, only when he is beginning to enjoy laughingly little pinches on the cheek, and otherwise to show a germ of a sense of fun. The light touches, reminiscent at once of unpleasant settlers, and of delivering fingers, would, one imagines, be exactly fitted to supply that dissolution into nothing of momentary apprehension indicated by our analysis of the mental factor in tickling.

With respect to Dr. Robinson's hypothesis, it may be acknowledged ungrudgingly to be a brilliant piece of hypothetical construction. But, as the writer frankly confesses, the facts, here and there, do not point in its direction. A very serious objection is the fact that the sole of the foot and the palm of the hand are not taken into account in his attempt to establish a correspondence between the ticklish areas of the surface and a high degree of vulnerability. In Stanley Hall's returns it is the sole of the foot which is most frequently mentioned as a ticklish area; and, as we have seen, it was the first to give rise to laughter in the case of one child at least.116

There is another and more serious objection to Dr. Robinson's theory as an explanation of laughter. One may urge that the occurrence of such violent movements would, by shaking the body and by inducing fatigue much earlier than need be, pretty certainly be detrimental to that prolonged practice of skill in attack and defence, to which Dr. Robinson attaches so much importance.

The supposition that tickling is a variety of play developed by natural selection among combative animals is, I think, highly probable. The play of animals, like that of children, is largely a form of social activity involving a playmate; and is apt, as we know, to take the form of attack and defence, as in chasing, throwing over, pretending to bite, etc. These playful attacks are, as we have seen, closely related to teasing; indeed, teasing may be viewed as merely a play-imitation of the first stage of combat, that of challenging or exciting to contest.117 Tickling pretty obviously finds a fitting place among the simpler forms of playful combat which have a teasing-like character. Moreover, these forms of social play all seem to show, in a particularly clear manner, the utility referred to in the preceding chapter.

Now, this idea will, I think, help us to understand how loud and prolonged laughter came to join itself to the combative game of tickling and being tickled. If play—pure, good-natured play—was to be developed out of teasing attacks, it would become a matter of the highest importance that it should be clearly understood to be such. This would mean, first of all, that the assailant made it clear that his aim was not serious attack, but its playful semblance; and secondly, that the attacked party expressed his readiness to accept the assault in good part as sport. It would be of the greatest consequence to the animal that chanced to be in the play-mood and wished to make overtures of friendly combat that he should be sure of an equally gamesome attitude in the recipient of the challenge. One may see this by watching what happens when a dog, unwisely trying to force a frolic on another dog, is met by a growl and possibly by an uncovering of the canine teeth. Now, what better sign of good-temper, of readiness to accept the attack as pure fun, could nature have invented than the laugh? The smile is, no doubt, a pretty good indicator in some circumstances. Yet one must remember that the rudimentary smile of an ape-like ancestor may, now and again, have been misleading, as our own smiles are apt to be. A laugh would presumably be less easy to affect in such circumstances than a smile; and, in any case, it would be far less liable to be overlooked.

In saying that the laughter which accompanies tickling and other closely allied forms of play in children owes its value to its being an admirable way of announcing the friendly playful mood, I do not mean that other signs are absent. Dr. L. Robinson reminds us that a tickled child will roll over on his back just like a puppy. The laughter and the rolling over seem to be two congenitally connected modes of abandonment to the playful attack. In the young of other ticklish animals, *e.g.,* the puppy, the rolling over may of itself suffice to give the friendly signal.

It seems not unlikely that this consideration, the utility of laughter as a guarantee to a playful challenger that his overtures will be received in the proper spirit, applies to the evolution of all laughter which enters into such forms of social play as the pretence to attack, to frighten, and generally what we call good-natured teasing. It has been suggested that teasing might well be taken as the starting-point in the evolution of play.118 By adopting this idea, and by regarding laughter, in its elementary form, as essentially a feature of social play, we might set out with this consideration of utility in constructing our theory of the evolution of laughter. One is tempted, too, to follow this course by the fact, recognised in common language, that much, at least, of the later and more refined laughter is analogous to the effect of tickling.119

Nevertheless, as we have seen, the best evidence attainable points to the conclusion that this simple form of the laughter of social play was preceded by, and grew out of, a less specialised kind of laughter, that of sudden accession of pleasure. We may conjecture that the laughter provoked by tickling was reached in the evolution of our race soon after this reaction passed out of its primal and undifferentiated form as a general sign of pleasurable excitement, and began to be specialised as the expression of mental gaiety and of something like our hilarity. The fact, noted above, that children only laugh in response to tickling when they are in a pleasurable state of mind seems to confirm the hypothesis that the love of fun, which is at the bottom of tickling and makes it perhaps the earliest clear instance of mirthful play with its element of make-believe, first emerged gradually out of a more general feeling of gladness.

CHAPTER VII.
DEVELOPMENT OF LAUGHTER DURING THE FIRST THREE YEARS OF LIFE.

Having examined the earliest and distinctly hereditary germs of the laughing impulse in the child, we may pass to the consideration of its expansion and specialisation during the first years. Although, so far as I am aware, the new child-study has not yet produced a methodical record of the changes which this interesting expression of feeling undergoes, we may by help of such data as are accessible be able to trace out some of the main directions of its development.

Two closely connected problems are involved here: (*a*) how the expressive movements, the laugh and the smile, themselves change and get differentiated; and (*b*) how the psychical process which precedes and excites these expressive movements grows in complexity and differences itself into the various forms of gaiety or amusement enumerated above.

In dealing with these early manifestations we shall, of course, look for reactions which are spontaneous, in the sense of not being due to imitation and the lead of others. Yet it will not always be easy to determine what are such. It has been pointed out above that laughter is one of the most contagious of the expressive movements. Children, therefore, who are much given to imitation may be expected to show this contagiousness in a particularly clear manner.

The difficulties are, however, not really so formidable as they might at first seem to be. If a child is, on the one hand, highly susceptible to the contagion of laughter, there is, on the other, no expression of his feeling in which he is more spontaneous. The swift directness of the "natural" or spontaneous laugh may be readily discriminated by a fine observer. Not only so, but a difference may be detected in the tone of the laughter when it is perfectly natural and real, and when it is merely imitative and artificial. The note of affected laughter is well known to careful observers of children. It is particularly plain where a child is not merely reproducing the laughter of others at the moment, but has it suggested to him by others that a thing is laughable. Miss Shinn's niece developed at the end of the second year a forced laugh on hearing the word "funny" employed by others.

The best safeguard against this error is to choose an only child who is well isolated from mirthful surroundings. This need not be so cruel an experiment as it looks. In the social world of the merry little Ruth, nobody, we are told, was a "laughing person". This circumstance gives great value to the observations made on this child. Her laughter was probably as purely self-initiated as anything in child-life can be.

It may be added that, even if we could not eliminate the imitative and the artificial element, there would still be a pretty wide field for careful observation in the child's own freer type of mirth. For, as all his friends know, his hearty laughter is frequently a response to things which leave us dull "grown-ups" wholly unaffected, or affected in quite another way.

With regard to the development of the expressive movements themselves I can find but few data at hand. These are enough, however, to show that the process of differentiation commences during the first year. Mrs. Moore tells us that her boy in the thirty-third week acquired a new form of smile "which gradually but not entirely supplanted the (earlier) broad open-mouthed smile. . . . The nose was wrinkled up, the eyes nearly closed. . . . This smile seemed to express an extreme and more conscious enjoyment."[120] Preyer remarks that his boy developed in the last three months of the first year "a more conscious movement of laughter," which, presumably, had a different character as an expressive movement. In the case of the boy C., of whom I have written elsewhere, a new and clearly differenced note was detected in the laugh of defiance (to be referred to later) which appeared early in the second year. Mrs. Hogan says she noticed a "mischievous laugh" at the age of fifty-five weeks, whereas Preyer remarks that the first "roguish laugh" occurred in his boy's case at the end of the second year. A more precise record of the phonetic changes in laughter during the first two or three years is greatly to be desired.

The movements of laughter are subject to the laws of movement in general, Repetition and Habit. They tend to perfect themselves by practice; and the result probably involves a strengthening and an expansion of the wide-ranging organic commotion which makes up the reaction. A child of four will laugh on being tickled much more vigorously than one of two.[121] Moreover, the effect of repeated exercises of the function would seem, as already hinted, to involve the setting up in the motor-centres, from which the discharge in laughter issues, a condition of high instability, so that a very slight application of the stimulus, or (as in the case of tickling) the mere threat to apply this, suffices to evoke the reaction. Lastly, this work of organisation will plainly involve a fixing of the connection in the brain-centres between the effect of the stimulation and the motor reaction. We say that the impulse of laughter has become associated with a definite kind of sense-presentation. The instant response of a child to the threatening fingers is a clear example of the result of such an associative co-ordination. Other examples are seen when a particular sight or sound takes on permanently a funny character. A child that has come to regard a figure in a picture book or an odd sound made by the nurse as funny will laugh whenever this recurs or is spoken of, provided that the mood of the moment is favourable. This is a noteworthy illustration of the way in which the action of the novel and unexpected—which, as we all allow, has a large *rôle* in the excitation of laughter—may be replaced by that of an antagonistic force, namely, habit, which itself appears to secure the hilarious response.

It may be added that so far as Habit comes in, reducing the importance of the initial psychical stage, and rendering the reaction automatic, the theory of Lange and James applies fairly well. The feeling of genial hilarity is in this case largely the reflex mental effect of the movements themselves, including the whole organic commotion brought about.

Coming now to the development of the psychical element in laughter, we may, by way of introduction, refer to certain principles which ought to be useful.

(*a*) To begin with, any variety of emotional reaction excited by a particular kind of presentation appears, as it is repeated, to undergo a process of development, taking on more of fulness and complexity. A feeling of attachment to a person or to a place, or of admiration for a cherished work of art, grows fuller and deeper with the establishment of a relation of intimacy. Dimly realised resonances of former like experiences melt into, and deepen the feeling, and new elements are woven into it by associative complication, and by growing reflection. This increasing complexity affects both the ideational basis of the emotion and the closely connected emotional tone itself.122

At first sight we might be disposed to think that the feeling of sudden joy at the back of a merry explosion would prove to be an exception to this law. Since an element of novelty, a sense of joyous mental collapse under a sudden, yet harmless stimulus, runs through all our laughter, there might seem to be no room for any increase of depth and volume. But this is not so. A child's feeling of the "fun of it" at the approach of the tickling hand seems to gain in volume and force with the repetition of the experience. The zest of the enjoyment of a laughing romp with the nurse, or, better, with the father, of watching the funny ways of a kitten, and so forth, grows fuller because of the increasing complication of the psychosis behind the laughter.123

(*b*) In the second place the development of an emotion is essentially a differentiation of it, not merely into a more definite kind of experience as a whole, but into a number of distinguishable sub-varieties of feeling. In other words, the reaction is called forth by new excitants and new modes of stimulation which give rise to mental complexes somewhat different from those caused by the earlier excitants. Thus, as we mentally develop, admirations having a richer ideational structure and more complexity of feeling-tone take the place of the first simple ones, which last die out or survive only as rudimentary processes.

This enlargement of the field of exciting objects, with the concomitant differencing of the emotional state into a larger and larger number of shades, is the outcome of the whole process of mental growth. It means, first of all, the growing differentiation of the child's experience, that is, of his perceptions and ideas, as well as the expansion of his reflective processes. In this way a modified admiration attaches itself to a new kind of object, *e.g.,* works of art, virtuous actions, when these come to be perceived and reflected on in such a way as to disclose their admirable side.

In all such extensions the emotional reaction remains in its essential elements one and the same experience. We may say, if we like, that the expression has been "transferred" to a new situation or a new experience, through the working of a force which has been called "the analogy of feeling".124

This process of extension by analogy of situation and attitude may be seen to be a constituent in the development of laughter. Taking its primitive form to be the expression of a sudden raising of the feeling-tone of consciousness to the level of gladness—which elevation may be supposed to involve at least an appreciable sense of relief from a foregoing state of strain or oppressive dulness—we may readily see how the reaction is passed on, so to speak, to analogous mental attitudes which are developed later.

Let us take as an example a child who, having reached a dim apprehension of the customary behaviour of things begins to laugh at certain odd deviations from this. Here the transition appears clearly to be a kind of transference mediated by the identity of the mental attitude with that of the laughter of an earlier stage, say at the sight of the new and entertaining baubles. Similarly when, after the consciousness of rule is developed, a child roguishly "tries it on" by pretending to disobey, we may regard the new outburst of the spirit of fun as a natural transition from an earlier variety, the laughing pretence of running away from mother or nurse.

Nevertheless, we have to do here with more than a mere transference. Such extensions always involve some amount of complication and enrichment of the mirthful experience. These later forms of mental gaiety depend on the development of more complex psychoses, both on the intellectual and on the emotional side. The first amusement at the sight of the ill-matched, the inconsequent, implies the advance of an analytic reflection up to the point of a dim perception of relations. A large part of the extension of the field of the laughable depends on this intellectual advance, a finer and more precise apprehension of what is presented, in its parts and so as a whole, as also in its relations to other things. With respect to the other condition, expansion of the emotional life, it is enough to remark that certain forms of laughter which fall within the first years of life arise directly out of a deepening of the emotional consciousness as a whole, *e.g.*, the awakening of the "self-feeling," as seen in the laughter of success or triumph; or, on the other hand, of tenderness and sympathy, as illustrated in the first rudiments of a kindly humour.

We see, then, that, as a feature in development, differentiation into a multiplicity of forms is inseparably connected with another feature, complication. The gradual appearance of a number of laughters variously toned, such as that of slightly malicious elation at collapse of dignity, of entertainment at an intellectual inconsequence, and of a kindly amusement at a petty disaster, means that the elemental feeling of joy is getting modified by accretions or absorptions of new psychical elements.

A final remark is needed to prevent misapprehension. Among the several processes of complication which underlie this differentiation of the laughing psychosis, some tend to arrest or tone down the reaction. It is thus that, when sympathy comes to be united with the laughing impulse, the gaiety of the latter is apt to become subdued into something between a smile and the gentlest of laughs. In addition to this inhibitory effect of heterogeneous emotional elements we have that of new conative attitudes. A child soon finds out that a good deal of his rollicking laughter is an offence, and the work of taming the too wild spirits begins.125

With these general considerations to help us, we may now look at the course of development of the laughing experience during the first three years.

It may be premised that the smile and the laugh only become gradually differentiated as signs of qualitatively dissimilar attitudes. In the case of Ruth the two expressions remained for a time interchangeable, and frequently alternated in the same fit of joyous delight. But about the 129th day the smile, it is remarked, began to take on one of its specialised functions, the social one of greeting.

Coming now to laughter, we have found that it begins at an early date to pass from a general sign of sudden increase of pleasure or good spirits into something akin to mirthful play. This has been illustrated in the early responses to tickling, and, a little later, to simple forms of a laughing game (*e.g.*, bo-peep).

By what process of change, one may ask, does the impulse to laugh when the heart suddenly grows glad pass into the laughter of play? Allowing, as seems certain, that the play-impulse is inherited, can we point out any psychological connection between the two?

The answer has already been given in substance in our general analysis of the causes of laughter. A sudden rise of pleasurable consciousness, when it possesses the mind and becomes gladness, say the infant's flood of delight at the swinging coloured baubles, necessarily dissolves, for the time, the tense, serious attitude into a loose, play-like one. The child's consciousness is now all gladness in face of his bauble; and play is just another way of effecting this dissolution of the serious attitude into a large gladness. Not only so, but the elemental mood of laughter resembles the play-mood, since it finds its satisfaction in pretence or make-believe. The gladdening object divested of all serious interest becomes a play-thing, a mere semblance of the thing of practical account which the child observed in the serious moments. Its greeting by the senses may be described, indeed, as a kind of play of these senses. Hence, the specialisation of the primal laughter of delight into that of fun would appear to be one of the simplest processes in the whole development of the emotion.

We may now briefly trace out some of the phases of development of these two primal forms of laughter.

With regard to the laughter of delight and jollity, we find, to judge from the careful record of Ruth's emotional utterances, that there is a rapid development during and after the fourth month.126 In this month, we read, the child was thrown into a state of vivacious delight—which expressed itself in smiles, in movements, in cooing and crowing—by the faces and voices which may be said to have "played" to her as she sat at table. The advent of the meal was that of a new joyous world, and, if the child could have spoken, she would probably have exclaimed, "Oh, what fun!" The large change effected by the return of a familiar face and voice after an absence was only another way of transforming her world into a merry one.

Towards the end of the fifth month, the note-book speaks over and over again of "jollity" and "high spirits," of the child's "laughing with glee when any one smiled or spoke to her," of "being exceedingly jolly, smiling, kicking and sputtering," and so forth. This growing gleefulness seemed to be the outcome of new expansions of the pleasurable consciousness, of a pure "Lebenslust". No doubt it had its obscure source in a pleasurable cœnaesthesis, the result of merrily working digestive and other processes of organic life. Yet it had its higher conditions, also, in the expansion of the life of the senses and in the growing range of the muscular activities. Laughter and shouts of joy would, we are told, accompany not merely the inrush of delightful sights and sounds, but the new use of bodily powers in exploring and experimenting.

This gaiety in taking possession of her new world showed itself in the greeting of friendly faces. The new appearance of her grandfather after an absence excited her laughter on the 133rd day. By about the middle of the year, the child had, like Preyer's boy, developed a jubilant greeting for her social belongings, nodding a friendly nod with all the signs of huge delight.

These outbursts of laughing joy may sometimes be seen to have been preceded by a distinctly disagreeable state of feeling. In the case of Ruth, we are told that the fit of jollity broke out, on one or two occasions, upon "instantaneous relief from great general discomfort". Again, on the 222nd day, having awoke and felt timid, she laughed with joy and a sense of relief when her mother came into the room. I have other evidence to show that this laughter of overflowing gladness is often to some extent a relief from constraint. Thus, a boy of one and a half years who had a new nurse, and for some days behaved with great gravity when with her, was during the same period "extremely hilarious" when alone with his parents.

The gladness of the world grew larger to this happy girl when, towards the end of the seventh month, she was taken into the open air, and, shortly after, allowed to lie on a quilt and roll on the ground. The wooing of the passing freshness, the play of sun and shadow, the large stir of life in moving and sounding things, all this possessed her and made her "laugh and ejaculate with pleasure". With this may be compared a note on a boy nine months old, who, lying in a clothes-basket in a garden one summer's day, looked up at the leaves dancing in the sunshine and laughed with "a hearty noisy laugh".

The development of bodily power in this same half-year brought our little maiden much gleeful laughter. Any experience of movement, passive as well as active, filled her with noisy hilarity. To ride on anybody's foot brought out, at the end of the fifth month, the unmistakable signs of hilarious rapture. A month later, the gleeful explosion was called out by the new frolicsome experience of being jumped and tossed. Similar expressions of mirth occurred when new active movements were accomplished. In the record of the middle of the ninth month, we are told of a medley of movements, tumbling on the floor or lawn, sitting up and lying down, raising herself on the feet and hands, etc., which brought her "singular joy".

A part of the gleefulness of this widening experience of movement is due to its unexpected results. It seems probable that the first successful experiments in crawling, climbing and the rest may give rise to new complexes of muscular and other sensations which come as a joyful surprise. Such delightful surprises grow more varied and impressive when the arms and hands begin to experiment. For example, a little girl, aged two and a quarter years, happened when throwing a ball at random to jerk it over her head, and was seized with a spasm of hilarity. The gleeful outburst is apt to occur, too, later on when a child first achieves the feat—half-wonderful, half-amusing—of walking, of running and of jumping.127

In these expanding processes of jollity or gleefulness we may detect the beginnings of more specialised forms of laughing enjoyment. Thus, in the outburst of merriment which winds up a successful attempt to climb, we recognise the germ of that mode of reaction which is apt to follow at the moment of sudden relaxation of tension on the attainment of an end. We may be sure that a child of nine months finds the effort to stand a very serious and exhausting strain; and may infer that the laughter which occurs in this case is largely due to momentary relaxations of this strain.

But again, these experiences clearly supply conditions favourable to the emergence of that "sudden glory" which enters into successful effort. The "shouting and laughing" of little Ruth (forty-five weeks) on completing the magnificent exploit of climbing the staircase had, as her aunt's epithet "exultant" recognises, something of the free-breathing jubilation of the successful mountain-climber. We are told further that, in the tenth month, Ruth would break into the same exultant laugh after some successful mental effort, such as pointing out the right picture when this was asked for.

Here, then, we have the laughter of a joyous feeling-tone complicated by new elements. These include, not merely the delightful feeling of relief after prolonged effort, but some dim form of an agreeable consciousness of growing power and of an expanding self. In the glee on mastering a new movement, *e.g.*, riding on somebody's foot, we see traces of a more distinctly playful mood. We may now follow out the development of this large variety of gamesome mirth.

The overflow of the health-filled reservoirs of muscular activity begins at an early stage to wear an unmistakable aspect of playfulness. The first exercises in crawling, accompanied by various sounds of contentment and gladness, are indeed recognisable by all as a kind of play. As the forces of the organism establish themselves a more manifest bent to a romping kind of game appears. This, as a game in which co-operation enters, involves a development of the social consciousness, and its gleefulness comes in part from the reverberations of mutual sympathy. A good example of the hilarity of a romping game is Ruth's uproarious delight, in the seventh month, when dragged about on a carpet, an experience which involved, of course, much loss of equilibrium and some amount of awkward bumping. That the bumps were of the essence of the enjoyment is confirmed by the fact that, in the tenth month, she would like to stand, holding on to a chair, and then deliberately to let herself go so as to "come down sitting with a thud," winding up the performance by "looking up laughing and triumphant". Another game involving exciting jolts was liked in the middle of the twelfth month. The child was shot in her carriage, now from the aunt to the mother, and now back, each little ride ending up with a jolt, over which she grew very merry. Later on, (at the end of the twentieth month) she laughed heartily on being knocked down by her dog in a too pushful bit of play; and she enjoyed in like manner some pretty rough play at the hands of a nine-year-old boy companion.

This mirthful treatment of romps, which must have involved a palpable amount of discomfort, is interesting as showing how laughter plays about the confines of the serious. This little girl seems, up to the age of three, at least, to have been curiously indifferent to pain. Yet she was not wanting in the common childish timidity. It looks, then, as if the fun of these rather rough games turned on dissolutions of nascent attitudes of apprehension, and, consequently, the laughter expressed something of a joyous contempt of fear. Indeed, it seems likely that an element of this joyous rebound from a half-developed state of fear entered into much of this child's laughter, already illustrated, on succeeding in a rather risky experiment, such as climbing the staircase. We read that, like other vigorous children, she was a keen pursuer of new experiences, even in cases in which she knew that some pain was involved. The passion for trying new experiments seems to have urged her on, in spite of nascent fear; and the final shouting and laughing may well have announced, along with the joy of successful effort, a sense of triumph over the weaker timid self. The ability, illustrated in these hardy experiments, to turn situations suggestive of danger into "larkish" play, was a singular proof of the firm foundation on which this child's prevalent mode of gaiety reposed.

In some cases Ruth's play would take on a form which clearly involved a triumphing over fear. Thus, we are told that when, on the 429th day, she was asked to find "auntie" in the dark she at first stood still and silent. Then, when her head was touched by somebody's hands, she broke into laughter and started off by herself to explore in the dark. Later on, with the growth of a bolder spirit, this laughing triumph over fear extended itself, so that in the twenty-ninth month she played at bear with her uncle, going into a dark room, with her hand in her aunt's, and enjoying "the exhilaration of unreal alarm"; and when the uncle sprang out from his dark hiding-place, growling fearfully, she "laughed, shrieked and fled all in one". If the uncle went a little too far in the use of the alarming she would check him by saying, "Don't do that again".

In these cases, it is evident, we have a complex psychosis with alternating phases. The awful delight which vents itself at once in a laugh and in a shriek and a flight is certainly of a mixed feeling-tone. The laughter is the note of a triumphant spirit, and yet of one in which, in the moment of triumph, the nascent fear leaves its trace.

In these laughing games we have clearly an element of make-believe. A firm persuasion, low down in consciousness, of the harmlessness of the coming bump and of the human bear in the blackness keeps the little girl's heart steady and turns the adventure into fun. At the same time, the play as "pretending" would seem to involve at least a half-formed expectation of something, and probably, too, a final taste of delicious surprise at the fully realised nothingness of the half-expected. In some forms of play-pretence this element of final annihilation of expectation becomes more conspicuous and the distinct source of the hilarious exultation. When, for example, in the eleventh month, Ruth sitting on the floor held out her arms to be taken up, and the mother, instead of doing this, stooped and kissed the child, there was a perfect peal of laughter again and again.

The increase of muscular activity shown in the laughing romps leads to the extension of mirthful enjoyment in another way. A vigorous child, even when a girl, grows aggressive and attempts various forms of playful attack. As we have seen, to tickle another is merely one variety of a large class of teasing operations, in which the teased as well as the teasing party is supposed to find his merriment. Regarding now the child as teaser, we see that he very early begins to exercise at once his own powers and others' endurance. The pulling of whiskers is one of the earliest forms of practical jokes. Ruth took to this pastime in the first week of the fifth month. By the end of the sixth month the little tormentor had grown aware of her power, and "became most eager to pull, with laughter and exultant clamour, at the nose, ear, and especially the hair, of any one that held her". The boy C., at the same age, delighted in pulling his sister's hair, and was moved by her cries only to outbursts of laughter. As intelligence develops, these practical jokes grow more cunning. Another little girl, of whom I have written elsewhere under the initial M., when seventeen months old, asked for her father's "tick-tick," looking very saucy; and as he stooped to give it, she tugged at his moustache, "and almost choked with laughter".

With this teasing of human companions we have that of animals. When sixteen months old, Ruth would chase the cat with shouts of laughter. Another child, a boy, about the same age, went considerably further, and taking the toilet puff from its proper place went deliberately to "Moses," the cat, who was sitting unsuspectingly before the fire, and proceeded to powder him, each new application of the puff being accompanied by a short chuckle.

There is no need of reading into this laughter the note of cruel exultation over suffering.128 Ruth's mischievous doings would take forms which had not even the semblance of cruelty. There was merely impish playfulness in the act of snatching off her grandmother's spectacles and even her cap, with full accompaniment of laughter, in the twenty-second month when lifted to say good-night. In much the same spirit the other little girl,

M., delighted, when two years old, in untying the maid's apron strings and in other jocose forms of mischief.

The laughing mood in these cases is understandable as a rioting in newly realised powers, a growing exultation as the consciousness of ability to produce striking effects grows clearer. Ruth, in her eleventh month, blew a whistle violently and looked round laughing to her aunt and the others present. Here, surely, the laughter was that of rejoicing in a new power. This sense of power implies a clearer form of "self-feeling". A child may grow keenly conscious of the self in such moments of newly tried powers, as he grows in "the moments of intense pain". This laughter, then, furnishes a good illustration of the sudden glory on which Hobbes lays emphasis.

I have assumed that in this laughing mischief we have to do with a form of (playful) teasing. The little assailant enjoys the fun of the attack and counts on your enjoying it also. The indulgence of others, even if they do not show an equal readiness for the pastime, removes all thought of disobedience, of lawlessness.

Yet things do not commonly remain at this point of perfectly innocent fun. The gathering energies of the child, encouraged by indulgence in games of romp, are pretty certain to develop distinctly rowdyish proceedings. Ruth, for example, when about twenty-one months old, scrambled defiantly on to the table at the close of a meal, seized on the salts, and scampered about laughing. About the same time this new spirit of rowdyism showed itself in flinging a plate across the room and other mutinous acts. Little boys, I suspect, are much given to experiments in a violent kind of fun which they know to be disorderly. One of them, aged two years eight and a half months, was fond of "trying it on" by pulling hair-pins out of his mother's hair, splashing in the puddles in the road, and so forth, to her great perplexity and his plainly pronounced enjoyment.

In these outbursts of laughing rowdyism we see more than an escape of pent-up energies, more than a mere overflow of "high spirits"; they are complicated by a new factor, something of the defiant temper of the rebel. A child of two has had some experience of real disobedience, and may be said to have developed simple ideas of order and law. We may reasonably infer, then, that in this turbulent fun there is some consciousness of setting law at defiance. The presence of this new psychical factor is seen in the alteration of the laughing sounds themselves. In Ruth's case, we are told, they were "rough" and unlike the natural and joyous utterance. It is further seen in the method of the fun, for, as Miss Shinn observes, Ruth "tried repeatedly to see how far she could go safely in roguish naughtiness".

I think we find in this behaviour a clear instance of laughter becoming an ingredient in the attitude of throwing off a customary restraint. It is the early analogue of the laughter of the rowdies bent on window-smashing, of the riotous enjoyment of the people at festal seasons when the lord of misrule holds sway.

The degree of conscious defiance of order may, no doubt, vary greatly. In much of what we view as the disorderly mirth of a child this ingredient of the laughing mood may be small and sub-conscious; yet at times it grows distinct and prominent. Thus, Ruth, in the eleventh month, developed a special expression for the attitude of defiance when disobeying, namely, a comical face with a wrinkling of the nose, together with laughter. The boy C., early in the third year, would give out a laugh of a short mocking ring on receiving a prohibition, *e.g.,* not to slap his dog companion. He would remain silent and laugh in a half-contemptuous way. Sometimes in his moods of defiance he would go so far as to strike a member of his family and then laugh. His laugh was sometimes highly suggestive of the mood of derision.

In this note of warlike challenge we have a point of kinship with the "crowing" laughter of the victor. Yet it is doubtful whether a child at this early age reaches the mental attitude of a mocking contempt. Preyer tells us that he has never observed scornful laughter within the first four years.129

When the consciousness of the unruly in these "high jinks" becomes distinct and begins to be oppressive, the laughter will be less boisterous and express more of playful pretence. The child learns to be satisfied with making a feint to rebel, with a make-believe unruliness. Ruth, on the 236th day, laughed when pretending to disobey by biting off the petals of flowers, and on the 455th day, by stuffing buttons into her mouth. The boy C., when about the same age, had his little way of turning disobedience into a game. In the seventeenth month, when he was bidden by his mother to give up a picture he had got possession of, he walked up to her and made a show of handing over his unlawful possession, and then drew his hands back with much laughing enjoyment.

A more complicated psychical attitude appears when such laughing pretence at disobedience takes on a "roguish" aspect. Here we have, not only an element of slight uneasiness, but one of self-consciousness, which together give a distinct complexion to the whole mental attitude and to its expression.

This ingredient of a timid self-consciousness or shyness under the scrutiny of others appears, as we know, some time after the simpler forms of fear. In Ruth's case it seems to have showed itself on the 123rd day in a distinctly "roguish" attitude. When at dinner and spoken to by her grandfather, she turned her head as far as she could. On the 141st day, too, when held in her nurse's arms, she smiled at her grandfather and others and then ducked her head. This expression of roguish self-consciousness had more of the look of a nervous explosion in the eleventh month, when the girl laughed on being set on her feet in a corner where she was much noticed; and again, in the thirteenth month, as she tumbled about and showed herself off. This laughter, with something of the *gêne* of self-consciousness in it, was, we are told, not to be confounded with the expression of a complacent self-consciousness.

The element of an awkward shyness comes into much of the early playful "trying it on". In the case of the boy C., just mentioned, it was seen in the sly, upward look of the eyes and the short, half-nervous laugh, when he was face to face with authority and disposed to play at disobedience. The fuller roguish laugh occurs frequently along with a risky bit of play, as when a boy of one and a half year would point to himself when asked for a finger-recognition of somebody else. In such cases the laughter seems like an attempt to get rid of the element of risk. When the masking of the impulse of fun by timidity is greater, the expression reaching only to a tentative smile, the roguishness of a child may easily wear a look of kinship with our grown-up humour.130

A full account of the development of laughter during these first years, as an ingredient of the play-mood, would be of great value. It would, in particular, help us to see how the reaction comes to be definitely co-ordinated with the sense of make-believe, and the attitude of throwing off the burdensome restrictions of reality. The vocal mirth of children, as they give reins to their fancy, attests to the weight of this burden and to the intense delight which comes from its momentary abandonment.

In seeking for the first traces of the laughter of play and of defiance, we are not greatly troubled by the interfering influence of others. No doubt this influence is at work even here. The nurse and the parents are pretty certain to laugh at much of the roguish "trying it on"; and this laughter will react upon the child's own merriment. In play, too, in which others usually take some part, there is this action of older persons' laughter. Still, in the main, the utterances are spontaneous, and at most are reinforced by way of some sympathetic rapport with another.

It is otherwise when we come to consider the first instances of laughing amusement at the presentation of "funny" objects. The lead of others now complicates the phenomenon to a much more serious extent. The recognition of an object as "funny" implies some detection of a quality which acts on others as well as on the self;131 consequently, it presupposes a certain development of the social consciousness. Hence, some cautiousness is needed in noting the first clear examples of a perception of the quality. Before language comes and supplies a means of self-interpretation, we cannot safely say that because a child laughs in presence of an object there is a recognition of something objectively "funny". As we have seen, such laughter may be fully accounted for by supposing that the object has an exhilarating or gladdening effect on the child's feeling. On the other hand, when language is added we have to cope with the difficulty, already touched on, that a child's pronouncements are apt to be controlled by what others laugh at and call funny. Nevertheless, here, too, the child's spontaneity and his way of discovering his own sources of amusement may enable us to overcome the difficulties.

Our study of the conditions of the perception suggests that a true enjoyment of presentations as oddities is not to be expected at a very early date. And this, first of all, for the reason that the new, especially if it is strange, even though fitted to draw forth a joyous laugh, may easily excite other and inhibitory attitudes. An infant, during the first year of life, if not later also, is apt to be disturbed and apparently alarmed at the approach of new objects, so as to be unaffected by its rejoicing aspect; or, if he feels this, the laughter may be accompanied by signs of fear. Ruth, on her 254th day, greeted a kitten which her father brought to show her with "all gradations from laughter and joy to fear". In the second place—and this is of more importance—the recognition of an object as funny presupposes the work of experience in organising a rudimentary feeling for what is customary. This, again, involves a development of the social consciousness and of an idea of a common order of things.

Now all this requires a certain amount of time. It hardly seems reasonable to look for a true apprehension of the laughable till some time after the appearance of an imitation of others' laughter and play-gestures, which was first observed, in the case of the boy C., in the ninth month. Nor could it well be expected until after a child had acquired some understanding of others' language, so as to note how they agree in naming and describing certain objects as funny, which understanding only begins to be reached in the second half of the year. Hence, I should hesitate to speak of a clear recognition of a laughable object as such before the last quarter of the year. It seems to me, for example, a little rash to say that a boy of five months, who always laughed inordinately when a very jolly-looking physician, the image of Santa Claus, paid him a visit, displayed a "sense of humour".132

When once the idea of objects of common laughter begins to grow clear a child is, of course, able to develop perceptions of the funny along his own lines. This he certainly seems to do pretty briskly. The freshness of his world, the absence of the dulling effect of custom which is seen in the perceptions of older folk, renders him an excellent pioneer in the largely unknown territory of King Laughter.

Among the sense-presentations which awaken the infantile laugh are new and queer sounds of various sorts; and they may well be selected for a study of the transitions from mere joyous exclamation to a hilarious greeting of what is "funny". Early in the second half of the first year, a child in good health will begin to surmount the alarms of the ear, and to turn what is new and strange into fun. About the 222nd day brave little Ruth was able to laugh, not only at such an odd sound as that produced when her aunt rattled a tin cup on her teeth, but at that of a piano. Preyer's boy, later in the year, was given to laughing at various new and out-of-the-way sounds, such as that of the piano, of gurgling or clearing the throat, and even of thunder.

Odd sounding articulations appear to be especially provocative of laughter about this time. As early as the 149th day, Ruth laughed at new sounds invented by the aunt, such as "Pah! Pah!" Queer guttural sounds seem to have a specially tickling effect.

After words and their commoner forms have begun to grow familiar, new and odd-sounding words, especially names, are apt to be greeted with laughter. The child M., when one year nine months old, was much impressed by the exclamation "good gracious!" made by her mother on discovering that the water was coming through the ceiling of a room; and the child would sometimes repeat it in pure fun "shaking with laughter". When she was two years seven months old she laughed on first hearing the name "Periwinkle".

In these and similar cases of the hilarious response to sounds we seem to have, well within the first nine months, a germ of a feeling for the odd or droll. The early development of this sense of the funny in sounds is aided by their aggressive force for the infant's consciousness, and by the circumstance that for the young ear they have pronounced characteristics which are probably lost as development advances, and they are attended to, not for their own sake, but merely as signs of things which interest us.

The psychical process involved in the transition may be described as follows. Sounds, while by reason of their suddenness and unexpectedness they are apt to take the consciousness off its guard and to produce a kind of nervous shock, are of all sense-stimuli the most exhilarating. The sudden rousing of the consciousness to a large joyous commotion is the fundamental fact. Nor will the jar of the shock, when the sense-organ develops and becomes hardier, interfere with this. On the contrary, it will add something in the shape of an agreeable rebound from a nascent attitude of uneasiness.133 The laughter of the child at the first sounds of the piano, which have frightened many a child and other young animal, is, in part, a shout of victory. There is here, too, an element of "sudden glory" in the rejoicing, as the new expanding self is dimly conscious of its superiority to the half-alarmed and shrinking self of the moment before.

In this case, it is evident, we have to do with a greeting of the laughable which will vary greatly according to the psycho-physical condition of the child. The same child that laughs at a new sound to-day will to-morrow, when in another mood, be disturbed by a quite similar surprise of the ear.

But more is involved in this laughter. The sudden and slightly disturbing attack of the ear by new sounds is apt to wear for the child's consciousness a game-like aspect. We have only to think of the nursery rhymes, alluded to by Miss Shinn, in which the excitement of fun is secured by an explosive shock at the end, games closely analogous to the rides which terminated in a good bump. In these rhymes the fun lies in the shock, though only half-unexpected—a shock which has in it the very soul of frivolous play, since it comes at the end of a series of quiet orderly sounds. May not the new sounds, the guttural utterances and the rest, affect a child in a like manner as a kind of disorderly play? For a child's ear, pitched for the intrinsic character of a sound, they may hold much which is expressive of the play-mood. This will apply not only to utterances like the "Pah! Pah!" which are clearly recognised as play, but to many others produced by a nurse or a mother who is given to entertaining. Perhaps the gurgling sounds which moved the mirth of Preyer's boy appeared laughter-like.

This tendency to look on certain sounds as a kind of play seems to supply a psychical link in the development of a feeling for the odd and out-of-the-way as such. We have seen how the play-impulse "tries it on" when the restraints of rule grow too irksome. I suspect that the mirthful appreciation of the queer and out-of-the-way grows out of this inclination to a playful disorderliness or law-breaking. A child is apt to feel oppressed with the rules of propriety imposed on him. By these rules quite a terrible multiplicity of noises is branded as "naughty," and the prohibition tends to fix the playful impulse precisely in the direction of the forbidden sounds. Children have a way, moreover, of projecting their experiences and their inclinations into things which we call lifeless. What more natural, then, that they should feel these incursions of violent and quite improper-sounding noises to be a kind of playful throwing aside of order and rule?

In the domain of the visible world, suddenness of presentation rarely reaches, perhaps, the point of shock or joltiness. Yet there is ample scope, here, too, for the working of the unexpected on the child's sensibilities. The first visual excitants of laughter, the sudden uncovering of the face in bo-peep, the unexpected return of the familiar face after an interval of absence, the instant transformation of the accustomed features when the mother "makes a face," show how directly the surprisingly new may act on the young muscles of laughter.

Here, too, we may see how the hilarious enjoyment of the new and out-of-the-way emerges out of play-mirth. The distorted face of the mother produces a laugh when it has ceased to alarm and is taken as fun.134 According to one observer, this making of faces grows into a standing pastime towards the end of the second year.135 Is not the greeting of the baby-face in the mirror, which in Ruth's case occurred on the 221st day (eighth month), and in that of Preyer's boy at the end of the ninth month, a kind of accost of a newly discovered playmate? Perhaps the laughter of a little boy, of one and a half year, already referred to, at the jumping of a ping-pong ball and at a spring-blind going up or coming down with a run, expressed a recognition of something play-like.

This co-operation of the play-inclination in the perception of the laughable in visual presentations is still more plainly illustrated in the effect of actions and postures. The quickness of the eye of mirth for expressions of the mood of romping play is seen in a child's laughter, already referred to, at the gambols of a horse or other animal. Ruth was much entertained on her 441st day by the antics of a dog. Especially enlivening is the appearance of quick, play-like movements in grave elders addicted to decorous deportment. The girl M., at the age of eighteen months, broke into boisterous laughter on seeing her father as he ran to catch a train, with his handkerchief hanging out of his pocket. This sudden revelation of the playful temper may come to the child by way of postures and expressions. The awful laws of propriety soon tend to give the look of playful licence to certain bodily postures, especially that of lying down. The boy C., when twenty months old, laughed heartily on seeing his sister lying on the ground out of doors. Making faces, pouting lips and the rest become playful just because they are felt to be improper, the sort of thing one only does in a disorderly moment, playful or other. May not the drolleries—to the child's consciousness—of animal form, for example the long neck of the giraffe, owe something to suggestions of improper jocose actions, such as trying to stretch oneself into Alice-like dimensions?

In this blithe recognition of the irregular in others' behaviour we have the rudiment of an appreciation of the laughable, not only as a violation of rule but as a loss of dignity. This is apparent in such cases as the boy's laughter at the prostrate form of his sister, illumined as it was by the observation that, at the age of twenty-six months, he expressed great contempt at the spectacle of a Japanese gentleman stretched on the grass in the suburban Heath, which was the child's daily resort, and which he seemed strongly disposed to subject to his own code of manners. Possibly, too, there was a touch of this appreciation of lowered dignity when the same boy, at the age of twenty-eight months, laughed greatly on seeing his father batter in an old hat. The laughter, complicated now by a new element of conscious superiority, probably took on a crowing note, though our dull ears may not be equal to a clear detection of the change. Not only so, it is possible that the laughter of children, common in the second year, at signs of disorderliness in the hair or dress of others, and especially superiors, implies a perception of something like lowered rank.

In this effect of the new in the visible world different tones of mirth are no doubt distinguishable. As the higher forms of perception begin to develop the primitive laughter of joy may persist and combine with later and more specialised kinds. Ruth's voicing of merriment, in the thirteenth month, on having a new pair of mittens put on her, was largely an outburst of joy, though some dim sense of the oddity of the thing probably combined with this. On the other hand, the laughter called forth in the little girl M., at the age of twenty-one months, by the spectacle of a doll that had lost its arms presumably had in it, along with a sense of something weirdly absurd in the mutilated form, a pretty keen sub-consciousness of dollish proprieties set at defiance.

Other directions in the development of this early laughter at entertaining spectacles may be said to have their origin in the fun of play with its pretence or make-believe. Mrs. Hogan's boy, at the age of two years and two months, would laugh at his nurse's pretended efforts to put on his shoes, which, instead of getting on, flew away wildly into freedom. This laughter was evoked at the fun of the thing, and probably involved an interpretation of the nurse's action as play. Yet it had in it also, I think, the trace of an appreciation of the absurdity of the farcical collapse of effort. This is borne out by the fact that the boy, about the same time, would also laugh when the nurse, not in play, tried by jumping to hang a garment on a nail just too high for her. He may, of course, have regarded this, too, as but a continuation of the play. Yet it seems reasonable to suppose that the merry current had one of its sources in the perception of the amusing aspect of failure, of effort missing its mark and lapsing into nothingness.

I confess to have been surprised at what looks like the precocity of some children in the matter of honouring the proprieties of conduct. The little girl M., when only fourteen months old, is said to have laughed in an "absurdly conscious way" at a small boy who stood by her perambulator asking for a kiss. That kiss, we are told, was not forthcoming. Was the laugh merely an incident in a mood of nervous shyness, or did it signify a dim perception of "bad form" on the part of the proposer? Much care is needed in the interpretation of such expressive reactions. A small boy of eighteen months laughed when his pants slipped down. But this may only have resulted from a sense of the fun of the irregularity of the proceeding, aided perhaps by others' amusement. A true feeling of shame is, of course, not developed at this age; yet a child may have caught from instruction a feeling of the shocking impropriety of an ill-timed casting aside of the clothes-trammels.

We may find in the laughter of the child, within the period of the first three years, pretty clear indications of the development of a rude perception of amusing incongruities in dress and behaviour. The young eye has a keen outlook for the proprieties in the matter of clothes. Ruth, who was in the thirteenth month amused at seeing her new mittens put on, showed amusement about the same date when her pink bonnet was put on her aunt's head. In this case, the play-significance of the action for the child's consciousness is apparent. It seems fairly certain, indeed, that this higher form of a recognition of the laughable grows out of the play-interpretation. When at play children not only throw off rules of decorum and do improper things, they put aside ideas of appropriateness and launch out into bizarre discontinuities and contrarieties of action and speech. The play-attitude, as lawless and free, tends to inconsequence. Hence the readiness with which a child interprets such inconsequences as play.

It is the same when a child laughs at droll stories of the doings of animals and persons. He may take fables and other fancies seriously enough at times, but if his mind is pitched for merriment, he will greatly appreciate the extravagant unsuitabilities of behaviour of the heroes of his nursery books. The little girl M., when two years seven months old, laughed gaily at a passage in a story about kittens, in which they are made to say, "Waiter, this cat's meat is tough;" asking in the midst of her merriment, "Did you ever saw such funny tits?"

Along with this rudiment of merry appreciation of the spectacle of the incongruous, we have the first crude manifestation of the closely related feeling of amusement at the absurd. Children are said to have no measure of the probable and possible, and to accept the wildest fancies in unquestioning faith. Yet experience begins her educative work during these first three years, and one may detect sporadic traces of a feeling for what is gloriously incredible. A boy, already alluded to, aged about one and a half year, laughed as his aunt asked him what the waves, which he was gravely observing, were saying. The boy C., when twenty-two months old, grew quite hilarious over the idea of flying up into the air. Some one had suggested his flying like a bird, and he proceeded to cap the suggestion, adding, "Tit (sister) fy air," "gee-gee (horse) fy air". The last idea of a flying horse especially delighted one innocent, as yet, of Greek mythology.

Lastly, a bare allusion may be made to the early development of an appreciation of word-play and the lighter kind of wit. That this grows out of the play-element, the love of pretence, is at once evident. Verbal fun, "trying it on" with an incorrect use of words and so forth, is a common outlet of the rollicking spirits of childhood. Mrs. Hogan's boy, at the age of one year eight months, developed a fancy for calling things by their wrong names, a knife a "fork," for example. Ruth did the same towards the end of the third year. The fun derived from punning seems to be immense in the case of many children at the close of our period, as when a boy on hearing his mother say she had just called on Mrs. Fawkes asked, "Did you call on Mrs. knives too?" This easy childish mode of satisfying a jocose bent is seen also in the use of false statements, not seriously, but "in fun," as the child has it. Ruth had a fit of such merry fibbing at the end of the third year. A child will often "try on" this kind of verbal game, when called up for a moral lesson.136

This same roguish impulse to "try it on" with the authorities leads to something like a play of wit in repartee. The merry interchange of intellectual attack and defence, which relieves so many serious relations of adult life, grows naturally enough in the case of children out of their relation of subjection to the grown-ups. The playful experiment in the direction of disobedience is frequently accompanied by pretty exercises in verbal fencing, the joke of which the perpetrator himself, at any rate, greatly enjoys. Such sportive dialectic may arise, too, by way of meeting serious correction. A girl of two and a quarter years was told by a foolish nurse that if she put out her tongue she would get spots on her face. After listening gravely she turned on her instructress and, putting her finger on a little pimple on the latter's chin, asked with "a most mirthful smile," "How Lizzie (the nurse) det dat 'pot dere den?"

Enough has been said, perhaps, even in this slight examination of children's laughter, to show that within the first three years all the main directions of the mirth of adults are foreshadowed. Humour itself, which is supposed only to come with maturity of feeling and reflection, begins to announce itself in a modest way during this period. The boy C., in his twenty-first month, had managed to twist his india-rubber horse, so that the head was caught between the tail and the legs. He laughed out loudly at first, then waxed tender, saying in a pitiful tone, "Poor Gee-gee," and so swung from the one emotional attitude to the other.137

This appearance of the two feelings, distinct though contiguous, is, of course, a very different thing from the highly organised sentiment which we call humour. Miss Shinn tells us that, in the case of Ruth, the period of infantile gaiety has been followed by one of serious practicality, into which humour does not enter. Perhaps it will come later. In any case we have to recognise in this laughter of the first years something far removed from the humour of the adult. It is a pure primitive gaiety, uncomplicated by reflection and sadness. It is enough for my purpose if it can be seen to disclose faint embryonic tracings of the main lines of differentiation in the development of human laughter.

CHAPTER VIII.
THE LAUGHTER OF SAVAGES.

In the last chapter we took a glance at the primitive forms of human laughter as illustrated in children. We may now supplement this by a brief inquiry into the merriment of the childhood of the race, so far as this is reflected in the laughter of those savage tribes which have come under the direct observation of the civilised man.

We shall expect the two domains to disclose similar features, spontaneity, absence of reflection, whole-hearted simplicity. At the same time we shall expect the study of the laughter of savages to bring us more directly in touch with the social conditions which help to determine the directions of mirth. The study of the savage mind is the study of a collective mind, that is to say, of a typical form of ideas, sentiments, and psychical tendencies generally, running through a community. Its modes of merriment, like its more serious emotional manifestations, have been observed as common traits of members of a tribal society.

A word may be said at the outset with respect to the sources of our information. It is a commonplace that civilised man finds all his powers taxed when he tries to get into touch with the mind of a savage. The difficulties of this access will naturally be greater when the trait to be observed is an emotion which, while it is wont to display itself with an instinctive directness so long as the surroundings secure freedom, tends to hide itself as soon as anything strange appears which induces a feeling of *gêne*. The presence of strangers, so far removed from the plane of life of savages as the missionaries or officials of a civilised nation, would, one supposes, act as such a check to their risible impulses. It is possible, too, that the stranger who visits a savage tribe may supply, quite unknowingly perhaps, in his look, dress, and manner of behaviour, a number of provocatives of laughter which are resisted from a feeling of what is due to a guest.

That there is some hiding of the merry mood here is not a mere matter of inference, since travellers distinctly testify to the fact. The undisciplined savage will now and again show a degree of self-restraint comparable with that which an educated Frenchman will show when in a Paris street he is addressed by a hardy British youth in what the latter cheerfully supposes to be the language of the country. The following story may serve as an example. A public meeting was being held in a native village in Africa. An Englishman who was present got up on a recumbent trunk of a tree, which is used as a seat in native villages. The log rolled and the Englishman fell heavily. Yet the whole meeting looked as grave as if the accident had been a part of the programme. An uninstructed observer might have hastily inferred that the tribe was wanting in a "sense of humour". The narrator of the incident knew better, and gives the incident as a proof of the great power of self-restraint displayed. The same writer observes that African savages, while allowing a European traveller to humour them and treat them as children, will "amuse themselves at his expense after he is gone, and, indeed, while he is present, if they know that he cannot understand their speech".138

These considerations will prepare us to understand how some have regarded savages as dull creatures, who know not how to laugh. That this view is commonly held by those who have not visited them is suggested by a passage in one of Peacock's stories. In *Crotchet Castle* Mr. MacQueedy puts forward the thesis that laughter is "an involuntary action developed in man by the progress of civilisation," and adds that "the savage never laughs".139

It is only fair to say that travellers themselves have not been so foolish as to uphold this view. At the same time, some of them have drawn hasty conclusions from the fact that they happened never to have heard members of a particular tribe indulge in laughter. A curious illustration of this reasoning from inadequate negative evidence is the dispute that took place, not so long ago, as to whether a people of Ceylon, known as Weddas (or Veddas), came into the category of the laughing animal. It was confidently asserted by a certain Mr. Hartshorne that they never laughed, even when they were experimented upon, and were confronted with the spectacle of others convulsed. Another visitor may help us to understand this by his remark that they vary "between a taciturn and almost morose mood when hungry, and a laughing reckless mood when not hungry". Hartshorne must evidently have observed them in a hungry mood. Could it have been that, unlike Mary Kingsley, as some of us remember her playfully observing, he had something about him which kindled appetite?140

Other illustrations of a too confident basing of a conclusion on failure to observe may be found. Thus it is said by one traveller, Bates, that the Brazilian Indians are of a phlegmatic, apathetic temperament. A more recent visitor, Von den Steinen, gives us a different impression, remarking in one instance that "the silent Indian men and women continually chattered, and Eva's laughter sounded forth right merrily" (lustig heraus).141

These apparent discrepancies in the notes of different observers point, I suspect, to something besides such accidents as the particular mood in which the tribe is found. The ability to provoke laughter is not possessed by all: witness the failure of many meritorious attempts by adults to excite children's merriment. Something of the easy good-nature which disarms timidity, of fraternal sympathy, and of the knack of making your audience believe you are like themselves, seems needed to draw forth all the mirthfulness of these children of nature.142 We must always allow for this factor in the personal equation of the observer of savage ways. It is refreshing to find that missionaries have so often succeeded in getting at the lighter moods of the heathen. It speaks well for their genial humanity.

The general impression one derives from these accounts is that savage tribes are certainly not given over to a sullen despair, but on the contrary have a large and abundant mirth. Like children, they appear to express their emotions with great freedom, and their laughter and other signs of good spirits are of the most energetic kind. Darwin tells us that his correspondents, missionaries and others, satisfied him on this point. Loud laughter accompanied by jumping about and clapping of the hands, and frequently carried to the point of a flooding of the eyes—these are conspicuous characteristics to be met with among the Australians and other savage tribes.143 Other testimony supports Darwin. Sturt, for example, tells us that the natives of Central Australia are a merry people, and sit up laughing and talking all the night long.144 The more recent observations of Lumholtz support the view that the natives are "very humorous".145 The Maoris (of New Zealand) are said by one traveller to be "remarkable for their natural gaiety: they are merry fellows: always laughing and joking, especially during the adventures of a journey".146 Of the Tasmanians we read: "There is not a little love of fun in the despised aborigine".147 Similarly, the South Sea Islanders are "more accustomed to jesting, mirth and humour than irritating and reproachful language".148 The natives of Tahiti, again, "jest upon each other with greater freedom than the Europeans".149 So, the Tongans have "a strong sense of the ludicrous" which they show in "the ordinary intercourse of life".150 Mr. Ling Roth, writing of the natives of Borneo, speaks of "the chaff and fun so dear to the heart of every Kanowit".151

In other regions, too, and among other races we light on the same exuberance of mirth. This is true of the natives of Africa, when they are unspoiled by Europeans. The Kafirs were said, by one who knew them earlier, to be generally speaking a good-humoured people with a keen relish for amusement, and ready to join in a jest.152 Visitors to the Gold Coast found that the natives dearly loved a joke, and had a most lively sense of the ludicrous.153 Miss Kingsley, as is well known, found in the West Africans a people still given to mirth and jokes. In a letter to me she writes: "I think the West African, unadulterated, the most humorous form of human being there is, and this makes him exceedingly good company for me".

Nor is this joyous exuberance confined to the natives of warm climates. We find examples of it in the chilly North. One who visited the Indians of the Canadian Red River (the Chippewas) about forty years ago says, that they are "full of frolic and fond of relating anecdotes; they laugh immoderately at any trifling joke or absurdity and seem thoroughly to enjoy existence".154

These recurring statements of travellers about the mirthfulness of savages are to some extent supported by other evidence. The writer on the Tasmanians, already quoted, gives us a number of their different local names for fun. When a people—and especially a savage people—has a name for a thing, it is a fair inference that it has some considerable acquaintance with the thing itself.

To say that this or that tribe is given to laughter and joking does not, of course, imply that the merry temper is the constant or even the predominant one. We are told, indeed, in certain cases that the mood is a changeable one, and that these undisciplined men and women resemble children in their rapid transitions from grave to gay. Thus one traveller to the Gold Coast remarks that the inhabitants will change suddenly from reckless gaiety to despondency.155 On the other hand, as may be seen from our quotations, the predominance of the gay temper, as expressed in the habitual smile and readiness to laugh, seems to be a distinguishing trait of certain savage peoples. One traveller, writing of the Patagonians, tells us that their faces were "ordinarily bright and good-natured," and that two of them in particular, whom he knew intimately, "always had a smile on their faces".156

On the other hand, there is reason to think that some tribes stand out from the general run of good-natured, merry folk by a habitual preponderance of the grave and austere in their bearing. Rengger, for example, remarks of the Indians of Paraguay that they are serious and gloomy (düster), laugh only rarely, and never break into loud laughter.157 There are probably serious savage tribes, as there are serious children in England and other civilised countries. It would be strange, too, if the treatment of American Indians and other aboriginal races by their civilised conquerors should not have developed now and again, even in naturally merry folk, something of a gloomy demeanour, at least in presence of the white man. Hence, these exceptional cases do not seem to impair our general conclusion, that laughter has a large dwelling-place among the uncivilised peoples of the earth.

The descriptions of the movements expressive of mirth, given by these visitors to savage tribes, are not as a rule full or exact. This might be taken to mean that the laughter of a savage is much like our own. Yet this would be a rash inference; for we must remember that it is not easy for one untrained in the finer kinds of observation to note with precision movements so complex and so rapidly changeful as those which express gladness and mirth. The apparatus of the photographic camera and of the phonograph has not as yet, I believe, been made use of for the purpose of registering these presumably primitive forms of laughter ere they vanish from the earth.

Darwin, as we have seen, has satisfied himself as to the flooding of the eyes. The concomitant movements of hands and feet seem to be common. A more precise account of these movements is given by Ling Roth. The Tasmanians, he tells us, accompanied their loud bursts of laughter with movements of the hands to the head and quick tapping movements of the feet.158 The loud, deep-chested character of the men's laughter is sometimes specially noted. A recent visitor to Central Africa regrets that, under European influence, the deep-chested, hearty laughter of men is being replaced by what is known as the "mission giggle" in the younger folk.159

I have come across, too, one attempt to describe with some exactness the expression of a happy mood when it flows on more quietly. The good spirits of the Andamanese, it appears, show themselves in a sparkling of the eyes, and a wrinkling of the surrounding skin, also in a drawing back of the corners of the mouth which remains partially open.160 It may be concluded that the facial movements and other changes correspond broadly with what we have seen to be the characteristic expression in the case of the children of civilised races; though differences of racial physique undoubtedly introduce a slight amount of dissimilarity into the expressive movements of laughter.161

Much of this savage laughter is just the outcome of a "gladsome mind," a flow of good spirits undisturbed by the thought of care or trouble. This persistent "cheerfulness," to describe it by our inadequate language, stands their possessors in good stead. The natural gaiety of the Maoris, we are assured, comes to their aid when they encounter hardship. They are full of fun even when short of food on a journey.162

But the laughter of savages does not appear merely as a general sign of gaiety and rollicking spirits. It has become specialised into the expression of particular mental conditions and attitudes similar to those which are expressed by the laughter of our own children.

For example, we find instances of laughter occurring as a recoil from something like timidity or shyness. Two boys, relates a missionary, had had the small-pox and had not seen one another for a month. When they met in the missionary's house they began by shyly hiding from one another their disfigured faces. At last they summoned courage, and after many side looks at one another they faced round and burst out laughing, the elder boy saying, "We are alike marked".163 Here escape from *gêne*, from a feeling akin to shame, was the primary condition of the laughter, though this was no doubt reinforced by a sense of triumph as each discovered that he was, at least, not worse off than the other. A writer tells us that in East Africa "a slave never breaks a thing without an instinctive laugh of pleasure".164 This laugh is set down to the love of destruction; yet it may be, in part at least, like that of a naughty child, a laugh of bravado hiding a consciousness of naughtiness, a mode of drowning a nascent sense of shame; for it is presumable, from what this same writer tells us, that an East African slave does not destroy his owner's property with impunity. At the same time, one must allow that the process of destruction in itself may be to a savage, as alas it often is to an English boy, an easy way to the attainment of a "sudden glory".

Savages appear to resemble children more clearly in their introduction of jocose attack into their play. Here we see an analogy between the mental attitude of a savage and that of an older child. Nothing comes out more plainly in the reports on these uncivilised peoples than their fondness for teasing, including practical jokes.

The love of teasing is testified to by more than one writer. A good authority tells us that savages "tease one another much more freely and jokingly (scherzhaft) than Europeans".165 This fondness for teasing comes out strongly in their mimicries of one another's defects, a point to be illustrated presently. In certain cases, the teasing, as with our own boys, is apt to take on a decidedly rough form. A lady, writing of the inhabitants of Funafuti, observes: "It is thought a good practical joke in Funafuti for a girl to saw an unsuspecting youth with a pandanus leaf," which produces a very painful scratch: "a good deal of laughter on the one side and volubility on the other is the usual result of this joke".166

Practical jokes grow out of the teasing instinct: they are new inventions which take the victim by surprise, if they do not distinctly mislead. The savage intelligence is quite boyish in the fecundity of its invention in this domain.

The younger folk seem to practise rude jokes very like those carried out by our own youngsters. Here is an instance. A young African negro, seeing an old woman carrying a pumpkin, approached her and shouted that there was something on her head. She forgot all about the pumpkin, shrieked at the thought of some hideous object on her head, and ran forward, allowing her tormentor laughingly to pick up the prize she had let fall.167 As is natural, these practical jocosities are sometimes directed, with a certain caution, of course, against the European. A young savage of Tasmania once slyly removed a bag of shell-fish laid down by a sailor at the foot of a rock, and let him search for it in vain, and, when tired of his joke, replaced the bag, showing himself "highly diverted" at the trick he had played the European.168

As with ourselves, these practical jokes are wont to be paid back, and with "interest". A story is told of certain Hottentots who played off a joke on some sleeping companions by shooting a couple of arrows close to them, which made them start up and hurry for arms to their waggons, where they were received with a shout of laughter. The victims of this false alarm afterwards paid out the perpetrators. They succeeded in terrifying them by a skilful imitation of the roar of a lion, which drove them into camp screaming with terror.169 In other cases the practical joke may be retaliative of some serious annoyance, and may even be inflicted on some European "superior". Miss Kingsley relates how some of her West African "ladies" had been piqued by the employee of a trading company, who tried to get them apart, when planting manioc, so as to hinder them from talking. They took their playful revenge by making a haycock over their tyrant and shouting: "Get along, white man! I 'spectable married woman," and so forth. She gives another instance of this disposition to playful punishment in her ladies. A young black official had been rude to some of them, whereupon they resorted to the broader joke of throwing him into "the batter that passes for 'water'".170

Closely connected with these modes of teasing, we have the practice of taking off bodily defects by mimicry and by nicknames. These modes of playful attack appear to be directed most commonly against outsiders, but instances are given of a discreet mimicry of a fellow-tribesman in his absence. It seems probable, though I have not found the fact brought out explicitly, that much of the amusement derived by these simple folk from their nightly talks, which are made gay with laughter, consists in teasing attacks on the bodily defects or peculiarities of certain members; though, from the evidence forthcoming, one would infer that a choral laughter over the stranger is the more usual feature in these social entertainments.

In all this mirthful teasing it is easy to see much that strikes us as cruel, or, at least, as unfeeling. It is only natural that the hilarity of peoples low down in the scale of culture should now and again take on this aspect; as when, for example, they are said to laugh exultantly at the struggles of a drowning man.171 Yet, on the whole, the merriment of these peoples, when the butt is a fellow-tribesman, though undoubtedly rough and often very coarse, does not seem to be so brutal as one might expect.

We can understand the diversion of so large an amount of savage mirth into these practical channels—teasing, bantering and playing-off jokes upon members of ones tribe, by reflecting that laughter is a social process, and plays, as we shall see presently, a large part in the smooth working, if not also in the very maintenance, of the social fabric.

In order to see the meaning of this teasing laughter, we must note the way in which it is accepted. There is no doubt, to begin with, that savages have by nature a lively dislike to being laughed at. It would be strange indeed if this were not so, seeing that both the monkeys below them and the white men above them display this aversion. This seems to have been specially noted in the case of certain races. The Weddas of Ceylon, who, as we have seen, have not impressed all visitors as laughter-loving, show a marked displeasure at being made the butt of a joke. We are told that they are much provoked (gereizt) when they are laughed at (ausgelacht). It is related of one of these men that, when during a dance he was thus treated by a European, he shot an arrow at the laugher.172 Poor old folk among ourselves will, we know, do much the same when they are jeered at by incautious boys, and even a youth has been known to shy a stone at a too robust jeerer. This dislike of being made the object of a facetious attention holds good of other savages as well. A writer tells us that a common fireside amusement among certain savages is to tease the women till they become angry, which always produces great merriment. The teasing, it is added, is of a rough and not very decent kind.173 Further evidence of this distaste for the douche of a voluble laughter is supplied by the curious ordeals of the Greenlanders, to be spoken of presently.

On the other hand, there is ample evidence to show that the rough jocosities of the teasing game are, as a rule, accepted in good part. The youth who bore the biting satire of the pandanus leaf seems to compare favourably in this respect with a London policeman, who recently complained in court of the soft attentions paid him by a lady of the East End in tickling some part of his official visage with her dainty feather. Sometimes we are distinctly told that jokes are taken in good part, so long as they are seen to be intended as such. So of the African Hottentots and Kafirs, according to the authority already quoted.174 Of the Tahitians it is said that the jests played off at their expense are never taken in ill part.175

It is evident that the rougher kinds of jocosity here described allow considerable scope for something of the spirit of superiority and contempt. One fears that this was felt to be present, for example, by the women victimised by the men's coarse teasing. As with boys, so with savages, we may suppose that playful attack does not always respect its limits, but that now and again it allows itself to be infected by the brutish element in man. Nor is this surprising when we remember how much of so-called humour in civilised men owes its piquancy to the same brutish ingredient.

This attitude of superiority and contempt seems, as one might have expected, to be more apparent in what may be called the extra-tribal direction of jocosity, more particularly in the common laughter at members of other rival and possibly hostile tribes. In certain cases we are told that this is of the nature of mockery and ridicule. Among savages and early communities, writes one authority, when their chieftain sat in his hall with his warriors, they amused themselves by turning enemies and opponents into mockery, laughing at their weaknesses, joking on their defects, giving them nicknames, and so forth.176 The savage—again like a boy—is apt to be a vain sort of fellow, and to think that his ways are a lot better than those of the rest of mankind. Hence he will, with something of contempt in his heart, laugh at the bungling efforts of men of another tribe to kill a turtle, and will give a nickname to the white man or take off with admirable mimicry some of his crazes, such as his passion for road-making or for bartering.

Yet it would, I think, be an error to treat this laughter at the outsider as a form of serious ridicule, with its feeling of the corrective superior. It is, even when lightly touched with contempt, savage play, and has for its chief ingredient the love of fun, and that delight in the mere contemplation of what is foreign and odd which the savage shares with his ethnic betters.

One characteristic of this savage jocosity is so frequently referred to by travellers that I cannot pass it by. We have seen that the teasing of the women is apt to take on an indecent form. We are told, again and again, that savage jokes are commonly low and immoral. The coarser the joke, we are informed, the better it is liked by the natives of the Gold Coast.177 The jests of the natives of the islands in the Pacific are said to be "low and immoral to a disgusting degree".178

Possibly the European is not permitted to know the worst of this aspect of savage mirth. It is easy, however, to give it too serious a significance. To the simpler feeling of savages, untrammelled by the laws of decency as civilised people know them, there may be no suggestion here of a delight in the immoral as such. Their laughter may well indicate the fact that for them an undisguised reference to what we insist on hiding up has in it nothing improper; that they are just within sight of the stadium of culture at which convention begins to brand such references as obscene. Young children among ourselves will, I believe, often laugh at such open and direct mention of unmentionable things and much in the same way. It is hardly more in many cases, I surmise, than a little bravado, a glorying in doing something unusual which they are beginning to suspect is forbidden, though this is no doubt apt to be accompanied by a perception of the indignity done by this uncovering to the person involved.179

We may now turn to those forms of savage laughter which involve a more disinterested contemplation of things, and a rudimentary sense of their ludicrous phases. There is no doubt that the enjoyment of the droll side of their world fills a large place in the life of savages. One may conjecture that it is a larger pastime in their case than in that of most boys; for though the intellect of a savage may not surpass that of a boy, his experience and matured good sense enable him to judge of the unseemly and the incongruous with considerable skill and quickness, and to derive much mirth from the contemplation of them.

The simplest form of this merriment, serving, as in the case of the child, as a bridge from joyous expansion under a new sensuous excitement to an appreciation of the odd, is the common laughter of savages at what is strikingly new to them, and at the same time takes their fancy. For example, the natives of Borneo were very much amused at a piano, and when they saw the dampers of the keys jumping up and down they "fairly laughed aloud".180 In like manner the Indians of Hudson Bay took a compass for a toy and laughed at it, refusing to accept the owner's account of its use.181 These are pretty clear examples of a mirthful delight at something which is new, devoid of import, and appealing to the play-appetite. The later stages of the laughter at the lively little compass-toy were, perhaps, more expressive of a dim sense of the absurdity of the suggestion that a dear wee play-thing could do such marvels. This gleeful greeting of what is at once new and exhilarating to sense answers in the case of these simple people to what in ourselves is joyous admiration. Thus, we read of certain African ladies, wives of a king, who expressed their delight at European works of art by repeated loud bursts of laughter.182 Our own children show us now and again how the new, when it not only captures the sense by its novelty, but holds it by its charm, may evoke this purely mirthful greeting, as free from the stiff attitude of curiosity as it is from fearsomeness.183

It is a good step from this childish abandonment to the fun of a new toy-like thing to the recognition of something as foreign and opposed to the tribal custom. In these simple communities the unwritten laws of custom play a most important part. Violations of them on the part of any tribesman are apt to be dealt with seriously. This at once tends to limit the range of savage laughter; the pressure of custom is too tyrannical to allow of a full display of the odd and irregular in human behaviour. These elements of the amusing have accordingly to be supplied from without; and they are supplied in good measure, partly by other neighbouring tribes whose manners are observable, and to a still larger extent by the Europeans who visit them with a virtuous intention to reform and civilise.

Let us first take a glance at the hilarious appreciation of the *other* tribe's ways. The spectacle of the foreigner will grow particularly entertaining when he seems to bungle in doing something which is perfectly familiar to the observer's own tribe. The Tahitians, it seems, are laughed at by the dwellers in the neighbouring islands when they try to kill a turtle by pinching its throat. As may be supposed, the trick, so useful to the beast, of drawing in the head gives a veritable look of the absurd to these attempts. So, too, the enlightened people of one island drew voluminous amusement from the news that those of another island who had just come into possession of the novelty, a pair of scissors, tried to sharpen them by baking them.184 These two illustrations show a dim apprehension of the fitness of things as determined, not by the relative standard of "my way," but by an objective standard.

The field in which they cull most of their facetious enjoyment of the doings of outsiders would seem to be the ways of their white visitors. There the differences, the departure from "our way" and the inability to acquire this are great enough to appeal strongly to their crude sense of the ludicrous. They see the odd white people do a number of things which strike them as extraordinary and quite useless. If the Englishman laughs at the foreigner for not taking his morning tub, the simple savage will turn the tables by making merry over our elaborate washings. Thus the Fuegians, though living much in the water, have no idea of washing themselves; accordingly "when Europeans first came among them, the sight of a man washing his face seemed to them so irresistibly ludicrous that they burst into shrieks of laughter".185 Here is an example of a rather more complex feeling in presence of new-fangled European ways. It seems that a South African Prince, presumably as a compliment to the white man's custom, wished to shave himself and, as our youths frequently do on first attempting the feat, cut himself. He then asked his European visitor to perform the office for him. The natives present "stood mute with admiration during the whole performance, gazing with the utmost eagerness in their countenances, and bursting at length into a general peal of laughter—this being their customary mode of expressing delight, astonishment, nay even embarrassment and fear."186 The last part of this statement is a little loose, since, as we have seen, it is not so much the astonishment, the embarrassment, or the fear in itself, which laughter expresses, as a relaxation of the strain involved in these attitudes.

The laughter excited is of a rather more intellectual kind when the action of the white man presents itself as absurd, not merely because it rudely diverges from the customs of the natives, but because it involves something out of the range of their comprehension, and so appears incredible. It is then that the white man shows his superiority in evoking laughter: his arts, his apparatus—when like the photographic camera they do not excite fears—are apt to evoke incredulous laughter. A traveller in South Africa had learned some sentences of the speech of a tribe (the Sichuana language) from his man. He then wrote them down and read them off before the man. This simple fellow laughed "most heartily" when his white master told him that it was the marks he had made in the book which showed him what he was to say.187 A child would pretty certainly join the savage in laughing at the idea of getting sounds out of the inert, stupid-looking word-symbols, if it were suddenly introduced to him in this way.

When the white man's doings are not absolutely new, he may expose himself to the laughter of these merry folk by the odd manner of them. One would like to know all the jokes which the natives of South Africa, of Polynesia, and the other abodes of the mirthful "Naturkind" have had over the dress, the gestures, and the speech of their white visitors. Yet this would be hard to get at. We do know, however, how they are wont to greet some of our highly civilised performances. This is the way in which some Tasmanian women behaved on a first introduction to the European manner of singing. They listened attentively while it lasted; then some applauded by loud shouts; others laughed to splitting, while the young girls, no doubt more timid, remained silent.188 This laughter was, presumably, more than the expression of a wild delight. Those who laughed may be supposed to have been the most susceptible to the absurdity of this unheard of manner of song. In the case of the closely allied art of dancing, we are distinctly told that our highly approved style may appear ridiculous to the savage onlooker. The Sumatrans, writes one authority, have very slow dances which are thought to be ludicrous by Europeans. Yet, funnily enough, they think our customary dances "to the full as ludicrous". They compared our minuets to the fighting of two game cocks.189 Did they also see a galop, one wonders, and if so, what did the lovers of slow dances say about this? The "refinements" of the arts of civilised men are ever apt to appear laughable to those lower down.

The laughter of these uninstructed people grows loud when the clever white man fails to achieve one of their own simple accomplishments. More particularly, his inability to pronounce the sounds of their language seems to be a prolific source of merriment. The Tasmanians, writes one whom we have quoted more than once, often laughed to splitting when, wishing to repeat their words, "I made mistakes or pronounced them badly".190 Another traveller, speaking of the natives of the West Coast of Vancouver's Island, writes: "That they had some standard of correct speech is evident from the readiness of the children to ridicule a stranger who mispronounces native words".191 A third example comes from Borneo. The girls, a visitor reports, made Europeans repeat sentences of their language after them, and burst out into loud laughter "either at our pronunciation or at the comical things they had made us utter".192 Nothing, perhaps, more clearly exhibits the ludicrous value of the violation of a perfectly uniform custom than a mispronunciation of language.193 Nor is this all. It seems absurd to a savage, just as it does to an average English child, that the foreigner should fail to do what seems to him not merely to require no effort, but to be something one cannot help doing, like laughing itself or crying. No doubt some feeling of superiority to the foreign ignoramus enters into the enjoyment here. Perhaps the children of Vancouver's Island felt this superiority most of all. In some cases, however, we are distinctly told that the ineptitude of Europeans, when it provokes laughter, calls out also the soothing accompaniment of kindly encouragement.

The exhibition of another kind of incompetence to do the thing "we do," highly provoking to the hilarious mood, is a breach of good manners; for here there comes in something of the sense of social superiority, and something of the joyous momentary relief from the burden of rules of etiquette. Just as "Society" gets nearest to a genuine laugh when confronted with the vulgarities of Midas as he pushes into her inner circle, so the savage keenly enjoys his opportunity of detecting *gaucherie* and want of *savoir faire* on the side of his white visitors. Indeed, he seems ready, when he is sure of not offending, to treat these breaches of etiquette with good-natured merriment. A traveller tells us that on visiting the house of an Indian chief in Canada he sat down on what he took to be a bundle of buffalo robes. The composure of mind proper to a guest of royalty must have been slightly disturbed at the discovery that the robes began to move and undulate beneath him, till to his utter confusion he felt himself projected into the middle of the tent among the embers. The chief, his three wives and the other native people in the tent "shrieked with laughter" at the catastrophe. The full measure of the good humour that lay behind this laughter revealed itself to the white visitor when he saw emerging from the heap of robes the fourth and youngest wife of the chief, who, to her credit be it said, joined in the hilarity.194

Something of the reflective element seems to peep out in one variety of this laughter at the odd ways of the white man. A missionary, one of the discerning ones as it would seem, found the Sea Dyaks disposed to treat the idea of our religious services as a joke. They were curious to learn what was required of the religious worshipper, and particularly wanted to know whether he was forbidden to laugh; and they explained their inquisitiveness by confessing that, like Mr. Barrie's "Humorist," they were far from sure of being able to restrain themselves.195 Solemn ceremony with its severe demands will be apt, when its meaning is hidden, to provoke in savages and in children alike a keen desire for the relief of a laugh.

A palpable ingredient of mind appears in the laughter of savages at the white man's ideas about the beginnings and the endings of things. The inquirer into their beliefs may present himself to them as a quite unreasonable sceptic, grubbing at the very roots of things which sensible men accept as self-explanatory. The members of a tribe in Central Australia (Arunta tribe) were immensely tickled by the question how their remote ancestors came by the sacred stones or sticks which they had handed down to them. The idea, that anything could have existed before these original ancestors, struck them as ridiculous. The ultimate explanation of any custom of the tribe was, "Our fathers did it, and therefore we do it". To try to go behind tradition was to challenge its sufficiency, and so to put forward an absurd paradox.196 Here we have a mental attitude at once like and unlike that of our children; for the latter are conservative of tradition and disposed to accept authority, but at the same time very energetic in pushing back inquiry into "what came before".

Intelligence would seem not merely to be stirring, but to be capable of adroit play when the savage detects the ridiculous in the white man's ideas of the future of his race. How many of the simple savages who are instructed in the dogmas of the Christian religion accept them unquestioningly it would be hard to say. Many, perhaps, fail to put any definite meaning into what they hear. Now and again, however, we meet with an instance of a daring laugh at what strikes the hearer as utterly absurd. A teacher of the native Australians had once tried to explain to an intelligent black the doctrine of the immateriality and immortality of the soul. He afterwards learned that his pupil had gone away from the lesson to have a hearty fit of laughter at the absurdity of the idea "of a man's living and going about without arms, legs, or mouth to eat".197 The crass materialism of this tyro's effort to assimilate spiritual ideas was much the same as we observe in our children.

In this laughter at our ways and our ideas we superior people are inclined to see merely the ignorance and narrowness of mind of the laughers. Yet it is possible that the savage may, once and again, in making merry at our expense show himself really our superior. His good sense may be equal to the detection of some of the huge follies in the matter of dress and other customs to which the enlightened European so comically clings. And he has been known to strike the satirical note and to look down upon and laugh "at the stupid self-satisfied Europeans who preached so finely but practised so little what they preached".198

We may now glance at the intra-tribal activity of the mirthful impulse. That this fills some place in the life of savage communities has been illustrated in our account of their teasings. We must not expect to find here a large field for the play of what we call the comic spirit. As we shall see presently, this spirit only begins to fly bravely when the movement of civilisation introduces more diversity of class, and, further, a greater liberty of utterance—for women as well as for men.

A pretty clear illustration of laughter directed to fellow-tribesmen is supplied by the merriment that is said to accompany athletic and other competitions in which skill is tested. Among the natives of Victoria, we are informed, a favourite amusement of the young men is the throwing of the spear and other similar exercises. The trials of skill are accompanied by a good deal of laughter, notwithstanding that the older men are present to instruct the boys and that some effort is made to preserve discipline.199 This merriment is no doubt largely the counterpart of our schoolboys' laughter in the playground. It is the expression of a keen enjoyment of the triumphs of the game. At the same time if, as one may assume, it is directed against blunders it has a sociological significance. It becomes a "social sanction," which urges a youth to do his best in the field. Another example illustrates the impulse to laugh at a comrade's failure to accomplish a feat for which he is totally unprepared. A member of a European party which was visiting the Weddas could move his ears. A native was asked to do the same; and the others, knowing what was to be done, watched him attentively. The man singled out for the feat looked blankly towards the sky, his ears remaining "as if nailed to his head"; at this moving spectacle one of the onlookers suddenly broke out into laughter, the others at once joining in.200 Here we have laughter at a fellow-tribesman, in face of Europeans too, exactly similar to that which is directed against the European himself. Doubtless, there is much of this kind of laughter at those who make an exhibition of their limitations, especially when the attempt is preceded by a display of vanity and boastfulness. In this respect, too, savage laughter has the ring of the merriment of the playground and of the circus.

One of the first forms of a reciprocal mirthful attack or bantering between classes is that between the Sexes. Savage life supplies us with clear cases of inter-sexual jocosity besides that of the teasing which, as we have seen, is a two-sided game. In a collection of sayings and stories of West Africa we find the following: A woman left her husband to look after a "pot-au-feu". On returning she found that he had skimmed off the bubbling foam and hidden it in a calabash, naïvely supposing that this was the cream of the dish. She twits him with it and discovers to his slow wits that the savory scum has melted into nothing.201 This reminds one of many a story of the Middle Ages, and shows how wide-spread is the exposure of the male incompetence to the lash of woman's merry wit.

These jocose thrusts at the opposite sex are interesting as illustrating the differentiation of class-standards. If the male is laughed at for his bungling at the mysteries of cooking, how much more when he actually fails to keep up with the women folk in his own domain! Mr. Ling Roth, whose eye seems to have been specially focussed for records of the mirthful utterances of savages, tells us that a boat-load of women who had been gathering oysters rowed a race with a visitors' crew and managed to beat them; whereupon there was a fine outburst of feminine hilarity and much quizzing of the men who had allowed themselves to be beaten by women.202 Here, surely, was a touch of a higher feeling, a dim perception at least of the permanent and universal forms of the fitness of things.

The clearest example, I have met with, of what we should call a dry humour is to be found in the work just quoted. It seems that a stupid old soothsayer once called together a large concourse of chiefs to deal with the problem of naming his children. These, he contended, were not properly his, but had been begotten by certain spirits (the Antus or Hantus). One of the chiefs did not enjoy having to come many miles to listen to this sort of stuff, so "he pretended in the midst of the soothsayer's discourse to faint away, and fell back gasping for breath, kicking his legs spasmodically in the air at the same time". This interruption brought the tedious proceedings to an end, and so saved the chief from further boredom. But this was not all: the disappointed humbug had to pay the chief who had spoilt his performance some fowls as a punishment for allowing the spirits to attack him.203 The story is instructive as illustrating the tendency, as soon as classes begin to be marked off, to score off a man of another class. Perhaps, indeed, we have in this jocose imposition on the imposer a suggestion of the merry-making of kings and peoples at the expense of the clergy which was so marked a feature in mediæval hilarity.

A word may well be expended on the subject of the organisation of the laughing propensity into regular amusements among savage tribes. One of the things which a white man can learn from these much-misunderstood peoples is the art of social entertainment. Without luxurious salons, without plate and rare wines, without the theatre and the concert hall, they manage to obtain a good deal of genuine, unpretentious conviviality. When, writes one traveller, they are relieved of the presence of strangers they have much easy social conversation. Round their own fires they sing and chat, and older men lie and brag about feats in war and chase. "Jokes pass freely and the laugh is long if not loud."204

A standard dish in these social entertainments is taking off the peculiarities of other tribes and of Europeans. Mimicry, the basis of the actor's art, is often carried to a high degree of perfection among these uncouth savages; and it is highly prized. When, writes a missionary of the tribes of the remote part of Victoria, a native is able to imitate the peculiarities of some absent member of the tribe, it is very common to hear all in the camp convulsed with laughter.205 The Indians of Brazil hold the peculiarities, *e.g.*, the beard, of other tribes up to laughter by means of a lively pantomime.206 This mimicry, as might be expected, embraces the odd ways of the white man. The natives of New South Wales used to be so skilful in this art that one wrote of them: "Their mimicking of the oddities, dress, walk, gait and looks of all the Europeans whom they have seen from the time of Governor Phillips downwards, is so exact as to be a kind of historic register of their several actions and characters".207 The same authority tells us that the Tahitians are acute observers of the manners, actions, and even looks of strangers; and if they have any singular imperfections or oddities, they will not fail to make themselves merry at their expense.208 Another traveller certifies to the fact that the aborigines of Victoria were splendid mimics, and would, after attending the white man's church, "take a book and with much success imitate the clergyman in his manner, laughing and enjoying the applause which they received".209 A turn for mimicry is found also among the North American Indians. The Californian Indians gave to the American whites the name "Wo'hah," formed from "whoa-haw," the sound they heard the early emigrants produce when they drove their oxen. "Let an Indian see an American coming up the road, and cry out to his fellows: 'There comes a wo'hah,' at the same time swinging his arm as if driving oxen, and it will produce convulsive laughter."210

Along with this skill in mimicry, savages show considerable readiness in the verbal arts of descriptive caricature, witty sayings and repartee. In practising these, we are told, they make ample use of the instrument of irony.

The possession of these rudiments of talent naturally leads to a certain amount of specialisation. It is attested again and again that our uncultured savage communities possess their professional pantomists, jesters and wits. Indeed, we read of crude forms of a comic art among savages so low in the scale as the Australians and the Tasmanians. Thus, Lumholtz writes of the pantomimic dances of the Australian blacks,211 and Ling Roth assures us that the Tasmanians have their drolls and mountebanks, who exhibit the peculiarities of individuals with considerable force.212 Among the Sumatrans, again, are to be found "characters of humour," who by buffoonery, mimicry, punning, repartee and satire are able to keep the company in laughter at intervals during a night's entertainment.213 In some cases jesters are appointed by a chief, just as a fool used to be selected by one of our kings. In Samoa every chief has his regular clown, a privileged person who, among other liberties, is allowed that of taking the food out of the chiefs mouth.214 A privileged buffoon in Kanowit, who had been given an old gun, told the Resident that he had killed fourteen deer with one bullet. The Resident being puzzled, he explained that he had cut the bullet out each time.215 Here we have the exact counterpart to the trick of the European clown of the circus.

Among the Eskimo of Greenland, it seems, there is a regular performance in which the aspiring "funny men" compete for popular favour. After a repast they get up, one after the other, each exhibiting his musical resources by beating a drum and singing, and adding a touch of the actor's art by making comical gestures, and playing ridiculous tricks with the face, head and limbs.216 Much the same kind of contest takes place in connection with their peculiar ordeals, already referred to. Each of the two litigants tries to make the other ridiculous, by singing satirical songs and relating misdeeds; and the one who succeeds in getting the audience to laugh most at his jibes or invectives is pronounced the conqueror. Even such serious crimes as murder are often expiated in this merry fashion.217

In one or two cases we read of more elaborate entertainments. Thus, some of the natives of the Western Pacific have a regular masquerade performed before the King, into which may enter a histrionic representation of a British sailor with his cutlass, acted by a leading buffoon, who combines with the *rôle* of a "premier" the "fool's" privilege of breaking through the strict laws of decorum by pointing to the King and asking ironically if that was the King—amid shouts of laughter.218

Other traces of a rudimentary art of the comic are to be found in the amusing songs and stories which can be traced to savage invention. The Australians had songs in which the peculiarities of Europeans were caricatured, the chorus being sung amid shouts of laughter.219 Another comic song, heard among some of the aborigines of Australia, took off the bodily peculiarities of some men—presumably of another tribe—in the graceful lines:—

Oh, what legs, oh, what legs!

The Kangaroo-rumped fellows.

Oh, what legs, oh, what legs! *

In these crude forms of art we probably find traces of the influence of European models. There are, however, stories which seem to be a perfectly spontaneous growth. Of these it is enough to refer to the originals of the delightful tales of Uncle Remus, the substance of which, as their author tells us, he obtained from the blacks in the American plantations.221 Miss Kingsley writes to me of these: "I know the tales are not made up. I struck the Tar Baby Stories in the Lower Congo". It may be added that the device of the tar baby is to be found in its essentials in a collection of African stories.222

Our study seems to tell us that savage laughter is like our own in representing different levels of refinement. Much of it is just naïve, unthinking gaiety, like that of the little girl spoken about in the preceding chapter. Co-existing with this infantile gaiety we have the coarse brutal forms of laughter which we associate with the rougher kind of schoolboy. Along with these lower forms we find higher ones, in which some amount of reference to social standards is discoverable. Lastly, we may detect here and there, as in the story of the man tickled by the idea of dead men going about *sans* arms, legs, etc., and of him who jocosely stripped a humbug of his disguise, germs of a more thoughtful laughter; and on the other hand, in the kindly tempering of the laughter of the girls at the Englishwoman's inability to make mats, a movement towards sympathetic laughter. In other words, we detect the dim beginnings of that complex feeling or attitude which we call humour. It seems probable that the quality, if not also the quantity, improves as we pass from the lowest and most degraded to the higher savage tribes.223

Hence, no doubt, the difficulty which has been felt by travellers in describing the common characteristics of the hilarity of savage tribes. Miss Kingsley writes to me with respect to the humour of the West African: "It is peculiar, it is not child-like—it is more feminine in quality, though it is very broad or coarse. It is difficult to describe. I can only say what seems to me an excellent joke seems so to him—there are many jokes neither of us can see the point of: others, we chuckle over, superior persons look down on and would call buffoonery."224

One practical reflection to close with. Any civilised community which has much to do in the way of managing the "lower races" would surely be wise to take some heed of their love of fun. And this, because it has been found that appeals to this side have been more effective than the harsher measures to which even a gentle Briton may think himself sometimes driven. An African missionary, already quoted, writes that in cases where a disposition to quarrel shows itself "one joke is worth ten arguments".225 This is borne out by one who has not much good to tell of his savages, when he says of the East African that he delights in a joke "which manages him like a Neapolitan".226 In a letter to me Miss Kingsley writes: "I have always found I could chaff them into doing things that other people could not get them to do, with blows—I could laugh them out of things other people would have to blow out of them with a gun".

CHAPTER IX.
LAUGHTER IN SOCIAL EVOLUTION.

In the two preceding chapters we have followed the earlier stages of the development of laughter in the individual and have glanced at its counterpart in the life of savage communities. If now we try to push the psychological inquiry farther, and ask how the mirth of the child develops into that complex sentiment which in these days we call humour, we find ourselves forced to pause. One thing is clear, however. No one of us would ever have acquired this valuable endowment but for the educative action of that advanced stage of social culture which is our intellectual and moral environment. It seems to follow that we shall need to look for a moment at the movement of social culture itself, to consider the impulse of laughter as one of the features in the life of a community, and to inquire how it has become transformed, almost beyond recognition, by the movement of social progress.

To attempt to give an exhaustive account of these social changes would clearly lead us very far. It may be argued with force that every one of the great directions of social evolution, such as that of intellectual conceptions, of moral sentiments, of political and social liberty, of wealth, of the differentiation of classes and ranks, has involved as its effect some change in the intensity, the mode of distribution, and the manner of expression in daily life and in art, of the laughing impulse. But we do not need to consider so deeply. It will be enough if we briefly retrace those phases of social evolution which appear to carry with them as their immediate accompaniments considerable modifications of the mirthful spirit.

We must in this inquiry begin by defining the social aspect of laughter. This was touched on in the last chapter in connection with our study of the mirth of savages. We have now to examine it more closely.

One of its most obvious characteristics is its contagiousness, already referred to.227 The potent appeal of laughter to a mechanical imitativeness is significant in more ways than one. It suggests how large a part of human hilarity is nothing but a kind of surface resonance, as empty of ideas as the infectious yawn or cough. But it suggests also that laughter is social in the sense that it is essentially choral and so uniting. A gathering of yokels at a fair laughing at a clown tends for the moment to become a coherent group; and the habit of laughing together will tend to consolidate the group.

When the conjoint laughter is less automatic and issues from community of ideas and sentiments, the contagious property still plays a part. It is as if the swift response of others' laughter, the drowning of one's own outburst in the general roar, effaced for the time the boundaries of one's personality. To rejoice together in the full utterance of the laugh, though it moves us less deeply than to weep together, is perhaps no less potent in cementing a lasting comradeship.

The social side of laughter comprehends, however, much more than this. It is commonly recognised that the feeling expressed has something human for its object. Now those who directly or indirectly serve as the butt are all the world over disposed, till the grace of a genial tolerance has been added, to dislike and resent the part thrust on them. So far, then, laughter would seem to be anti-social and dividing, and, alas, the history of literature will furnish the student with notable illustrations. Yet this hurtful edge in laughter becomes one of its valuable social properties. As the despised Greenlanders may teach us, laughter supplies a mode of punishment which combines with effectiveness, economy and humanity, a good deal of enjoyment for the onlookers. In all societies, if not exactly in the Greenland fashion, it has been accorded an important place among the agencies which, by castigating vices and follies, seek to lower their vitality.

The sharp edge of laughter represents, however, only one of its effects on the sensibilities of the butt. Savage life has given us illustrations, not only of its disagreeable consequences turned to judicial purposes, but of its agreeable consequences in cajoling others out of attitudes of hostility and stubbornness. This curious effect, as it may seem, of a mode of treatment which is primarily hurtful is to be explained in the main by its playful function. To substitute a joke for argument or coercive pressure is, like tickling, to challenge to play, and tends to call up the play-mood in the recipient of the challenge. The mutual teasings of savages serve, as we have seen, as a training, an ἄσκησις, in simple and estimable virtues, such as the maintenance of good temper, toleration, and the setting of comradeship above one's private feelings.

One other social aspect of laughter illustrated by savage life needs to be touched on. In the instinctive tendency of the savage to ridicule the customs and ideas of outside folk we have one expression of the self-protective attitude of a community against insidious outside influences. Just as the Hebrews ridiculed the religious ideas of the worshippers of Baal and so helped to keep their national faith intact, so these tribes low down in the culture scale have in their laughter at what is foreign a prophylactic against any contamination from outside peoples. No doubt this tendency in laughter will help to preserve once useful tribal characters when altered circumstances, introduced, for example, by the coming of the white man, require new adaptations. In this we see the essentially conservative function of laughter in the life of societies. On the other hand, as we have seen, novelties in dress introduced by the white man may attract and delight. In dealing with the connection between social progress and laughter, we shall need to consider very carefully the attitude which the mirthful spirit takes up towards social changes.

Now these aspects of laughter point, as we have seen, to a social utility in laughter. As offspring of the play-impulse, it might, indeed, be expected to share in those benefits which, as recent research has made clear, belong to play. In our study of its development and persistence in the life of progressive communities, we shall have occasion to illustrate this utility much more fully. That laughing is good, physically and morally, for its individual subjects has become a commonplace, at least to the student of literature. Here we shall be concerned with its distinctly social advantages, such as the maintenance of customs which from the point of view of the community, or of some class of the community, are to be regarded as good, the keeping down of vices and follies, and the furtherance of social co-operation.

The question how far this utility extends is one which cannot be answered simply. It will be found that societies, so far from universally recognising laughter as a useful habit, have taken vast pains to restrain it. Indeed, our study of the fortunes of mirth in the advance of social life will show us that it has had throughout to struggle for its existence.

From what has just been said it will be clear that we shall have to consider the history of laughter and the movement of social evolution as inter-connected. Not only does a change in ideas, sentiments or institutions tend to modify the expression of the mirthful mood, there is a reciprocal influence of laughter upon ideas, sentiments and institutions. Such interaction holds good generally between amusements and serious pursuits; the recreations of a community serve in important ways to determine the measure of the vigour thrown into serious activities. In the case of laughter this reciprocal influence is much more marked, owing to the circumstance that mirth has been wont to play about serious things, to make these the target for its finely tipped shafts, now and again going so far as to shoot one into the midst of the solemnities of social life.

In the savage tribe we find but little of class division. The perception of what is unfit and the laughter which accompanies this are directed, for the most part, to members of other communities. The laughter is choral because it is that in which the whole tribe joins or is prepared to join; but for that very reason it has a monotonous sound. Some differentiation of groups within the community seems necessary, not merely for the constitution of a society, but for the free play of the laughing spirit. Diversity in thought and behaviour is a main condition of the full flow of social gaiety.

The germ of such diversity is present in the lowest conceivable type of human community. The institution of male and female in which Nature, as if to combine divine work with human, at once joins together and puts asunder, has been with us from the beginnings of human society; and it might be an amusing pastime to speculate how the males of our ape-like ancestors first gurgled out their ridicule of female inferiority, and how the females managed to use their first rudiment of speech-power in turning the tables on their lords and masters. Some differentiation of rank, too, must have been found in the simplest human societies in the contrast between the old and the young, and the closely connected opposition of the rulers and the ruled. But it would be hazardous to reason that, in the early stages of social evolution, much in the way of exchange of fun passed between those who were presumably kept solemnly apart by the sense of their relative station.

It is only when we move on to a society with a considerable amount of class differentiation that its relation to the nurture and distribution of the spirit of mirth grows apparent. In glancing at these divisions we may conveniently adopt M. Tarde's expression, "social group". Such a group may be either a class, the members of which have like functions and a common character connected with these, such as priests and traders; or it may be a set constituted merely by community of knowledge and taste, as the members of a society standing on a particular level of culture. Although this double way of dividing social groups necessarily leads to overlapping, it seems desirable to adopt it here, so as to give an adequate account of the relation of group-formation to the particular directions of social laughter.

The development of distinct groups within a community influences the behaviour of the laughing impulse, first of all, by introducing diversity of occupations, abilities and intelligence. In this way it enlarges the field for those relative judgments about competence and fitness with which, as savage laughter illustrates, simple forms of mirth have so much to do. Thus, the establishment of distinctions of employment and mode of life between the sexes has contributed copiously to that mirthful quizzing of each by the other which seems to have been a prime ingredient in human jocosity from the lowest stages of culture. The slightly malicious laughter of the male at female incompetence, which is seen in the schoolboy's treatment of his sister, is illustrated throughout the course of literature. And good examples are not wanting of a turning of the tables by the female on the male. The story of King Alfred's misadventure with the cakes—of which we have found the counterpart in savage life—is an example of the more shrewish criticism of the male ignoramus by the female expert. When the sense of injury is less keen, and the impression of the folly of the performance fills the soul, the shrewish note is apt to fall to the genial pitch of laughter. The differentiation of industrial and other employments, such as those of countryman and townsman, of landsman and seaman, of soldier and civilian, serve to develop new centres of concerted laughter, and new points of attack.

The formation of social groups further enlarges the material and the opportunities for laughter by introducing noticeable and impressive differences of behaviour, dress and speech. In this way the field of the odd, the absurd, that which contradicts our own customs and standards, has been made wide and fertile. A mere difference of locality may suffice to generate such differences. Not so many years ago, one could hear in the West of England the jibes which the people in one small town or district were wont to hurl at those in another. We read that in the Middle Ages, when local differences of dress and speech were so much more marked than now, satires on people of particular localities were not uncommon—though probably much more than a perception of the laughably odd was involved in these rather fierce derisions.228

The immediate utility of this mirthful quizzing of other sets would, like that carried out by one savage tribe on another, consist in the preservation of the characteristics of one's own set. But the play of laughter about class-distinctions illustrates another of its benefits. When one set gets used to the distinctive ways of another, it tends to regard them as right and proper for the latter; and it may carry its regard for their propriety so far as to support the inner sentiment of the other group by deriding those members who do not conform to their group-customs. Distinctive customs have been conserved not only—to adopt ethical terms having a somewhat different meaning—by "internal sanctions" in the shape of serious penalties as well as ridicule administered by fellow-members of the set, but by "external sanctions" in the shape of outside mockery. The imposing soldierly attitude has perhaps been kept up quite as much by the merry quizzing of civilians as by any military discipline and *esprit de corps*. A poor tottering hero in uniform could, one opines, never have escaped the eye of citizens lying in wait for the laughable.

The finer opportunities for this mirthful screwing up of men of other groups to their proper moral height would occur when the peculiarities of the mode of life imposed a special rule of behaviour, and, particularly, when this rule was a severe one. The hollow hero, trying to hide the poverty of his courage in braggadocio, has been a favourite figure in comic literature, classic and modern. A notable illustration of this situation is the laughter heaped on the clergy by the people during the Middle Ages. The caricatures of the monk—representing him, for instance, as a Reynard in the pulpit with a cock below for clerk, and the many *Contes* which exposed his cunningly contrived immoralities, and frequently visited them with well-merited chastisement, show pretty plainly that the popular laughter in this case had in it something of hate and contempt, and was directed in part to the exposure and punishment of the celibate class. This may be asserted, even though it must not be forgotten that in these *Contes* the holy man by no means infrequently emerges from his dangerous experiment unscathed: a fact which suggests that in the popular sentiment there lurked, not merely something of the child's mirthful wonder at daring cunning, but a certain sympathetic tolerance for a caste, on the shoulders of which was laid a somewhat weighty yoke. The mental attitude of the narrator rather suggests here and there that of an easy-going Englishman when confronted with the spectacle, say of a drunken sailor or soldier.229

Another class having high pretensions, which has come in for much of the "screwing-up" kind of laughter, is the physician. Next to the healer of the soul, he undertakes the most for mortals. In *Gil Blas,* in the comedies of Molière, and in other works, we may see how his ancient methods and his pedantries were apt to affect the intelligent layman with mirthful ridicule.

So far nothing has been said of the rank of the groups thus formed. The differentiating of a higher from a lower caste, with more or less of authority on one side and subservance on the other, will turn out to be the most important feature in social grouping in its bearing on the calling forth of social laughter. As we have seen, our merriment has much to do with dignities, with the claims on our respect made by things above us; while, on the other hand, the contemptuous laugh which has had volume and duration implies a relation of superior and inferior—if only the fugitive one created by the situation of quizzer. All stages of group-formation seem to involve something of this distinction between an upper and a lower class. The simplest conceivable structure of society includes a head and ruler of family, clan or tribe, and subjects. Hence, the vast significance of social grouping as a condition of choral laughter.

How far persons in positions of authority have gratified their sense of superiority by derisive laughter at those below them, it would, of course, be hard to say. When power is real and absolute there are other ways of expressing contempt. Literature undoubtedly furnishes examples of the ridicule by the social superior of the ways of a lower class, as in the Provençal poem of Bertran de Born (*c.* 1180) in which the villains are treated contemptuously. Yet the larger part of literature, not being produced for a ruling caste, does not throw much light on this subject.230 One can only infer with some probability, from the relations of parents and adults, generally, to children, and of white masters to their coloured slaves, that power has always been tempered by some admixture of good-nature, which composition has produced a certain amount of playful jocosity, at once corrective and cementing.

The derisive laughter of the superior is particularly loud in certain cases where the authority is not so real as it might be. Man's ridicule of his not too obedient spouse may be said almost to shriek adown the ages. We may read in papyri of Egypt of the fourteenth or thirteenth century B.C. of the misfortunes of a husband, named Anoupou.231 The Greek comedians thought no abuse of the sex too bitter or too coarse.232 In Latin literature we have satirical portraits of different types of women, drawn under the figures of various brutes, a fox, a mare, etc.233 In mediæval society, the low opinion of women entertained by their lords is illustrated in the firm persuasion that the only way to treat them was to beat them—watching them was quite vain—so that they might be occupied all the day with crying.234 Sometimes, as in the *Arabian Nights,* this contempt takes the form of bitter denunciation; but, for the most part, it has laughed in the brighter key of comedy. Even the satire here is wont to lose all trace of savageness, and to assume the tone of a good-natured acceptance of the incurable.

While the formation of social ranks has thus secured a wide range for supercilious mocking of inferiors, it has guaranteed these ample opportunity of avenging themselves by laughter at the expense of the authorities.

How soon in man's history any such laughter became possible, it would be hard to say. In the simpler types of community, the severe restraints laid on youths by the men of the tribe must, one supposes, have been fatal to any indulgence by sons in laughter at the expense of fathers, such as is illustrated in comedy both ancient and modern. The penalties attached to breach of ceremonial rule must have stifled any impulse of laughter, if it happened to arise. It is said that when the chief of a certain tribe chanced to stumble, his subjects were bound to pretend to stumble in order to cover up his defect.235 The utility of this quaint custom may have lain in its effectual suppression of the risible impulse. This theory, however, postulates a kind of courtier widely removed from the modern, of whom it seems safe to say that he might be trusted to see stumblings and worse without feeling an over-mastering temptation to laugh.

One can only conjecture that men began to discern and enjoy the amusing side of authority and its solemn ways of asserting itself, in their free moments, at a safe distance from tell-tale eyes.

What is known of the hard-worked slave of antiquity is suggestive not merely of play after toil, but of a safe turning on task-masters. When, as we read, the Egyptian workman got fun "out of the smallest incident in the day's work—an awkward apprentice cutting his finger, a comrade sleeping over his task whom the overseer lashes to awaken him," and so forth, did not something of a spirit of malicious crowing over the overseer express itself too? The analogy of the judiciously half-smothered laughter of the

English schoolboy in playground or dormitory suggests the answer. We must not wonder if these dangerous excursions of the spirit of fun have failed to be recorded. Still more significant is another picture from the same hand, representing a tussle between overseer and workmen in which "the stick vainly interferes," so that "at least an hour elapses before quiet is re-established".236 This looks like the rollicking laughter of schoolboys at the spectacle of an orderly ceremony suddenly turned to disorder. The interpretation is borne out by the fact that these same Egyptians were able to enter into the fun of a loss of dignity in a solemn function, for example, the upsetting by a collision of the richly supplied table in the funereal boat, and the falling of a mummy on a priest during the ceremony of conveying it to its resting-place.237

The return of contemptuous laughter from the slave to his master was certainly allowed to some extent among the Romans. It became a well-recognised privilege during one of the chief annual festivals (Saturnalia). The slaves in the plays of Plautus treat the tyranny under which they live "in a spirit of gay bravado".238 Nor need we be surprised at these liberties if we remember that the modern schoolmaster must almost be perfect if he does not find it expedient, not merely to permit his pupils *desipere in loco,* but to allow them now and again to have a mild joke at his expense. The cajoling by means of jokes, which Miss Kingsley found so serviceable for managing the West African, may of course stop short of this, and its virtue lie in the substitution of a light, laughing treatment for bullying. Yet genial laughter, when the contempt has been vaporised out of it, necessarily tends at the moment to a levelling of planes, as is seen in the immediate assertion of the right of reciprocity. This is perhaps the main reason why the schoolmaster is, in general, chary of introducing the method of jocosity. His laughter is apt to sound as if it held some of the gritty deposit of contempt.

The really delightful illustration of the turning of the tables on masters by those in subjection is to be found in woman's retort on man's contemptuous treatment. She has again and again managed to outwit him, as we have found him dolefully admitting, and has had her full laugh at his cumbrous attempts to manage her. The mediæval *fabliaux* are certainly disposed to award success in strategy to her, rather than to her lord. Her ways of befooling him, too, have often been so simple—as when she persuades him that he has been dreaming what he fancies he has observed—that the poor dupe ought, one supposes, to have died of chagrin. And, when there has been a call for the finer sort of manœuvring, she wins the unprejudiced reader to her side by displaying an admirable ingenuity and subtlety of invention, qualities which Mr. Herbert Spencer would probably regard as secondary sexual characters evolved during ages of marital tyranny. Of her modes of turning on him in these latter days there is no need to speak. The shout of contemptuous laughter seems to have passed from the one side of the eternal fray to the other. But this hardly belongs to the present division of our subject.

It may be added that the laughter of the laity at the clergy illustrates, in addition to the impulse already dealt with, the itching of spirited mortals to turn on oppressors. The denunciations and anathemas of this class, backed, as they asseverate, by supernatural sanctions, have always been trying to untamed men and women. And the appetite of our ancestors for stories disgraceful to monks and priests drew some of its keenness from this rebelliousness of the natural man against spiritual tyrannies. Here is an illustration of the feminine retort: A woman was chatting with a gossip of hers in church: bidden by the preaching friar to hold her peace she exclaimed, "I wonder which babbles most of the two?"239

Still another variety of social laughter springs out of this distinction of superior and inferior groups. The impulse of exalted persons to assert themselves and to strike their inferiors with awe—an impulse by the way which the peacock and other birds will betray in the presence of their inferior, man—is apt to be disallowed by those for whom the display is intended. It is one thing, they feel, to acknowledge true authority, another to bow down to the exaggeration of its claim, to the boastful exhibition of power and rank. Hence, perhaps, some of the quickness of the mirthful eye for the entertainment latent in all braggadocio. The soldier who needlessly emphasises the fact that he possesses the height and spirit of his calling by strutting, by imposing vociferation and the rest, has probably always been a source of comic merriment, as the *Miles gloriosus* of Plautus and the Bobadil of Ben Jonson may remind us.

It will be evident that all this laughter of inferiors at superiors, whether these are so really or merely in their own opinion, must, so far as it has got home, have had a valuable corrective function. If the derision of the lord helps to keep in place his inferior dame or vassal, much more does the laughter of his inferior serve to hold him to what befits his rank. *Noblesse oblige* is a rule largely maintained by the demands of those below who are expected to pay homage. These, as we know, have been much employed in claiming modest rights from their "betters". The curbing of a king's tyrannies may have required a rebellion of his barons, or a riot of his people: yet a good deal of checking of tyrannic propensities has been carried out by the unalarming expedient of ridicule. Even in a free and enlightened country we may observe in officials a tendency now and again to inflate their dignity unduly; so that one infers that the restraining force of the laughter of inferiors still counts.

The results of this spirited turning of the worm have been considerable. The impish spirit of mirth has taken up its abode with the common people, and instructed them in the rich sources of the laughable which lie in all rank and dignity. On the other hand, the "high and mighty" have, from a true instinct of self-preservation, waged fierce war with this irreverent attitude of the multitude. The struggles between the two will be spoken of presently.

The scope for laughter which, given the disposition, these divisions of group and of rank bring with them is further widened by the vital circumstance that, as groups in the same community, they have to enter into various relations with one another. A judicious mixture of opposition and harmony of interest seems to be most favourable to a rich production of mirth. This is illustrated even in such masterful relations as that of the overseer and the commanding officer, who may find that the compulsion of the rod is inadequate to the extraction of the required amount of work, and so have to cast about for other instruments.

The good effect of a skilful use of the cajoling laugh has already been illustrated. It is seen with particular clearness in the relation of husband and wife; for the fun of the situation is that, in spite of profound differences of taste and inclination and of a sharp antagonism, the necessity of common interests and ends holds them together in daily association. This necessity, ever present to the wiser of them, has tempered the contempt and forced the derider to at least a pretence of good humour. The same may be said of the relation of the sexes in general. The quality and range of the fun which is wont to lighten a talk between a young man and a young woman on a first introduction are pretty closely determined by the consciousness of sexual relation on either side. Shyness, a disposition to regard the other suspiciously as opponent, together with the instinct to please and win admiration, and the desire to strike on points of sympathy—all this helps to bring about, and is reflected in the peculiar wrigglings in which the mirthful spirit expresses itself on such an occasion.

One of the best examples of the combined effect of hostility and a desire to agree is to be found in the humours of the market place. The relation of buyer and seller seems to be pregnant with opportunities for merry fooling on either side. The direct and sharply felt opposition of interest is apt to beget a good deal of the rough sort of "taking down". Not only will the tongue be stirred to derisive attack, the situation may even beget retaliations in the shape of practical jokes. The merchant, as the expert, has always had the upper hand in the contest of wits. His customer has had to find consolation in satires on the cheat, such as those which were common in the Middle Ages.[240] On the other hand, the need of coming to an agreement has served to bring into the haggling process a good deal of the conciliative kind of laughter. The vendor has always known the value of good-natured banter as an instrument of persuasion. This overflow of the spirit of fun into the channels of serious business may still be seen as a faint survival in front of a cheap-Jack's van. George Eliot has given us a charming picture of the play of this spirit in the south in her chapter on "The Peasants' Fair" in *Romola*.

The same intrusion of fun as an auxiliary into the business relations of groups is seen in many other cases where opposition has to be toned down and a *modus vivendi* arrived at, as in that of opposed political parties, religious bodies and the like. The appearance of the laughing imp, if only he behaves himself, in these rather warm encounters of groups serves to cool the atmosphere and to temper animosity by at least a momentary experience of genial contact. It does much, indeed, to tone down the uneasy and half-suspicious attitude which members of any group are apt to take up on first having to do with those of a strange group, especially one of higher rank.

We may now summarise the chief social utilities of the reciprocal laughter of classes at the ways of other classes. In the first place, it helps, like the laughter of the savage tribe at the ways of other tribes, to counteract any tendency to imitate the manners and customs of foreign groups. What we have laughed at, we are not likely to adopt. This is the self-protective function of laughter. To laugh at the ways of another group is, moreover, in most cases at least, to indulge in a feeling of our own superiority; and this attitude would have a further conservative tendency, especially when it is the laugh of the expert in his own department at the outside ignoramus.

Let us now glance at the effect on the group whose ways are being laughed at. To be the object of another set's ridicule, especially when we have the right of retort, so far from necessarily weakening our hold on that which is ridiculed may strengthen it. When we are strongly attached, others' laughter may make us cling the more firmly to what we cherish. Laughter in this case is, indeed, as we have seen, an excellent training in a good-natured suffering of others' ridicule, a training which has in it the virtue of a moral tonic.

Yet this inter-groupal laughter is not wholly subservient to the maintenance of characteristic differences. In all the higher forms of society, at least, such ridicule has an assimilative action as well. It manages to some extent, by inducing self-criticism, to get rid of useless excrescences. Thus, it helps to keep down class-vanity, the professional narrowness which cries, "There's nothing like leather!" a narrowness which is so delightfully satirised by Molière in the wranglings of M. Jourdain's professors.

The correction of this exclusive feeling of self-importance of a group by outside laughter has always been at work, helping to keep groups in friendly touch, and hindering the sectional or professional *esprit de corps* from overpowering the larger social consciousness which we call national sentiment, and the common-sense of the community. Of this last more will be said presently.

So far, we have illustrated the bearing on the ways of laughter of what may be called the structural features of societies. There has been no reference to the effects of social movements, of all that is meant by the successive changes of fashion in manners, dress and so forth, and of those more persistent movements which make up what we call social progress. The least reflection will show that in this continual flux of things social, the unceasing modifications of the head-covering and the rest, and the trampling down of old beliefs and institutions by the resistless "march of intellect," we have at least as large a field for the gambols of the laughing spirit as in the distinctions and oddly combined relations of classes.

We may best begin by referring to the movements of fashion. These may be defined as changes in dress, manners and so forth, which are marked off from the improvements entering into progress by two circumstances: (1) that they are capricious, not the products of a rational choice of the best; and (2) that they are of comparatively short duration. When we call a mode of doing a thing a fashion, we imply, quite unknowingly perhaps, that it has not the cachet of a change for the better, and that as such it has no security of tenure.

A fashion differs from a custom in being essentially communicable from one group to another, and even from one nation to another. Its development thus belongs to a comparatively late period of social evolution. Its hold on men and women is explained by the fact that it appeals to two of their strongest instincts, the craving for novelty and the impulse to imitate superiors.

Keeping to the intra-national diffusion of manners, we note that the movement of fashion is normally from the highest rank or ranks downwards. This movement may well have commenced far back in the evolution of communities where class-distinctions were rigorously enforced. The attitude of reverence towards superiors has for its psychological concomitant the impulse to imitate. Just as children will copy the voice and gestures of one whom they look up to, so savages will copy the ways of Europeans who manage to make themselves respected. In the ceremonies of primitive tribes and even of highly complex societies, *e.g.*, church ritual, a good deal of scope is offered for this flattery of imitation. We may infer, indeed, that the impulse to adopt the ways of exalted personages must always have been at work. In the earlier stages of human history this impulse was checked by the force of custom and of law, *e.g.*, sumptuary laws. This imitation from below must strike at the root of those external differences, such as style of dress, between group and group, observance of which has helped greatly to maintain class-distinctions. It could only have made way against these barriers gradually. So difficult, in sooth, does the feat appear to be, that Mr. Herbert Spencer suggests that fashion, as the imitation of those of high rank and authority, began in a change of custom; as in the rule already alluded to that when the king slipped the onlooking courtiers should at once imitate his awkwardness.

It is probable that the imitation of what is distinctive and fixed in the costume and manners of the higher class preceded by some interval the imitation of the changes we call fashion. How the two are connected does not seem to be quite clear. Did the rulers and those immediately about them, piqued at the adoption of their ways by the vulgar, try to steal a march on imitation by changing their customs? To judge from what takes place to-day, one would answer "yes". I am told that ladies strongly object to go on wearing a fashionable hat as soon as it becomes generally worn by factory girls, or other inferior group. However this be, it seems certain that the "leaders of society," while they reserve for special ceremonial occasions a distinctive dress, mode of speech and the rest, choose to alter these from time to time for other purposes. Such alterations may be the result of the caprices of a "leader," guided by some inventor, or they may take the form of an assimilation of a foreign mode. Lastly, the leaders may include others besides the Court people: the universities are accredited with the origination of many of the pretty bits of slang, the use of which is supposed to betoken a certain social altitude and "up-to-dateness".

In the midst of these changes of fashion something of custom may be seen still to persist. Taking the dress of woman to-day, we note that in spite of experiments like those of the Bloomers, skirts continue to be a permanent feature in female attire. Fashions in respect of width, and even of length, may come and go, but the skirt as skirt seems to go on for ever.

Even when the impulse to adopt the dress and behaviour of the upper class was allowed a certain play, it was probably long before it acted on all ranks. Each rank, whilst keen in its imitation of the ways of the class above it, would naturally resist any further descent of the imitative movement.

In this descent of fashion from higher to lower ranks we see a mutual modification of fashion and permanent custom. In some cases imitation from below may be stopped pretty early through lack of means for giving effect to it. The joy of wearing pearls, or other precious stones in fashion at the moment, is denied the young seamstress. Yet there are solaces here in the shape of "imitations". Again, the lower middle class, not to speak of the cottagers, are, for obvious reasons, not likely to be affected by a craze for the Queen Anne style in domestic architecture. Even in the case of dress, fine limitations which the "mere male" might find it hard to define, seem to be imposed, for example, on the architecture of the hat, when a new style is assimilated by lower ranks. Here, again, fashion is clearly restrained by class-custom. Ideas of neatness, of an unaggressive quietness appear to be valued, in theory at least, in milliners, domestic servants, and others who minister to the wants of the titled and the wealthy. The very expression "the fashionable world" implies that the full magnificence and luxury of fashion is a monopoly.

The imitation of the manners of high life by the middle class is in most cases a pretty clear acknowledgment of a superior social quality. One of the most amusing examples of this thinly-veiled snobbism is the elevated hand-shake lately in vogue. A fashion like this easily reaches the eye of the vulgar, focussed for the first appearance of a new characteristic of "high life," by way of the theatre or of the illustrated paper. A point worth noting here is the exaggeration of what the imitators regard as of the essence of the new "mode". It would be curious to hear what symbolism (if any) those who appeared so eager to get the hand-shake up to the level of the eyes assigned to this fashionable rite.

This eager and almost simian mimicry of the ways of society's leaders must, it is evident, tend to the obliteration of recognisable class-distinctions in ordinary life. We only need to compare the spectacle of a crowd in London to-day with that of a mediæval city crowd, as represented in a drawing of the time, to see what a depressing amount of assimilation in dress the forces of fashion have brought about.

The connections between these movements of fashion and the spirit of laughter are numerous and pretty obvious. Even the primal movement, the adoption of a fashion by the head of a community from abroad, offers a rich spectacle for those who lie in wait for the coming of the ludicrous. How finely the folly that lurks in a slavish submission to fashion grins out at us from the story of those New Zealand chiefs who, goaded by the fashion set by others of giving great feasts, would often push their feast-givings to the point of causing a famine among their peoples![241] The following of a foreign fashion by a court has in it, moreover, always something to prick the spirit of malicious laughter in the subjects. Not so terribly long since, the importation of customs from one European court to another, and a reciprocation of the loan, by way of family connections, was the subject of a rather malicious laughter in each of the countries affected.

It is, however, in the downward rush of fashion from rank to rank, and the incidents which attend it, that the seeker for the laughable will find his satisfaction. The eagerness of persons to be in the van of the movement will of itself produce a crop of ludicrous aspects: for the first sudden appearance of a large and capturing novelty, say in a high-branded bonnet or manner of speech, brings to us something of the delightful gaiety which the sight of the clown brings to a child. It is a huge folly, which we greet with the full, unthinking roar of hilarity. Never, indeed, does the inherent non-rationality of a large part of human behaviour reveal itself so directly and so unmistakably as when a fashion which has reigned long enough to become accepted as right is thus rudely thrust aside in favour of an interloper: whence the laughing contempt poured on new fashions by comic poets and satirists.242

Nor is this all, or the best. The behaviour of the ardent aspirant has its absurd aspect even for dull souls. The form of self-assertion which consists in stepping out of one's rank is always viewed by those of the deserted rank with an acidulated amusement; and those who are too manifestly eager to appropriate a new fashion are wont to be regarded as persons who are trying to get above their set. If the fashionable cosmetic is laid on thickly, as it pretty certainly will be by those seized with the more vulgar form of social ambition, the fun will wax still greater. The display in this case adds to the delightful transformation of the clown a touch of the bombast of the mountebank.

New possibilities of mirth arise out of the collision between the imitative impulse to be fashionable, and respect for the customs of one's group. An exaggeration of something in dress or speech which savours of an attempt to break through class-barriers cannot but amuse the onlooker disposed to mirth. Middle-class house-wives are, one hears, wont to enliven the dulness of their Sunday afternoons by a stealthy quizzing of their "maids" as they set out for their parade. The maid's village acquaintance—if it could succeed in stifling envious admiration—would doubtless draw a more rollicking enjoyment from the spectacle. In general, any appearance of craning one's neck so as to overtop one's set is greeted by a slightly malicious laughter; and the bold donning of fashionable array is the most easily recognisable manifestation of the craning impulse. For a more purely disinterested spectator, too, the situation has its entertaining drollness. The struggle in the panting bosom of a young woman, whether of white or of coloured race, as the passionate longing for some bewitching novelty—recommended, too, by the lead of her superiors—is sharply confronted with the sense of what befits her, and possibly a vague fear of being plunged by a fiery zeal into the morass of the laughable, has its comic pathos for the instructed eye.

One further contribution to the fun of the world made by this hot eagerness to pay homage to rank is perhaps worth a reference. Like the verbal kind, the flattery of imitation is often visibly hollow. When the soul of man or woman is held captive by the necessity of doing what is done by others—especially by others higher up—there is no room for thought of sincerity: whence, among many results, this one, that for him who can be pure spectator responsive to the amusing aspects of things, the spectacle of a great national demonstration of loyalty cannot fail to have its diverting aspect.

No doubt the pushing worshippers of fashion, if they only wait long enough, get their chance of laughing back. As soon as the new thing, so charged with rollicking gaiety at first, settles down to a commonplace habit, there comes the moment for ridiculing the belated imitator. That popular figure on the stage, the "old dowdy," is commonly represented as ridiculously behind the times in respect of attire. Yet the range of jocosity inspired by respect for mere newness, on the value of which reason has had nothing to say, is evidently limited.

We may now turn to those deeper currents of change which together make up social progress; including all distinct advance from lower to higher forms of intelligence, sentiment and character, as well as from lower to higher types of social life; and, along with these, the growth of institutions in which these changes express themselves.

We may assume that these progressive changes arise, either from the adoption of the products of superior mental capacity appearing in individuals who are members of the community, or from the propagation of ideas, inventions, institutions from one country to another.

To say precisely how the production and circulation of a social improvement takes place is not easy. Men of imaginative minds, with an exceptionally large mechanical, legislative, or other insight, or with a fine feeling for the subtle things of beauty or of the moral order, there must be. Against all attempted innovation, however, whether from within or from without, the attitude of conservatism sets itself as a serious obstacle. Here, too, we seem to perceive the charm and influence of rank. It is only when some recognised authority proclaims the value of the new discovery that the multitude, which was perhaps a moment before doing its best to trample on it, turns deferentially and kneels. The free adoption of it as true or as good commonly follows much later.

A startlingly new idea, whether in science, religion, or the utilities of life, finds in its intrinsic reasonableness no defence against the attacks of malicious mirth. The ordinary mind when it laughs, just as when it is serious, judges things by the standard of what is customary. What violently jars with this is viewed as legitimate game for ridicule. The history of ideas and of the social movements growing out of them is one long illustration of this truth. The idea of a larger freedom and higher functions for women was treated by the theatre of ancient Greece as matter for wild hilarity. The idea came up again and again after this, thanks to the zeal and courage of isolated advocates. But it continued to excite the loud laughter of the crowd. And less than half a century ago, when J. S. Mill advocated the spiritual and legal emancipation of women, the response was at first largely an expression of amusement. Only to-day is a part of the civilised world beginning to recognise the naturalness and fitness of the idea that women should have their share, both in the intellectual gains of the more advanced education, and in the larger work of the world.

We may see by this illustration how mighty a force every new idea of a large revolutionary character has to meet and to overcome. Darwin's idea of the evolution of man seemed in the sixties to the mass of Englishmen, including a bishop of Oxford and many another high up in the scale of intellectual culture, very much as some of the teachings of our missionaries strike a keen-witted savage. The figure of the monkey, which is, by the way, one of the oldest symbols of caricature, rendered excellent service to those who, naturally enough, greeted the proposed topsy-turvyness of Darwinism with boisterous cachinnations.

It is much the same with the attitude of the crowd towards the first use of practical inventions. Much merriment accompanied the introduction from abroad by the gallants of the Restoration of so simple an innovation as the use of the fork243—a fact to be remembered by the English tourist abroad when he is disposed to laugh at the sight of a too lavish use of the knife. In such cases, the first adopters of the novelty are laughed at very much as in the case of a new fashion. The absurdity of the adoption in either case turns on the delightful freshness and the glorious irregularity of the proceeding.

On the other hand, we meet here, too, with a recoil of laughter upon the laugher. Though a respect for the customary prompts us at first to ridicule any sudden and impressive change in ideas or habits of life, yet, when the change is in a fair way of becoming fixed, the same feeling will urge us to make merry over those who show an obstinate prejudice in favour of the old. Laughter finds one of its chief functions in ridiculing worn-out ideas, beliefs that have been proved illusory, and discarded habits of life. Nowhere, perhaps, is the elation of mirth more distinctly audible than in this ridicule by an advancing age of survivals of the discarded ways of its predecessors. Art gives us many examples of this merriment over what is decaying and growing effete. Every age of stir and commotion has probably had its satirical literature, striking with boisterous mirth at the disappearing phantoms. The broad and genial comedy of Aristophanes pushed against the tottering mythology of his time, and the fall evoked a large outflow of mirth. The great work of Cervantes and the satires (pasquins) of the same period poked fun at the sentimental clinging to the decaying order of chivalry and feudalism.244

Merry-making over the death of outworn ideas and institutions has frequently been reinforced by the deep and refreshing expiration which accompanies relief from pressure. This elemental form of laughter has entered into all those happy moments of national life when the whole people has become closely united in a joyous self-abandonment. Plautus, the comedian of the people, reflects in his broad merriment the rebound of the spirit after the second Punic War from a long continued state of tension, and the craving of the masses for a more unrestrained enjoyment of the pleasures of life.245 The popular art of the Middle Ages, in which the demons seem to play the harmless part of the policeman in a modern pantomime, illustrates the rebound from an oppressive superstition. A like relief of tension and outburst of pent-up spirits are recognisable in the literature of the Reformation and of the English Restoration.

The same exhilarant aspect of the vanishing of the outworn moves us in a quieter way when we ridicule the survivals of customs and rites which have lost their significance. This form of hilarious enjoyment, which implies a piercing through of appearances and a searching into meanings, will be more fully considered later on.

It seems to follow from what has been said that laughter reacts in a double manner upon changes of social habit. First of all, it resists the wildness of the craving for the new (neomania). As schoolboys are wont to treat a newcomer, it applies its lash vigorously to a proposed innovation, in order to see what "stuff" it is made of, and whether it can justify its existence. In this way it moderates the pace of the movement of change. On the other hand, it completes the process of throwing off an outworn habit by giving it, so to speak, the *coup de grâce*. It thus combines the service rendered to a herd of sheep on the march by the shepherd who walks in front, with that rendered by the sheep-dog which runs back again and again to the laggards. It seems to be enforcing Goethe's maxim:—

"Ohne Hast

Aber ohne Rast."

We may now glance at some of the workings of this complex movement of social progress on the formation of social sets, and on their reciprocal attitudes.

It is evident that, by introducing much more subdivision of employment and exclusive knowledge of experts, progress will tend to widen the area of mutual quizzing and chaffing, already dealt with. It is of more importance to point out that the advance of a community in knowledge and culture will lead to the formation of new groups involving certain differences of rank. The importance of this kind of group-division shows itself in classic comedy. Juvenal expresses the lively contempt of the urban citizen for his provincial inferior,246 and our own comedy of the Restoration, taking town life as its standard, pours ridicule on the country gentry.247 It is illustrated also in the relation of the clergy as the learned class, to the ignorant laity. As the *contes* amusingly suggest, a large part of the authority of the clergy during the Dark Ages rested on this intellectual superiority. If we view culture widely we may speak of an indefinite number of levels composing a scale of intellectual dignity. These levels are commonly supposed to coincide with such groups as the professional class, the man of business (Kaufman), and the lower class. But no such coincidence can be assumed when once education has become a common possession. A large portion of our "upper" class—which is determined no longer by descent but to a considerable extent by wealth—is neither cultured nor even well-informed. A clerk will often be found to have more general knowledge and literary taste than his well-dressed employer, and a working man, in spite of the limitations of poverty, may know more about such subjects as philosophy and history than the great majority of the middle class. We see then that the strata representing gradations of culture are largely independent of commonly recognised divisions. These older distinctions may, indeed, be very much toned down by the culture-movement. The ancient line of division between the superior man and his inferior spouse has been half effaced by the admission of women into the higher culture circle. The culture divisions are real social groups, each being bound together by a large community of ideas, tastes and interests; and their importance in the system of social grouping tends to increase.

The development of culture groups introduces a new and important change in the standards of fitness, to which laughter is, so to speak, tied. When superiority is lacking in a clearly recognisable basis of reason, its ridicule of inferiors can only have its source in a pride which may be, and often is, of the most foolish. When, however, it resides in the possession of greater spiritual wealth, more refined ideas and a more acute sense of the fitting, the laughter itself shows a finer quality. It is less boisterous, more discerning, and more penetrating. As such, we need not wonder that, though it is felt to be irritating, it is not understood. The *nouveau riche*, whose vulgarity reveals itself as soon as he appears in a society having refined manners, may wince under the half-repressed smile, though he seems for the most part well protected by an insensitive tegument. As Schopenhauer has observed, the man of mediocre intelligence very much dislikes encountering his intellectual superior; and it so happens, for the gratification of merry onlookers, perhaps, that social ambition not infrequently precipitates its possessor into a sharp encounter with those who have a whole world of ideas of which he knows nothing.

Not but that the inferior here, too, may now and again have his chance of laughing back. The possession of ideas and of an exacting taste is apt to appear affected to one wanting in them. Midas, accustomed to measure values by incomes, and to identify intelligence with the cleverness of the money-maker, not unnaturally regards a habit of appealing to ideas as an eccentric superfluity; and so laughter may come consolingly to him who is utterly beaten in the encounter of wits. The "common-sense" of the average Briton scores many a loud laugh in its confident self-assertion against any proposed introduction of ideas into the sphere of practical affairs.

A further effect of the movement of culture on group-formation is seen in the divisions into sects, a phenomenon which seems to be conspicuous in the communities built up by our race. This tendency to a minute subdivision of religious, political and other bodies introduces a new kind of relation. We cannot well say that one section surpasses its rivals in intelligence. This may or may not be the case, but the rules of the social game require us to leave the question open. On the other hand, this differentiation of organised opinion into a number of particular creeds or "views," the shade of opinion being often fine, leads to a new bifurcation of "higher" and "lower" groups. The "higher" here is the mass or majority which naturally laughs at tiny minorities as faddists and cranks. Yet again, the fine impartiality of the god of laughter, to whom, since mankind for the greater part is other than wise, the difference of the many and the few may hardly count, occasionally gives the despised minority its chance; for minorities do sometimes represent ideas which are born for sovereignty.

While the progress of a nation in ideas and institutions thus serves in a manner to multiply groups, and so to introduce new opportunities for the indulgence of group attack and retaliation, it tends on the whole to break down their barriers. It does this by means of the pulpit, the press, and the educational agencies which help to circulate new ideas through all classes. These conduce, both directly and indirectly, to a certain assimilation of groups; and assimilative action is going on rapidly to-day. Yet, as we have seen, it leaves ample room for different grades of culture, since natural differences of coarseness and fineness in the intellectual fibre will always secure the broad contrast of the cultured and the uncultured.

The spread of knowledge and culture through all classes acts indirectly on group-distinctions by throwing open the occupations of one class to members of others, and more particularly of "lower" ones. The workman's son who has a brain and cultivates it may, as we are often told, find his way to the university and take his place unchallenged among the lawyers, the doctors, or the exalted "dons" themselves.

Now all sudden changes in class, especially such as involve elevation, are apt to appear laughable. Even when promotion comes by royal favour, we feel the leap into a higher sphere to be anomalous, and are wont to examine the grounds of the new title with some care. The conservative instincts of men oppose themselves laughingly to the appearance of new dignitaries very much as they oppose themselves to the appearance of new ideas, and some temporary unfitness in the person for his new social niche is to be expected. In the comedy of the Restoration, we are told, "no measure is kept in pouring contempt on the mushroom growths of yesterday, the knights of recent creation".248

Something of this impression of the incongruously new is produced for a moment even in the case of a well-earned rise in the social scale. The young aspirant's family and connections, living on in the less brilliant light, will perforce laugh, though perhaps with something of sympathetic admiration, at the oddity of the sudden elevation; and the rising young man will be singularly fortunate if he does not now and again betray an amusing unfamiliarity with the ways of the company he has joined.

Yet the confusion of ranks due to the universalising of education is small and unimpressive when compared with that arising from another cause. The great destroyer of fixed class-boundaries is the force which tends to transmute a community into a plutocracy. This tendency may, no doubt, illustrate in a measure the effect of a diffused education; for the successful fortune-builder will sometimes have attained success by scientific knowledge skilfully applied. Yet the presence—or the absence—of other qualities than the intellectual seems to have much to do in these days with sudden elevations in the plutocratic scale.

As the comedy of Molière may tell us, the spectacle of a man standing at the foot of the social ladder and looking up wistfully at its higher region has something entertaining in it both for those on his actual level and for those on the level of his ambition. Later, when the wistful glance is followed by actual climbing, the unrehearsed performances may grow mirth-provoking even to the point of tearful mistiness. Nor does the attainment of the goal make an end of the fun, since the maintenance of a decorous equilibrium at the new altitude may turn out to be even more precarious than the climbing, especially when relatives and other accidents of the humbler state persist in their attachment.

On the other hand, these climbings exhibit much in the way of amusing imposture; for men, as Schopenhauer tells us, have been known to push their way, unqualified and impious, even into literary circles, and snatch a kind of reflected distinction by the use of arts at once ancient and vulgar.

The spectacle of changing one's class exhibits the amusing aspect of fraud in another way. When leaders high up in "society" pay homage to the deity of the climbing money-maker by betaking themselves to trade under assumed names, the mirth of Midas and of his whole despised caste may find its opportune vent.

We may now briefly indicate the general effect of the social movements just sketched upon the quality and the mode of distribution of the hilarious moods of a people.

(*a*) To begin with, the advance and wider spread of the wave of culture will clearly tend to effect a general raising of the standard of taste, and to develop an appreciation of the quality of the ludicrous. This result, though effected in part by the development of art and the extension of its educative influence, is in the main the direct outcome of intellectual progress and of that increase in refinement of feeling which seems to depend on this progress. One may describe this change by saying that the standard of ideas tends gradually to gain ground, hemming in if not narrowing that of custom. The primal laugh, void of intellectual content, becomes less general, the laugh of the mind more frequent. This effect of an introduction of ideas holds good in the case of members of all classes in so far as they enter into the higher culture group. In this way particular standards of locality and of social group begin to count less in our laughter.

This effect of expansion of the intellectual view is reflected in all the more refined varieties of comic art. Any manifest insistence on dignity of rank, more especially when the group is not of imposing aspect, whether the *petite noblesse* in a small "Residency" town on the Continent or the families which compose "Society" in an obscure town in England, is felt to be on the verge of the ludicrous. On the other hand, a magnifying of the dignity of a person or a class by those below, when accompanied by a cringing demeanour, is apt to take on the amusing aspect of flunkeyism, the due appreciation of which presupposes a certain maturity of the laughter of the mind.

The general tendency of this advance of ideas is as yet very imperfectly realised. The march of mind, like some military marches, is not quite so uniformly triumphant as it is wont to be represented. A considerable part of the laughter among what are called the educated classes is still but little influenced by the finer and deeper perception of ludicrous quality; while, as for the uneducated majority of all social grades, it would be hard to find in their mirth any distinct traces of a deposit from the advance of the culture-stream. One might venture on the supposition that the appreciation of the ludicrous shown to-day by the frequenters of a "high class" Music Hall in London is, both as to its intellectual penetration and as to its refinement of feeling, but little, if anything, above that of a mediæval crowd which gathered to see and hear the jokes of the *jongleur*. So slow a process is the infiltration of refining influence from the higher strata of culture downwards.

(*b*) This change in the quality of social laughter through an infusion of ideas has undoubtedly been accompanied by a change in its quantity, as seen in a decline of the older, voluminous merriment of the people. This fall in the collective outburst, already touched on, and recognised by all students of the past, is largely due to a toning down of the simpler and heartier utterances of the common people. This change is so important as to call for a short investigation.

In simpler types of society, the more hearty and voluminous laughter probably came from the lowest strata. It is enough to recall the mirth of the Egyptian and the Roman slave. Later on, the large scope for indulgence in laughter was supplied by an *organisation* of mirth in the shape of shows and other popular entertainments. There was possibly the germ of such an organisation in the annual celebration "in honour of the most jocund god of laughter" referred to by Apuleius.249 One may instance the merry-makings at the harvest and vintage festivals out of which Greek comedy took its rise, and the rollicking fun of the multitude at fairs and festivals during the Middle Ages. That the people were the true experts in the secrets of laughter is further suggested by the fact that slaves, both Greek and Roman, were selected as jesters and wits by well-to-do people. The fools kept by Orientals were probably from the same class.250 The later "fools" of European courts were drawn from the simple folk.

The characteristics of this early type of popular mirth can be summed up in the word childishness. The slave or other oppressed worker could without effort throw off ideas of toil and chastisement in his play hour. Towards his master and his treatment of him, his attitude seems to have been on the whole the resignation of a life-long habit. He might, not improbably, enjoy a quiet joke at the expense of his overseer, but he seems to have entertained towards him none of the deeper animosity.

This naïve form of popular laughter gave way to a less childish type when "the common people" began to include a goodly number of free-men who were able to form opinions of their own, and bold enough to assert the right of expressing these. It follows from what has been said above that the newly gained freedom would naturally give rise to some laughter-bringing criticism of authorities. This tendency of the mirthful mood of the crowd was instantly perceived by the authorities who waged war against it, using the weapons of a repressive censorship. We have an example of this censorship in the police regulations which hampered the introduction of comedy from Athens into Rome. It was required by the authorities that the scene of the play should always be laid outside Rome as if to guard against a direct attack on Roman institutions and persons.251 A like hostility to the pranks of a free and quite unfastidious mirth was shown by the mediæval church. This may well have been in part the outcome of honest moral reprobation of the scurrilities of the songs, the *contes* and the rest. Yet it looks as if the prohibitory enactments originated for the most part in the alarm of the ecclesiastics for the security of their hold on the mind of the people.

It was not, however, an easy matter to silence popular laughter when this had once heard itself and recognised its force. Aristophanes and his laughing public were, for a time at least, stronger than the demagogue whom they ridiculed. No doubt the civil and the ecclesiastical power have again and again succeeded in half-stifling for a time the ruder sort of laughter. Yet the complete suffocation of it in free communities has proved to be impossible. In the Middle Ages, we are told, the atmosphere of fun would rise now and again to a kindling heat, so that holy men themselves would join in the not too decent songs.252 The modern history of Political Satire abundantly illustrates the force of popular laughter. Thus, in the Stuart period, satires were produced which were a popular protest against the grievance of monopolies.253 How firmly it maintained its ground is illustrated by the fact that the politicians, when they have failed to oust it from the stage, have endeavoured to turn it to their own ends.254 If the more scurrilous sort has now been driven from the stage, political caricature flourishes vigorously and has dared to attack royalty itself within a measurable period.255

The people has undoubtedly been the upholder of the wholesome custom of mirth. Taking the peasantry, the workmen, and the lower middle class as representing the "people" of to-day, one has to confess that its merry note seems to have been lost. The reservoir which in the past supplied the stream of national gaiety has certainly fallen and threatens even to dry up. But of this more by-and-by.

(*c*) As a last effect needing to be emphasised here, we have underlying the laughter of a people a curiously composite attitude. By this I mean an agglomeration of mental tendencies involving different *manières de voir,* and different standards of the fit and, consequently, of the laughable.

In the preceding chapter we saw how the choral laughter of the savage followed the directions of the self-conservative tendencies of his tribe. This unconscious self-adaptation of the mirthful mood to the ends of the tribal life has persisted through all the changes introduced by the play of fashion and by the movements of social evolution. We of to-day who travel so much more than our ancestors in foreign lands, and may even learn to speak their languages, retain the tendency to resist the importation of what strikes us as un-English. In certain seasons, say when the war-temper heats the blood and foreigners criticise, this feeling for what is national grows distinct and vivid, and reflects itself unmistakably in the manifestations of such mirth as seems to be compatible with the mood of the hour.

This point of view of the tribe has always coexisted with the narrower and more relative one of the group, illustrated above, though it has in ordinary circumstances been less prominent in men's mirthful utterances. The mediæval laughter at the priest, one may conjecture, was now and again directed from the national or patriotic point of view, as the people began to discern in him the servant of a foreign power.

Not only so, but in much of a people's laughter at what it deems the "absurd"—the laughter of "common-sense," as we may call it—it is the point of view of the tribe or society which is still adopted: and this holds good of the larger part, at least, of a community in the van of the march of civilisation. When we smile at what appears to us a far-fetched view, or a quaint habit of life, we are really guided by the standard, "what people round about us say and do and expect us to say and do". This contented reference to a vaguely formulated custom, without any scrutiny of its inherent reasonableness, holds good, indeed, of the judgments passed by ordinary men on the laughable aspects of the immoral. Promptness in paying one's debts, for example, will for most men wear a reasonable or a foolish aspect according to the custom of their tribe—though here two class-standards make themselves distinctly felt; and so the laugh may be turned, as the custom changes, from him whose tardiness in discharging liabilities suggests straitened means otherwise carefully concealed, to him who displays an ungentlemanly haste in matters of a contemptible smallness.

It seems to follow that the adjustments of laughter to more universal norms, to ideas of an inherent fitness in things, are a kind of artificial addition to deeper and more instinctive tendencies. The ordinary man, even when he enjoys the spectacle of some laughable folly or vice, hardly transcends the point of view of custom, from which what all men do is seen to be right. It is only when a higher culture has made apparent the universality of the laughable, as of its opposite the reasonable, that a conscious resort to ideas becomes frequent. This clarifying of our laughter by the infusion of ideas is, in a special manner, the work of experts, namely, the moralist, the literary critic, and, most of all, the artist whose business it is to illumine the domain of the ludicrous. This function of art will form the subject of a later chapter.

In this chapter we have dealt merely with what I have called choral laughter, that of groups, smaller or larger. There is, however, another kind, the private laughter of the individual when alone, or in the company of sympathetic friends. This also has its pre-conditions in the processes of social evolution just touched upon.

Such independent laughter would, it is evident, be impossible in the lowest stages of this evolution. In the savage or quasi-savage state an oddly constituted member of a tribe—if such a being were possible—liable to be seized with a spasm of ridicule at the absurdities of tribal ceremonies would certainly encounter serious risks. It has needed ages of social progress to establish the conditions of a safe individual liberty in the indulgence of the jocose temper.

This freedom in choosing one's own modes of laughter has gradually asserted itself as a part of all that we mean by individual liberty. Perhaps, indeed, it may be regarded as the highest phase and completion of this liberty.

This is not the place for a full inquiry into the complex conditions on which the development of a freer individual laughter depends. It may be enough to point to the need of an advance in ideas and the capability, among the few at least, to form individual judgments, which this advance implies. A man who would laugh his own laugh must begin by developing his own perceptions and ideas.

A fuller understanding of the pre-conditions of an independent laughter will only be possible to one who has carefully examined its characteristics. In the following chapter I propose to analyse that variety of the laughing temper which seems in a peculiar way to be an attribute of the developed individual. This attribute is what is specially designated in these days by the term humour.

CHAPTER X.
LAUGHTER OF THE INDIVIDUAL: HUMOUR.

In the preceding chapter we have seen how the advance of civilisation has tended to still the louder choral voice of laughter. Yet man's best friend is not of the sort to take an affront too seriously. Driven out from the crowd, he has known how to disguise himself and to steal back into the haunts of men, touching here and there a human spirit and moving it to a quieter and perfectly safe enjoyment of things laughable. This new endowment, this last inspiration of the mortal by the god, is what we mean by Humour.

Perhaps hardly a word in the language—and it seems to be exclusively an English word—would be harder to define with scientific precision than this familiar one. It is often used with the greatest degree of looseness, as when a man is endowed with humour because he laughs readily.256 Yet any one who takes pains in using words knows how far this is from being accurate. A chronic garrulity of laughter, typified in what Mr. Meredith calls the "hypergelast," stands, indeed, in marked contrast to what careful speech indicates by "humour". As its etymology might teach us, the term connotes, not so much the common endowment of "risibility," as a certain kind of temperament, a complexion of sentiment, nay, more, a mode of psychical organisation. We cannot, therefore, think of the race as humorous, and should even find it difficult to generalise the endowment so far as to speak of humorists as a class. The humorous man or woman is so, primarily and essentially, by the unpurchasable possession of an individual mind.

This fact of a quite peculiar mixture of elements in the humorous person must never be lost sight of. It dooms this person to a comparative solitude in the vocal expression of a feeling which is primarily social and communicative. The idea of a large unison of utterance among humorous persons is not entertainable. A man who has developed his humorous bent will be thankful if he finds in his social circle one or two who can understand, and, now and again, join in his quiet chuckle.

Yet, though essentially in every individual case a unique blend of elements, humour has certain common characteristics. What sort of temperament and mind are we thinking of when we agree to call Shakespeare, Cervantes, Goldsmith, Sterne, Lamb, Dickens, and George Eliot humorists?

One thing we can say confidently, that it is wanting in certain characteristics of the more diffused laughter. It is far removed from the swift reflex gaiety of the child and the unthinking adult. Its laughter is not only quieter but has a slower movement, and it is charged with a deeper meaning. Again, its utterance differs in tone from the old brutal and contemptuous shout. It voices itself in low and almost tender tones. It is the laughter altogether farthest removed from the standpoint of the interested person: there is in it nothing of the crowing over the vanquished, hardly anything of a consciousness of the superiority to which the uplifting of laughter may at the moment make valid claim. Hence, one may hesitate to apply the name humorist to a writer in whose laughter—though it is commonly spoken of as humour—a note of derisive contempt begins to grow prominent.

These contrasts point clearly enough to certain positive characteristics of the moods of humour. A quiet survey of things, at once playful and reflective; a mode of greeting amusing shows which seems in its moderation to be both an indulgence in the sense of fun and an expiation for the rudeness of such indulgence; an outward, expansive movement of the spirits met and retarded by a cross-current of something like kindly thoughtfulness; these clearly reveal themselves as some of its dominant traits.

At first it seems impossible to view this subtle and complex mental attitude as a development of the naïve and rather coarse merriment of earlier times. Yet a slight examination of the choicest examples of what the discerning call humour would suffice to show that it finds its pasturage very much where the Greek or the mediæval populace found it. Topsy-turvyness, especially when it involves the fall of things from a height; stumbling and awkwardness of all kinds; human oddities when they grow to provocative dimensions; all self-inflation with a view to force a reluctant notice; the manifold masqueradings of mortals; the unfitnesses of things to the demands of circumstances; extravagances, perversities, and the multitudinous follies of men; these which move the rough man to his unconsidered cachinnation move also the humorous man to his slower and *sotto voce* note.

As our great woman humorist has it: "Strange as the genealogy may seem, the original parentage of that wonderful and delicious mixture of fun, fancy, philosophy and feeling, which constitutes modern humour, was probably the cruel mockery of a savage at the writhings of a suffering enemy—such is the tendency of things towards the better and more beautiful!"[257]

In asserting that gentle humour has its descent from such an uncouth ancestry, we must not be supposed to imply that its genesis has been a sudden or a simple process. As has been suggested, the sentiment is highly complex. It presupposes in its possessor the presence of a particular assemblage of qualities which may be expected to be rare; and a study of the development both of the individual and of the race tells us that this grouping of qualities is, of all the products of nature's laboratory, one of the most delicate, one exacting from her a very special effort of preparation.

Although humour is correctly described as a sentiment, its most apparent, if not most important condition, is a development of intelligence. It is plainly an example of what Mr. Meredith calls "the laughter of the mind," an expression which makes the large presupposition that we have this mind. It thrives best at the level of ideas. Yet the element of intellect which is vital to humour does not imply subtlety of mind, still less the presence of ideas remote from the plane of ordinary men's understanding. What is needed is a mind given to musing on what it observes—it may be that of a shrewd housewife—having a sufficient life and independence of movement to rise above the dull mechanical acceptance of things, to pierce these with the ray of a fresh criticism.

The distinguishing intellectual element in humorous contemplation is a larger development of that power of grasping things together, and in their relations, which is at the root of all the higher perceptions of the laughable. More particularly, it is a mental habit of projecting things against their backgrounds, of viewing them in their complete settings—so far as this involves those relations of contrariety which, as we have allowed, are of the essence of the ludicrous, in the stricter sense of the term. This comprehension of the setting is dependent on a process of *imaginative reflection;* for the background which humour requires is not the same as the visible background, but has, to a considerable extent, to be reinstated, or rather to be constructed.

This introduction into humour of something in the nature of a thinking process or reflection has this curious consequence, that it does not merely play about the realm of the serious, as the earlier and simpler laughter does, but comprehends, assimilates, and becomes toned down into half-play by something of the weightier import of things, of their value and their bearing on our welfare. This is the paradox, the secret of the humour-loving soul, irritating at once to the merely serious person and to the light-hearted trifler. In order to understand how this is effected, we shall, as will be seen presently, need to look at other elements besides the intellectual. Yet we shall do well to note the fact that the possibility of this meeting of the playful and the serious in the mood of humour has its intellectual condition in an enlarged mental grasp of things.

Our analysis of the objects which entice the laugh from man has suggested that the risible aspect nearly always coexists with other aspects. The kind of physical defect which is amusing may also be wrong æsthetically or hygienically, and so on of the rest. And though writers from Aristotle to Bain have been careful to point out that the laughable defect or degradation must in its magnitude be below the threshold of the painfully ugly, the blameworthy and so forth, it is perfectly clear that given a quick and comprehensive perception, and a turn for musing on what is perceived, the serious tendency in that which amuses us will come into the margin of the field of vision.

In this way, in the case of those who have developed the requisite combining organ, a kind of binocular mental vision has become possible. We enjoy pensively the presentation of Don Quixote, of Uncle Toby, and the other great humorous characters, just because we are in a mood in which, while giving ourselves up to an amusing spectacle, we nevertheless embrace in our reflective survey, and are affected by, something of its deeper meaning.

A full account of the humorous way of regarding things would trace out all the subtle interpenetrations of merry fooling and serious inspection, of a light and merry fancy and a sober reason. A hint, only, on their modes of combination, can be given here.

A finer appreciation of contrasts, and of relations generally, will often serve to enrich the impression given by a palpable instance of the laughable. A small plump child falls on the floor with sonorous effect: the sudden flopping down is fraught with entertainment for all men. The observer who can contemplate thoughtfully, enjoys the fall also, but more quietly and with a larger process of mental assimilation. His mind discerns in the trivial incident such things, perhaps, as the compact sturdiness of nature re-establishing itself by vigorous efforts duly announced by grunts, and the harmlessness of falls when bones and joints are young, as compared with those of the old, of which in many respects the child's fall may remind him. It is a train of ideas of this kind, though only half-consciously pursued, which gives to the thumping fall much of its value for the humorous observer.

Again, the development of the intelligence to a large and varied activity will, by quickening the faculty of seizing relations, open up new and spacious fields for the humorist's quiet contemplation. To one bringing a mental eye focussed for the amusing juxtaposition, and a temper disposed to muse on what he sees, how much of the entertaining may reveal itself in common sights, such as that of a thin wheezy man joining in shouts of a full-blooded Jingo crowd, or that of a woman, whose head has just been pommelled by her rightful lord, turning upon and "slanging" the bystander who has foolishly tried to curb an excessive assertion of marital rights.[258] The possession of ideas, again, will help a man at once sympathetically to realise and to transcend limited points of view when they come into collision, and so to gather much ruminating amusement. How large a scope, for example, for such quiet entertainment opens up in the rejoinder of Mrs. Flynn, an Irish lady who had been brought before a magistrate for assaulting her husband, and commiserated by that compassionate functionary on her sad plight with one eye closed and the head bandaged: "Och, yer worship, just wait till yez see Flynn". The recognition of the real proportions of a zest for battle and a taste for compassion in the stalwart Irish dame, unsuspected by kindly magistrates, at once gives us the point of view for a half-serious, half-amusing contemplation of human relations.

As these illustrations suggest, the point of view of the humorous observer is not a fixed one. Sometimes the freshness, the sense of liberation from the stupidly commonplace, will come by applying a rational idea to things which are not accustomed to the treatment. At other times, when the intelligence happens to be more sprightly, the new point of view is reached by a flight of fancy which loves to perch itself on some outlook far from that of a rational criticism. The humorous sort of mind delights in the play of inverting ordinary arrangements, say, of making man and beast, father and son, exchange places, or, as in Lewis Carroll's delightful instance of an ideal experiment, of putting the sane people in asylums and allowing the lunatics to go at large.259

It follows that humorous contemplation will have many shades of seriousness. In some instances, the proportion of the rational element leads us to speak of it as wisdom laughing,—"ridentem dicere verum"; in others, in which the predominance of a capricious fancy brings the expression near that of sportive wit, to describe it rather as laughter sobered by a word of wisdom. Yet it may be said that in every state which we describe as one of humorous enjoyment the rational element itself, affected by its alliance, puts on a half-festive attire, so that after all the whole mind may be said to join in the play.260

The humorous state is, however, much more than a peculiar modification of the processes of intelligence. It cannot be constituted by a mere train of cold perceptions and ideas. It means that the whole consciousness is for the time modified by the taking on of a new attitude or mood. The play of young fancy about the grave elderly form of reason, which is half-coaxed to play too, comes from this new tone of the whole mind.

This mental tone involves a peculiar modification of the conative processes. All laughing scrutiny of things, as a play-attitude, is a sort of relaxation of the set concentration of a conative purpose. Whenever we laugh, if it be only with a child at the jocosities of a clown, we are freed from the constraining force of the practical and even of the theoretical interests which commonly hold and confine our minds when we observe closely. In such moments we abandon ourselves to the tickling play of the object on our perceptions and ideational tendencies. In humour this self-abandonment takes on a shade of seriousness, not because the relaxation of the conative effort is less complete, but because the self-abandonment is that of a mind so habitually reflective that, even when it is at play, it does not wholly lose sight of the serious import of the thoughts which minister to its entertainment; because it dimly recognises the worth of the standard ideas, by the lightest allusion to which it is able to indulge in a playful criticism of what is presented.

The deeper secret of the mood of humour, however, lies in a peculiar modification of the feeling-tone of consciousness. In this, it is at once evident, we have to do with a special example of complexity. The laughter tinged with something akin to sadness is a mixture of feeling-tones; of tones, too, which seem directly opposed and likely to be mutually repugnant.

The gaiety of laughter begins to be complicated with an undertone by the half-intrusion into consciousness of the serious import of things. To be aware, however indistinctly, that the world has its serious side, is to lose the child's note of pure mirth, is to have a touch of sadness added to our laughter.

The more serious complication comes, however, when the regrettable side of the laughable object makes itself felt. The effect of this on the humorous person has nothing in common with that of the exhibition of folly on the contemptuous person. It is the very opposite to the feeling of one who rejoices in another's discomfiture as such. It is a sense of the implicated "pity of it". A person completely humorous is essentially sympathetic, skilled in the humane art of transporting himself to others' standpoints, of comprehending men's doings and words in the warm light thrown by the human affections. By some, indeed, sympathy is regarded as the great distinguishing characteristic of humour.261 But it seems well to add that it is the infusion of a proportionate amount of the sympathetic into our blithe survey of things which carries us far in the path of humorous appreciation. A sympathy of a step too quick for the sense of fun to keep abreast in friendly comradeship will, as Flaubert says happened in his case in later life,262 make an end of laughter.

It is but a step from this recognition of the regrettableness of what amuses us to a discernment of what, in its turn, tones down the sadness of regret, of the fine threads which attach the laughable defect to elements of real worth. Humour, of the richer kinds at least, certainly includes something of consideration, of a detection, in the laughable quality or its attachments, of suggestions of what is estimable and lovable.

The disposition to think well of what amuses us may come in the first instance from an impulse of gratitude. So ready are we in general to acknowledge another's entertainment of us that, even when the pleasure bestowed is known to have been given quite unwittingly, we cannot quite check the impulse to tender thanks.

Again, that which amuses us will often, when thoughtfully considered, show itself to be bound up with what is really estimable. It is exaggerations of good qualities which are so amusing, especially when through sheer obstinacy they tend to become the whole man, and to provoke while they entertain. Comedy will sometimes—in the figure of Molière's Alceste, for example—exhibit to us this clinging of the laughable to the skirts of excellence. But it is only to the more reflective mood of humour, to which comedy, as we shall see, does not appeal, that this coexistence of the quality and its defects, fully discloses itself.

Sometimes, too, even though we fail to discern its partial redemption through an organic connection with a worthy trait, a laughable defect may take on the appearance of a condonable and almost lovable blemish of character. Thus it is with the small imperfections seen in men recognised to be substantially good, imperfections which bring them nearer to us and so make them comprehensible. Thus, too, is it with the ignorances and simplicities of children, which, even while they bring the smile, disclose their worth as pure expressions of child-nature.

By speaking of a sentiment of humour we imply that the kindly feeling somehow combines with the gaiety of laughter in a new type of emotional consciousness. This combination, again, seems to involve a simultaneous presence in consciousness of the two elements, and not merely a rapid alternation of two phases of feeling. It is this simultaneous rise and partial fusion of a gay and a sad tone of feeling which differentiates humour proper from the feeling of ages to which the proximity of the laughable and the pathetic in things was familiar enough, as we may see, for example, from Pope's lines on Addison:—

> Who but must laugh if such a man there be?
>
> Who would not weep, if Atticus were he?

Again, as a harmonious blending of elements the sentiment of humour contrasts with that mere mixture of pleasurable and painful ingredients which Plato thought he detected in all laughter.263

The psychology of the emotions is still in a backward state, and we know very little about the laws of their fusion.264 One or two points may, however, be touched on.

It must be remembered that two feelings simultaneously excited may clash and refuse to combine in a peaceful whole. This commonly happens, indeed, when they are repugnant in kind, *e.g.*, pride and tenderness, and when both are powerfully excited. Emotional fusion means that this repugnance is somehow overcome, that the constituent emotive processes combine in some new current of consciousness. Not that the elements need be wholly submerged in the product; they may remain as tones remain in a chord, half-disclosed, though profoundly modified by their concomitants. Such a state of partial fusion may be illustrated in our moods of memory, in which delight in the recovery of lost experiences is tempered with regret.

The conditions of such a peaceful, harmonious confluence of dissimilar feelings are various. The effect may be furthered by the presence of points of affinity among the elements; whence the sentiments which dignify their objects, such as love and admiration, readily combine. This holds good to some extent of the constituents of humour, since amusement and something like tender regard for him who amuses us are plainly allied. Yet this consideration does not seem to help us in understanding how the two polar moods of hilarity and sadness should be able to combine.

We may be helped here by setting out from the fact of a simultaneous appeal to the dissimilar feelings by the same presentation. When this occurs again and again, it is probable that organic modifications may be effected by the simultaneous action of the double stimulus. Nobody begins by feeling amused and sorry at the same moment. The boy and the savage may have a moment of mild pity for an ugly piece of deformity; but this moment comes after the laughing is over. The co-presentation of the sad and the amusing had, we may be sure, to be repeated during many generations of men before the two currents could join in one smooth flow.

Those who find the core of an emotion in a widely diffused organic process may reason that such repetitions of a complex emotional stimulation may modify the nervous system in some way, so as to allow of the combination of some parts at least of the bodily resonances characteristic of the emotional constituents. For one thing, the fact, already alluded to, that there is a certain community of physiological process in the case of laughter and of the expression of grief, may help us, to some extent, to understand the combination.265 Yet mutual inhibition by the two sets of organic processes involved seems to be the principal agency in the case. The more energetic movements of laughter are without doubt restrained by an admixture of sympathy. Perhaps if we understood the physics of organic processes, we might speak here of an "interference," or, at least, of some antagonistic action between the motor-impulses of the laugh and of the sigh.

One other condition seems to be important. Where emotions are widely dissimilar and likely to be antagonistic, it is necessary that they should not both be excited in a high degree. We may succeed in getting a blend between a gentle laugh and a mild pity, though certainly not between a state of mirthful excitement and one of deep compassion. The moods of humour run in low keys, laughter and kindly sentiment being each toned down as if for smoother confluence. This need of a reduction of the force of consorting emotions may, too, find its explanation in the conditions of the organic processes which have to be combined. This does not imply, however, that the two feelings which unite in humour are of equal strength. As hinted above, humour seems always, even when an almost poignant sadness pierces it, to maintain itself at the level of a quiet enjoyment. It answers to the mood which has been called the luxury of pity, in which the sense of pain has shrunk away to a scarcely heard over-tone, while the ground-tone of alleviating tenderness sounds out clear and full.

This analysis may help us to understand why Mr. Meredith has called the laughter of Shakespeare and Cervantes "the richer laugh of heart and mind in one".266 It may help us, too, to interpret some things said by the German metaphysicians about laughter. Kant, for instance, redeems the poverty of his general theory by a memorable passage on the amusing aspect of a naïveté of behaviour which does not know how to hide itself. He allows that in this case there is mingled with the laughter—which he supposes to arise from an annihilation of the expectation of the customary—something of earnestness and of respect, as we reflect that what is infinitely better than accepted codes of manners (Sitte), namely, purity of natural disposition (Denkungsart), is not wholly extinguished in human nature.267

Our analysis of humour may help us to understand some well-recognised facts. It teaches us that a sentiment, at once complex and implying a mature reflection, must not be looked for in the young; it is the prerogative of the years which have hoarded experiences and learned to reflect. Nor, as implied in what was said above, is it to be sought for in the youth of the world. That humour is—in its clearest and fullest utterance at least—the possession of modern times, the period ushered in by the appearance of the great trio, Rabelais, Cervantes and Shakespeare, is explained by saying that, like music, it fits itself into the ways of our new spirit.

The apprehension of this complex basis of humour helps us, further, to understand somewhat the curious variations of the attitude among races and peoples. There are regions of civilisation where, so far as literary expression gives us the key, laughter seems to remain at, or at most only a little above, the level of the child's simple merriment. This appears to be true of certain portions of the East, where a considerable love of fun coexists with a predominant gravity of mind without interpenetration, almost without contact.268 Among certain races of Southern Europe, too, which have produced a rich literature of amusement, the blending of the serious and the playful, which is of the essence of humour seems to be but very imperfectly reached. The gaiety of the mediæval *Conte* is the gaiety of the Frenchman who, in spite of one or two literary exceptions, likes to keep his thinking and his mirth distinct, in their original purity and *netteté*.269 Frenchmen, such as M. Taine and M. Scherer, have fully recognised the fact that what we mean by humour is a product of the *triste nord*. What racial characteristics have served to further its growth in this region, it may not be easy to say. Perhaps, the closest approximation to an explanation may be found in the hypothesis that a vigorous germ of laughter fertilised by a disposition to brooding melancholy always tends to generate something of the nature of humour; and that, as we shall presently see, utility does something for its preservation.

The consideration of the complexity of the sentiment may throw light, further, on its modifications among the peoples which are correctly spoken of as endowed with it. These differences are roughly accounted for by saying that the proportions of gravity and gaiety, of serious reflection and playful fancy vary indefinitely. They are certainly different, let us say, in the case of the Englishman, the American, the Scotchman and the Irishman. Yet this consideration does not account for all the dissimilarity. Since humour is playfulness modified by the whole serious temper of a man, we should expect it to differentiate itself into many shades according to the trend of the ideas, interests, impulses and the rest which distinguishes one sort of mind or character from another. We can only fully understand the contrast between American and English, or between Irish and Scotch, humour, when we understand the differences of character. An amusing Irish or Scotch story, one, that is to say, which is produced for home-consumption, seems to be redolent of the whole temperament, mind and character of the people. It is this complexity of the sentiment which makes the amiable effort to illustrate the humour of other peoples by published selections a pathetic futility. How can one expect, for example, the ordinary Englishman to get into touch with that fine product of child's fun, quick fancy, alert sympathy, open-heartedness, and a deep brooding sentiment which meets him in the humour of the Irishman? It is enough to remember how he is wont to laugh his superior laugh at an Irish bull, as if this were necessarily an unconscious "howler," whereas it may be, in reality, a charming expression of a most amiable trait of character.270

A due recognition of the complexity of the sentiment discloses to us a point of capital importance: humour, in the sense of a perfect fusion of play and gravity, of the aggressiveness of laughter and kindly consideration, is, as already hinted, pre-eminently an endowment of individuals rather than of races. It presupposes a basis of temperament which, though it may be favoured by certain racial characters, is only realised where nature hits upon a particular proportion among the elements by the mixing of which she produces an individual; and so nice an operation is this mixture, that humour, of the full rich quality at least, is perhaps less frequently handed down from parent to child than specific forms of talent.

The old writers treated humour by help of their general theory of temperaments as compounded of certain physical elements. The learned Burton, for instance, in the chapter already quoted, discourses agreeably of pleasant vapours which break from the heart, and thinks that these may explain why the melancholy are witty, as Aristotle suggested. The passage is valuable as indicating that antiquity recognised the connection between laughter and the melancholy disposition. Modern testimony might be added. Thus Savage Landor remarks that genuine humour, as well as true wit, requires a sound and capacious mind, which is always a grave one;[271] and Tennyson notes that humour "is generally most fruitful in the highest and most solemn human spirits".[272]

The need of this deep and massive seriousness, if not of a marked tendency to sombre reflection, seems to be borne out by what we know of the great humorists. Sainte-Beuve regards Rabelais, who was a grave doctor, and who worthily represented in his public lectures at Lyons "the majesty of science," as writing with the quite serious purpose of throwing out in advance certain ideas of deep import (*de grand sens*) "dans un rire immense". Much the same is true of Cervantes, who is said—though the assertion has been challenged—to have conceived of his delightful romance in the dreary surroundings of a sponging-house.[273] The germination of a mirthful sense in the soil of a serious character has been noted, indeed, in the case of some who represent the lighter moods of comedy—a fact which points to the more general relation of laughter to seriousness spoken of in an earlier chapter. Thus Sainte-Beuve, writing of Molière, says that he was called "the contemplative"; and was wont to be taken with sadness (*tristesse*) and melancholy when he was alone.[274] Victor Hugo has somewhere spoken of him as "ce moqueur pensif comme un apôtre". It was remarked of Sheridan and other dealers in the mirthful by those who knew them that they seldom even smiled.

It is easy to see that the transformation of laughter which we find in humour will carry with it a large modification of the range of enjoyment. While, as has been admitted, the changes of feeling and mental attitude involved will tend to restrain the earlier reckless merriment, they will also add vast regions to the territory of the amusing.

With regard to restriction, one must protest against the common misapprehension, that the development of humour spoils the taste for simple modes of mirth. I have known sad-looking humorists who were well endowed with the valuable capability of joining in children's fun. What humour does undoubtedly restrain is any tendency in laughter which smacks of the brute and the bully in man.

On the other hand, the field of objects over which humour wanders bee-like gathering its honey is vastly greater than any region known to the rougher and more brutal merriment. The introduction of a reflective element and of higher points of view expands the horizon to an incalculable extent.

This change in point of view means at once that we penetrate below the surface of things, reaching the half-veiled realities, and that we envisage them in a network of relations. The former is illustrated in the humorist's finer contemplation of behaviour as a revelation of character. An amplitude of enjoyment is secured by the circumstance that, even in the case of the self-vigilant, intellectual and moral weaknesses have a way of peeping out which is most convenient for a humorous onlooker who has his mental eye duly accommodated. When, for example, a young teacher, asked by an examiner to explain "congenital tendency," wrote, "It is the tendency to be congenial and pleasant: children vary in this characteristic," the entertainment of the error for the reader lay in the naïve disclosure of the preoccupation of the writer's mind with the chequered fortunes of her profession. Or again, when another candidate from the same class, in describing the qualifications of a teacher, wrote: "He should be as intimately acquainted with the workings of a child's mind as the engine-driver is with the engine," the fun of the comparison for the reader came from the detection of an unscientific habit of mind, natural enough in an over-zealous worker, intruding, unobserved, into theoretic reflection.

These innocent self-revelations meet the watchful eye of the humorist everywhere in the haunts of men. They lie like hoar frost in the sun on his surroundings, on which he unwittingly casts a reflection of the habits of his mind and of the directions of his taste; as when in a large town bizarre juxtapositions of the vulgar heroic strike the observer's eye in the names of streets, or of loose engines on a railway.

To this finer penetration the humorous faculty adds a vision for relations which distinguishes the higher kind of judgment. What we call the ludicrous in character is, indeed, always to some extent a matter of relations. As implied above, it is the view of some trait set in a particular milieu which brings the smile. The hidden weakness may entertain because of its juxtaposition with something that is worthy, or at least has an appearance of worth. In a certain kind of impulsive person, for example, there discloses itself to the humorous eye an almost admirable consistency in the recurring inconsistencies; while, on the other hand, in another sort of character, that eye will rather spy an inconsistency within the limits of a quality, as when a person, on the whole generous, lapses into a kind of niggardliness in certain small particulars of expenditure, as if to show that even a moral quality, firmly planted, needs the sunlight of intelligence. In many cases the entertainment in observing character comes, not so much through a perception of the juxtaposition of something worthy and something slightly unworthy, as through a detection of some discrepancy between the character and the *rôle* assumed at the moment, as when a self-assertive sense of justice, in "a child of larger growth," reveals itself in the quaint exaggeration of doing more than justice to oneself. No better terrain, indeed, for a chase after the imperfectly masked will be found than that of the manners of persons who are quite above suspicion of serious fault. Perhaps it is a certain kind of woman who shows the greatest skill in this humorous reading of character, as when she sets herself to decipher the palimpsest of manners in one educated rather late in life, detecting traces of the earlier cramped hand below the thin caligraphy of a later culture.

To a finer perception of relations, again, must we ascribe the readiness to enjoy the large and variegated presentment of unsuitabilities of men to their circumstances. The situations in which the merry god, who seems to arrange the puppet show, often chooses to place us are pregnant of ironical suggestion to the contemplative eye of humour. The necessity of confronting what nature never intended that we should confront makes us an amusing spectacle to the twinkling eyes above us. How delightful for example is the variety of social juxtaposition which brings embarrassment to the encounterers. When it is not accident but a man's foolish impulse, unmindful of limitations of capability, which pushes him into the awkward situation, as when his civility plunges him into discourse in a foreign language with a fellow-traveller, or when the most undecided of men attempts to make a proposal of marriage, the value of the situation for the humorous observer is greatly enhanced.

As with the topsy-turvyness of momentary situation, so with more permanent incongruities between character and surroundings. In this case a more special gift of humorous insight is needed; for to the many what lasts grows seemingly right by its mere durability. You may make a highly unsuitable person a bishop, or the editor of a comic journal, and you will find that, for most onlookers, time will soon begin to invest the position with a sort of suitability. Even an ill-matched connubial pair will take on something of mutual appropriateness through this influence of the customary on human judgments. But the eye of the humorous onlooker, guided by ideas, entertains itself with stripping off the trappings of convention and use.

This humorous quizzing of the characters and of the revealed mental processes of those about us has grown, in the case of a few, into a chief pastime. The development in these days of a keener interest in character, which is partly reflected in, partly the product of, modern fiction, has led these few to something like a sustained and methodical survey of their acquaintances and their friends, in which the quiet laughter of the humorist may find ample room. A part of the temperate mirth in this case springs out of the delightful surprises—the result of the complexity of organic products and of the limitations of our powers of prediction. The appearance of a moral metamorphosis when a man comes under the influence of some new force, say a wife, or the invasion of his social world by a war-craze, may amuse a humorous observer much as the semblance of a physical transformation amuses him. In this habitual contemplation by a humorous person of those he knows, there is, evidently, a blending of amusement with kindly interest. That is, indeed, the note of much of the "psychologising" at which many, instructed by the best fiction, now try their hand. The combination of the playful with the respectful attitude is nowhere more plainly seen than in our new estimates of diversity of character and of individuality. The contemplation of the result of some new experiment of nature in the variation of the human type, will always bring something of the gaiety which is provoked by the sight of a fresh oddity; yet our new regard for individuality, as discriminated from eccentricity, brings down the mirthful utterance to the low tones of humour.

There is another way in which the development of the humorous faculty enlarges the sphere of the risible. In the simple nature of children and uncultured adults, fun and seriousness tend to dwell apart. The introduction of a serious element into the mood of amusement, which is at the basis of humour, makes a breach in the dividing wall. As a consequence, the humorist, though a profoundly serious person, will show a readiness in the midst of grave occupations to digress for a moment at the prick of some ludicrous suggestion. Good talkers and letter-writers, including women with the quick ear for the bubblings of fun, are thus given to momentary interruptions of serious discourse by side-glances at amusing aspects, and many persons who take themselves to be humorists are apt to be shocked at the proceeding. Yet, in truth, the extent to which a man succeeds in making laughter permeate the sphere of the serious, without loosening its deep-laid foundation of gravity, is one of the best measures of the vitality of his humour. It is this resolute yet perfectly respectful invasion of the domain of the serious by humour which has made a good deal of modern literature possible. Of this, more anon: it may suffice for the present to call attention to a work of a friend of mine dealing with a subject which might well seem to be dismally serious—logic itself, a work which attempts with conspicuous success, while maintaining the dignity of the science, to relieve its heaviness by a good number of amusing remarks and illustrations.275

Yet the expansion of the range of enjoyment when mindless mirth gives place to humour is not wholly due to the absorption of a serious element. One chief limitation of the more common kind of laughter arises from the circumstance that it is apt to be disagreeable to the person who is its object. This dislike, again, is due, as we have seen, to a natural feeling of resentment at being taken down and treated as an inferior. So long as the laughter retains a distinct vibration of the old note of contempt, we must resist it; but when it grows mellow and kindly we are ready to withdraw the objection. There is nothing so terrible in having fun poked at our foibles, or even at our petty misfortunes, so long as we know that a friendly face is hiding behind the laughing mask. If a person only gives the assurance in his way of laughing that contempt is drowned in a more genial sentiment, he may laugh at his children, aye at his parents, too, even when they grow old and infirm. Nor is a previous knowledge of friendly disposition always needed. There are a few whose mellow laughter will instantly disarm resistance in a stranger—in the street boy, for example, though he has the double sensitiveness of the poor and of the young.

From this frank acceptance of others' overtures of a friendly laughter to the practice of a humorous self-criticism, there would seem to be but a step. If humour always involves some degree of sympathetic self-projection into the object of contemplation, it should not be difficult to turn the humorous glance upon one's own foibles. Self-inspection is a thing of various kinds, and there are varieties of it (for example, the performances of the "moi spectateur" in the case of that curious young lady, Marie Bashkirtseff) which are removed by the amplitude of the sky from humorous self-quizzing. The last is perhaps the most rarely practised. Before he can accomplish it, a person must not only have developed a "higher ego" capable of criticism in the light of ideas, but have learned to see himself as others—especially humorous onlookers—see him, a feat hardly less difficult than that of getting a glimpse of the crown of one's head.

That the doings of the lower ego, or rather cluster of egos, are fitted to afford an ample supply of the amusing goes without saying. Human nature is so oddly compounded, even in the best of us, that it only needs the clear vision to detect incongruity and the masking of the real. Thus, it is frequently easy to spy the stealthy advances of rudimentary tendencies which seem hardly to belong to us, and which we are disposed to disown; still more frequently, to light on a whole crop of little inconsequences which are due to the complexity of our soul's workings, and to the irremovable circumstance that, however predominant some better part of us seems to be for the moment, the suppressed forces turn out to be only half-suppressed. It is well when such self-scrutiny can be carried on without any risk of encountering forms of ugliness and of ill omen, which would make speedy end of the amusing exercise.

The quiet fun that may be enjoyed by occasional glances at ourselves is so palpable, that it hardly seems conceivable how any true humorist should fail to pluck the tempting fruit. Yet when one finds a man who is wholly incapable of accepting another's playful laughter, it seems a fair inference that he will be found lacking in the disposition to amuse himself with conning his own doings. The resentment which a distinguished purveyor of mirthful entertainment will sometimes exhibit at being treated with a humorous freedom, say by a lady interviewer whose overtures have been rejected with needless emphasis, suggests that a mind may train itself in the detection of the ludicrous in the larger show outside, and yet remain blind to all the comic aspects of the microcosm within. Perhaps every humorous contemplator of things has some "blind spot," of the existence of which he is just as ignorant as of his retinal blind-spot; and if this failure of sensibility chances to render invisible the whole of the humorist's own behaviour, the contraction of the field of vision is certainly a considerable one.

We have seen that the earlier forms of human laughter have their uses as contributing to the stability or the improvement of a society or social group. When, however, we turn to the milder and more complex sentiment of humour we appear to lose these social benefits. As has been implied, the development of the sense of humour in any vigorous and fruitful form is a rarity, so much so as to condemn its possessor in a large measure to a solitary kind of satisfaction. The change may be expected to effect a transformation of the serviceable function of laughter, to make it, in the main, a thing wholesome, refreshing and edifying of character, to the individual himself.

It is true, no doubt, that a refined humour is capable of being turned at times to the same social uses as its ancestor, the elemental laughter of the people. One may see, in the journalism and literature of the hour, foibles, exaggerations and other amusing things dealt with in a humorous or quasi-humorous temper. The gentleness to which humour inclines allows, indeed, of attacks on parties, schools and personalities which would otherwise run the risk of being condemned as "bad form". Yet something of a serious practical purpose, namely, to hold up to ridicule, can always be detected in this kind of writing: whence it is correctly designated, not as humour, but as "social satire".

On the other hand, the moods of humour are admirably fitted for that *indirect* adaptation of the individual to social conditions which we call self-criticism. This humorous self-quizzing may be started by the spectacle of comedy, as Lessing and others suggest; yet this, as we shall see later, is not to be counted on. If a man wants promptly to detect the first flecks of dust on the bright surface of character, he must be habitually ready to note this surface.

This office of humour in helping us to nip evil tendencies in the bud may be viewed, in part, as the vicarious discharge by the critical self of the restraining function of the community on the individual. None of us can safely wander far and long from the point of wholesome contact with the community, that is to say, with the good sense and the right feeling embodied in a community. To master the not too easy art of seeing ourselves as others—for whose judgment we should care—see us is surely eminently fitting for those who desire to laugh at what is objectively laughable.

Nevertheless, it must not be supposed that in such private self-correction we are always at the social point of view. Humour is the outgrowth of a pronounced individuality; its possession seems always to imply that a person forms his own ideas of the value of things, guided of course by the world's teachers, but caring little whether his views agree with those which happen to obtain in his community at the moment. Here, again, in the high service rendered by a vigilant humour, we find the work of reflection carried out by the help of ideas or ideal conceptions, which are in part a product of the individual mind. The laughing rebuke administered to some folly, which lifts its head once more after many repressive blows, comes from the ideal self; which, though it must have nourished itself in some "communion of saints," becomes in the end free and self-legislative. "Correction" seems too strong a word to use for this prophylactic function; for, as we have seen, humour does not readily lend itself as an instrument to serious purposes. What the habit of a quick humorous perception does for its subject here is best described, perhaps, as the fostering of a pure and wholesome atmosphere in the soul, in which disease-germs must perforce die of inanition.

We may now turn to those uses of humour, into the conception of which the thought of a practical aim can hardly intrude. Humour as amusement is something agreeable and cheering. It has the refreshing properties of primitive laughter and much more; for, as a mood that feeds itself on reflective contemplation, it is consolatory and sustaining in a way in which mere gaiety, even when it persists as a temper of mind, cannot be. Apropos of Voltaire's saying that heaven had given us two things to counterbalance the many miseries of life, hope and sleep, Kant remarks: "He could have added laughter, if the means of exciting it in reasonable men were only as easily attainable, and the requisite wit or originality of humour were not so rare" (as some other endowments).276

When the humorous bent is lively and "original," it will stand its possessor in good stead in more than one way, amid the toilings and moilings of life. Seeing that laughter is always in a measure a throwing aside of serious pressure, we should expect it to come to our aid in the workaday hours. But it is only when the eye for the sparkling of fun in things has been instructed by humorous reflection that the alleviating service of mind-play is fully realised.

For one thing, the possession of a large humorous insight will greatly extend the scope of the conciliative function of laughter. All cajoling must be good-natured, or at least conceal the sting of laughter; but the finer disarming of men by banter requires the reflective penetration of the humorist. One may easily see this in the art of conciliating opponents, political and other. The winning force of a manifested good-nature will sometimes act on those who are far from appreciating the play of mind involved. The *gêne* introduced by an awkward situation,277 the tendencies that make for loss of interest, for weariness, for a falling away from a perfect sympathetic touch, in all human relations—these things find their most effective counteractive in occasional intrusions of the humorous spirit. I think here of one no longer among us, with whom I once had the privilege of co-operating in a long and difficult piece of public business; and of how all weariness was kept out of sight by laughing side-glances at threatening absurdities, frequent enough to have suggested a premeditated plan had they not been so delightfully spontaneous.

Perhaps, the stoutest obstacle to the smooth flow of social intercourse is the tendency in men to lay stress on their personal importance. The superior airs, which seem with some to be as much *de rigueur* as their correct attire, are sadly inimical to companionship, whether the would-be companion be a man's wife or a contributor to his journal. The one sure safeguard against the stupid clogging of the social wheels, which this chronic stiffening of the figure introduces, is the gift of a lively humour, whose alert eye would at once note a possible laughableness of deportment for onlookers. One may see this function of humour illustrated in that instinctive readiness of one who has had a perfect social training to dismiss laughingly from conversation the first appearance of an allusion to himself and his claims.

In all this, though there may be no conscious aiming at an end, social utility is not wholly wanting. Yet just because it is an individual temper, humour confers its chief benefits on its possessor in the privacy of life. Its solacings and its refreshings come to him through the channel of a new and genial manner of reflecting on his mishaps and his troubles.

Most men who have developed any appreciable fund of humour must know how the petty annoyances of life can be laughed away, almost as soon as they are seen advancing. When, for example, your lost pencil is discovered in its hiding-place between the leaves of a rarely consulted book; or, on the other hand, after endowing it with various sorts of mischievous flight, you perceive it lying close by you on the desk, where it has been dutifully complying with its proper law of inertia; you may snatch a compensating laugh from a moment's reflection on the small ironies of things, or on the vast wastefulness of the world in the matter of hypotheses. Your vexation at the children who are at play in the road in front of your bicycle and refuse to retire till your bell rings a third time, instantly gives way to an agreeable smile as you sympathetically shift the point of view by recalling the fact that they are on their proper playground. The dreary ugliness of a London street in winter will now and again be lit up as with sunshine for you if your eye is focussed for the amusing, as when the driver of a slow van goes on nodding in blissful ignorance, while the driver of your 'bus behind, justly proud of his vehicle's speed, pelts him mercilessly with the most awakening of epithets.

It is much the same with the small vexations inflicted by our social world. We may no doubt feel hurt just for a moment when, at a concert, we see a big hat thrust itself betwixt our eyes and a face which has held them captive, wearing a look of the tragic muse as it leans yearningly over the violin from which it seems, like a mother's face, to draw the sobbing tones. Yet, even as the nerve smarts, we may half-seize the glorious absurdity of the hat and its bobbings. Or, again, when an untimely call interrupts some bit of nice thinking and leaves the nerves tingling, we may smile for a moment as we catch a glimpse of the simple faith of the visitor in the supreme importance of the cause he pleads, a glimpse sufficient to make us half-aware of a like "subjectivity" in our own estimation of selected tasks. Social bores are vexations which, perhaps, ought not to be called petty. Humorous persons, one suspects, are specially exposed to their attacks, since they are a tolerant folk, preferring on the whole to suffer rather than to hurt others. But here, also, the humorous have their remedies. It suffices, for example, to reflect for a short moment on the droll pathos of the circumstance that persons, between whom and ourselves we find no attaching sympathies, should select us for their importunate attentions. Even when the destinies throw us together with men and women from whom we instinctively recoil, as from creatures of a species at once closely akin to ours yet sundered from us by impassable boundaries, a reflective humour may devise alleviations. The aggressive self-assertion of a plutocrat, with his "buy-you-up" sort of stare, and the rest, may wound for half a moment; but a laughing solace comes on the heels of worry; for there is a quiet pleasure in looking back and discovering the clumsy construction of the vulgar "snub;" and in any case a playful half-glance at higher measures of worth restores the equanimity.

Even greater troubles may, to the trained humorist, disclose amusing aspects or accompaniments, so that refreshment reaches us even while the blow still hurts. The relieving smile may come by way of a playful contemplation of ourselves as pitted against our mighty superior, circumstance; for it is possible to find something amusing, as well as irritating, in the ironies of destiny. The idea of a struggle with fate, which gives the zest of life to brave hearts, helps, too, to bring the reflective mind back to the play-mood. The readers of Miss Kingsley's *Travels* need not to be reminded of the fecundity of amusing reflection which her humour showed in circumstances which would have depressed many a man.278 It was with a like readiness to smile that Goldsmith's genial spirit faced the blows of destiny, giving back, as his biographer has it, in cheerful humour or whimsical warning what it received in mortification or grief. In his celebrated character, Mark Tapley, Dickens has no doubt illustrated how in the rough waters of his youth he learned to draw humorous entertainment from massive troubles. It is this playful shimmer of a light thrown by an entertaining idea on the surface of a misfortune which rids it of the worst of its gloom.

By a line of humorous reflection already suggested, we may in all cases of worry and moral disturbance reach the consolatory idea that the trouble has, in the first view of it, been grossly exaggerated. At the moment when the sensitive tissue is lacerated the shock of pain blinds us to dimensions; our disappointment fills the outlook, like a thunder-storm. The healthy nervous organism will show its vitality in the rapidity of the recuperative process; and this is often effected by a quick turning of the thoughts to other and brighter parts of the scene which the trouble has for a moment blotted out, and to the proportions of the one to the other. A trouble—like the all-enveloping thunder-storm—begins to retire almost smilingly as soon as we discern its boundaries.

In much of this alleviating service of humour the laugh which liberates us from the thraldom of the momentary is a laugh at ourselves. Indeed, one may safely say that the benefits here alluded to presuppose a habit of reflective self-quizzing. The blessed relief comes from the discernment of a preposterousness in the forcing of our claims, of a folly in yielding to the currents of sentiment which diffuse their mists over the realm of reality. The coming of the smile announces a shifting of the point of view; the maladjustment, which a moment ago seemed to be wholly on the side of our world, showing itself now to be on our side as well.

How far humour will help a man in throwing off troubles one cannot say. Even when the flash of bright reflection fails to dispel the darkness, it may secure a valuable moment of respite. When the trouble has real magnitude, the dismissive smile grows hard for all save the elect. Few of us, perhaps, could rise to the height of serene irony attained by a German musician whose wife had eloped with his master.279 Many might be disposed to think that the woman who, after nursing her husband through a fatal illness, remarked that it was only a sense of humour which had kept her from failing, was less than human. Yet it is highly risky to infer, from the fact of an intrusion of the humorous temper into calamity, the existence of a low degree of moral sensibility. It may rather be that those who suffer most are beholden in an exceptional degree to this kind solacer of men's woes.

This service of humour, at once consolatory to suffering and corrective of one-sidedness of view, is perfected by a development of that larger comprehensive vision which is reached when the standpoint of egoism is transcended. Even the beginning of humour implies some getting away from the point of view of the individual, so far as to gain a momentary comprehension of others' points of view. The great educative value of being laughed at is that it compels attention to the fact of a multiplicity of such points. How good a lesson, one thinks, it must have been for the Scotch professor to hear his disgusted caddie remark: "Anybody can teach Greek, but gowf needs a heid".

There remains for brief illustration another service which humour renders its possessor, though in truth it may turn out to be only a further development of the one just dealt with. Laughter at things, being primarily an accompaniment of observation, remains in its highest forms chiefly an amusement at outside spectacles. The resources of a mature faculty of humour may lend themselves to the end of an enjoyable contemplation of one's social world, both in its parts and as a whole. The value of humour to the individual can, indeed, only be rightly measured when the large possibilities of entertainment which lie in criticising one's surroundings are borne in mind.

The enjoyment which a humorous observer is able to gather from the contemplation of the social scene implies that he make his own standpoint, that he avoid the more turbulent part of the social world and seek the quiet backwaters where he can survey things in the calm light of ideas. One who lives wholly in the giddy throng will never be able to see things in the perspective which humorous appreciation requires. Nor is this all; if he live, move and have his being in the commotion, he will be forced to repress mirthful impulses and to show the hurrying figures about him a certain respect, since any generous indulgence in the joys of laughter would be likely to bring him into unpleasant collisions.

That there is much in the social spectacle which falls only to the eye of one half-retired is certain. The vagaries of "society," in the conventional sense of the term, are one of the traditional matters of laughter; our comic journals have enlightened even dull minds on this point. It is pleasant to a humorous contemplation to note the high pretensions of the "fine world"; how naïvely, for instance, it assumes that it holds all the men of brains and all the good talkers in its service;280 pleasant, that is to say, to one who bears in mind some of the characteristics of this world, such as a certain emptiness in the matter of ideas, together with something of the readiness of a certain kind of dog to follow any self-appointed leader, and an amiable impartiality in crowning any sort of "hero" that happens to be trumpeted, whether potentate from the East or showman from the West. It is entertaining, too, to note how enclosed it remains within its purely arbitrary standards, being rather shocked, for example, to find when it travels that there can be such a thing as "society" in Italy which is not a "dining society". This, and much more, will often draw the eye of humour, oddly enough, in the same direction as that of an awe-struck flunkeyism.

It is an agreeable pastime, too, for our half-retired observer to watch the fierce struggles of men and women in these days to gain a footing within the charmed circle. Here, surely, the gyrations of the moral figure reach the height of absurdity. Nowhere does there seem to reflection to be quite such a disproportion between effort and its doubtful reward as in these labours of the hot and panting to win a footing on the fashionable terrain.

What makes the scene the more pathetically droll is that success never seems to satisfy; the necessity of getting in is followed by a no less dire necessity of keeping oneself visible in the tightly-packed crowd. The sensitiveness of men of high position to the least sign of neglect in their goddess is something that cannot fail to tickle a humorous fancy. It is said that high officials once passed unhappy days and nights waiting for an invitation to dinner. The occasion was a national festival, when some inventive dames, taking themselves apparently quite seriously as representative women of the age, proceeded each to invite a representative male. So do the gods give us harvest of laughter by sowing vanity with its small spitefulnesses in the minds of men, and setting "society" to lure them to her thraldom.

To the dispassionate eye of reason, no "society" which is founded on birth or on a mixed basis of birth and wealth has seemed quite worthy of this servile attitude. Certainly in these days, when, as the Berlin Hofschneider is said to have observed to Prince Bismarck at the Opera Ball, society is rather mixed (*ein bischen gemischt*), rational men might be expected to leave this kind of homage to the weak-minded. No doubt men of mind caught in the snare have been ready to admit this; yet it may be questioned whether, when they set down their endurance of the boredom of the diner-out to the social ambition of their wives, they evade the laughter of the gods.

Pity may find a place at the side of laughter when she visits these absurd scenes. A peep behind the masks will, it has been said, show here, too, the thinnest pretence of gaiety. Dull with something of the dulness of death are many of the older faces, even when they force themselves to produce grimaces and spasmodic cacklings, thin and anæmic like themselves. It looks as if it were a dram of excitement, and not pleasure, which these loyal worshippers of society are seeking; only to find, perhaps, that the hope of excitement itself has grown illusory.

Yet, in speaking of the entertaining aspects of the social spectacle, one need not confine oneself to the fashionable scene. "Society," charmingly irrational as she is, has no monopoly in the matter of the incongruities. The doings of the Great Middle Class and even of the Masses have their amusing aspects for the unprejudiced eye. All phases of social life, indeed, may yield rich entertainment to one who has the mental vision justly accommodated.

What first strikes the eye here, perhaps, is the fine display of human oddities. The newspaper, fully alive to the value of things new, gives welcome to the self-revelations of human folly, perverted ingenuity, and uncontrollable vanity. The struggle for its coveted column seems hardly less violent than that for the fashionable gathering. Apparently, the supreme necessity is to show yourself, to win the pestered and rather jaded eye of a crowd, if only for an instant. Many and wonderful are the movements and sounds to which children, feeling themselves overlooked, have been known to resort in order to compel notice: yet the frantic efforts of men and women to advertise themselves to the public eye are, surely, not less numerous or less strange. Even when they have left the social scene these self-advertisers will sometimes still try to seize your eye by sending you an autobiography, consisting largely, it may be, of an account of all the dinner parties attended—a priceless thing for the historian, perhaps, if only the writer had happened to be a politician.

The vanity in this self-advertisement does not always lie on the surface, a partial self-blinding being of the humour of it. A person may be pushed on to the advocacy of a bottomless craze by a belief in a special mission so earnest, as completely to hide from him the inflated self-estimation which lurks in the attitude; and the recognition, by the quiet onlooker, of this malicious way of Nature's, in hiding from men so large a part of their own motives, draws back the corners of the mouth yet farther.

The absurdity of this forcing of oneself on the notice of the public, like that of pushing one's way into "society," grows clearer when we reflect on the real value of the object of pursuit. It is the fashion just now to deify public opinion. Yet spite of the classical dictum, it is not always flattering to the deity to identify the two voices. A modern democratic society is apt to exhibit very much the same plasticity to the hand of the crafty moulder as that on which the wise Greek sprinkled his dainty irony. To be able to see through the pretty pretence that the demos "forms" its opinions, and that its verdicts on statesmen, generals and other notabilities are consequently sacred, is to have one chief qualification for enjoying the fun of the show. How entertaining, for instance, is the proceeding when an editor invites a census of opinion on books, or other things which postulate some discernment. In this case, too, the humour of it lies in the circumstance that the good people who are lured into the trap honestly think that they are giving their own individual judgments. Still more delightful do these performances become when an editor, with his sense of the value of names fully awake, applies to celebrities, and entertains us, say, with a church dignitary's conception of the ideal Music Hall, or with a popular jockey's views on the proper dimensions of a scientific manual.

These exhibitions of authority for the guidance of the public sufficiently testify to its docility before any kind of proffered leadership. The very bigness of the modern demos, assisted by its "holy simplicity" of mind, lays it open to the wiles of the charlatan. How can one expect the worthy tradesman reading in the solitude of his back parlour to gauge the authority of his newspaper guide? It is more than he can do, perhaps, to take the measure of his Sunday instructor. He who reflects thus will find much to entertain him in the way of make-believe, when he examines the foundations of imposing reputations, or of the proud boast of political leaders that they carry "the Country" with them.

The newspaper, highly respectable institution as it undoubtedly is, entertains those in search of humorous enjoyment in other ways too. Its very standpoint as issuer of news leads to an amusing exaggeration of the importance of anything which happens to thrust its head up at the moment. An idea, aye and a fallacy too, old as the ages, will secure attention if only somebody with a name happen to bring it up anew. Whence comes the neomania which we see on all hands, the absurd exaltation of the latest novel and the rest. Yet more exhilarating to humorous inspection is the naïve assumption of the newspaper and its clients that everything happens in order to furnish them with news. I remember a paper, not of a low class, seriously contending, when a disagreeable *cause célèbre* had to be re-tried, that, since everybody had made up his mind on the case, a new trial was most regrettable. The frank suggestion that the proceedings of our law courts have their final cause in the satisfaction of a craving for news in readers of journals was, doubtless, an editorial slip; yet the assumption is often discoverable to a penetrating eye. The point of view reminds one of the joyous antics of the Italian children who follow the cavalcade of the diligence and its "supplements" as it descends southwards to the level of the olive-groves, sure in their glee that the rattling procession, and the "soldi" too, have come for their delight. In view of the entertainment afforded by the press in these days, one may sometimes wonder whether the expression "comic journal" is not growing into a pleonasm.

Humour will keep at our elbow, too, if we push deeper, and, lifting the wrappings of convention, insist on seeing the realities. The involutions of public utterance when, say, a dubious appointment has to be defended, are in themselves no less entertaining an exhibition of naïveté disclosed through elaborate wrappings than the romancings of a naughty child beating about for an excuse. No kind of spectacle, perhaps, is more uplifting to a spirit given to the right sort of reflection, none too which has a larger promise of unwearying variation, than the wrigglings of the human mind when tangled in awkward appearances, and forced to find something which looks like a way of logical escape.

As all who read are aware, the vagaries of "society" and the drolleries of public life are no new spectacle. Other times and patterns of society have had their entertaining aspects fixed for us by the half-retired chronicler. Yet there is much to suggest that the social scene of to-day bears the palm, as illustrator of the volume and the many-sidedness of the laughable. The bigness of our social scheme, its instability and "go-aheadness," its reckless activity—these and other features, aided by the eagerness of people to gain publicity for their doings and a corresponding readiness of journals to accord it, appear to secure for the quiet onlooker to-day the enjoyment of an exuberant crop of personal oddities, pushful pretences, disparities between position and qualification, and the other amusing features of the social scene.

Much of the drollery of the social spectacle here touched on may be enjoyed with a certain detachment, and even with a *soupçon* of the malice which characterises the laughter of those outside the social group, within which the merry showman is erecting his stage. The kindlier note of humour enters here only as a subordinate element, as a good-natured toleration of folly, supported by a more or less distinct comprehension of it under the head of worthy qualities sadly perverted. It must be otherwise if the bizarre and provocative spectacle of folly's head obtrudes itself into a season of national storm and stress, say of war-commotion, when the observer of things cannot, unless he be an unsocial cynic, any longer consent to be detached. The very possibility of a laugh, or even of a smile, might seem to be excluded as a desecration. If it is possible, it can only be through the discovery of a *modus vivendi* between the mirthful impulse and some of the deepest and most absorbing of our feelings and impulses. Our analysis of humour has prepared us for a considerable penetration of the mellowed kind of mirth into the heart of the serious, for a fine and rapid detection by the practised eye of amusing aspects of situations and experiences which appeal directly and powerfully to the acuter feelings and to the sterner attitudes. We may, perhaps, find the crowning illustration of this interpenetration of the serious and the playful in the possibility of a humorous glance at things which must stir the heart-depths of every true citizen.

The truth, that a state of war will develop in citizens much that is good and admirable, has, perhaps, been sufficiently recognised; while, on the other hand, its ravages and its sufferings have been a frequent theme of the eloquent lip and pen. Less attention has, for pretty obvious reasons, been paid to those aspects and accompaniments of the state which seem to some, when regarded from the point of view of the normal type of consciousness, to illustrate human folly in one of its larger manifestations. These aspects which, when seen if only for an instant by the qualified observer, must entertain, may be said to grow in distinctness as a community rises in the scale of civilisation. Since, moreover, the humorous person has trained himself in the swift detection of the accompaniments and the relations of the objects which he inspects, and has a habit of looking at the neglected sides of things, it may be expected that he will be found now and again among those who in the troubled atmosphere preserve something of the faculty of clear observation.

The fundamental factor in the situation for a humorous observer is the temporary hypertrophy of the most powerful of man's instincts, having its roots deeply seated in the primal impulse of self-conservation, appearing in the organic *milieu* of a higher type of social consciousness with its fixed habits of estimating and judging things. The state of hypertrophy gives rise to a group of extravagances which have something of the dimensions of a burlesque. The many expansions of the boastful, self-sufficing temper, the exaggerated forms of hatred, with its brood of suspicions, denunciations and vilifications, the swollen dimensions of credulity, and of a correlative incredulity, with regard to things which touch the patriotic passion—this and much more is probably an inseparable accompaniment of the national psychosis, certainly so if the dignity of "our cause" is challenged, whether from within or from without.

In these larger manifestations of the war-temper such organic *milieu* as the surviving normal consciousness can supply takes but a small part. What movements of intelligence are observable are pretty plainly of an intelligence subjugated by the dominant passion, and made to work for it by foraging far and wide for food-stuffs to satisfy its appetite for provocatives and solaces.

Yet this is but a small part of the humorous aspect of the situation. It is the collision between the new temper and the habit of feeling and judging nursed into vigour and endurance by a long course of civilisation which introduces the really amusing feature. For the quaint thing is that drowsy intelligence will now and again try to sit up and give a nudge to its rather noisy bed-fellow. It is the juxtaposition and interaction of two tendencies of widely removed moral levels, and quite disproportionate in their strength which supplies the rich variety of the entertaining. In this way, for example, we obtain the droll spectacle of an over-confident advocate of the cause suddenly brought to silence by a foggy suspicion that his hearer is not responsive enough, a suspicion which instantly brings to light the residuum of the normal man's desire for others' support. Or again, the powerful impulse to belittle the enemy—older than the age of Goliath—may, when it runs away with a patriot, carry him to the point from which he dimly discerns the edge of a dialectic precipice, the fatal concession that victory is robbed of all its glory. Or the fancy portrait of the enemy—preferred to a study from life because it is so dear to the war-temper—may bring its possessor into the quandary that he finds himself quite incapable of carrying out the necessary business of understanding that enemy's aims and methods.

A slight examination will show that the spectacle will illustrate most of the forms of the laughable recognised in a previous chapter. The whole situation may tend to assume the look of a big "mess," from which the participators vainly seek to extricate themselves. The high-strung emotional and conative attitude is certain to lead to futilities, as when confident predictions strike against the hard substance of fact. The situation will, further, be prolific of contradictions, including, not only the fundamental one already dealt with, but the discrepancies of statement which arise as the ratio of the intensities of the normal and the abnormal varies within the limits indicated above.

That the psychological situation will give rise to a large display of pretence, has been already suggested. The survival of a partially stupefied intelligence in the bellicose patriot will, indeed, be chiefly manifested in the somewhat onerous task of covering the unsightly faces of things with veils, bespangled ones if possible, in dignifiying the aims and the methods of the war. These efforts will plainly show themselves, to calm observation, for the most part, at least, not as conscious hypocrisies, but as self-deceptions following from the interaction of the two selves so strangely forced to consort.

It is hardly needful to say that disorder, topsy-turvyness, confusions of *rôle*, and, generally, inversions of normal relations, form an essential feature of the spectacle. A world so altered from the normal pattern that men given to a golden silence take to a speech which is hardly silver; that "leaders" assume the droll aspect of shepherds forced onwards by unruly flocks; that a certain kind of moral inconsistency appears to have won its place among the virtues; and that those versed in the divine have to assume the inverted part of justifying the ways of men to God, cannot fail to look disordered to a calm eye trained by the orderly. There would seem to be no room in such a scene, where men are wont to divest themselves of their individual characteristics, for a display of personal oddity. Yet a closer observation will show that, in spite of the powerful tendencies which make for uniformity of behaviour, shreds of individuality survive. The prevailing temper seizes on men, as a fever seizes on them, according to their individual constitutions; and one may watch the process of assimilation of parties, sects, and individuals to the type of the hour, much as a shrewd physician might watch the quaint modifications of a malady in a case of strongly marked family or individual peculiarities.

It was said above that the possibility of this humorous observation implied the discovery of a *modus vivendi* with the serious and more sensitive part of us. This means that the observation can be no quiet, prolonged pastime, but must rather resemble the momentary intuitions of the amusing side of things, which help us when we battle with life's worries and encounter its greater troubles. Such appreciation of the laughable as is possible in the case is rightly called humorous when it accompanies a complex serious attitude which, on the one hand, discerns both the hurtfulness and the pitifulness of the folly that brings the smile, and on the other, makes an effort to hold fast to that which repels and to descry estimable qualities hidden away under it. The smile will bring a momentary relaxation of strain, as in other cases where mental and moral tension is high. The humorist will suffer it to steal upon him because reflection enables him, in a sense, to comprehend, by recalling, for example, what Plato, Montaigne and others tell us as to what is likely to happen when men are captured by a crowd. He will be more inclined to be tolerant, if history comes to his aid, as the history of a patient may come to that of an anxious physician, assuring him of recovery and resumption of normal functions; still more, if a time of civic division, lacerating to the social part of him, has brought him near men and women whose gentleness seems to sweeten the ferment of the hour, and whose faces will henceforth appear to him in comforting vision—

earth's angel faces whose smile comes not with the brightening morn but with the deepening blackness of night.

CHAPTER XI.
THE LAUGHABLE IN ART: COMEDY.

We have traced the development of laughter in the individual and in the community with as little reference as possible to the influence of Art. It has been assumed that the feelings which move us to laughter are primal, and capable of expanding and deepening independently of this influence. At the same time, it is certain that the educative lead of the artist has been at work from a very early stage of human development. We have found even in savage life the figure of the "funny man," the expert in lifting the sluice gates of social laughter by means of jest and pantomime. Within the historical period, the practice of engaging jesters for banquets, and social entertainments generally, appears to go back to remote times and very simple social conditions.281 The finer and more methodical exercise of men's gift of laughter by these skilled choragi must have been a potent factor in its development. We may now glance at the evolution of art on its amusing and comic side.

This is no occasion for probing to its dark bottom the problem of the function of art. If we keep to the beginnings of the art of ministering to men's laughter, as we may study them among savages and our own children, the theories which look to art for the expression of an idea, or even of an emotion seeking for resonance, seem to have but little relevance. It looks as if the amusing art grew out of that simple social act which I have called a play-challenge, as illustrated in the game of reciprocal tickling. Hence, the play-theory of art serves particularly well for our present purpose. The quality of beneficent productivity which is an essential of art may be supposed to have grown distinct, as soon as an individual of superior cunning in playing on the mirthful organ found himself *vis-à-vis* with an audience. No social impulse of an art-like character strikes out its visible and audible effect more directly and more impressively than the desire to raise a laugh.

Taking this view, we see that the art which moves us to mirth illustrates the conative process in art-production. To amuse men, to raise their spirits to the treble pitch of gaiety, pre-supposes the desire to please. In all simple art-performance, this essentially social motive works consciously and directly: the partly unconscious art of the "fool" being here, of course, overlooked. In higher forms, the will to move men merrily is, I believe, always present in normal cases, and controls the whole art-process, though it may not be consciously realised at every moment. In the case of the comic actor, at any rate, a volitional control of his own feeling and its expression seems to be a prime necessity. This is sufficiently illustrated in the solemn aspect commonly assumed by the popular jester, in order to add to the mirthful effect of his utterance.

It would be an interesting inquiry, if our limits allowed of it, to examine the means which art, as a whole, possesses for moving us to laughter. This would open up the curious question of the symbolism of colours and tones, and of their combinations, as expressive of mirthful feeling and of jocose intention.

That laughter has for its proper excitant men and their doings, at once suggests that only those arts which represent human ideas and actions on a large scale have a considerable field for the exhibition of the ludicrous. Architecture, apart from sculpture, is heavily handicapped here. Music, as the expressive art *par excellence,* has a certain though narrowly limited range of effect, as may be seen in the characteristic rhythms, such as combinations of light staccato with deep-pitched notes, incompleted phrases and so forth, which do duty in comic opera. Some of this tickling effect is certainly due, not to an expression of jocose feeling, but to the bizarre aspect of the combination of sounds. And the same is probably true of the slightly amusing effects of such grotesque combinations of colour as are common in the costume of the harlequin, of the prince of mockers, and of other more or less comic figures. The grotesque and amusing in dress, that of the clown for example, is manifestly based on its suggestions, especially those of wrong sex, wrong age and the like.

Passing by the comic directions of pictorial art, including the highly developed process of modern political and other caricature, the great *rôle* in stimulating men's laughing susceptibilities falls to literature, and pre-eminently to dramatic literature and its interpreter, the stage. Here, only, can the procession of human follies display something of its variegated amplitude. Hither must we come, if we would fain laugh our fill and know what resources art possesses for playing on the whole gamut of our "risibility".

It would be well if we knew the beginnings of jocose literature. It may be that the jest-books preserve for us forms resembling those which these beginnings have taken. A short descriptive story of some practical joke, or of some smart bit of repartee, may have grown naturally enough out of the evening fire-side talk and become fixed and handed down to new generations. The Mediæval Contes (fabliaux) may be viewed as a slight expansion of such stories and fragments of talk. This short anecdotal story would allow a certain scope for mimicry and a crude art of elocution. A rudimentary form of comic acting, with its mimic gestures and its facetious dialogue, would naturally take its rise in the rehearsal of such a story by an acknowledged expert. The bits of dialogue, at least, would enforce a certain amount of mimicry of tones and gestures.

The beginnings of comedy, so far as we can get back to them, bear out these conjectures. The humble birthplace of Greek comedy was the village revel—a sort of merry harvest home—of the vintagers. At first, we read, there was no actor, only a leader "who let off coarse and scurrilous impromptus".282 Or, as another writer has it, Greek farce began with mocking songs and ironical speeches during processions, the Greeks being quick to mimic and to improvise.283

The dawn of our own comedy shows a somewhat similar process. It was in an atmosphere of mirth that the child, half-seriously quizzing things in order to laugh the more, was born. This may be seen by a reference to the mirthful societies and their riotings which were a feature of mediæval English life. The "feast of fools" was the great occasion for satirical songs, and, later on, for dramas in which the clergy were more especially taken off. No doubt, as we shall see, there existed in the old miracle-plays and moralities a simple dramatic form capable of being transformed into comedy. Yet this transformation was made possible by the spirit of mirth and revelry, which had some time before rudely broken into the solemnity of the miracle-play.284

The full rise of the comic drama has had its social conditions. Mr. Meredith has pointed to some of them, particularly the existence of an intelligent middle class, and the recognition of woman's status; to which one may add, that of her conversational wit.285 To these social conditions might be added a national mood of gaiety, coming from some new sense of lightened shoulders and a freer breathing.

The value of comedy as chief ministress to our laughter may be seen by a mere glance at its many resources. It seems able to present to the eye and ear all varieties of the amusing. As a show, it carries on the fun of children's make-believe play. It can set before us the most grotesque aberrations of dress, carriage and manners. In its human figures, again, it presents to us in forms of its own choosing the full variety of laughable traits of mind and of character. Lastly, it can exhibit in its plots the whole gamut of teasing and practical joke which amuses ordinary men in real life.

We may defer illustration of the comic treatment of laughable traits of character, and look for a moment at the ways in which the incidents of comedy carry on the movements of primitive fun.

A glance will tell us that these incidents are woven out of the play and the practical jokes of merry youth. The boisterous fun of the spectacle of a good beating, for which the lower savages have a quick sense, and which is a standing dish at the circus, is a frequent incident in comedy, both in the popular and boisterous variety of Aristophanes and Plautus, and in the quieter and more intellectual one of Molière.286

Another variety of amusing incident drawn from child-play and the popular fun of the circus is a repetition of words, gestures or other movements. These repetitions grow particularly funny when they take the form of an alternate going and coming, or of ending and recommencing a discourse. Amusing already in their semblance of purposeless play, they sometimes grow more droll by assuming a look of irrepressibility, as when the philosopher Pancrace in *Le Mariage forcé* is again and again pushed behind the coulisse and returns to renew his discourse. It has been pointed out that such movements have something of the amusing character of the toy known as Jack-in-the-box.287

Another class of repetitions, which we may call imitations, also frequent on the comic stage, seems in like manner to reproduce easily recognisable features of child's play. Nothing is more characteristic of the play-mood in young animals and in children alike than an imitative propagation of movement. The child's game of making faces is an excellent example. The liking of the stage for these imitations shows how closely it remains in touch with primitive fun. This is plain enough when the action imitated is disorderly, as we may see in the rebuffs and counter-rebuffs of the circus. The repeated beatings of the wife-beater in *Le Médecin malgré lui* have something of this diverting effect

The amusing repetitions wrought into the mechanism of comedy are, as Molière may tell us, commonly far less aggressive. The reproduction of the series of exclamations of Cléonte on the perfidy of his mistress by his valet, Covielle, in *Le Bourgeois gentilhomme,* and the counterpart to this, the slightly varied repetitions of the reproaches of Cléonte's mistress by her maid, are quite delightfully suggestive of a plot on the part of Love to reduce his victims to one level of imbecility.288

Comedy, both ancient and modern, is full of trickery and dupery. A whole play may be one big piece of fooling, ending for the most part in a merry scene in which the deluded victim or victims come to their senses again. The spectator, who is in the secret, enjoys sympathetically the laughter of the plot-maker.

One of the simplest and earliest comic devices, another outgrowth from child's play, seems to be a disguise. The figures of comedy towards whom our laughter is guided are not gifted with the finest of visions, and a small amount of disguise, especially when it meets and flatters their desires, suffices for complete deception. Classic comedy and that of Shakespeare make large use of such trickery.

But a strange dress and other means of disguise are by no means always necessary for the befooling. When the credulous mood is on, the victim, whether fish or man, will rise to the crudest of artificial imitations, and comedy fastens on its victims when they are in this mood, as in the case of Malvolio, M. Jourdain and the rest.

Sometimes the comedian prepares for the needed deception by throwing its victim into a fit of absent-mindedness. A good example may be found in the scene between Arnolphe and the notary in Molière's *L'École des Femmes*, where the tongues of the two make a pretence of running on together, while the two brains that move them remain in a state of perfect mutual misunderstanding. It is another kind of amusing self-deception when the comic figure, again showing his descent from the clown, undertakes to do something, and instantly displays a complete inability to carry out his undertaking. This is illustrated in a less obvious manner in *Le Bourgeois gentilhomme* by the behaviour of Cléonte, who, after quarrelling with his mistress, and begging his valet to "lend a hand" to his spite and to sustain his resolve to bear down any remains of his foolish love, instantly afterwards protests against the obedient servant's depreciations of the lady.

The comic person must be mercilessly attacked now and again, if the spectator is to get his fill of merriment. Molière again gives us the illustration. The scene in which the miser's son, Cléante, playfully holds the father as in a vice, as he takes off the ring from the old gentleman's finger and offers it as if in his behalf to the lady they both desire to wed, has the full flavour of the retaliative joke.

The laugh which is "malicieux" though not "amer" comes in a large wave when the deception is a kicking over of traces which have become galling. The tricking of the severe guardian, parental or other, illustrated by Terence in the *Adelphi*, and by Molière in *L'École des Femmes*, *L'École des Maris* and other works, yields a lusty gratification as a practical joke directed against an oppressor.

A good deal of the fun of comedy may easily be seen to flow from a bizarre placing of a person, especially the setting of him in a situation where he has to do what he is not accustomed to do. If false appearances have to be kept up, so much the better. The tricks by which the sham doctor Sganarelle tries to play up to his part in *Le Médecin malgré lui* are of the broadly comic. A diverting situation may be obtained in other ways, as when lovers who have fallen out and are in the most doleful of moods have to meet. The subjection of the arch-hypocrite Tartuffe to the watchful eye of Orgon's son is pregnant of comic effect.

As already hinted, comedy reflects those movements of social laughter which have been dealt with in a previous chapter. The works of

Aristophanes are a storehouse for one who seeks illustrations of the popular attitude towards the new, when this lends itself to a buffoonish inflation. The comic stage is conservative in the sense that it is ready to ridicule whatever wears the look of a bizarre novelty. The importation of foreign dress and manners has been a well-recognised source of merriment in modern plays.

With grotesque innovations may be set the affectations of superior manners, fashions of speech and the rest, for which the laughter-loving public has had a quick eye. The exposure of an excessive fondness for using fine expressions, especially foreign ones, has always, one suspects, had an exhilarating effect on an educated audience. The preciosity of Molière's dames lives as the great example of a culte of "the fine shades," carried to the point of the irresistibly droll.

The well-recognised social antagonisms, again, lend to comedy all their store of the amusing. The droll side of the bloodless feud between man and woman comes into view in all stages of the development of the art. It will, of course, vary in its mode of presentment with the social conditions of the time it represents, and more especially with the status of woman. In the comedy of Aristophanes, the mutual chaff of the sexes is a constant source of incidental effect and a main motive of two plays.289 Yet the part taken by woman in the dialogue is exceedingly small.290 The Greek assumption of her inferiority meets us with a charming frankness. The notion of her rising to a higher place in civic life is handled with a buffoonish extravagance which must have delighted conservative husbands. When the poet wishes to show up the folly of the Athenian war-party he invents a revolt of the dames, who by certain effective measures, connubial and other, manage to the lasting shame of their betters to bring about peace. The triumph of the inferior here reminds one of the hilarious victory won by the savage women in the art of rowing. The Greek comedy as a whole treated women, including hetaerae, with copious abuse;291 yet in Latin comedy, at any rate, the woman now and again gets the better of the man. In the *Asinaria* of Plautus, an amorous old man, one of the favourite figures of comedy, is finely chastised by the wife who surprises his secret.

The interminable contest of man and woman carries with it the rivalry of the home and the tavern—or, as we should say to-day, the Club. In Plautus, who goes for a large licence in pleasure, the opposition is emphasised. Terence, by introducing a more becoming conception of feminine nature and married life, prepared the way for a more equal intercourse between man and woman. It is, however, only under the improved conditions of modern family and social life that the verbal duel of the sexes in comedy has grown keen and brilliant.

Another and primitive relation, that of old and young, or, in its special form, of father and child, amply displays its possibilities of fun on the comic stage. In the newer Attic comedy, we are told, representations of the old became frequent, now as austere and avaricious, now as fond and tender-hearted.292 The contrast of the severe "Governor" and the fond "Papa," which we have seen illustrated in Terence and Molière, clearly points to the fact that comedy, as play designed expressly for merry youth, favours the son's case, and seeks to relax the paternal leading strings.

Just as the too weighty rule of a father is apt to be laughingly pushed aside by comedy, so is that of the master. The intriguing, cheating valet of Latin comedy is the ancestor of many a domestic swindler, down to the Mr. Morgan whose sudden disappearance was regretted by Major Pendennis. The outwitted master, like the outwitted husband, is a comic figure that excites but little pity; perhaps, because the getting the better of one in power by his subordinate is never wanting in the agreeable look of a merry equalising of things. Other "humours" of social groups, that of trader, money-lender, and their clients, for example, are, as suggested in an earlier chapter, reflected in comedy.

The same flavour of fun, the same kinship to child's play, is recognisable in the speech of the comic stage. Word-play here is merely the lighter interlude in what as a whole has much of the character of a game, the contest of rapier-like tongues in comic dialogue.

Men have written weightily on the nature of wit and its relation to intellect in general and to humour. Their discourses seem hardly to capture its finer spirit. Locke started the discussion by his well-known distinction between wit and judgment, the former consisting in a bringing together of ideas with quickness and variety wherein can be found any resemblance or congruity; the latter in discriminating and separating ideas.293 Addison, who accepts this definition in the main, is bound to add that, though wit is generally produced by resemblance and congruity of ideas, it is very often produced by their opposition.294 Hazlitt follows Addison in including likeness and opposition. Wit, according to him, "is an arbitrary juxtaposition of dissonant ideas, for some lively purpose of assimilation or contrast, generally of both."295 All this, though it hints at a distinctive manner of intellectual activity, misses the mark by busying itself in the main with the question of a particular kind of relation of ideas.

The rather solemn treatment of puns by these serious writers is characteristic. Addison deals with them under the head of false wit, and bravely attacks the ages for upholding the practice.296 For thus spurning the humble pun, he was rendered blind by the god of laughter to the real nature of wit, as essentially a mode of intellectual play.

As the etymology of the word suggests, wit is not so much a special faculty concerned with a particular class of relations, as an attitude or manner of behaviour of the intelligence as a whole. It illustrates her most lively and agile gait, and is characterised by readiness of mind, quickness of perception, ingenuity in following out hints of quite unexpected contrasts, similarities, aims, causes, reasons, and the other apparent belongings of an idea. As tending to sportiveness, it loves an intellectual chase for its own sake, and revels in sudden transitions, doublings, and the whole game of verbal hide and seek.297

According to this view, wit is a talent which has been especially developed by a proper exercise of one of the chief functions of the social animal, conversation. This has its light and entertaining variety, talk, which when it reaches the perfection of an art becomes a kind of game. A subject is tossed out like a ball and each side then tries to strike it in turn and so keep the game going. Something of serious purpose may be behind, as a half wish to illumine the subject, but the main interest lies in the game itself, in the exhilarating pleasure of crossing the intellectual foils with a worthy opponent.

Yet, though a game, talk is commonly carried on by persons who are not merely fellow-players. As we have seen, witty dialogue flourishes when some force of repulsion as well as of attraction is involved, as that between a would-be seller and his needy yet stand-off buyer, or between a wooer and a woman concerned not to make winning too easy. Where, as between two rivals, the situation is conducive to warmth, the wit will be apt to grow pungent. As Addison reminds us, wit is often developed in an unequal game, between a "butt" and his assailants, the butt knowing now and again, like Sir John Falstaff, how "to get the laugh of his side".298

The art of witty exchange, like that of using foils, clearly implies self-restraint; and in both cases the desirable coolness is greatly furthered by the presence of the impartial spectator. It is possible that husband and wife first learned to spar jocosely by having to carry on disputes in the presence of outside hearers.

Taking this view of wit, we may see how word-play inevitably comes into it. The pun of childish years, which merely tricks the ear by an accidental doubleness of meaning, need not be considered here. It is only when the ambiguity has value for laughter, when it can be turned to some merry purpose, that it comes under the eye of art. Word-play clearly tends to run into thought-play. Some of the best-known "mots" will be found to involve the double-sense of the pun, like the praise awarded by the witty King to one of his courtiers in the remark that he was never in the way and never out of the way. It is the deep sense discernible through the verbal appearance of a self-contradiction which charms and entertains here.299

It seems to follow that the laughter excited in spectator or reader by a display of wit is slightly complex. It has in it something of the child's laughter of admiration at what is new, rather startling, and fine, of his gay response to a play-challenge, and of a sympathetic rejoicing with the combatant who, by showing his skill, obtains an advantage over his antagonist.

The dialogue of comedy and of the fiction which adopts the comic point of view will make use of these verbal sports, these doublings of the intellectual chase, at the hint of ambiguous language. They are refreshing, they enlarge the scope of the witty combat, and they help to maintain the mirthful temper of the spectator. Their use may be illustrated throughout the history of comedy. Thus, we find in the comedy of Aristophanes much chaffing of the sexes and punning. The same is true of Plautus. In the merry comedy of Shakespeare we have still an abundance of puns, also a great advance in the art of the verbal foils, especially as crossed by man and woman, more particularly on the side of the latter. Molière's quieter and more thoughtful discourse, though now and then it finds room for a pun, illustrates the finer art of witty combat, in which the foils seem to have been tipped with a softer button.

We have so far dwelt on those elements of comedy which seem plainly derivable from simple forms of fun, as seen in child's play and the laughter of primitive folk. There remains what is in some ways the most interesting feature, the comic presentation of character in action and speech.

It is customary to classify comedies into those of Incident, of Manners and of Character. Such a division must not, however, mislead us. The three ingredients are present in every comedy. If Aristophanes depends largely on incident, he only gets his fun by choosing comic characters—the sophist, say, or the commercial explorer endowed with wings. In the so-called comedy of Manners of Congreve and his school, the persons, such as they are, undoubtedly form a main support of the entertaining action. Molière, though he relies chiefly on character, can only give us comedy by inventing situations in which his figures will have flashed on them the droll light of the comic stage. What is meant by the above classification is pretty plainly that in some comedies the characters are more central, are more finely evolved, and attract a much larger attention.

That the evolution of comedy has, in the main, been an advance in the presentment of character, as judged both by the variety and the complexity of the personalities depicted, and by the fulness and definiteness of the presentation, is just what we might have expected. It seems certain that, with the progress of civilisation, men and women have grown more complex and more varied, both intellectually and morally, and further that the interest in character and the capability of understanding it have developed concurrently.

A word on the general conditions of a presentation of character in comedy. For one thing, dramatic construction, as compared with that of prose fiction, has certain obvious limits set to the delineation of character. The art is too wise to attempt a full presentment of so complex a group of traits as we find in a developed individuality. It illustrates, however, degrees of fulness in the presentation of personality, and the finer art of drama may produce its impression of a concrete person very much as a skilful painter does within the limits of a rough sketch by a few master strokes. Yet without the actor's visible embodiment of the part, the full impression of a concrete individual would be difficult within the limits of dramatic construction.

In the case of comedy, moreover, there is another reason for the limitation of the art of developing individual character. The superlative æsthetic value of the ludicrous aspect of character imposes on the writer an unusual degree of simplification, of something like a reduction of the concrete personality to an abstraction. The comic entertainment afforded by the presentation, say, of a swelling vanity, springs from our keeping the mental eye fixed in merry expectation of the coming developments of the laughable trait. If, then, only this core of the character, as the mood of the spectator estimates it, is clearly presented and sufficiently illustrated, both in its immediate manifestations and in its effects on the rest of the man, a very shadowy reinstatement of this remainder will suffice.

This conclusion seems clearly borne out by the common way of speaking of the great comic figures as "types"; for to view a character as typical means that we are interested in the person, less as a particular individual, than as an example of a certain sort of person. The common practice of writers of comedy, ancient and modern, of marking their characters by appropriate names, the Braggadocio, the Miser, the Misanthrope, and so forth, shows that authors recognise this typical function.

Such comic representation of type will always have in it something of the nature of exaggeration. The laughable trait, in order to raise the tide of merriment to its full height, must itself be raised to a higher power and displayed in the hypertrophic volume it tends to assume when the balancing forces of the normal man are greatly reduced. Yet, to say this is not to say that the common distinction between a lifeless abstraction and a living character has no meaning in comedy. There is a vast difference between the rigid abstractions of early modern comedy, before the art had extricated itself from the leading strings of the morality plays, and the relatively full and freely moving figures which we encounter in Molière's plays. On the other side, the always controlled expansion of an amusing trait in the comic character is to be clearly marked off from that forcing of expression up to the dimensions of a distortion which is the essence of caricature.

A glance at the history of comedy will show us how, with its development, there has grown a finer recognition of the comic value of character and a corresponding skill in the presentation of it.

The comedy of Aristophanes illustrates the art of comic character-drawing in its infancy. Here, where the comic muse has not yet left behind her the Bacchanalian rout; where the scene is apt to be violently transported, now to mid-air, now to the abode of the gods, and now to Hades; where the boisterous fun in its genial onslaught spares neither deity, poet nor statesman; and where the farcical reaches such a pass as to show us competitors for the favour of Demos offering to blow that worthy's nose; there would seem to be no room for the portrayal of character. And, in truth, the problem of constructing character was in a way obviated by calling in living or historical personages familiar to the spectators. Yet even in this riotous atmosphere, where the eyes of the spectator must have been half-blinded by laughter, we may discern the dim beginnings of the art of comic portraiture. Not only have we now and again, as in the litigious old gentleman in the *Wasps,* hints of a typical comic figure, we have illustrated in the historical figures themselves, Socrates, Cleon, Euripides, a rude art of type-delineation.300

In the later Greek and the Latin comedy we find ourselves in a less turbulent scene where the air is clearer, and things can be viewed with some steadiness. In Plautus, the poet of the masses and the taverns, the spirit of riotous buffoonery proved itself to be still alive. Yet the confinement of the scene not only to earth but to its familiar haunts, and the introduction of the love-motive, even though in its baser form, gave new scope for the exhibition of comic varieties of character. Even in Plautus we find sketches, not, indeed, of a moral type as we find elsewhere, but of a representation of some social class or calling, with its characteristics forcibly set forth, as in the boastful soldier, the cheating servant, and the stingy money-lender. An approximation to the illustration of a moral type may, perhaps, be detected in the amorous old man in the *Asinaria.* It is, however, in the work of Menander and his Roman adapter Terence that we must look for the real advance. In the plays of Terence, written for the educated Romans, the figures assume something of respectability. Thus the father ceases, as with Plautus, to be a sort of football for filial buffoons to kick about, and grows into a character worthy of study; and the contrast between a foolish excess of authority and a wise lenience, given us in the two fathers in the *Adelphi,* has been the model for more than one modern writer. In Terence, too, the family begins to come by its own in its tussle with the rowdyism of the tavern, and this is no small gain for the comic delineation of character.301

The circumstance that modern comedy took its rise in the moralities, with their personifications of evil and the rest, readily explains how certain broad types of ignoble character were set in the forefront of its scene. These appear already in the later moralities, for example, "Like will to Like". In the work which marks the full transition from the interlude of the didactic morality to the comedy, "Ralph Roister Doister" (*c.* 1550), we have outlined one of the valuable figures in the comic world, the vainglorious cowardly man, the victim of the most entertaining of delusions.302

In the comedy of the Elizabethans, Ben Jonson and Massinger, it is easy to trace this influence, disguised though it is sometimes by that of classical comedy. In Jonson's "Every Man in his own Humour," said to be the first important comedy of character in our literature, the source of entertainment is laid, not in a merry plot, but in the presentation of a variety of characters which display themselves in odd fashions and novelties of conduct. It may be roughly true, as Taine says, with Molière present to his imagination, that the method pursued is to take an abstract quality and put together all the actions to which it gives rise.303 In other words, the object-lesson of the morality is still too near, and the dramatist has not learned how to make his comic characters move and grow under the spectator's eye. Yet, if we compare Bobadil with a braggart of Plautus, we may see that real progress has been made in the comic grasp and manipulation of character.

In the comedies of Shakespeare a superficial reader might, so far as drawing of purely comic characters is concerned, suppose himself to be moving backwards. The glowing air of romance, the removal of the scene from the workaday world, the partial abandonment to the moods of poetry and dream-delight, all this would seem to exclude the setting up of well-defined figures fitted to entertain the mood of a gay contemplation. The supposition would not be utterly wrong. The "mixture of tones," which comes into the poet's comedies as well as into his tragedies, does undoubtedly tend to limit the portrayal of purely comic traits.304 The romantic background cannot, like the fixed arrangements of homely society, throw the follies and perversities of the figures into sharp relief. Think for a moment how different æsthetic significance and value would have attached to the figure of the melancholy Jaques, if it had been encountered, not in the solitary forest, but in one of Molière's orderly homes.

The mixture of tones introduces a softening, transforming influence which affects our attitude towards the queer figures themselves. Benedick and the other men who are gently brought to reason by schooling women have in their very perversity something amiable. Even Malvolio and the other figures, whose folly is exposed with something of the unsparing extravagance of an older comedy, catch a saving ray from the warm glow which is diffused over their world. We laugh heartily; yet the pre-dominant sentiment of the play moves us at the same time towards tender condonation.

Must we then say that because he rarely allows us to look on folly and vice in the pure attitude of amused observation, Shakespeare is no comic poet? It does not greatly matter how we answer the question so long as we reflect that in the world he has here created for us, at once beautiful and touched with a tender melancholy, and yet charged with the electric current of mirth, we possess something quite as delightful as the well-defined comic scenes of a Molière. Now and again, moreover, where the rosy warmth of romance gives place to the colder light of realities, as in "The Merry Wives" and "The Taming of the Shrew," we see how keen an eye our poet could turn to the comic possibilities of character. Nor must we forget how great a contribution he made to comic character-drawing in his dialogue, where the man and the woman, at once attracted and repelled, use their witty tongues with excellent effect, and where woman, though now and then chastised, has a large part assigned her in curing man of his follies and developing what is best in him.

For the comedy of character, in its highest and purest form, we are told, and rightly told, to go to Molière. In his world, not only is the uproarious, dust-raising mirth of classic comedy silenced, but the fun of extravagant plot with its disguises and errors, though not absent, is kept within measure. It is the familiar domestic world, into which we can readily transport ourselves. It is peopled for the most part with the sober and sensible. Upon this orderly scene is brought one or more of the great typical representatives of human folly. In some cases it is an old entertaining figure revived, the exacting and anxious miser, for example, or the voluble braggart. But the comic idea also incarnates itself in a rich variety of new forms, such as the *faux dévot* and his victim, the critic of society who turns a sour face on its conventions, the wrong-headed educator of woman, the ready-tongued quack, the crazy pedant and the others.

Nor is the enlargement of the gallery of portraits the only or the chief advance in the comedy of Molière. The fineness of the drawing is what fixes the eye. All trace of the old rigid abstractions has disappeared. Typical they all remain, as is their function: yet they are individualised in a way that satisfies all the conditions of the art.305

Molière's supremacy in the comic use of character is seen, first of all, in the selection of his types, which have each a large amusing aspect inherent in the character itself, and capable of being set forth in a sufficient variety of manifestation. We see this at once by comparing his best-known characters with those of his predecessors. In Molière we have, what Coleridge tells us is wanting in Ben Jonson, the presentation of the laughable defect as "a prominence growing out of, and nourished by, the character which still circulates in it".306 The simple-minded ambition of the Bourgeois gentilhomme, the pious over-confidence of Orgon, the intractable misanthropy of Alceste—these, as traits broad-based in the character, offer large possibilities of comic development.

The next point to be noted in this new art is the mode of presentation of the character which is to hold the eye in amused contemplation. The pointing effect of contrast is present, as in all good art; what is noteworthy is the admirable simplicity of the method of contrasting. This is rendered possible by the type selected and the point of view adopted. To Molière, the man taken with vain conceit, the opinionated prig, the unsociable critic of society and the rest, are aberrations from a normal type, the socially adapted person. The Harpagons, the Orgons, the Arnolphes, the Alcestes, the Sganarelles and the others, have their amusing lop-sidedness, their characteristic tendency swollen to the ridiculous proportions of a tumor, defined from the first by the antithesis in which they are set to the normal members of society. The orderly world, pleading for a reasonable accommodation to the usages of men, is sometimes represented by the judicious friend, *e.g.,* Alceste, Arnolphe; not seldom by the wife, *e.g.,* Madame Jourdain; at other times by the brother, *e.g.,* of Sganarelle; and, now and again, even by the privileged and saucy maid, *e.g.,* of Orgon, of M. Jourdain.

In this juxtaposition the comic poet exhibits clearly enough the antisocial tendency of the inflated characteristic. The outrage to woman in the rigorous treatment of their wards by Arnolphe and Sganarelle, the harshness of Alceste's demands on the high-spirited girl he woos, the menace in Jourdain's craze to the stability of the home, the cruel bearing of Harpagon's avarice on his son—all this is made quite plain to the spectator; and the exposure of this maleficent tendency in the perverse attitude serves somehow to strengthen the comic effect.

In thus presenting the hypertrophy of a moral tendency, Molière gives movement to the embodiment by disclosing the organic action of the disordered part on other parts of the man. The avarice of Harpagon renders him fearful of a theft, as if this would ruin him. He takes it as an insult that he should be called rich, asserting that "nothing is more false". This points to that effect of perverted passion which Molière everywhere emphasises, intellectual blindness, the result of a mastery of the mind by compulsory ideas (*idées fixes*). The often-quoted indication of mental deafness in Orgon, when, to the servant's announcement that his wife is ill, he dreamily iterates the ejaculations "Et Tartuffe?" and "Le pauvre homme!" illustrates the full comic value of such a detachment of mind from the realities which are seen by others to be rapping at the doors of sense.

This state of the intelligence reduced to something resembling "mono-ideism" carries with it a loss of the normally clear self-consciousness. The foolish Arnolphe, who, in order to guard himself against the risk of a faithless spouse, subjects the girl he means to wed to intolerable restraints, has the delusion that he is a great reformer, striking the hyper-pedagogic note when he says that a woman's mind is soft wax.307 Here and elsewhere the spectator is made to see that the queer creature is acting like a somnambulist, quite unaware of the consequences of his actions. It thus becomes an exhibition of human folly, and of the droll obliquity and bombastic extravagance which are folly's inseparable concomitants.

There is, no doubt, somewhat of abstraction here. To give a tendency complete dominance and to reduce intelligence to the menial position of its servant is to destroy the organic complexity of the man. All the same, this method of uncovering the drollness of moral obliquity is not adequately judged when it is called abstract. The simplified mechanism still lives, in a sense. One might say that the mature mind is reduced to the level of the child's. There is, indeed, something suggestive of the child in a lull of naughty temper in Harpagon's inquiry of his coachman, what people are saying about him. A still more striking approach to the childish occurs when M. Jourdain shows off to his wife and his maid his newly acquired superiority through the discovery of the meaning of "prose".

It may be added that an escape from the rigidity of the abstract is secured by the development of the obliquity itself. As long as things are seen to grow, they are taken to be alive. The expansion of the ridiculous ambition of M. Jourdain endows him with a certain plenitude of life. It may all be very one-sided, and, by comparison with the life of a normal man, remind us of the inflexibility of a machine; yet it is still a deranged organism that acts, and not a mechanism.308

It is to be noted, too, that though they resemble distinctly morbid aberrations from the normal pattern, these characters do not reach to the full height of mania. M. Jourdain, no doubt, gets near the boundary that separates sanity from insanity in the closing scenes of the play;309 but the comic intention is careful to keep the droll figure on the right side of the boundary.

A frequent termination of the action in this comedy is a climax, in which the folly of the comic character rises to an outburst so voluminous and torrent-like as to throw the onlookers in his world into uproarious mirth. The final befooling of M. Jourdain is an example. Molière was too good an artist, and too wise a man, to try in every case to compass the end of "poetic justice" by giving to society in its struggle with a mighty and obstinate perversion of humanity more of a victory than the laugh. Unhappy Alceste has to rush into the desert without his Célimène amid the hilarity of onlookers. Arnolphe and Sganarelle are no doubt found out and disappointed; and Tartuffe is unmasked and gets into trouble. Yet there is no evidence of a general intention to punish. Orgon, though he is cured of his pious delusion by a rough surgical operation, receives no more chastisement than M. Jourdain receives for having brought alien interests and an alien master into the home. Nor does even that embodiment of an ugly vice, Harpagon, get anything worthy of being called a trouncing.

In all this, the master shows us how well he knew how to keep at the point of view which he had selected as the comic. Let us try to define this after our study of his plays.

When we contrast the world, quiet and orderly for the most part, presented in these comedies with the hurly-burly scenes of a play of Aristophanes, we are tempted to say, as has been said, that Molière sets before our eyes the realities of everyday life. Yet the comic figures blown out into ridiculous volume are certainly not taken straight out of our familiar world. They are always transformations, to this extent, that they are the simplified embodiments of fully developed tendencies which only show themselves in germ-form, and complicated more or less by balancing tendencies, in the real world which is said to be imaged here. We seem thus to have an element of the unreal thrown against a background of the real.

There is no anomaly here when once we get at the comic point of view. In Molière's plays, the source of laughter lies in this very intrusion of the ill-shapen into a community of well-rounded forms. It is the intruder on whom we fix the eye, for whose unpredictable antics in a world for which he is not made our expectation is set. The serious background is there, but does not take a strong hold of our minds: we are not greatly moved, for example, by the spectacle of the sufferings of the daughters and the wards of testy old gentlemen, or even of the wearing housewifely anxieties of Madame Jourdain. The proper world, into which the absurdly ill-fitted is here pitchforked, is but a background, rendering the valuable service of backgrounds by throwing into relief and so sharply defining the form for which the spectator's eye is accommodated.

It is hardly an exaggeration to say that the whole plot of one of these comedies consists in the showing up of the grotesque unsuitability of the comic character to its environment. It groups its persons and arranges its scenes as if with the intention of demonstrating the futility of the attempt of this droll figure, lop-sided, and of an awkward gait, to move about in our ordered world. This helps us to understand why Molière, though, as observed above, he now and again resorts to older and more elemental sources of mirth, is able to be so economical in the use of disguise of improbable encounters, and of the other mechanical devices of the entertaining show. The situations themselves as well as the action seem to arise out of the fundamental facts, the given characters and their relations. Thus, one is hardly surprised to find Harpagon in the ignoble part of a money-lender, to whom the son he has pinched betakes himself.

The enjoyment of the comedy here provided presupposes a trained faculty. There must be the quick observant eye that catches in side-glance all the relations, and yet remains accommodated for the laughable. There is no place for a mixed tone, for a blend of laughter with melancholy sentiment. The serious is envisaged less as the serious, than as the framework within which the comic figure moves. The mood is one of a purely gay observation, which has no room for pity, indignation, or any other emotion; which is brightly and coldly intellectual; which is content with just looking and being amused.

For a right understanding of the scope of laughter in comedy, we need to glance at another of its developments. In the so-called "Comedy of Manners," as illustrated in the English plays of the Restoration, we have undoubtedly to do with a very special trend of the comic spirit.

In the art of Molière we have for the most part the presentation of an individual grotesquely transformed from the common social type which surrounds him. It is only in a few comedies, as *Les Femmes savantes* and *Les Précieuses ridicules,* that we have spread out for mirthful contemplation the characteristics of *a set* of persons. In these, the moderate sensible world, against which the cultivation of "the fine shades" looks so entertaining, is still indicated, though, of course, less immediately and fully.

In the plays of Congreve and his contemporaries, we meet with a comic treatment of more widespread "manners" of the hour. The sources of their fun are pretty obvious. There is something of the utter abandonment to disorder and revelry which we met with in the works of Aristophanes.310 The ordered world, with its interaction of normal characters, seems blotted out of existence. The plot is, as with Plautus, a love-intrigue, and has much of the coarseness and the degradation of situation which mark the popular Latin comedy. Yet it is at least marked off by the feature that it frees men from the sordid business of sending menials to bid for the prize, and sets them face to face with the women they are bent on obtaining. The women, again, are not shy maids, but range from experienced wives to the would-be simpletons fresh from the country. They are, moreover, while saucy and disposed to make good show of resistance, untrammelled by any sentimental or other attachment to their chains.

It seems undeniable that this "artificial" comedy can make good its claims to be entertaining. It has vivacity and stirring movement, the full frolicsomeness of the practical joke, and it abounds in scenes of voluminous gaiety. Its dialogue at its best has, along with its coarseness, an unmistakable brilliance of wit.

But how are we to define the point of view where there is no ordered world as background? There seems no question here of laughing at the affectations of a few, who are viewed as comic aberrations from a reasonable type. The whole world is affected with frolicsome disorder.

We are not now concerned with the mental attitude of the spectators for whom these comedies were written. To them, no doubt, the spectacle was a merry one as bringing a sense of relief from the gloom of the Puritan's reign. It may, as Taine suggests, have been served up as a kind of "Appetitsbischen" between meals, in order to stimulate the palates of the gallants who frequented the theatre; though it is difficult to attribute this function to what by common consent was intended to provoke mirthful laughter. What is of more importance is to get at the point of view of Charles Lamb and others who avow that they find a true comedy here.

Lamb himself has told us what attitude a man should bring to the appreciation of this comedy. He is to regard these "sports of a witty fancy" as "a world of themselves almost as much as fairyland". His moral feelings are left at home with his morning suit. He goes to the play in order "to escape from the pressure of reality". For him the figures that pursue one another across the stage have no moral substance, and are proper subjects neither for approval nor for disapproval. In other words, Lamb tells us that the comedy of Congreve and his school is to be taken as a pure show, holding no relations to the real, everyday world.

This view has been spurned by Macaulay, in a well-known Essay, as subversive of morals. To him, the comedy of the Restoration is a thing that is inherently anti-moral in spirit and intention; and he proceeds to pound it with weighty invectives.

The argument would have been relevant if the question had been a practical one of this kind: shall we put this comedy on the stage to-day for our boys and girls to see it? As against Lamb's plea it seems to me to be a curious case of missing the point. When, for example, Macaulay complains that in these comedies the husbands are treated as objects of contempt and aversion, whereas the gallants are decked out with all the graces, he might have remembered the old *Contes* and bethought him that this was an elementary condition of the artificial world, which is created solely for amusement. His answer to Lamb, that recollections of morality do steal now and then into this fantastic world, does not touch the latter's main contention, and only shows (so far as it is just) that the creators were not perfect architects, and tried to combine incompatible styles. The moral order is still in the background, dimly perceived, even here: the fun of the thing is at bottom, as Lamb says, a sense of momentary escape from rules which we know cannot be set aside in the real world. But this idea of an escape implies that what we fly from must not be dragged into the show.

Our study of comedy and of the sources of laughter has prepared us to accept Lamb's view. The comic spectacle appeals to the man in the play-mood. When there, he may see the fun of the turbulent world of Aristophanes and not be troubled by the thought of the undesirability of its realisation. Even when he is entertained by a play of Molière he does not take the background quite seriously, waxing indignant, say, in sympathy with Harpagon's ill-used son, or with M. Jourdain's ill-used wife. The least swerving from the point of view of comedy, a turn of the mental "eye-glass," would spoil all. He would begin, with Rousseau, to protest against presenting so good a man as Alceste in a ludicrous light. The Restoration comedy appeals to the same playful mood simplified by the temporary inhibition of all outside tendencies.

It is, I conceive, a profound error to suppose that either the writer of a comedy or his audience is at the moral point of view, envisaging behaviour as morally commendable or the opposite. Possibly, the influence of the didactic morality on early modern comedy may have helped to foster this error. It is true that Molière finds his comic material in certain defects of character. Yet the selections made by comic art are not determined by degrees of moral turpitude. As hinted above, very small and comparatively harmless vices may be preferred as having the drollest look on the stage.311 Vanity, the richest of all moral blemishes in its comic possibilities, and therefore greatly employed by comedy, both ancient and modern, is not judged as heinously immoral, like hatred and cruelty, for example.312 This may suffice to show how wide an interval separates the point of view of the spectator of a comedy from that of the moral judge.

It seems to me to be much more correct to say, with M. Bergson, that comedy takes up the social rather than the moral point of view. By this I mean that the comic poet is thinking of the look of things to the trained apperceptive organ of the social kind of person, according as they appear to be well or ill adapted to the common practices and opinions of society as discerned and interpreted by its more intelligent representatives. Yet, in speaking of the social point of view, I must not be taken to mean that either the author or the spectator of the comic scene is seriously judging of the behaviour of its figures by a reference to social values. There is, undoubtedly, an approach to this, not only in the early modern comedy, but in the later serious variety, including some plays of Molière; but the art-impulse of the writer, where it is clear, prevents the approximation of points of view from becoming a loss of distinctness. Comedy addresses itself to a mood of æsthetic contemplation which, though it has room for keen penetration, and even for a dim discernment of a serious import in the background of the puppet show, remains on the whole a playful attitude. The spectator is agreeably occupied with the look of things; and such social consciousness as is awake in him serves merely to give to his perceptions a precise measure of the seemly, or at most to enable him to glimpse something of a sharply corrective expression in the puckered visage of the comic showman.313

In comedy, the moral comes into view as "mores," as a part, and a principal part, of the customary, as we have it in a civilised society. Yet it is not disengaged and held up as moral. Molière, the Comedian of Society *par excellence*, shows us clearly enough that he is not trying to distinguish the more permanent and universal basis of society in morality from the variable accidents which enter into the manners of a particular society at a given date. The "gushing" mode of accost adopted by mere acquaintances which irritates Alceste is accepted by the poet as a standard of the fitting, just because as a fashion it is a social institution, to be good-naturedly accepted by the social kind of person. When M. Jourdain tries to step out of his bourgeois rank, the laughter he provokes depends primarily on the unseemliness of his ambition. Yet, at the end of the nineteenth century in Paris or London, such ambition is so common and meets with so large a success that we have almost forgotten to smile at it. Hence, when Taine talks of Molière as a "philosopher" illustrating "universal truths," he commits an error which may be pardoned, as due to the natural inclination to stretch the achievement of a great compatriot.314 What Molière does is to secure for the rather oddly formed group of customs and practices adopted by the particular society he is depicting, adequate exponents, who, in their advocacy of the social system against the socially perverse, not only disengage and give clearness to the unwritten laws, but may—so long as they do not raise the question of their deeper grounds—seek to recommend them by the most enlightened presentment of the common-sense attitude.

Now, in substituting the social for the moral point of view, the writer of comedy necessarily tends to slacken the cords that bind us in society. Nothing comes out more plainly in Molière's plays than the good-natured accommodation of social requirements to human infirmities. The author distinctly rejects the idea of going above this standard, of trying to improve on social customs—for example, in the comic treatment of Alceste and of Arnolphe. At heart, like his Roman predecessors, he takes sides with indulgence against all irksome restraint. He has the large tolerance, the readiness to excuse and to pass by, of the easy man of the world. Célimène's coquetries, for example, are accepted as natural in one who "is twenty years old". So it must be; for comedy is written to put us into an easy frame of mind, in which we are perfectly content with the world as it is.

From this point of view, we may see that the comedy of manners is not, fundamentally, so different from that of character as is often maintained. It breaks with the moral order of stable societies, no doubt, and turns its back rather rudely on this order. Yet it may still, in a sense, be said to adopt the social point of view. That is to say, it envisages the seemly as that which falls in with the code of manners which happens to obtain at the time. Its standard of fitness is, like that of the savage and of Molière, the customs of the tribe. It is the sour-tempered and suspicious husband, for whom Macaulay expresses so droll a concern, who in this inverted world becomes the anti-social kind of person. The large indulgence of this society is but an expansion of the indulgence common to Terence and to Molière. A sub-conscious awareness of the topsy-turvyness of things is with us as we look; and the quaint fancifulness of the inversion—if only like Lamb we can refuse for a moment to take serious views—is distinctly refreshing.

In saying that we go to meet comedy in the play-mood, in which our habits of moral approbation and disapprobation, and even of estimation of social values, are lulled to a sleep more or less profound, it is not meant that these serious tendencies in us can be ignored by the writer of comedy. As implied above, they mould our forms of the seemly, unknowingly to us perhaps, even as we look. And more, though inhibited by the play-like mood, they have force; and should the showman go too far, say in the direction of stripping off the veil of decency, they may wake up and make an end of the comic enjoyment. Just as tragic fear and pity may give way to physical revulsion when horror obtrudes itself, so when in comedy the unclean thrusts into view its ugly head, a sort of physical revulsion may silence laughter. The latitude in these matters conceded from time to time to comic art will, it is evident, vary greatly with the particular ratio between the vigours of the mirthful and moral tendencies.

The presentation of the comic aspects of men's behaviour on the stage is narrowly limited. As Sainte-Beuve reminds us, a whole people may have a fit (*accès*) of mania. If this happen to be the war-fury we shall have given us, as pointed out above, unmistakable elements of comic situation and character. Indeed, if a person who has just been in the midst of a wild "Jingoism" without losing his head will read Molière's plays he will not fail to be struck by numerous resemblances. And here, as in comedy, the figures have their comical contours and poses thrown into relief by a social background, as much superior to any single community at a particular moment, as a community to one of its members. Yet no national comedy could in these days follow Aristophanes and use such promising material, nor are we likely as yet to have a comedy for the civilised world.

Before leaving comedy, we may glance at other forms of literature which seem to approach its point of view. Of certain kinds of the so-called serious comedy of recent times I do not propose to speak. It seems more important to remark that prose fiction may now and again draw near the comic point of view. It sometimes presents us with a texture of fantastic situations and adventures which reminds us of the Aristophanean burlesque, as in the "Tartarin" series of Alphonse Daudet. This type of fiction gives us elemental laughter, uncomplicated by anything in the nature of sad reflection—though a little of the tenderness of humour may steal in. Or the tone of the story may approach that of the more sedate comedy, making, indeed, the one hardly distinguishable from the other, save through the narrative form. This holds good, for example, of the novels of Miss Austen. The social point of view is sharply defined and steadily adhered to, and critical reflection is confined to the *rôle* of giving a fuller and more lucid interpretation of the standards of the society illustrated.

The comic point of view may intrude, too, and tend to become supreme in fiction which has something of the deeper and more thrilling import. It seems to have been present, at times at least, to Balzac, and to Thackeray. But it is in Mr. Meredith's novels that we may study a new and a finer employment of the comic attitude in connection with the more enthralling kind of interest. The very subjects—for example, the egoist entangled in the situation which makes large demands for consideration; the father with a pedagogic system of his own concoction; the tailor more successful in soaring than his client M. Jourdain, with certain consequences to his family; the gallant cadet of an ancient house affected with the zeal of radicalism—these sound like the titles of comedy. And though the writer may allow the reedy tone of humour to be heard now and again he gives prominence to the fluty note of comedy, with its simplicity and clearness, and something of its sound of sharp correction, too. Occasionally indeed, as in *Beauchamp's Career,* this characteristic note will be distinctly heard at the end of a story which closes on a tragic disaster.

Yet a closer inspection will show that though the point of view of these writers may approximate to that of the comic poet, it remains distinct. This distinctness, moreover, is not due merely to the presence of a large serious interest which gives gravity to the story. It arises out of the circumstance that the writer of prose fiction, by addressing himself to the reflective mood of a solitary reader, and not to the apperceptive attitude of a spectator, will, even in presenting the comic aspects of his subject, unavoidably tend to transcend the standards of fitness adopted by a particular community, substituting for these the ideal standards of a community of the wise and good.

In comedy we have the appeal to laughter in its purity, the child's laughter at the funny show guided by an intelligent grasp of social customs. It addresses itself to the many, united by common modes of judgment and a common standard of fitness. Literature gives us, however, appeals of another kind. The writer who amuses us may seem, at least, to be very far from the social point of view, and the mood he induces may be by no means that of pure gaiety. After what has been said in the preceding chapter, a few words must suffice to indicate these other literary expressions of the laughing spirit.

We may distinguish two main varieties of this mixed tone: (*a*) the combination of laughter with the attitude of serious attack, as illustrated in satire; (*b*) its combination with mellowing feelings in what we have recognised as modern humour.

The distinguishing note of satire is the angry one of reprobation. Here vices and follies are no longer set before us as a diverting spectacle, but emphasis is laid on their moral indignity. The satirist is at the point of view of the moral judge; only, instead of the calmness of the judge, he has something of the fierce attitude of the prosecutor who aims at exposing and denouncing the turpitude of an offence.

This being so, we see that laughter enters into satire as an expression of contempt and as an instrument of punishment. It assumes its most pungent and most dreaded form, ridicule or derision. It is thus less a spontaneous feeling than a volitional process: the satirist wills to mock. As satirist he controls his personal indignation by an artistic purpose, such a presentment of his victim as will excite in his hearers or readers the full laughter of contempt. Hence, the large license he takes, in the employment of exaggeration and the devices of caricature, in the invention of degrading situations, and in the appropriation of humiliating comparison, figure of speech and the other resources of his art.

It is clear that the mirthful spirit when it thus lends itself to the purpose of damaging attack becomes modified to the point of transformation. To laugh with Juvenal or with Swift is to feel more of a bitter malignity than of gaiety. We may say that satire takes us back to the brutal laughter of the savage standing jubilant over his prostrate foe. Or we may describe the laughter as a feeling of "sudden glory" deeply tinged by the dominant angry attitude of the laugher.

Yet the intrusion of laughter into invective, just because it is the solvent of all serious moods, tends, as we have seen, to develop, if only for an instant, a lighter tone. Hence the gamut of dissimilar tones in satire, which at the one end is furiously denunciatory, at the other almost playful and good-temperedly jocular. The early popular "farce" of the Greeks, with its mocking and ironical speeches, and the satirical songs of the Middle Ages were apparently pieces of rollicking fun, like the comedy of Aristophanes, in which the satirical note was half-drowned in buffoonish laughter. Where, however, the composition is palpably a satire, the serious purpose may be seen to dominate and to colour the whole expression.

The characteristics of satire, thus roughly indicated, hold good alike whether the vices exposed be those of an individual, of a social class, of a society at a particular moment, or of mankind as a whole. In any case, the point of view is clearly that of a supposed moral judge and sentencer.

The presence of a purpose of serious exposure is not by any means equally clear in all cases; whence the denotation of the term satire is not sharply bounded. Comedy itself has been said to have a strong satirical element, and this seems certainly true of the compositions of Aristophanes, which, as Bergk remarks, contain in their mixture of tones a "biting scorn" and a "bitter irony".315 Romances, as pictures of men and their manners, are often described as satirical, presumably because a free delineation of human vices is taken to imply the condemnatory attitude and the intention to castigate. Yet here the castigation may be of the mildest, as in *Gil Blas*, which, according to Sainte-Beuve, does not hold up men in the mass to ridicule as wicked and foolish, but rather exposes their meanness and dulness.316 M. Taine finds the satirist's lash laid on heavily in the English school of fiction, even in the writings of Thackeray.317 Yet judgments as to a writer's intention based on the prevailing tone of the world he portrays are apt to seem subjective and capricious.

Satire proper, where the purpose of ridicule is confessed, is a very different thing. We see this in the works of Juvenal, of whom Prof. Tyrrell writes, "He is always in a rage and a laugh seems to sit strangely on his lips".318 In this more serious and poignant satire the laugh takes on a shrill note of malignity from its mental *entourage*. The virulence of the satire of antiquity has since been softened. This is frequently effected by allegorical disguise. The mediæval satires, such as that on cunning and treachery in the fable of the Fox, are examples. The satires of Voltaire and of the English satirists, including the bitter and unsparing Swift, illustrate the same tendency.

This throwing of a fierce attack, whether political or moral, into the form of an allegory, though it seems to veil the direction of the assault, really gives it more point. In the attacks of derision, at least, a back-handed blow may often hurt more than one straight from the shoulder. The reader's satisfaction includes no doubt an element of admiration for the finesse of art: yet more seems to be involved. Swift could not have shown us the absurdities in our social and political institutions half as well by any direct attack on them as he has shown us by the indirect attack in *Gulliver's Travels*. The indignity of a familiar vice or folly seems to be made palpable when it is thus ridiculed under the guise of some new semblance. Further, our laughter at the vice is reinforced by that which comes from the detection of the make-believe of the allegory. The playful element probably takes on something of malice from the prevailing tone of the satire, and in the end we may laugh yet more cruelly at the victim who is ever being anew detected, so to speak, under the literary mask.

Much the same kind of remark applies to the effect of simile, innuendo, irony, and all that we mean by wit in satire. We have touched on the playful side of wit under the head of Comedy. But this is only a part of what the word commonly implies. Even in comic dialogue there is something of attack, and the witty women of the Restoration and other writers have now and again a rasping tongue. Yet it is in satire that we see the deep malignity of wit. The witty sarcasms of Voltaire and the rest seem to be imps of malice disguised as toys. The sally of cruel meaning out of what looks harmless nonsense, or a mere verbal slip—as in the polished rebuke of a Master of Trinity to a too confident Junior Fellow, "we are all fallible, even the youngest of us"—has a wounding force greater than that of a direct mode of statement. The effect is still greater where failure and disgrace are exhibited under a thin ironical veil of glorious achievement, as in Pope's lines on the Lord Mayor's Show—said by Leigh Hunt to be the finest piece of wit he knew:—

> Now night descending the proud scene is o'er,
>
> But lives in Settle's numbers one day more.

In all such ironical inversion the satirist manages by a suggestion of the worthy and honourable to drive home with added force the humiliating truth; as in the remark of Cicero, apropos of an elderly dame who said that she was but forty years old: "I must believe her, for I have heard her say so any time these ten years".319 The presentation in this case of something hidden, immediately followed by an uncovering, may evoke an echo of the "bo-peep" laugh of infancy, which should, one supposes, tend to introduce a milder and playful tone into the attack; yet, owing to the predominance of the attitude of fierce derision, this very element of playfulness appears, somehow, to give a new pungency to the satirical thrust.

Nothing could be more unlike the laughter of virulent satire than that provoked by the expression of humour in literature. As our analysis would lead us to expect, we find in the truly humorous writer the mellowing influences of good nature and sympathy, and a large understanding and acceptance of that against which he pokes fun. While satire, sarcasm and their kind seem to be trying to push things away, or at least to alter them, humour, curiously enough, looks as if it were tenderly holding to the world which entertains it. Yet while all humorous writings illustrate these tendencies, the subjective and personal quality of humour is seen in the circumstance that every writer brings to bear on what he sees a new temper and attitude.

The contrast of the satirical and the humorous point of view may be conveniently studied by glancing at the current and much-discussed distinction between wit and humour. That these do not logically make a pair of contrasting species has been implied in our analysis of the two. Perhaps nowhere do we find the human mind to have been more strangely misled by the fact of the existence of two words than in this case. Wit, as essentially a manner of deportment of the intelligence, can stand in no simple and direct relation to an emotional mood like humour.

No doubt there are facts which give colour to the idea of an opposition in this case. Thus, it is indubitable that whereas humour specially favours certain kinds of imaginative and reflective activity, wit seems always to prefer, even in its play, something in the shape of an incisive logical process.320 But I suspect that the deeper ground of the distinction is to be found in the circumstance that the wit which is most brilliant, of keenest edge, and most effective in its stroke, appears always to grow out of, and so becomes associated with, those moods of satire and mordant mockery, to which humour as good-natured and tolerant is directly opposed. So it is with the wit of Voltaire and of others of his century.

A closer examination will, however, show that there is nothing incompatible between the humorous sentiment and the witty mode of behaviour of the intellect. As play indeed, wit quite naturally allies itself to the attitude of humour. It will be found that much that is commonly described as wit discloses the softening effect of humour, and might, indeed, just as well be called an illustration of humour. Those who really know the Irish will sometimes hesitate whether to speak of their wit or of their humour. The same applies, I feel sure, to a large number of Shakespeare's "witticisms".321 In all such cases, the wit, which when set in the fierce mood of the satirist has a nasty sting, not only becomes harmless, but may take on something of positive kindliness when it is tempered by an infusion of genial humour. The remark apropos of a very correct person, "He has not one redeeming vice," may illustrate the point. It may even, in this harmless form, come into a laugh which tells against the humorist, as in the observation of an idler, "I don't like working between my meals".322

Yet though in their well-marked forms thus dissimilar, the satirical and the humorous mood may shade one into the other in a way that makes it difficult to draw the boundary line. Heine, in some of his writings, *e.g.*, the poem *Deutschland*, tempers his mockery with sentiment and humour in such a way that one finds it hard to think of it as a satire. In places, indeed, this genius, so simple-looking yet really so profound, seems to become a consummate humorist, bringing out with a single touch all the laughter and all the tears of things. Was Lewis Carroll a satirist when he threw behind the fun of his children's stories some deeper meaning which for ever eludes us? or was this semblance of a meaning a part of his fun, his playful way of punishing the "grown up" for reading a child's book?

In modern literature, the interesting point to note is the growing interpenetration of the laughing and the serious attitude, and the coalescence of the mirthful spirit with sentiment. The two processes, though distinct, may run on together, as we may see in Shakespeare's plays. The humorous element introduced by the fool in "Lear" and elsewhere at once relieves the tragic tension, and gives a moment's play to that disposition towards a lighter laughing criticism which is always active when we survey colossal folly, even though the mental eye is at the moment focussed for its catastrophic effects. The laughter is controlled and kept tenderly humorous and half-sad by a large reflection, which does not lose sight, even at the relieving moment, of the lamentable ruin. It is only another way of combining the "fun" and the "pity" of it when the master brings a genial humour into comedy and makes us, with his faithful follower Bardolph, half-love and more than half-pity the faulty knight who so merrily entertains us.

As we have seen, prose-fiction may illustrate the comic spirit and something of the fiercer temper of satire. Yet laughter comes into it in another form. It has to accommodate itself to the presence of serious interests, and of a plot which involves sympathetic fear and strain. Hence it appears in stories which have a mixed tone, as it does indeed in comedy when this is not pure—for example, "heroic comedy," as illustrated by M. Rostand's *Cyrano*—in the guise of humour. That is to say, its gay treble note is complicated by an undertone, a resonance of the sadness of its *milieu*. One needs only to think how one laughs at Moses and his purchase of spectacles in the *Vicar of Wakefield*, or at the disfigurement of the hero in *Cyrano*.

A novel may, of course, present the grave and the gay in mere juxtaposition, so that the interaction and modification here spoken of are only very imperfectly realised. The notion of a good story entertained by many is of one that bears the imagination of the reader swiftly through a series of diverse scenes, now grave and pathetic, now gay and mirthful. A large part of modern fiction satisfies this need. Stories of wild adventure from *Gil Blas* to *Tom Jones* are "humorous" to the multitude in this sense. Even in the case of a real humorist like Dickens, whose amusing figures are there to touch the heart as well as to entertain the imagination, the perfect harmonising of tones may sometimes seem to be wanting. A humorist of another complexion, Laurence Sterne, seems to have missed the judicious mixture of laughter and sentiment in his *Sentimental Journey*.323

The art of humorous writing consists in part in selecting characters, incidents and the rest in such a way as to exhibit the intimate connections between that which amuses and that which touches the serious sentiments, respect and pity; and to develop the reflective consciousness which sustains the mood of humour. Goldsmith's history of the Vicar and his family is one of the best examples. Scott's Antiquary and Fielding's Parson Adams are characters which at once entertain and win us. Such humorous types involve, as Leigh Hunt has pointed out, a striking contrast within the characters, *e.g.*, the gullible and the manly in Parson Adams;324 and the sharpness of this contrast turns on that of the feelings excited by the constituents. The characters selected by humorous fiction may be consciously amusing, after the manner of the Merry Knight, or wholly unconscious of their laughter-provoking power. A valuable part of this amusing portraiture consists in bringing out the fresh and odd-looking characteristics not only of individuals, but of classes and even of races.

In addition to this objective presentation of the humorous aspects of character and its relations, the writer may further the effect by striking now and again undertones of quaint reflection and so introducing an element of subjective humour. The notion that such reflection is out of place in narrative art seems strange to a student of the history of literature. If there was room for the comments of the onlooking chorus in Greek drama, and for the yet deeper reflections supplied by the acting onlookers in Shakespeare's plays, there should be room for it in a prose narrative. In truth, some of the best writers of fiction, Fielding, Thackeray and George Eliot among others, make excellent use of this reflective accompaniment. In the best works of the last-named writer we have something of Shakespeare's art of adding a pregnant observation which, so far from disturbing, rather furthers the mood needed for a due appreciation of the action.

In the great humorous writings, those of Rabelais, Cervantes and— removed by an interval no doubt—Sterne, we appear to find presented a largeness of subject and of treatment which makes direct appeal as much to reflection as to perception. You must know the Middle Ages, which are being laughingly kicked aside, before you will even care for Gargantua; you must envisage Don Quixote and his squire, not as two individuals or even as two types of character, but as embodiments of two remote levels of culture, and more, of two opposed ways of looking at the world, before you will begin to feel all the humour of these juxtapositions. And so of the great contrast between Mr. Shandy and his brother, the Captain. There is no need for the interpolation of reflection: the scale, the breadth of treatment, the wealth of ideas poured out, these compel us to reflect. The laughter which comes from the perceptions of the utter incongruity of the mental and moral structures thus juxtaposed and attached is saturated with this reflection. And more, so right, so likeable, so estimable even is each of these contrasting characters, with its well-marked temper and *manière de voir,* that our sympathies go out towards both. Thus we leave the perceptual level and the relative point of view of comedy far behind us, reaching a standpoint near that of the thinker who embraces all particular points of view, and yet may manage to have his own laugh in the end. When, as in Jean Paul's *Siebenkäs,* and yet more clearly in Carlyle's *Sartor Resartus,* the contrast seems to open up the great collision in human experience between sentiment and prosaic reality, idealism and the earth-binding instincts of practical life, we stand, indeed, on the border-line between the humour of fiction and that of philosophy.

Humour has its place, a respectable one too, in essays and other forms of literature which deal directly with reality and are products not so much of imagination as of thought. In these, the contrast between the serious and the playful appears in transitions from a perfectly grave to a humorous kind of reflection. Marked differences of tone are observable here also. The humorous remark may be but a momentary diversion of the attention, a playful side-glance, in a serious argument. In some writings, *e.g.,* those of Sir Thos. Browne and of Lamb, the humorous element hardly amounts to a digression, or even to a momentary interruption, but is fused into and half lost to sight in the serious argument.325 Among more recent writers, too, including some yet living, we have admirable examples of historical narrative and criticism lit up here and there with soft glow-worm points of humour. In other cases, the humorous feature may be so large as to modify the colour of the whole, as in Miss Kingsley's *Travels in West Africa.* An Essay, again, may be as a whole a *jeu d'esprit* and the fun seem to preponderate, while the manner is throughout that of grave argument; or, in more subtle work, as some of Charles Lamb's, it may be best described as fun sandwiched in between a look of seriousness on the surface, and a real seriousness of meaning below. The fusion of tones leaves much to be desired in the case of many writers who are popularly regarded as skilled humorists. A mere interruption of serious thought by a sort of playful "aside" does not prove the existence of the gift of humour, which is essentially the power of playing on moods not only dissimilar but usually antagonistic in a way that avoids all shock and sense of discontinuity.

CHAPTER XII.
ULTIMATE VALUE AND LIMITATIONS OF LAUGHTER.

Our study has taken us through various regions of research. In looking for the germ of laughter we found ourselves in the wide and misty plains of biological speculation. In tracing its development we took a dip into the pleasant vales of child-psychology and anthropology, and then tried to climb the winding paths of social evolution. Having reached in this way the heights of modern civilisation, we made a special investigation into the social organisation of laughter, as represented in the art of comedy, and into the gradual appearance of a new type of laughter, essentially individual and independent of the social standard, to which is given the name of humour. Throughout this voyage of discovery we have kept in view the question of the function of the laughing spirit in the life of the individual and of the community. It remains to determine this function more precisely.

In order to assign its proper place and its value to a large spiritual tendency such as runs through human mirth, we must for a moment push our investigation into a yet more difficult and obscure region, that of philosophy. This is necessary for more than one reason. To begin, we can hardly hope to reach a clear view of the worth of the laughing impulse without the help of some clearly thought view of life as a whole; and such a "Weltanschauung" seems only to be attainable at the level of philosophic reflection. There is, however, a second reason for entering this more remote and private domain of knowledge. Philosophy is a carrying forward to its highest point of development of that individual criticism of life, with which, as we have seen, the quieter tones of laughter associate themselves. It would thus seem to be desirable to inquire how far along the road of philosophic speculation this companionship of the mirthful spirit in her quieter mood is possible. This inquiry may conveniently be pursued at once as supplementary to our discussion of humour.

As pointed out in the chapter on the subject, reflective humour grows out of a mutual approximation of two tendencies which seem to the unexamining person to be directly antagonistic, namely, the wholly serious turn for wise reflection and the playful bent towards laughter. In philosophic humour, touched on in our survey of the laughable in literature, this antagonism seems at first sight to be particularly sharp. The plain man, to whom philosophic speculation presents itself as something remote from all human interests as he conceives of them, may well receive a shock when he hears that it holds potentialities of a smile at least, if not of a laugh—for the person who engages in the occupation, that is to say, and not merely for him who looks on. It seems to be incumbent on us, therefore, to try to make this drawing together of impulses which look so hostile a little more intelligible.

The humorist, as we have viewed him, is able through the development of his individuality to detach himself from many of the common judgments and much of the common laughter of the particular community of which he is a member. He develops his own amusing mode of contemplation, which involves a large substitution for the standards of custom and "common-sense," of the ideal standards of reason. The habit of philosophic thought may be said to complete this uplifting of the individual to ideal heights, and its concomitant process, the expansion of the view of the irrational, the essentially unfitting, the amusing. A word must suffice to indicate the way in which it does this.

Philosophy, as we know, going boldly beyond the special sciences, pushes on to a deeper knowledge of things, and of these in their totality, of what we call the universe. In this effort it has to envisage things in a way essentially different from that of everyday observation. The modern philosopher may do his best to reach his conception of the reality of things by a careful analysis of experience; yet in the end his theory seems to have transformed our familiar world beyond the possibility of recognition.

In this philosophic re-construction of the real world, man, his relation to nature, and his history have to be re-considered. It illustrates a powerful tendency to view human life and experience as a phase of a larger cosmic movement determined by an ideal end. The introduction of ideal conceptions, by lifting us above the actual, seems to throw upon the latter an aspect of littleness, of futility, of something like the dishonour of failure. The ideal requirement proves hopelessly inapplicable to much, at least, of our everyday world; so that, as long as we remain at its point of view, familiar things—say the persons we happen to be thrown with, and a good deal in ourselves, social experiments growing out of some passing trend of "popular thought," and even long periods of history—take on the aspect of contradictions, of futile things that at least do not count, if they do not actually delay the fruition of the ideal.

So, too, when philosophy becomes distinctly practical. Whether we take happiness or moral perfection or self-realisation as the ideal end of men's conduct, a large part of the conduct which unfolds itself under our eyes, including much of our own, begins to look sadly poor and shabby, as soon as we venture seriously to apply an ideal as test. Much at least of what men praise as virtue shows itself to be of doubtful value, and at any rate to have received a laudation quite disproportionate to its true worth.

Lastly, this belittling effect of ideas on everyday realities is seen when philosophy constructs for us the ideal type of human society, and of that confederacy of civilised states of which, now and again, it has had its dream. Under the searching rays of these ideal conceptions even the "common-sense" to which "advanced" communities hold so tenaciously may begin to look something compacted rather of darkness than of light.

The situation would seem to offer room for some of those modes of transforming the aspects of things which we have found to be excitants of laughter. If philosophic contemplation effects a reduction of great things to littleness, of substances to illusory shadows, of the elevated glories of men to the level of barely passable dignities, it should, one may reason, help men to laugh. Yet the fact that a philosopher has been known to the ages as the laughing one suggests that mirth has not been a common characteristic of his kind.

In order to understand this, we must recall one or two facts. For one thing, though seriousness *may* combine with a taste for the laughable, it is and remains fundamentally opposed to the playfulness of mirth. Philosophers are serious persons: their constructive thought is of the most arduous of human activities, and imposes on those who undertake it an exceptional amount of serious concentration. Little wonder, then, if we so rarely find in them a marked fondness for the playful. The great and ineradicable gravity of the philosopher has been sufficiently illustrated in his theoretic treatment of our subject.

In addition to this general reason, there are others and variable ones, differing with the kind of philosophic creed adopted, and with the temperamental attitude of the individual towards it. To begin with differences of creed, we must remember that a philosopher's doctrine, while it may invest our common world and our common life with an aspect of indignity, may at the same time reduce these to mere semblances by setting them in contrast to the ideal region which it regards as the sphere of the veritable realities. In this way, as in Plato's Idealism, we may see a quasi-religious tendency to lift men above the follies, deceptions and seeming evils of the world to the sublime verities. Such a doctrine, if consistently held, reserves but a small place for laughter—save perhaps for the happy smile of release or escape. Plato, the thinker of many moods, was able to adapt his doctrine to attitudes widely different from the half-poetic, half-religious one to which on the whole he leaned; and some of these proved to be compatible with a delicate vein of mirth. Perhaps one may find in Plato a reflection of the different attitudes of the gods—to communion with whom his spirit aspired—towards luckless and erring mortals: the serene indifference of those on the height, and a mild good-natured interest in what is seen below, which lends itself to the softer kind of ironical banter. What is told us of the laughter of the deities is always, perhaps, a little difficult to reconcile with their remote altitude and the detachment of spirit which seems proper to this; being, either in its mocking virulence, or in its good-natured familiarity, rather too suggestive of a close attachment to our race; for which reason, by the way, philosophers, if they wish to soar god-wards and still to keep a laughing down-glance on their fellows, should beware lest they soar too high.

How high-pitched speculation tends to silence laughter by withdrawing the philosopher too far from the human scene may easily be seen by a glance at the historical schools. The Stoic and the Epicurean alike, widely dissimilar as were their views of the good and their moral tempers, took into seclusion the philosophic life which Aristotle had bidden them combine with a discreet participation in the social life about them; seeking, each in his own manner, to realise its self-sufficiency and its consolations. There, no doubt, they reflected much on the follies of the unwise who remained in the crowd. Yet the Stoical temper, with its striving after a passionless imperturbability, excluded the idea of a laughing, quite as much as of a pitying, survey. On the other hand, the Epicurean, though his theory of life accentuated the value of the tranquil pleasures, did not apparently find in his Garden a corner for the quiet amusement of a laughter-bringing contemplation.

In this way philosophy, by substituting a new and ideal mode of thought and life for the common mode, is apt to dismiss it as void of significance and unreal, and so to be unable to laugh at ordinary humanity just because it has ceased to be interested in it. Yet all philosophising does not thus belittle the realm of reality, as common men regard it. Philosophers have been known to regard as realities the same particular things that Plato contemned as mere shadows, and to reconstruct and to justify as rational what the plain man accepts as his world. When this goes so far as to insist on the goodness of things human, and to say that the world as a whole is as perfect as it can be, and thus in a new way, as it would seem, to break away from the common view, it seriously threatens the *locus standi* of the laugher. Nothing, indeed, in the way of a theory of life would appear to be more fatal to a mirthful temper of the mind than an out-and-out optimism. At most, laughter would take on the aspect of the serene gaiety of a happy and thoughtless girl; as it does, I suspect, in the case of Abraham Tucker, for whom Sir Leslie Stephen claims the character of a "metaphysical humorist".326 It is true, as I have elsewhere shown,327 that a genial and tolerant laughter may predispose a man, should he begin to philosophise, to adopt an optimistic theory of the world. Nevertheless, I believe that a firm grasp of such a theory would tend to reduce very considerably the scope of his laughter. It is just as well, perhaps, that R. L. Stevenson—whose predominant inclination to a hopeful and cheerful view of things is clearly shown in his idea that every man carries his ideal hidden away, as the Scotch boys used to carry lanterns in a silent ecstasy—did not go farther than his letters show him to have gone, along the path of philosophic construction.

If, on the other hand, the manner of philosophic speculation at once accepts the common facts of life as real, and yet as inherently and hopelessly bad, laughter is even more effectually excluded. There may, it is true, be room in the pessimist's creed for a grim irony, of which, indeed, we find a trace now and again in the writings of Schopenhauer and his followers; but for laughter pure and simple, or even for laughter mellowed by the compassion which the pessimist bids us cultivate, there seems to be no breathing-space. The state of things is too tragic to allow even of a smile.

It remains to determine the relation of one other tendency in this high thinking to the possibilities of laughter. In philosophic scepticism, with its insistence on the relativity of our knowledge and on the impossibility of attaining to rational certainty, we seem to find a denial of all philosophy rather than a particular species of it; nevertheless, as the history of the subject shows, it is the outcome of a distinct and recurrent attitude of the philosophic mind. Now scepticism does undoubtedly seem to wear a rather malicious smile. This smile may be said to express an amusement at the spectacle of illusions pricked, which tells at least as much against the high-soaring thinker as against the man of common day who relies on the intuitions of his "common-sense". The sceptic's attitude leans, indeed, more towards that of common-sense, in so far that, while destroying the hope of absolute knowledge, it urges the *practical* sufficiency of such conjectural opinion as we are able to reach.

Scepticism thus introduces another standpoint for the laugher and adds to the sum of laughable things. This is the standpoint of the practical man and of what we call common-sense, so far as this is knowledge shaped for the guidance of men in the ordinary affairs of life. This common-sense, as its name plainly tells us, is essentially a social phenomenon. Here, then, within the group of tendencies underlying reflection—that is to say, the kind of intellectual activity which marks the highest development of the individual point of view—we encounter the contrast between this and the social point of view. So far as we are able in our philosophic moments to "see the fun of it," as R. L. Stevenson says apropos of a modern philosopher, we join the choir of common-sense laughers—the laughing realists as distinguished from the laughing idealists.328 From their point of view, as the history of comedy plainly illustrates, all highly abstract speculation looks amusing because of its quaint remoteness from their familiar realities and interests; because, too, of a keen suspicion of its being a vain attempt to soar above the heads of common mortals. To pull down the speculative soarer to his proper footing on our humble earthcrust is always a gratifying occupation to the lovers of mirth. Even the soarers themselves will sometimes give one another a kick downwards, the man of science loving to have his joke at the expense of the unverifiable conceptions of the metaphysician, and the latter being sometimes lucky enough to turn the tables by showing how physical science itself may, by its abstract methods, manage to strip material things, the properties and laws of which it sets out to explain, of the last shreds of reality.329

A word may serve to define the relation of philosophic humour to the tendencies just indicated. Humour, we have found, is characterised by an inclination to reflect, and to take the large views of things which embrace relations; further, by a mirthful caprice of fancy in choosing for play-ground the confines of issues felt all the time to be serious. It grows distinctly philosophic when, as in Jean Paul or his disciple, Carlyle, the contemplation of things breaks through the limitations of the viewer's particular world-corner, surmounts "relative" points of view, and regards humanity as a whole, with oneself projected into the spectacle, as nearly as possible as disinterested spectator.

We need not look for the philosophic humorist among zealous adherents of the schools. In these, as elsewhere, a fervid devotion tends, through its narrowing effect on ideas and its rigid fixation of the point of view, to shut out humour, which even in its most serious vein loves an ample reserve of space for free wanderings in search of new aspects of things. The humorist is much more likely to be found among students of philosophy who retain a measure of scholarly impartiality in relation to the competing creeds.

A full development of humour in the philosopher seems to be impossible, save where the amusing aspects of speculative soaring are dimly recognised. This may come through a study of the history of the subject; for it is hard not to smile at the spectacle of a man refurbishing and possibly adding a new handle to one of the "systems" which have had their day (and more, perhaps) and undertaking once more to use it as a deadly weapon against the adversary. A dash of the sceptical spirit, also an ability now and again to see the pretentiousness of it all, would appear to be needful for a large humorous enjoyment. One should have, too, at least a side-glance for the fun of the proceeding when the human pygmy tries the giant's stride by offering us a definition of the absolute.

It would seem, then, as if the philosophic humorist needed to combine two opposed points of view; that of the thinker who criticises actual life in the light of ideas, and that of the practical man who takes his stand on the fact of primal human needs and seeks an interpretation of things which will satisfy these. He should be able to soar with the Platonist to the realm of Ideas, so as to enjoy the droll aspect which men's behaviour assumes as soon as a glimmer of light is made to fall on it from the Universal Forms; and he should be no less capable of taking up the standpoint of everyday reality and common-sense, so far as to discern the element of a practical irrationality which lurks in any undue insistence on these Ideas.

This combination in philosophic humour of two opposed tendencies is illustrated in its attitude towards the question of the worth of life. Since a humorist is characterised by a certain depth and range of sympathy, he is not likely to accept the optimist's easy way of getting rid of the sufferings of humanity. At this point, at least, he will be alive to the obstinate and inexpugnable reality of our concrete experiences. Yet, just because he insists on never losing his hold on his buoyant laughter, he will not sink into the pessimists depths of complaint. He will see that even the large spectacle of human struggle, in which there is much to sadden a compassionate heart, begins to wear the shimmer of a smile as soon as we envisage it as a sort of game played by destiny against our race. Just as a glimpse of the provoking, almost malicious aspects of the circumstances which irritate us in our smaller world may stifle the rising imprecation, by bringing up a smile or even a *sotto voce* laugh; so, when a philosophic humorist looks out upon the larger human scene, he may find the starting sigh checked by a glance at the playful irony of things. The reflective mind will indeed readily find in the scheme of the world traces of an impish spirit that must have its practical joke, cost what it may. With a fair appearance of wise purpose, the destinies have contrived to combine just the amount of bungling needed to convey an intention of playful though slightly malicious teasing.

Thus, in the final evaluation of the world, humour may find its place. Perhaps it is not too much to say that the last word on man and his destiny leaves an opening for the humorous smile. So quaintly do the rational and the irrational elements seem to be interwoven in the structure of our world, that a humorist, for whom, as we have seen, the spectacle must always count as much, might almost construct a new Theodicy and say: "The world is at least the best possible for amusing contemplation".330

We have spoken of philosophy as hovering aloof from our common life, and this idea might seem to exclude all possibility of a utility in the exercise of a philosophic humour. Yet even when men philosophise and so appear to erect about them a new cosmos, they remain in their human world and are doing something towards shaping their relations to it; so that, after all, we may not unreasonably look here, too, for some self-corrective function in laughter, some aid rendered by it to that adjustment of the self to its surroundings, which is enforced on us all—the exalted thinker no less, let us say, than his faithful quadruped, whose world his master's strange habits make sadly complex.

The first service of such a philosophic humour is to complete the process of a laughing self-correction. It is only when we rise to the higher point of view of a philosophic reflection and see our own figure projected into the larger whole, that we are able to estimate ourselves and our concerns with some approximation to justness. As we look down the vast time perspective we first fully discern our flitting part in the world. And the glimpse of the dwarfed figure we cut in the vast assemblage of things, followed by the reflection how well it can work out its hidden purpose whether or not we happen to be on the scene, may suffice fully to reveal to us the absurdity in the crude exaggerations of our dignity, of our usefulness and of our troubles, and bring to the lips the corrective smile, even if it fail to evoke the yet more valuable self-purifying laugh.

A like helpfulness is brought us by philosophic humour when we contemplate the whole human lot. In estimating our world as a dwelling-place for man, there is surely room for the exaggeration which comes from a natural indignation at what hurts us, or from a natural impatience at being able to do so little to better our estate. Similarly, when we undertake to pronounce on the moral worth of our species. It is, after all, our world, and, so far as we know, our only one; and a side-glance at the requirements of a practical wisdom may suffice to bring the smile which instantly corrects a disposition to decry it overmuch. Such a glance may save us alike from the sentimentalities of the cultivator of *Weltschmerz*, from the foolish bitterness of the misanthrope, and from the sadly unbecoming vanity of the "philosopher" who teaches that the world and the institutions of human society exist for the sake of the man of genius. A friend of Carlyle tells me that the gloomy sage would sometimes, after pouring out one of his long and savage tirades against things in general, suddenly hold breath, and then let himself be swiftly borne downwards to more familiar levels on the rapid of a huge laugh, almost as voluminous, perhaps, as that of Teufelsdröckh, which he has so vividly described for us. In this way, one conjectures, there came to him a moment of perfect lucidity, in which he saw the absurdity of the overstrained attitude likely to be produced by undue violence of emotion, aided by an irrepressible turn for preaching to one's fellows; a moment when, perhaps, the stubborn realities, which his words had made a show of demolishing, were seen securely standing and ironically smiling at his impotent rage.

In the foregoing account of laughter and its uses, we have sharply separated the individual from the social point of view. Fifty years ago, such a distinction would have required no justification. It seems, however, just now to be the fashion to think of the individual as merely an anatomical detail, too small to be really distinguished, of the "social organism," and of his part on the earthly scene as consisting merely in making a small contribution, which at its best is a negligible quantity, to the efficiency of this organism.

This is not the place to argue so serious a matter. At the risk of appearing unfashionable, one may venture to keep to the old notion that in counting human values we must assign a high one to individuality; that, for the sake of the community itself, a proper freedom for the full development of a man's own mind, tastes, and character, is something which should be secured even at great cost; and that, were this not so, society's claims on the individual have well-defined limits, beyond which every man has the right, and owes it to himself as a primal duty, to develop himself in the way which his natural inclinations enlightened by reflection may suggest to him. To insist further on this point would almost be to cast a slur on our literature, which contains some of the masterly pleadings for individual liberty.

This freedom for individual self-development clearly includes a perfect right to form one's own view of one's world, and to derive as much amusement as one can from a humorous contemplation of it. It could only be something akin to an awe-struck flunkeyism which would make a person hesitate here. To one who has cultivated the requisite observation and taste in the fellowship of one or two congenial friends, the following of the tortuous movements of the laughable in all domains of human industry and of human indolence is one of the crowning felicities of life: the fun is always old in its essence, wherefore we respond so quickly; yet it is always new in its embodiments, wherefore we go on relishing it with an unabated keenness.

The indulgence in this mode of amusing contemplation is, I readily grant, in a sense anti-social, that is to say, opposed to what the laugher's community at the moment accepts as fitting and as good. When a tranquil observer of his social world laughs at the pretences, at the futilities, or it may be at the vagaries of its high dignitaries, he may not improbably feel half-terrified at the sound of his laugh; so firmly has our early schooling set in us a tendency to regard as insolent upstarts all small things when they challenge big ones: whether a "cheeky" schoolboy standing up to his big senior, or a small country confronting a big one, or a "petty" anti-war minority facing a "practically unanimous" people. Insolence it may be, yet perhaps to the eye of reason not more contemptible than the genuine ὕβρις in which great things are wont to indulge freely as well within their right. It is indisputable, as urged above, that the verdicts of the many, when they appear to fix the permanent demands of social life, or to store away some of the precious fruit of experience slowly maturing with the ages, are entitled to respect; and a wise man will not hastily dismiss any popular opinion which promises to have persistence. On the other hand, it is no less clear that the views of minorities—whether singular or plural in number—are exposed to special risks of their own. Yet this, and more, does not affect the contention that popular opinion, just because it is popular, is almost completely relieved of that necessity of finding reasons for its assertions which presses heavily upon a minority; and, what is more serious, is subject to various and potent influences which are just as likely to lead to error as to truth. An opinion which may be seen to result from a mental process palpably warped by prejudice does not grow valid merely by multiplying the number of those who adopt it; for the increase may easily be the result, either of the simultaneous working of a like prejudice, or of the contagion which propagates psychical states, as well as physical, among perfectly inert members of a crowd.

At the risk of appearing insolent, then, one must urge that the individual and the society have their reciprocal claims. The most extravagant adulator of his community would, perhaps, allow that she has her favourites, and that some of the obscure "Judes" have no particular reason for bearing her affection. The limbs of the body politic which find themselves emaciated by under-feeding, while the belly is bloated with over-feeding, may perhaps be forgiven for not joining in the pæans on the glories of the social organism. Yet one need not urge this line of remark. Little chance, alas, of our Judes or our starvelings betaking themselves to a laughter which even approaches that with which we are now dealing. Those who would enter the gateway of this haunt of quiet amusement must leave outside all grudging and sense of failure. Happy he who having played the social game and lost can, with a merry shrug of the shoulders, and at least half a laugh, betake himself to such a calm retreat. He will find one into which the garden of Epicurus may be said to open, where he can gather about him, at any rate, the congenial friends who are always ready to hold sweet discourse with him through their books; patient friends whom he cannot offend by an unwise interruption, though unhappily they are out of reach of the gratitude which he would fain tender them. Here he may now and again glance through the loopholes in the wall and see each new day enough of the drolleries of the social scene to deepen his content.

The evolutionist has accustomed us to the idea of the survival of the socially fit, and the elimination of the socially unfit sort of person. But more forces are at work in the world than our men of science dream of. There is, oddly enough, a force which favours the survival of the unfit, widely different from that supplied by others' preservative benevolence: the impulse to adapt one's environment to the peculiarities of one's organism by turning the world into a plaything. How many men in one of the highly civilised communities of to-day may have learned to keep their heads above the water by the practice of a gentle laughter, no one knows or will ever know. It is enough to say that there are such, and that after fully cultivating their gift of humour they have found a world worth coming back to, with their part in which they will be perfectly contented. Some of these, who would probably be called social failures by the faithful adherent to conventional standards, have been known to me, and have been reckoned among the most delightful of my companions and most valued of my friends. Society's neglect of them, or their neglect of society, has at least permitted them to develop the gift of a wise and entertaining discourse.

I am far from suggesting, however, that this gay solitude—*à deux,* or *à peu de gens*—is only for the social failure. Even in our much-extolled age a philosopher will sometimes be found who is perverse enough to hold with Plato that the mass of society are wrongheaded, and that he will best consult his well-being by seeking a wall for shelter from the hurricane of wind and dust. Such an one may do worse than betake himself to our retreat. And a wise man who, like Montaigne, feels that he has lived "enough for others" and desires to "live out the small remnant of life" for himself may appropriately draw towards its entrance, not minding the shouts of "Old fogey!" which come from behind. Nay, more, as already hinted, a man who feels that his place is in the world may be advised now and again to enter the retreat, if haply he may find admission as a guest.

It may, however, be objected that even when a man thus detaches himself as spectator from his society he perforce remains at the social point of view in this sense, that the critical inspection which brings the coveted laugh involves a reference to an ideal community. The objector might find colour for his statement in the fact that it is Frenchmen, that is to say, members of the most sociable of modern races, who have chiefly dwelt on the delights of retirement from the crowd. I am not greatly concerned to dispute with such an objector; it is enough for my purpose to say that the point of view of our supposed contemplator is far-removed from that habitually adopted in any community which one could instance. As such, it stands clearly enough marked off as individualistic. To this it may be added that in that kind of laughter at the social spectacle which presupposes philosophic reflection, the point of view is no longer in any sense that of a particular community: it has become that of a human being, and so a citizen of that system of communities which composes the civilised world.

I do not doubt that during this laughing contemplation of the social whole, of which at the moment he is not serious enough to regard himself as a part, the individual will feel society pulling at his heels. The detachment from his community, though it fall far short of the abandonment of the recluse, will, as already hinted, be felt to be a revolt. When, glancing back at the crowd wreathing itself in a dust-cloud, he laughs with his large laugh free from rancour, he may catch a glimpse of the absurdity of his critical performances. Here, again, we meet the final contradiction between ideal conceptions and obdurate everyday facts. It is a droll encounter when the foot of pure intellect, just as it is parting from the solid earth, strikes against the sturdy frame of philistine common-sense, of "that which subdues us all," philosophers included. The individualism of the point of view in a laughing contemplation of one's social world is only surmounted when a large philosophic humour thus draws the laughers self into the amusing scene.

We may now better define the attitude of the humorist in its relation to that of the comedian and of the satirist. The comic spirit, placing itself at the social point of view, projects as laughable show an eccentric individual, or group of individuals. Satire, when it attacks the manners of an age, may be said to project the society, turning it into an object of derision. Humour, as we have seen, sometimes does the like, though in its laughter at the social scene it is neither passionately vindictive nor concerned with the practical problem of reforming a world. To this may be now added that as a sentiment nourished by sympathy it tends, when something of philosophic width of contemplation is reached, to combine the social and the individual mode of projection by taking up the self into the spectacle of the whole.

Enough has been said, perhaps, on the developments of individual laughter. Its point of view seems on inquiry to justify itself as a distinct and a legitimate one. With some idea of the ways of this, as well as of the larger laughter of societies and groups, we should be able to form an estimate of the final significance and utility of the laughing impulse.

Laughter, born of play, has been seen above to possess a social character. Throughout the evolution of communities, from the first savage-like tribes upwards, we have observed it taking a considerable part in the common life, helping to smooth over difficulties of intercourse, to maintain what is valued, and to correct defects. It remains to ask under this head, what is its whole value to-day as a social force, and what indications of the future can be discovered in the tendencies which we note in its later social developments.

These questions appear to be best approached by a reference to the results of our study of comedy. This, in its higher forms, has shown itself to be the clear expression of the attitude of a community, when it would laugh away something in its members which it sees to be unfitting, though it may not regard it as serious enough to call for a more violent mode of ejection. That which is thus lightly dismissed is always something which looks anti-social, whether or not it takes on for moral reflection the aspect of a vice.

A common tendency among writers on comedy is to claim for it the value of a moral purgative, to attribute to it the power of effecting directly a process of self-correction in the spectator. Even Congreve and Vanbrugh, in their defence of their plays against Jeremy Collier, pretended that they were reformers of the world.

This agreeable supposition will not, one fears, bear critical inspection. One objection, just touched on, is that comedy does not deal a blow straight at the immoral, as the language of Aristotle and of some of his citers appears to suggest. This circumstance seems to stand seriously in the way of its effecting a moral purification. Nor does the holding up to merry contemplation of the tendency of men to stray too far from the customary social type, imply a serious purpose of correction behind. Though she may wear a shrewishly corrective expression, the Comic Muse is at heart too gay to insist on any direct instruction of her audience. A glance at her stern-eyed sister, Satire, will convince us of this. On the other side, we meet with another and more fatal objection: the mental pose of the spectator at the comic show makes it extremely unlikely that he should at the moment apply the object-lesson so as to discern the laughable side of his own shortcomings. One remembers here that a man is all too slow in making such a self-application even in the serious surroundings of a church, where a remark, pointed perhaps with a significant turn of the finger (I speak of ruder times), is recognised by all but himself as specially aimed at him; and if so, how can we expect a spectator at a comedy, in the playful mood which has no room for any serious thought, to rub in the moral medicament supplied him?

Such purification as is possible can, it is plain, be only indirect. When Lessing writes "the whole of morality has no more powerful and effective *preservative* than the laughable" he seems to imply this indirectness. So far as the provocative lurks in the immoral, we can say that our laughter at the comic exhibition may serve as a useful prophylactic. By tracing out, with the guidance of the comic poet, the unsuspected developments and effects of a failing, we may be furthering our moral salvation through the setting up of a new internal safeguard. If the tendencies should later on thrust up their ugly forms in ourselves, the fact of our having laughed at them may make a considerable difference in the swiftness and energy of the movement of repression. The fear of becoming ridiculous, which grows better defined and so more serviceable in one who has made acquaintance with comedy, is a valuable side-support of what we call moderation and reasonableness in men; and comedy is entitled to her modest meed as one of our health-preservers.

Yet we may easily go wrong here, doing an offence to our gay enchantress by taking her words too seriously. She looks, at any rate, as if she wanted much more to please us than to improve us. In considering her aim one is reminded, through a relation of contrast, of what Aristotle said about the connection between pleasure and virtue. The good man, he tells us, though aiming at virtue, will be the more satisfied if pleasure comes by the way, giving a kind of unexpected finish to the virtuous achievement. The art of comedy merely reverses the order: she aims directly at pleasure, but is far too good-natured and too wise to object to furthering virtue if this comes as a collateral result of her entertainment.331

The comedy, at once wise and gay, of a past age seems to have parted from us; and one would look in vain to newer developments of the art for any considerable instruction in the lesser social obligations. Nor is the corrective function of a large communal laughter likely to be carried on by such new forms of art as our "social satire," in so far as these can be said to keep at the point of view of the good sense of a community. The tendency to-day seems to be rather to force a laugh from us at some bizarre extravagance of manners, which we could never think of as a possibility for ourselves; or, on the other hand, to bring us near a cynical point of view, at which the current of our laughter becomes shallow and slightly acidulated, a point of view which has little, if any, promise of a moral stiffening of the self against insidious attack.

In spite of this, laughter, or the potentiality of it, remains a social force. A measure of faith enables one to believe that even a political leader is sometimes checked by the fear of laughter—on the other side. It is probable that the men of good sense in every community are kept right more than they know by the faintly heard echo of the "dread laugh". If there is a danger just now of a conspiracy between a half-affected over-seriousness on the one side and an ignorant pretentiousness on the other, in order to banish the full genial laugh of other days, we may be allowed to pray fervently for its failure.

We have seen a tendency to claim too much in the way of serious function for the laughter of comedy. This desire to emphasise its practical utility, which is to be looked for perhaps in a people too pragmatic to seize the value of light things, is illustrated in a curious and mostly forgotten dispute as to the fitness of ridicule to be a test of truth. The debate was opened by Shaftesbury, who maintained its fitness, and was carried on by Warburton, Karnes and others. Much of it reads quaintly naïve to-day. Shaftesbury's paradox almost sounds like a malicious attempt to caricature the theory of Prof. W. James, referred to in an earlier chapter of this work. To suggest that we know a piece of folly, say that of Malvolio, to be folly because we laugh at it, is surely to be thrusting on our laughter a dignity which is quite unmerited, and, one may add, does not become it. This point was not held to in the discussion, which, as I have shown elsewhere, soon became a contest about the rights and the restraints of laughter.332

There is a like risk of exaggerating the useful function in estimating the service of laughter to the individual. No deep penetration of mind is needed for perceiving that a lively sensibility to the touch of the ludicrous will expose a man to considerable loss. To all of us, so far as we have to live in the world and consort with those who, being both solemn and dull, are likely to take offence, if not with those who, like Mr. Meredith's entertaining ladies, cultivate the fine shades, a quick eye for drolleries is likely to bring situations of danger. This drawback must be considered in appraising the total value of laughter to a man.

With respect to its function as aiding the individual in a healthy self-correction, enough has been said. It is, in truth, no small advantage to be able to blow away some carking care with a good explosion of mirth. And if the world is much with us, we shall be likely to need laughter now and again as a protection from contact with much that is silly and much that is unwholesome. Yet, in this case, too, the chief value seems to reside in its immediate result, the gladdening and refreshing influence on the laugher, which has in it a virtue at once conciliatory and consolatory. This it is which makes it so good to step aside now and again from the throng, in which we too may have to "wink and sweat," so as to secure the gleeful pastime of turning our tiresome world for the nonce into an entertaining spectacle; amusing ourselves, not merely as Aristotle teaches,333 in order that we may be serious, but because our chosen form of amusement has its own value and excellence.

It is one thing to assign to laughter a definite ethical or logical function, another to ask whether it has its place among the worthier human qualities. We have seen how some have denounced it, indiscriminately as it would seem, as a thing irreverent if not unclean. That view does not come further into the present discussion. We have only to ask what kind of dignity it has.

It is assumed here that we exclude the more malignant and the coarser sorts of laughter. A considerable capacity for the pure mirth which the child loves—and comedy may be said to provide for the man who keeps something of the child in him—supplemented by a turn for the humorous contemplation of things is, I venture to think, not merely compatible with the recognised virtues, but, in itself and in the tendencies which it implies, among the human excellences. This is certainly suggested by the saying of Carlyle: "No man who has once heartily and wholly laughed can be altogether irreclaimably bad".334 We may not be able to rise to the point of view of R. L. Stevenson, when he wrote, "As laborare so joculari est orare;"335 yet we may be inclined to think that it is impossible to construct the idea of a man who can be described as decently complete without endowing him with a measure of humour. Whatever our view of the "Good," reasonable men of all schools appear to allow some value to a capacity for pleasure, especially the social pleasures, among which laughter, even when it seems to retire into solitude, always keeps a high place. On its intellectual side, again, as the play of mind, the mirthful disposition has an intimate relation to such valuable qualities as quickness of insight and versatility.336 In the light entertaining form of witty talk it takes on a social quality of no mean value.

Best of all, laughter of the genial sort carries with it, and helps to develop, kindly feeling and the desire to please. It is too often forgotten that a mirthful spirit, though it may offend, is a large source of joy to others. He who produces a laugh of pure gladness brightens the world for those who hear him. Fertility in jests may qualify a man to become one of the human benefactors; and it has been claimed for Falstaff, with some reason, that he "has done an immense deal to alleviate misery and promote positive happiness".337 It is this implied wish to entertain which gives to laughter much of its value as an educator of the sympathies. Nothing, indeed, seems to promote sympathy more than the practice of laughing together. Family affection grows in a new way when a reasonable freedom is allowed to laugh at one another's mishaps and blunders. One reason for this, perhaps, is that the consciousness of our having laughed at our friends and been laughed at by them, without injury to friendship, gives us the highest sense of the security of our attachments. When a friend laughs "as love does laugh"—to quote Mr. Meredith's Rosamund—with the laugh which only half-hides a kindly sentiment, say, a wish to help you to laugh away what will vex or harm you, it binds hearts yet more securely. Even our comparatively solitary laughter at things, when no appreciative sharer is at hand, may, if only it has the tolerant good-natured tone, connect itself with and bring into play the sympathetic side of us.

If there is in laughter this element of a deeper humanity, we shall do well to view jealously any undue imposition of restraints. The history of popular mirth points to the dangers of this.

That some regulation of the impulse, both external by social pressure and internal by a man's own self-restraint, is required, does not need to be argued. The laughing impulse, when unchecked, has taken on ugly and deadly forms. If men have endowed their deities with mirth they have also endowed their fiends. Society is right in her intuitive feeling that an unbridled laughter threatens her order and her laws. Specific injuries done by ribald jests, *e.g.*, to religious convictions, may have to be dealt with by the magistrate. This all men know, as also that society acts wisely when she seeks to maintain the dignity of social converse by putting down with a gentler hand all unworthy and unbecoming laughter, and to observe vigilantly the "hypergelast"—a species that includes others besides Aristotle's low jesters (βωμόλοχοι)—who, if he does not, either maliciously, or through sheer heaviness and awkwardness of gait, kick sharply against some sensitive place, will at least weary decent men with all the weariness of the bore and something more.

Yet it is well to bear in mind that such imposition of restraint by external authority should be also self-restraining. If laughter has its uses, not only for him who laughs but for him who is laughed at, these should be borne in mind in determining the amount of restriction desirable. This wise caution is especially needed when the laughter which authority seeks to repress is likely to be directed against itself. It would never do, for example, if the fine world were at liberty to put down satires on its vulnerable manners. Divines of the solemnity of Barrow and Warburton might do much harm, if they could succeed in silencing the ridicule of the half-believers and the sceptics. Those in authority have a special reason for remembering here the maxim "noblesse oblige"; and even should they be lacking in a wise care for the well-being of the commonwealth, a measure of shrewdness will advise them that they will do well to pass a self-denying ordinance. Let them not be more afraid of laughter than their predecessors, but rather welcome it, not merely as a symptom of vitality in those who indulge in it, but as a sign of alertness in citizens against surprise by stealthy-footed evil. Perhaps when the story of the modern "emancipation of women" comes to be written, it will be found that the most helpful feature of the movement was the laughing criticism poured upon it; a criticism which seems not unnatural when one remembers how many times before men have laughed at something like it; and not so unreasonable to one who perceives the droll aspects of the spectacle of a sex setting about to assert itself chiefly by aping the ways of the rival sex. A statesman, having a large majority behind him, would probably best show his wisdom by discouraging the laughter of his own side and instructing it how to welcome that of the despised minority. Yet the quaint look of such a suggestion reminds one that the idea of adding wisdom to statesmanship is as far from realisation to-day as in the time of the Greek philosophers.

I have spoken of a community's self-restraint in relation to the laughter of its individual members. Of the duty of controlling its own mirth in view of the feelings of other peoples who seem to have a right to their slices of the planet there should be no need to speak. It may be enough to hint that a comic journal will do well, when touching on international matters of some delicacy, to exclude from its drawings irritating details, such as the figure of a monkey; not only lest the foreigner consider himself to be insulted, but lest one of the very gentlemen for whom it writes, stung in some old-fashioned impulse of chivalry, feel tempted to give a too violent expression to his indignation.

Of the control of laughter as a part of the self-government of a wise man, little need be said. A keen relish for jokes, especially one's own, may entangle the feet even of a kind-hearted man in a mesh of cruel consequences. The witty have been found to be trying to their families, so importunate is the appetite of wit in its demand for regularity of meals. There are the duplicities of laughter which may sometimes impose even on one who is in general a kindly laugher, the note of malice stealing in unnoticed. It is only when the lively tendency to mirthful utterance is found in a sympathetic nature, side by side with a cultured susceptibility to the pain of giving pain, that an adequate self-regulation may be counted on. Each of us, perhaps, has known of one man, at least, deserving to be called a laugher in whose mirthful utterances one would look in vain for a trace of malice, and who seemed never to be surprised by the temptation to risk a touch on sore places. I cannot but recall here one already alluded to—one who seemed to embody the ideal of his teacher Aristotle not only as the just man, who of set purpose acts justly, but as the refined and gentlemanly man who regulates his wit, being as it were a law to himself—from behind whose wistful eyes a laugh seemed always ready to break. If one knows of no such kindly laugher, one may study the characteristics of the species in the *Essays of Elia*.

A perfect self-control in the matter of laughter pre-supposes much more than a dread of inflicting pain upon the hearer, whether he be the object of the laughter or ready to identify himself with that object. It calls for a fine sense of the seemly, of what is fair. It is not too much to ask of one whose *rôle* is the detection of the unseemly in others that he should himself avoid unseemliness. He will do well to remember that nothing is worse than a jibe at the wrong moment:—

Risu inepto res ineptior nulla est.

When serious things are being discussed the attempt to hide poverty of argument under what might flatteringly be called an "argumentum ad risum" is one of the actions which belittle men.

The wariness proper to one who bears so keen-edged a weapon will go farther and prompt him to ask whether the thing which entertains the eye is meet for laughter. For example, our poor language being what it is, the use of a form of words which may be shown by another's elaborate dissection to hide under its plain meaning a second meaning derogatory to the speaker, does not, perhaps, make the latter quite legitimate quarry for the former's ridicule. It needs a fine sense of justice to detect the line which divides what is fair from what is unfair in such a case.

A perfectly wise direction of laughter will call for other fine discriminations. A word or action may be quite proper game for laughter when it smacks of conceit, though but for this it should have been passed by. So rampant indeed is conceit among men, so noxious is it, and so low a degree of sensitiveness in the moral integument does it connote, that even the discreet laugher may allow himself unstinted indulgence in view of one of its unmistakable eruptions. On the other hand, a sense of the true values of things will lead the wise to abstain from laughter where some manifestation of the beast in man obtrudes itself and requires a less gentle mode of expulsion.

Nor will a good man's self-regulation cease when there are no hearers. He will see how the habit of a reckless mirth may have a bad reflex effect on his own nature; how, for example, it may rob him in one moment of the perfection of an old reverence for something beautiful; how, instead of sweetening the fountains of affection, it may introduce a drop of bitterness; how it may smuggle in something of that pride and that contempt which dissociate men.

I have here emphasised the higher moral reasons which will urge the good man to restrain his laughter. One might add certain prudential reasons. If, as has been maintained here, laughter is an escape from the normal, serious attitude which living well imposes on us, its wise cultivation means that we keep it within limits. Only where there is a real earnestness and good feeling at bottom, will our laughter be in the full sense that of the mind and the heart. To laugh in this full way at a collapse of dignity means that we retain a respect for the true dignities. If the laugh grows too frequent and habitual this respect will be undermined, and, as one result of this moral loss, our laughter itself will shrink into something void of meaning and mechanical. The perpetual giggler, to whom nothing is sacred, never knows the flavour of a good laugh.

The impulse to laugh will always take its complexion from the moral nidus in which it germinates; and the good man, tender, and mindful of the dues of reverence, ennobles the mirthful temper. It seems, indeed, in such a moral *milieu* to become an expression, one of the most beautiful, of goodness. It assures us somehow of the genuineness of virtue, and brings it nearer to us as something human to be loved. Free from all touch of pride and malice, it takes on the look of a child's joyousness made large and beneficent by expansive sympathies.

It is to be maintained, then, not only that a full rich laughter may thrive in the soil of a good man's soul, but that this soul will remain incompletely developed without it. This doctrine seems flatly to contradict great authorities, Pascal and the rest. Yet it may be shown that there is really no contradiction here. The laughter which Pascal, Addison, and the others denounce, is not the genial and humorous kind, but the coarse and brutal sorts, and, what is hardly a jot more sufferable, the reckless output of "the vacant mind".

Laughter, then, may be claimed to be one of the possessions of men to which they should jealously cling. It brings gaiety into what is always tending to grow a dull world, and of which at times the onlooker is disposed to say what Walpole said of the doings of the fashionable æsthetes at Bath, "there never was anything so entertaining or so dull". It supplies diversion in youth and still more in age, and it may with a few, as it did with Heine and R L. Stevenson, remain a bright comrade on the sick-bed. It is the manna on which good fellowship loves to feed. And, so many-sided is it, it may be recommended as a planer for moral ridges, and it may add the last touch to the character-picture which every man is engaged in painting. It will graciously accompany us when we visit the nursery and try our cumbrous hand at the art of entertaining childhood; and will not forsake us—if we care for its company—when we betake ourselves to the graver occupations.

If this is true it would seem as if, instead of trying to put it down, we should seek to promote the laughing habit in ourselves and in others. Yet here one must be careful. For one thing, the man to whom it counts as a considerable ingredient of happiness can hardly be expected to assist in an effort to render all men of an equal quickness in mirthful response. He knows better than any one else that the spectacle of folly, of make-believe and of self-inflation, on which his laughter is fed, implies a lack of all the finer laughter of the mind in the great majority of his fellows. It would be an act of suicidal madness, then, on his part, to try to transform his social world into a body of laughter-loving men and women. Happily for the "gelast," such a transformation is beyond the powers of any conceivable society of laughter-promoters. Humorous men must continue with perfect serenity of mind to put up with being a "contemptible minority".

Not only in the interests of the lover of laughter is it well that he cannot impose his merry habit on all men alike. The wise man will remember that it takes all sorts to make our social world, and that the desirability of the laughing capacity varies greatly with a man's disposition, habits of mind and circumstances. To those, for example, who are of sensitive feeling and keen perception, especially if called on to lead an oppressively dull life, or, like Goldsmith, to wrestle with circumstance, a broad and quick appreciation of the laughable may be a real need. Some hearts of many chords, resonant to all the notes of life's music, might break but for the timely comings of the laughter-fay with her transforming wand. On the other hand, many worthy people not only do very well without it, but might be at a disadvantage by possessing the endowment. This seems to be true of many excellent men and women whose special bent is towards a rigorous concentration of thought and moral energy on some mission. Such persons appear ever to dwell in the subduing shadow of their cause; they bear about with them a special kind of self-consciousness, a sense of their indispensableness to the world. Laughter is not for these, we say with half a sigh. Nor can it, one supposes, find the needed air and sunlight in persons who hold imposing rank or office, and have to be daily concerned with maintaining a proper awe in others; or in those who have a deep-placed and imperturbable self-complacency, or those who are solemnly preoccupied with the momentous business of raising their social dignity. Probably nobody, save perhaps a waiter, has to be set more securely above the temptation to laugh than a man qualifying for his first dinner parties.

The case of these hopelessly confirmed "agelasts" is a very strong one. Those of us who prize the free circulation of laughter as that of a sea-air, and are disposed to object to the closeness of mental atmosphere which seems to enfold the devoted, shall do well to remember how much the world owes to a lack of humour in its citizens. If Rousseau had been a great laugher we should certainly never have had his picturesque and instructive attack on civilisation and all that flowed from it. Would Dante and Milton and the other builders of the vast and sombre architecture of verse have achieved their task if the laughing imp had been pulling vigorously at their coat tails? How many of our valuable social institutions would have been built up if the beginners had been keenly alive to the absurd aspects of the bunglings which are wont to characterise first attempts? Let those who laugh, therefore, be ready, not only from an enlightened self-interest, but from a becoming esteem for alien virtues, to allow the "agelasts" their place in the world.

The foregoing considerations suggest that in any effort to promote laughter we should move cautiously. A man may waste much precious time in trying the experiment on a member of his family. A waggish schoolmaster, too—and to the credit of the profession he is to be found—may, if he experiment in this direction, meet with nothing but disappointment. Perhaps some good "tests of humour" would be helpful here; but the daily papers have not yet succeeded in inventing a satisfactory one, and the psychological laboratories have, wisely perhaps, avoided the problem. Moreover, the business of testing would comprise some examination of the quality of the "humour" expressed, lest the pedagogue should be fostering in a boy a kind of growth which he is much better without. Perhaps, indeed, this testing of quality, were it possible, should be undertaken for more serious purposes: since the saying of Goethe, that the directions taken by a person's laughter are one of the best clues to his character, may be found to apply, differences being allowed for, to the raw stripling. In undertaking any such investigation of youthful mirth, the investigator would need to note the quality of the expressive sounds themselves; for one may suspect that in these days of early sophistication a young laugh, as pure and clear of tone as it is full and unhindered, is a rarity. For a first attempt at gauging a boy's humour the schoolmaster might, perhaps, do worse than select the following test, suggested by a remark of one of my most learned and most respected friends, that the situation referred to is the one which, in his case, excites the most hearty merriment: "Supposing you made a call, and having placed your hat on a chair inadvertently proceeded to sit on it; how would you feel?"

A more manageable problem for the pedagogue would seem to be to try, now and again, to force back the bolts of discipline and approach the boy with a judicious overture of fun. It is refreshing to find that this has recently been recommended by a highly respectable journal of the profession which writes: "It is no inherent dislike to work or to the teacher, but the absolute necessity of relieving a dull lesson by a bit of fun, that is accountable for many a difficulty in discipline".338 Next to this, the aim would be to encourage boys to bear the discipline of others' laughter, so that they fall not below the moral level of the estimable savage. This part of the schoolmaster's business is certainly not neglected in our country, and perhaps has even been a little overdone.

The gift of humour will save a man from many follies, among others that of attempting the office of prophet. This has its proper domain, for example in astronomy, though even in certain ambitious departments of physical science it begins to look like presumption. To bring it into the region of human affairs smacks of a juvenile confidence which has not begun to define its logical boundaries. Hence I shall not risk the illustrating of my subject by a forecast of the future of laughter.

It may be enough to say that, at the fraction of a second of the cosmic clock at which we happen to live, certain tendencies are observable which appear to have some bearing on this question. The most cheerful of men would perhaps hardly call the present a mirthful moment. We seem to have travelled during a century or more very far from the serene optimism which dwelt fondly on the perfectibility of mankind. If we grow enthusiastic about man's future at all, we let our minds run on the perfectibility of his machines. This fact in itself suggests that we are not likely to find an exceptional exuberance of the mirthful spirit. Writers, too, have emphasised the fact that the age, if not dull, is certainly not gay. An essayist, not long taken from us, has written sadly about the decline of the old frank social laughter;339 and another, writing of Falstaff says that, though by laughter man is distinguished from the beasts, the cares and sorrows of life have all but deprived him "of this distinguishing grace, degrading him to a brutal solemnity".340

That the old merry laughter of the people has lost its full resonance has been remarked above, and it may be possible, while avoiding youthful dogmatism, to conjecture to some extent how this loss has come about.

To begin, it seems fairly certain that the decline of popular mirth is only a part of a larger change, the gradual disappearance of the spirit of play, of a full self-abandonment to the mood of light enjoyment. We may see this not only in the rather forced gaiety supplied by the gorgeous "up-to-date" pantomime and other shows. It is illustrated in the change that has come over our out-of-door sports. Where is the fun, where is the gaiety, in the football and the cricket matches of to-day? Could anything be less like an "amusement" than a match at Lord's—save when for a moment an Australian team, forgetful of its surroundings, bounds into the field? Even the clapping of hands by the solemn-looking spectators sounds stiff and mechanical.

This reduction of the full stream of choral laughter of a past age to a meagre rillet may readily be supposed to be due altogether to a growing refinement of manners in all classes. Leaders of the "high society" tell us, as we have seen, that loud laughter is prohibited by its code of proprieties. The middle class, in which the imitation of social superiors grows into a solemn *culte*, has naturally adopted this idea from the upper class: and the classes below may be disposed on public occasions to consider Mother Grundy so far as to curb the froward spirit of fun. Still, the decline seems to be much more than any such artificial restraint would account for. The evidence available certainly favours the conclusion that, even when unfettered, the people does not laugh long and loud as it once did.

This is not the place to attempt an explanation of a change which is perhaps too recent to be easily explained. Yet we may hazard the suggestion that it is connected with other recent social tendencies which seem to be still operative. It is probably one phase of a whole alteration of temper in the mass of the people. It looks as if only the more solid material interests now moved the mind, as if sport had to have its substantial bait in the shape of stakes, while comedy must angle for popularity with scenic splendours which are seen to cost money. Other forces lying equally deep may not improbably co-operate. The mirth of Merry England was the outgoing of a people welded in brotherhood. The escape from the priest, and later from his Spanish champion, had begotten a common sense of relief and joyous expansion. No such welding pressure has come in these latter days pushing all ranks into a common service of mirth. The sharp class-antagonisms of the hour, especially that of employer and employed, leave but little hope of the revival of such a choral laughter of a whole people.

This decline of the larger choral laughter, including the reciprocal laughter of social groups, appears to have for one of its consequences a falling off in the part played by mirth as a tempering and conciliatory element in authority. Any gain arising from the introduction of a "humouring spirit" into our government of the young is, one fears, more than neutralised by the loss which ensues from the banishment of the cajoling laugh from the relations of master and workman and mistress and maid. Perhaps, too, in our terribly serious purpose of conferring the blessing of an incorporation into a world-wide empire upon reluctant peoples of all degrees of inferiority, we are losing sight of the conciliatory virtue of that spirit of amicable jocosity, the value of which, as we have seen, was known to some who had to do with savage peoples.

The seriousness of to-day, which looks as if it had come to pay a long visit, may be found to have its roots in the greater pushfulness of men, the fiercer eagerness to move up in the scale of wealth and comfort, together with the temper which this begets, the discontent—

The weariness, the fever, and the fret

which kill the capacity for a whole-hearted abandonment to simple pleasures.

So far as this is the case, what laughter survives may be expected to take on the tone of a forced utterance with something of a sigh of weariness behind it. It is as though men had no time to laugh. Even at a social entertainment you will find men and women who meet your playful challenge only with a niggardly giggle which they instantly suppress: poor distracted souls unable for a moment to free themselves from the chaos of social claims which haunts them.

A yet more sinister characteristic of this later social laughter, reflected more or less clearly even in much of what now passes for comedy, is its cynicism. By this is meant more than the hollowness of the laughter of the world-weary: it implies a readiness to laugh at a new sort of thing, or at least at the old sorts in a new way. Thus, we may hear the unscrupulous member of a profession laughing at some "amusing" bit of conscientiousness in another member. The laughter has its readily distinguishable tones: now the thin wiry note of contempt which issues from the superior person, now the rough brazen sound burred by the bolder lips of the roué. Such laughter is in the case of an individual, of a class and of a nation alike, the revelation of the attitude of a mind which has not yet completed the process of discarding its old obligations.

The tendencies here touched on illustrate how closely the moral forces encompass our laughter, how directly they determine its key and the depth of its sincerity. They suggest, too, how much more the evil inclinations menace the healthy vigour of our mirth than the good, even though these should be cultivated up to the confines of the saintly.

These signs may well make the friend of laughter sad. There is nothing unreasonable in the idea of a death of all the more joyous and refreshing mirth. The utilities—on which, perhaps, I have insisted too much—give us no pledge of a final survival of the merry impulse. However considerable its benefit to a society, we have examples of highly efficient communities which seem to do very well without it. And the like is probably true of individual laughter. A few persons may, as I have suggested, owe to it their persistence on the human scene; yet the evolutional efficacy of this utility is probably very narrowly circumscribed.

In spite of these sinister indications, an eye patient in search may descry others which point to the persistence of a wholesome laughter. Even if comedy and satire seem tired and slumbering, the humorous spirit is awake and productive. We have in the literature of more than one country the promise of a development of new tones of quiet, reflective laughter. The growth of a wider appreciation of other literatures than our own is overcoming the obstacles, already touched on, to an international appreciation of flavours, so far at least as to allow of a *rapprochement* of the larger-minded members of civilised nations in a reciprocal enjoyment of their humorous writings.

For the rest, we may put our trust in the growing volume of what I have called private laughter. It is not unlikely that in the future, men who think will grow at once more tenacious of their ideals, and more alive to the ludicrous consequences which these introduce. If so, they will become still less like gay-hearted children than they now are, and will have to brighten the chamber of life, as it loses the blithe morn-given light, with the genial glow of humour. They will be able to keep the flame alive with fuel drawn from the storehouse of literature. In this work of conserving human laughter they will do well, while developing the thoughtfulness of the humorist, to keep in touch with the healthiest types of social laughter, the simple mirth of the people preserved in the *contes* and the rest, and the enduring comedies. If a few men will cultivate their own laughter in this way and do their best to make their private amusement that of an inner circle of friends, we may hope that it will not die—though the death of what we love were less terrible to face than its debasement—but be preserved by a few faithful hands for a happier age. They will have their reward in advance, since pure and honest laughter, like mercy, blesses him that gives, and him that takes.

NOTES

1 Article on "Humour" in the *Cornhill Magazine*, vol. xxxiii., pp. 318–26.

2 See B. Bosanquet, *History of Æsthetics*, p. 360, where we are told that serious modern comedy, such as Molière's *L'Avare*, is, according to Hegel, wanting in this characteristic.

3 *Die Welt als Wille und Vorstellung*, Band II., Erstes Buch, Kap. viii.

4 *Le Rire*, published by Félix Alcan, 1900.

5 See an article "Pourquoi rit-on?" by Camille Mélinaud, in the *Revue des deux Mondes*, 1895 (Tom. 127, p. 612 ff.). The theory of M. Mélinaud seems to resemble closely that of Jean Paul Richter and others, which Lotze criticises, *Geschichte der Æsthetik*, p. 346.

6 M. Bergson furnishes some striking illustrations of the forcing of a theory on reluctant facts in his treatment of the laughable aspect of the red nose and the black skin, *op. cit.*, p. 41 ff.

7 The references here are to one of a series of articles entitled "Psychologie der Komik" in the *Phil. Monatshefte*, Bd. XXIV. See p. 399 ff. The articles have been elaborated in a volume, *Komik und Humor*. The point here dealt with is touched on in this volume in Kap. iv., s. 558.

8 The point that when we judge two successive impressions to be different we do not necessarily represent both simultaneously, has been recently emphasised by G. F. Stout and T. Loveday, who quote the views of Wundt and Schumann. See *Mind*, N.S., ix. (1900), pp. 1–7, and p. 386.

9 Dr. Lipps seems half to perceive this mode of interaction among parts of a complex presentation when he says that the cylinder appears to renounce its dignity (Würde) as man's head-covering when it stoops to adorn the head of a child (*loc. cit.*).

10 *Geschichte der Æsthetik in Deutschland*, p. 343.

11 *Versuch einer Theorie des Komischen* (1817), s. 23.

12 See Darwin, *Expression of the Emotions*, p. 199.

13 See among other authorities, Raulin, *Le Rire*, p. 28.

14 See art. "The Psychology of Tickling, Laughing and the Comic," by G. Stanley Hall and A. Allin, *American Journal of Psychology*, vol. ix., p. 1 ff.

15 *Purgatorio*, Canto xi., lines 82–3; *cf.* Canto i., line 20, where the fair planet (Venus) is said to have made the whole East laugh—a figure copied by

Chaucer, *The Knightes Tale,* line 636. Addison touches on this poetical use of "laughter," *Spectator,* No. 249.

16 Gratiolet, *De la Physionomie,* p. 116. Benedick instances as interjections of laughing "ha! ha! he"! *Much Ado About Nothing,* IV., i.

17 See an article on "Organic Processes and Consciousness," by J. R. Angell and H. B. Thompson, in the *Psychological Review,* vol. vi., p. 55. According to these researches, a hearty laugh, causing sudden and violent changes in the breathing curve, is accompanied by the sharpest and most marked vaso-dilation, as tested by capillary pulse drawing; though in one case the opposite effect of constriction was produced.

18 *Anatomy of Melancholy,* Pt. 2, sec. 2, mem. vi. subsec. 4 ("mirth and merry company").

19 Laughter is pronounced a "good exercise" by Dr. Leonard Hill in his useful work, *Manual of Human Physiology* (1899), p. 236. The physiological benefits are more fully treated of by Dr. Harry Campbell in his publication, *Respiratory Exercises in the Treatment of Disease* (1898), p. 125.

20 "*Positions,*" ed. by Quick, pp. 64, 65.

21 Angell and Thompson in the article quoted above suppose that the whole dilation of the capillaries during laughter is a secondary effect of sudden changes in the breathing. This seems a reasonable conclusion. Yet since, according to these writers, smiling as well as mild laughter causes gentle changes of the same kind, it seems possible that we have here, in a disguised form, the working of the general law stated by these writers: that agreeable experiences are accompanied by dilation of the peripheral blood-vessels.

22 See *The Expression of the Emotions,* chap, vi., p. 163. It is curious to note that Mulcaster and the recent physiologists referred to above claim a beneficial influence for "a good cry" as well as for laughter. But they do not seem explicitly to put them on the same level as occasional exercises.

23 Maria's words in *Twelfth Night,* "If you desire the spleen," seem to point to some supposed organic disturbance due to immoderate laughter.

24 *Op. cit.,* pp. 207 and 213.

25 Prof. James seems to admit this in his smaller work, *Psychology,* p. 384.

26 On the Contagion of Laughter, see Raulin, *Le Rire,* p. 98 ff.

27 It has been pointed out by an ingenious French writer, L. Dugas—whose work, *Psychologie du rire,* has appeared while my volume is passing through the press—that even a wild, uncontrollable laughter, "le fou rire," in spite

of its elements of suffering, remains to a large extent a pleasurable experience (*see* pp. 25, 26).

28 The French language is particularly rich in its vocabulary under this head, including expressions like "rire du bout des dents" and "du bout des lèvres" (*cf.* Homer's expression, ἐγέλασσεν χείλεσιν), "rire dans sa barbe," and others like "rire jaune".

29 *Sartor Resartus*, Bk. I., chap. iv.

30 Article on "Ticklishness" in the *Dictionary of Psychological Medicine*. He adds that ticklishness is not locally coincident with sensitiveness to pain. On the other hand, Dr. Charles Richet remarks that the parts most sensitive to tickling are the parts richest in tactile nerves. Article "Chatouillement," *Dictionnaire de Physiologie*.

31 See Wundt, *Physiolog. Psychologie* (4te Auflage), Bd. i., pp. 434–5. According to this authority the propagation of the stimulation may be either direct from one sensory fibre to another, or indirect, involving muscular contractions and muscular sensations.

32 See Külpe, *Outlines of Psychology*, p. 148.

33 See the article on "The Psychology of Tickling, Laughing, and the Comic," by G. S. Hall and A. Allin, in the *American Journal of Psychology*, vol. ix., p. 1 ff. These returns do not make it quite clear whether "ticklishness" is taken to mean the non-laughing as well as the laughing varieties.

34 My references to Dr. Robinson's views are partly to the article in the *Dictionary* already quoted, and partly to notes of lectures given before the British Association and the West Kent Medical Society, which he has been so kind as to show me. I have made much use of his interesting and often brilliant suggestions in dealing with the subject of ticklishness.

35 Both of these are included by Dr. Richet among the most sensitive parts (*loc. cit.*).

36 How far the results are complicated by the action of the muscles which serve to erect the separate hairs on the body, and are said by Lister to contract near a tickled surface, I am not sure.

37 *E.g.*, Külpe, *op. cit.*, 147.

38 *Expression of the Emotions*, p. 201.

39 In using the expression "ticklish period," I do not imply that ticklishness necessarily disappears after a certain period of maximal intensity. Like play, it probably persists in a certain number of persons as a susceptibility to which the laws of propriety leave but little scope for exercise.

40 *Op. cit.,* pp. 201, 202. The restriction I have added enables us to include the case of the sole of the foot.

41 *Loc. cit.* Dr. L. Hill confirms the observation and offers the same explanation.

42 In this connection an observation sent me by Dr. L. Hill is significant. His little girl first responded with laughter to tickling under the armpits at the same age (two and a half years) as she first showed fear by crying on being put into the arms of a stranger.

43 G. Heymans, *Zeitschrift für die Psychol. und die Physiol. der Sinne,* Bd. xi., ss. 31 ff.

44 Heymans, *loc. cit.*

45 The abnormal forms of automatic laughter, including the effects of stimulants, are dealt with by Raulin, *op. cit.,* $2^{\text{ème}}$ partie, chap. iv., and $3^{\text{ème}}$ partie.

46 Given in the returns to Stanley Hall's inquiries. This explosion of laughter on receiving sad news occurs in cases of cerebral disorder. See Dugas, *op. cit.,* p. 16.

47 Quoted by Dugas, *op. cit.,* p. 12.

48 Shakespeare makes Lady Macbeth perpetrate a pun in a moment of intense excitement when Macbeth's hesitation goads her into a resolve to carry out the murder herself:—

> "I'll gild the faces of the grooms withal
>
> For it must seem their guilt".

Did he mean to illustrate by this the way in which emotional strain tends to lapse for a brief moment into laughter?

49 *Op. cit.,* pp. 163, 208.

50 See *Les Passions de l'âme,* $2^{\text{ème}}$ partie, art. 25.

51 Co-operative teasing, when it methodically "nags" a boy because he happens, for example, to take the unfashionable side in some political dispute, making his school-life a torment, had—with all deference to apologetic headmasters, be it said—better change its name.

52 Given by Stanley Hall in the article, "The Psychology of Tickling," etc., already quoted.

53 Valuable beginnings may be found here and there; for example, in the entertaining volume of a French comedian, *Le Rire*, par (B. C.) Coquelin, cadet.

54 *Iliad*, ii., 212 ff.

55 *Loc. cit.*

56 There is, of course, often a reciprocal effect in these cases, the non-compliant intruder serving to show up the absurd monotony of the row.

57 See an article, "The Analytical Humorist," by H. D. Traill, *Fortnightly Review* (N.S.), vol. lx., p. 141.

58 Mr. Kipling suggests that the want of a proper nose in a family is regarded as a disgrace among the Hindoos (*Kim*, p. 81).

59 It may be well to add, by way of caution, that the feeble semblance of laughter which a modern theatre-goer is apt to produce when he sees something *risqué* is not a simple form of laughter at the indecent. It is the outcome of a highly artificial attitude of mind, in which there is an oscillation of feeling between the readiness of the natural man to indulge and the fear of the civilised man that he may be carried too far.

60 *Op. cit.*, p. 45.

61 Compare above, pp. 13 ff.

62 As our mode of classification shows, we may regard these as primarily instances of laughable degradation. Nevertheless, some apprehension of contradiction is clearly involved.

63 From a speech delivered by Sir John Parnell in the Irish House of Commons, 1795. See W. R. Le Fanu, *Seventy Years of Irish Life*, ch. xvi. ("Irish Bulls").

64 See Bergson, *op. cit.*, p. 45.

65 *Poetics*, v. i. (Butcher's translation).

66 A further and most important enlargement of Hobbes' principle is made by Bain when he urges that the spectacle of degradation works upon us, not merely by way of the emotion of power or glory, but by way of the feeling of release from constraint. This point will more conveniently be dealt with later.

67 Compare above, p. 100.

68 Kant's contribution to the theory of the ludicrous is contained in a single "Remark" appended to a discussion of the Fine Arts and Taste. See Dr. Bernard's translation of his *Kritik of Judgment*, pp. 221–4.

69 Article "On the Philosophy of Laughing," by the Editor, *The Monist*, 1898, p. 255.

70 I find after completing this paragraph that the point dealt with, namely, that surprise, in the sense of the effect of mental unpreparedness, is not an invariable antecedent of our response to the laughable, has been urged by a French writer, M. Courdaveaux. His critic, M. Dugas, does not seem to me to have effectually combated it. (See Dugas, *op. cit.*, p. 63 ff.)

71 See above, p. 6.

72 Compare what was said above *à propos* of the child and the hat, p. 14.

73 *Cf.* above, p. 114; also the article in *The Monist* already quoted.

74 *English Comic Writers*, lect. i., "Wit and Humour".

75 "The Physiology of Laughter," *Essays*, i., p. 206.

76 According to Fouillée, contrast is the formal element, faultiness ("le défaut"), the material. See Dugas, *op. cit.*, p. 85 ff.

77 Hazlitt defines the ridiculous as the highest degree of the laughable, which is "*a proper subject for satire,*" *loc. cit.*

78 Compare Ribot, *La Psychologie des sentiments*, p. 344.

79 M. Bergson has a glimpse of the co-operation of "child's fun" in our laughter, *op. cit.*, p. 69; but he fails to see the magnitude of this factor.

80 See *The Emotions and the Will*, "The Emotions," chap. xiv., §§ 38–40.

81 *Cf.* Dugas, *op. cit.*, p. 128 ff.

82 *Wit and Humour*, p. 7.

83 See p. 76, ff.

84 Prof. Groos does not, I think, bring out clearly enough the distinction here drawn, though he may be said to half-recognise it when he speaks of "joy in conquest" as the end of play combats (*Play of Animals*, pp. 291, 292).

85 This restriction sometimes takes on a look of a conative process of self-control, *e.g.*, when an older cat, not used to play, is importunately challenged by a lively kitten.

86 On this "divided consciousness" in play see Groos, *Play of Animals*, p. 303 ff.

87 On the uses of animal play see Groos, *The Play of Man*, Part III., sect. 2, and Lloyd Morgan, *Animal Behaviour*, chap. vi., sect. 2.

88 Among previous writers on the subject M. Dugas seems to be the one who has had the clearest apprehension of the essentially playful character of laughter (*op. cit.*, chap. vi., especially p. 115 *seq.*).

89 Karl Groos connects both the tusslings and the tearings of young animals with the instinct of sex-competition (*Play of Animals*, p. 35 ff.).

90 *The Psychological Review*, 1899, p. 91.

91 *Descent of Man*, Part I., chap. iii.

92 *Animal Life and Intelligence*, p. 407. The author strikes me as almost excessively cautious in accepting these evidences of canine jocosity.

93 W. Preyer, *Die Seele des Kindes*, p. 197.

94 Quoted by Lloyd Morgan, *loc. cit.*

95 *Expression of Emotions*, p. 208; *cf.* p. 132 ff.

96 See Darwin, *The Descent of Man*, Part I., chap. iii.

97 So in *The Expression of the Emotions*, pp. 211, 212. In the notes contributed to *Mind*, vol. ii. (1877), p. 288, two infants are spoken of, one of which smiled when forty-five, the other when forty-six days old.

98 The references are to his work, *Die Seele des Kindes*, 4te Auflage.

99 Champneys and Sigismund are quoted by Preyer. Miss Shinn's observations are given in her work, *Notes on the Development of a Child*, p. 238. Mrs. Moore's are to be found in her Essay, *The Mental Development of a Child*, p. 37. Dr. L. Hill writes that he noted the first smile in his boy when he was three weeks old, and in his girl when she was some days older.

100 See especially what he says about an unusual expression, including "a strongly sparkling eye" which occurred in the eighth week, *op. cit.*, p. 194.

101 I am indebted to Miss Shinn for a sight of her complete original notes; and some of my references are to these.

102 It is regrettable that Preyer does not describe with some precision the sounds produced by his boy on the twenty-third day.

103 Miss Shinn insists that the laugh did not develop out of the chuckle, since apparently it appeared, as many articulate sounds appear, with something of a sudden completeness. But this is just what we should expect if the laugh is an inherited movement.

104 *Op. cit.*, p. 197.

105 Preyer puts this at the end of the first half-year, which seems to me to be late.

106 *Op. cit.,* p. 96.

107 On the point of the priority of the smile in the process of evolution see Th. Ribot, *La Psychologie des Sentiments,* p. 346.

108 Darwin, *Expression of the Emotions,* p. 133.

109 A. Lehmann, in his interesting account of the development of the emotions and their expression in the individual, suggests that the first imperfect smile of the infant, which expresses the pleasure of sweetness, is genetically related to the movements of sucking (*Hauptgesetze des menschl. Gefühlslebens,* ss. 295, 296).

110 Darwin, *Expression of the Emotions,* pp. 134, 135.

111 As pointed out above, the French *e* sound seems to be the common one in children's laughter. Preyer tells us that the corresponding sound in German (*ä*) occurs in the first infantile babble (*Development of Intellect,* p. 239).

112 *Expression of the Emotions,* pp. 132–3.

113 See the article already quoted on "The Psychology of Tickling, Laughing," etc., p. 33.

114 See the article already quoted.

115 Dr. Robinson considers that another agreeable effect of tickling may be an inherited echo of the caresses of man's progenitors.

116 Stanley Hall also suggests that the most ticklish parts, which, according to his inquiries, are *the sole of the foot,* the throat, etc., are the "most vulnerable". But he does not explain what he means by vulnerable here, and certainly does not appear to use the word in the sense given it by Dr. L. Robinson.

117 Groos deals with the teasing of animals under the head of "Fighting Plays" (*Play of Animals,* p. 136 ff.).

118 H. M. Stanley, *Psychological Review,* 1899, p. 87.

119 This idea, that when we laugh at ludicrous things the process is fundamentally analogous to that of being tickled, has been made the basis of a curious and suggestive physiological theory of laughter, developed by a German writer. See Ewald Hecker, *Die Physiologie und Psychologie des Lachens und des Komischen.*

120 *Loc. cit.,* p. 39.

121 I am indebted for this fact to Dr. L. Hill. I believe a like remark applies to all the laughter of play.

122 The nature of the process of emotional development is more fully treated, and the relation of its effect to that of the dulling action of repetition is indicated, in my work, *The Human Mind*, vol. ii., p. 75 ff.

123 Of course, increase of volume might arise through a widening of the sensational factor in the experience, due to the larger diffusion of somatic stimulation, which, as already remarked, is an element in the expansion of laughter.

124 This expression is commonly used only where an expression is passed on to a palpably dissimilar feeling. But an essentially similar process takes place, according to my view, within the limits of development of what we call the same emotion.

125 The application of the principle of arrest to the changes in emotional states has been made with great success by Th. Ribot in his volume, *Psychologie des Sentiments*, p. 260 ff.

126 Miss Shinn's observations are recorded in Parts III. and IV. of her *Notes*.

127 For a pretty reminiscent description of a first experience of running and jumping, see Pierre Loti, *Roman d'un Enfant*, ii., p. 4 ff.

128 The nearest approach I have met with to a suggestion of a wish to inflict pain in this early practical joking is the following: The child M. when two years old stood on her mother's foot saying, "Oh, my poor toe!" But it seems reasonable to say that in such moments of frolic pain is quite unrepresentable.

129 *Op. cit.*, p. 196. I have heard of it occurring in a girl at the age of three and a half. The point should certainly be determined by more precise observations.

130 Preyer first observed roguish laughter at the end of the second year (*op. cit.*, p. 196). He does not define the expression "schelmisches Lachen".

131 Compare above, p. 83.

132 See Mrs. Hogan's *Study of a Child*, p. 18.

133 *Cf.* what was said in chap. v., p. 142, apropos of Leigh Hunt's theory.

134 Ruth's laughter at the mother's face was certainly very early.

135 Hogan, *op. cit.*, p. 71.

136 See my *Studies of Childhood*, pp. 274–5.

137 Most of the observations here quoted, on the laughter of the boy C., have appeared before in a chapter of my volume, *Studies of Childhood*. The

reader who is familiar with this chapter will, I feel sure, pardon the repetition.

138 Rev. Duff Macdonald, *Africana* (1882), i., pp. 266–7.

139 It is true that this astounding proposition is answered somewhat ironically by Rev. Dr. Folliott, who says, "Give him modern Athens, the learned friend (Brougham) and the sham intellect Society—they will develop his muscles". Yet it seems odd that this confident assertor was not taken to task for his amazing ignorance.

140 The dispute may be followed by the curious by turning up the following: *Indian Antiquary*, vol. viii., p. 316; cf. E. Deschamps, *Pays des Veddas*, pp. 378–9; *The Taprobanian*, vol. i., p. 192 ff. The German visitor, Sarasin, upholds the writer in the latter periodical, and says that the Veddas "lachen gerne," though some of them are bad tempered, and laugh but little. *Naturforschungen auf Ceylon*, pp. 378 and 540.

141 Carl von den Steinen, *Unter den Naturvölkern Zentral-Brasiliens*, p. 61.

142 This applies, of course, to the detection of the whole of the social qualities which make up good-nature. F. Nansen attacks the missionary Egede for his misrepresentation of the Greenlanders in calling them cold-blooded creatures. See *Eskimo Life*, pp. 100, 101.

143 *Expression of the Emotions*, p. 209.

144 *Central Australia* (1833), ii., p. 138.

145 *Among Cannibals* (1889), p. 291.

146 Angas, *Australia and New Zealand* (1847), ii., p. 11.

147 Bonwick, *The Daily Life of the Tasmanians* (1870), p. 174.

148 Ellis, *Polynesian Researches* (1832), i., p. 96.

149 Turnbull, *A Voyage Round the World* (1813), p. 372.

150 Erskine, *The Western Pacific* (1853), p. 159.

151 *Natives of Sarawak and Brit. N. Borneo*, i., p. 84.

152 Rev. Jos. Shooter, *The Kafirs of Natal* (1857), p. 232.

153 Cruickshank, *The Gold Coast of Africa* (1853), ii., p. 253.

154 Hind, *Canadian Red River Exploring Expedition* (1860), ii., p. 135. Other examples of the mirthfulness of savages are given by Herbert Spencer, *Descriptive Sociology*, Div. I., Pt. 2—A.

155 Cruickshank, *Gold Coast of Africa, loc. cit.*

156 Musters, *At Home with the Patagonians* (1873), p. 167.

157 *Saugethiere von Paraguay* (1830), s. 10.

158 *Aborigines of Tasmania* (2nd ed.), p. 38.

159 Johnston, *British Central Africa* (1897), p. 403.

160 E. H. Man, "Aboriginal Inhabitants of the Andaman Islands," *Journal of Anthropol. Institute,* vol. xii., p. 88.

161 See Raulin, *op. cit.*, p. 94 ff.

162 Angas, *loc. cit.*

163 Ling Roth, *Natives of Sarawak*, etc., i., p. 81.

164 Burton, *Lake Regions of Central Africa*, ii., p. 331.

165 Waitz, *Naturvölker,* 6ter Theil, s. 102.

166 Mrs. Edgeworth David, *Funafuti*, p. 230.

167 Shooter, *The Kafirs of Natal* (1857), p. 232.

168 Ling Roth, *Aborigines of Tasmania* (2nd ed.), p. 29.

169 Wood, *Natural History of Man*, i., p. 261.

170 From an article, "West African Women," contributed to the *Daily Telegraph.*

171 This is stated by Prof. Bain in his *English Composition and Rhetoric*, p. 237. I have been unable to verify the statement; but Mr. Ling Roth assures me that the statement is probably correct; and says that he remembers having read recently an account of the amusement of Chinese bystanders on such an occasion, one man putting out a boat—merely to save a hat!

172 Sarasin, *Forschungen auf Ceylon,* s. 537.

173 Sproat, *Scenes and Studies of Savage Life* (1868), p. 51.

174 Wood, *op. cit.*, i., p. 261, and Shooter, *op. cit.*, p. 233.

175 Turnbull, *op. cit.*, p. 372.

176 Wright, *History of Caricature and Grotesque*, p. 2.

177 Cruickshank, *loc. cit.*

178 Ellis, *op. cit.*, i., p. 97.

179 How easily one may overcharge this indictment of coarse immorality is illustrated by what Von den Steinen says of the laughter of the Brazil Indian women when he asked them the names of the several bodily parts. Some

would have taken this to be the low joking of brazen-faced women. He distinctly tells us that it was "just simple innocent laughter," *op. cit.,* p. 65.

180 Ling Roth, *op. cit.,* i., p. 72.

181 Barrow, *Hudson's Bay,* p. 32.

182 Lichtenstein, *Travels in Southern Africa,* ii., p. 312.

183 Compare above, pp. 72, 73.

184 Ellis, *op. cit.,* i., p. 97.

185 Wood, *op. cit.,* ii., p. 522.

186 Lichtenstein, *op. cit.,* ii., p. 308.

187 Burchell, *Travels in Southern Africa* (1822), vol. ii., p. 339.

188 Ling Roth, *op. cit.* (2nd ed.), p. 134.

189 Marsden, *History of Sumatra,* p. 230.

190 Ling Roth, *op. cit.* (2nd ed.), p. 36.

191 Sproat, *Savage Life,* p. 266.

192 Quoted by Ling Roth, *Sarawak and British North Borneo,* i., p. 93.

193 Compare above, p. 104.

194 Hind, *Canadian Red River Expedition,* ii., p. 135.

195 See Ling Roth, *Sarawak and British North Borneo,* i., p. 75.

196 Spencer and Gillen, *The Native Tribes of Central Australia,* pp. 136, 137.

197 Quoted from Gideon Lang by Bonwick, *Daily Life of the Tasmanians,* p. 174.

198 Nansen asserts this with respect to the attitude of the Eskimos towards the Danes who settled in Greenland in 1728. See *Eskimo Life,* pp. 106–7.

199 Brough Smyth, *Aborigines of Victoria* (1878), ii., p. 278.

200 Sarasin, *op. cit.,* iii., p. 540.

201 Burton, *Wit and Wisdom of West Africa,* p. 52.

202 Ling Roth, *Sarawak and British North Borneo,* i., p. 83.

203 Ling Roth, *op. cit.,* i., pp. 83–4.

204 Sproat, *op. cit.,* p. 51.

205 Quoted by Darwin, *Expression of the Emotions,* p. 209.

206 Von den Steinen, *op. cit.*, p. 71.

207 Turnbull, *op. cit.*, p. 88.

208 *Op. cit.*, p. 372.

209 Brough Smyth, *op. cit.*, i., p. 29.

210 *North American Ethnology* (J. W. Powell), vol. iii., p. 410.

211 *Op. cit.*, pp. 239, 291.

212 Ling Roth, *Tasmania* (2nd ed.), p. 38.

213 Marsden, *op. cit.*, p. 230.

214 Quoted by Waitz, *Naturvölker*, 6ter Theil, p. 102.

215 Ling Roth, *Sarawak and British North Borneo*, i., p. 84.

216 Hans Egede, *Nat. Hist. of Greenland*, pp. 156–7.

217 F. Nansen, *Eskimo Life*, p. 187; *cf.* Egede, *loc. cit.*

218 Quoted from Jackson's Narrative (1840) by Erskine, *Western Pacific*, p. 468.

219 Bonwick, *op. cit.*, p. 29.

220 Grey, *Two Expeditions in Australia* (1841), ii., pp. 307–8.

221 J. Chandler Harris, *Uncle Remus and his Friends*.

222 R. E. Dennett, *Folklore of the Fjort*, pp. 92–3.

223 Mr. Ling Roth has pointed out to me that the laughter of the Australian at the absurdity of the idea of a dead man going about without legs, etc., occurs in a race usually placed among the lowest in the scale. Yet this apparent exception does not, I think, affect the validity of the generalisation in the text. The intellect displayed in this ridicule is not of a high order; and, further, we are distinctly told that the scoffer in the case was an "intelligent" native, that is to say, one of more than the average intelligence of his tribe.

224 Mr. Ling Roth writes me that he agrees with Miss Kingsley as to the difference between the laughter of savages and of children. I should be quite ready to accept this view so far as it concerns the special forms and directions of the mirth. The differences of capacity, experience and habit involved in the difference between the child and adult will, of course, introduce many dissimilarities into their manifestations of the mirthful temper. I hold, however, that as regards the fundamental psychical processes involved, the similarity is real and great.

225 Macdonald, *op. cit.*, i., p. 266.

226 Burton, *op. cit.*, ii., pp. 338–9.

227 See p. 42.

228 Wright, *History of Caricature and Grotesque*, p. 181.

229 M. Jos. Bédier in his interesting study, *L'Esprit des Fabliaux*, though he argues that the fabliaux in general had no social aim ("portée sociale"), has to admit that in the case of the treatment of the priests these "contes à rire en vers" betray a genuine hatred, a hatred which (he adds) runs through other forms of literature of the Middle Ages.

230 Bédier points out in the work quoted that the writers of the fabliaux, which issue from the burgher class, and are written for this class, take sides with the weak villains rather than with the strong knightly class (see p. 291 ff.). *Cf.*, however, Wright, *op. cit.*, p. 114.

231 See Maspero, *Les Contes populaires de l'Égypte*, Introduction ("Conte des deux frères").

232 Percy Gardner, *Greek Antiquities*, p. 353.

233 Tyrrell, *Latin Poetry*, p. 220.

234 Bédier, *op. cit.*, p. 279 ff.

235 H. Spencer, *Principles of Sociology*, "Ceremonial Institutions," pp. 205, 206.

236 Maspero, *Life in Ancient Egypt and Assyria*, chap. i.

237 Wilkinson, *Manners and Customs of Ancient Egyptians*, iii., pp. 447, 429.

238 Simcox, *Hist. of Latin Liter.*, i., p. 46.

239 Given in Hazlitt's *New London Jest Book*, pp. 31, 32.

240 Wright, *op. cit.*, p. 133. A good story of a retaliative practical joke, carried out by a bachelor on a tavern keeper who had spilt some wine on serving him, is given by Bédier, *op. cit.*, iii., p. 272 ff.

241 H. Spencer, *op. cit.*, p. 208.

242 Curtius remarks of the Greek comic poets: "It was primarily against the novel fashion of the day that they aimed their blows" (*Hist. of Greece*, ii., p. 539).

243 See Ward, *Engl. Dram. Poets*, ii., p. 401.

244 Wright, *op. cit.*, chap. xix.

245 Sellar, *Roman Poets*, p. 167.

246 Tyrrell, *op. cit.*, p. 52.

247 Ward, *Engl. Dram. Poets*, ii., pp. 398–9. The Restoration comedy also made fun of the "cit" as the inferior of the West-end gentleman.

248 Ward, *op. cit.*, ii., pp. 399, 400.

249 *The Golden Ass*, Bk. III., ch. 55.

250 Doran, *History of Court Fools*, pp. 18, 37, 75.

251 Tyrrell, *Latin Poetry*, p. 43 ff. The scurrility of the early Greek comedy led to its being discountenanced by Pisistratus. As Prof. P. Gardner remarks, "Tyrants have no sense of humour, and dread ridicule" (*Greek Antiquities*, p. 666).

252 Wright, *op. cit.*, p. 44 ff.

253 Ward, *Engl. Dram. Poets*, ii., pp. 392–3.

254 Colley Cibber's satire "Non-Juror" is said to have brought him a pension and the office of Poet Laureate (Wright, *op. cit.*, chap. xxii.).

255 George III. was caricatured again and again by Gillray (Wright, *op. cit.*, chap. xxvii.).

256 This has no doubt arisen in part from the fact that no other single English word expresses directly and clearly the subjective feeling or disposition which lies behind laughter.

257 George Eliot, *Essays*, pp. 82, 83.

258 The opening scene of *Le Médecin malgré lui* shows that Molière had observed this quaint form of wifely loyalty.

259 *Sylvie and Bruno*, Part II., p. 132.

260 Hence Addison's remark (*Spectator*, No. 35) that humour should always be under the check of reason seems, in what one is tempted to call a characteristic way, to miss the mark.

261 See, for example, Höffding, *Outlines of Psychology*, pp. 294, 295.

262 Quoted by Dugas, *op. cit.*, p. 98. Flaubert here indicates, perhaps, one great limiting condition of the growth of the composite sentiment of humour.

263 *Philebus*, Jowett's translation, iv., p. 94 ff.

264 One of the best recent discussions of this subject will be found in the work of A. Lehmann, already referred to; *see* pp. 247–251 and 259.

265 *Cf.* above, p. 70.

266 *Op. cit.*, p. 95.

267 For the whole passage, written perhaps with an unconscious reminiscence of the Rousseau period, see the *Kritik of Judgment*, Dr. Bernard's translation, p. 227.

268 The absence in the East of the comic spirit as expressing itself in the art of comedy, a point noted by Mr. Meredith, is of course not conclusive with respect to the existence of the humorous disposition.

269 M. Bédier has a delicate characterisation of this French spirit in the *Contes;* touching on its want of depth and *arrière-pensée*, its spice of malice, its joyous good sense, its irony, which though a little coarse is yet precise and just, *op. cit.*, p. 278.

270 This redeeming quality of the Irish bull is indistinctly perceived by the Edgeworths in their essay on the subject, in which they speak of the Irishman's habit of using figurative and witty language. See *The Book of Bulls*, by G. R. Neilson (in which the Edgeworths' essay is included).

271 Quoted by Meredith, *op. cit.*, p. 87.

272 See his son's *Life*, chap. vii. (vol. i., p. 167).

273 The question is left an open one by his biographer, J. Fitzmaurice-Kelly. See *Life of Cervantes*, p. 207.

274 *Causeries du Lundi*, vol. iii., pp. 3, 4.

275 *Logic Deductive and Inductive*, by Carveth Read.

276 Bernard's translation of *The Kritik of Judgment*, p. 226.

277 Good illustrations will be found in the story of Mr. Bernard Capes, *The Lake of Wine*, chap. ii. and chap. xxxii.

278 See for one among many instances *Travels in West Africa*, chap. ix. ("The Rapids of the Ogowe").

279 The story of Hans von Bülow's almost superhuman behaviour under these circumstances is told in the *National Observer* of 17th Feb., 1894.

280 See, for example, a letter from a titled lady in *The Times* of the 1st June, 1894, in which this claim of "society" to the services of "the pick of blood and brains" is prettily assumed.

281 On the employment of buffoons and dwarfs in the palace of the Egyptian king see Maspero, *Dawn of Civilisation*, pp. 278, 279. On the Greek and Roman jesters (γελωτοποιοί, ἀρεταλόγοι, mimi, scurræ) see P. Gardner, *Greek Antiquities*, p. 835; [*cf.* Doran, *Court Fools*]. On the mediæval jester or fool see Wright, *op. cit.*, chap. vii.; Lacroix, *Middle Ages*, p. 238 ff.; and Jusserand, *English Wayfaring Life*, p. 187.

282 P. Gardner, *Greek Antiquities*, p. 666.

283 Bergk, Griech. *Literaturgesch.*, iv., pp. 9, 10.

284 See Wright, *op. cit.*, chaps. xii. and xiv.

285 *Essay on Comedy*, pp. 24–5 (on Molière's audience); pp. 8, 47 and following (on the recognition of woman).

286 Examples will be found in *Le Médecin malgré lui*, *L'Avare* and others. A delightful introduction of the all-round beating of the circus is that of the Professors in *Le Bourgeois gentilhomme*.

287 M. Bergson, who gives a delightful account of these mechanical aids to the effect of comedy, seeks to connect them with his theory that the laughable consists in the substitution of the monotony of the machine for the variety of the organism (*op. cit.*, p. 72 ff.). I suspect, however, that they owe much of the spell they cast over our laughing muscles to suggestions of child's play.

288 Compare the breezy fun of the scene in *Le Tartuffe*, where the maid, Dorine, has to tackle in turn each of a pair of lovers urging the same grievances in almost the same words (Act II., Sc. iv.).

289 Moulton, *Ancient Class. Drama*, p. 344.

290 "In Aristophanes the very few maiden figures that appear are dumb" (Neil, *The Knights of Aristophanes*, Introduction, p. xiv.).

291 P. Gardner, *Greek Antiquities*, p. 353.

292 Mommsen, *History of Rome*, vol. iii., p. 144.

293 *Essay*, Bk. II., chap. xi.

294 *Spectator*, No. 62.

295 *English Comic Writers*, Lect. I., "Wit and Humour".

296 *Spectator*, No. 6.

297 *Cf. supra*, pp. 112, 113.

298 *Spectator*, No. 47.

299 An elaborate classification of the various kinds of word-play may be found in an article by Dr. Emil Kräpelin, in Wundt's *Philosoph. Studien*, 2er Band, s. 144 ff.

300 Bergk observes that these are at once individuals and types (*Griech. literaturgeschichte*, Bd. IV., s. 91).

301 Mommsen observes that in Terence we have a more becoming, though not yet moral, conception of feminine nature and of married life (*Hist. of Rome*, Bk. IV., chap. xiii.).

302 Courthope, *Hist. of English Poetry*, vol. ii., pp. 345 ff., and 356.

303 *Eng. Lit.*, Bk. II., chap. iii.

304 On this mixture of tones see Moulton, *Shakespeare as Dramatic Artist*, p. 291.

305 Mr. Meredith touches on the way in which Molière developed his characters out of persons known to him (*op. cit.*, p. 53).

306 *Lectures and Notes on Shakespeare*, p. 416.

307

"Comme un morceau de cire entre mes mains elle est,

Et je lui puis donner la forme qui me plaît."

308 M. Henri Bergson (*op. cit.*, chap, iii.) seems to me to push his helpful idea of a mechanical rigidity (*raideur*) in Molière's characters a little too far.

309 The play closes with the "aside" of Covielle: "Si l'on en peut voir un plus fou, je l'irai dire à Rome".

310 Mr. Meredith remarks that it was "here and there Bacchanalian beyond the Aristophanic example" (*op. cit.*, p. 11).

311 See above, p. 92 f.

312 Coleridge saw clearly enough how far comedy is from making morality its basis. He remarks that the new comedy of Menander and the whole of modern comedy (Shakespeare excepted) is based on rules of prudence (*Lectures and Notes on Shakespeare*, Bell's Edition, 1884, p. 191).

313 *Cf. supra*, p. 139.

314 *Hist. of Eng. Lit.*, Bk. III., chap. i. Mr. Meredith is nearer the mark when he speaks of the comic poet as being "in the narrow field, or enclosed square of the society he depicts" (*op. cit.*, p. 85).

315 *Op. cit.*, Bd. IV., s. 2.

316 See his "Notice" to *Gil Blas*, pp. xii, xiii.

317 *Hist. of Eng. Lit.*, vol. iv., p. 173.

318 *Op. cit.*, p. 240.

319 Quoted by Bacon, *Essays*, "Apothegms," 181.

320 This is well illustrated by George Eliot, who observes rightly that wit is allied to ratiocination (*Essays*, "German Wit," p. 81).

321 I remember discussing the point with the late Henry Sidgwick—no mean authority—who admitted that several quotations which he had proffered as examples of wit might with equal appropriateness he described as humorous. The germ of the view put forward in the text is contained in some pithy remarks by the late Professor Minto (*English Prose Literature*, Introduction, p. 23).

322 The reference in the text is to humour and wit, regarded as subjective, as elements in the writer. Considered objectively as an attribute of a character, wit of a kind may become one ingredient in a humorous presentation, as in the homely and rather borné wit of the countryfolk in the novels of George Eliot and Mr. Hardy.

323 See Mr. Traill's criticism, *Sterne*, p. 156 ff.

324 *Wit and Humour*, p. 11.

325 See Canon Ainger's Introduction to *The Essays of Elia*, p. 8.

326 *English Thought in the Eighteenth Century*, vol. ii., p. 110.

327 See my work on *Pessimism*, p. 428.

328 See Dugas, *op. cit.*, pp. 109, 110.

329 See, for an excellent example of this retort, Dr. James Ward's *Naturalism and Agnosticism*, vol. i., Part I.

330 M. Scherer may possibly mean something like this when he speaks of the humorist's point of view as the justest from which a man's world can be judged (*Essays on English Literature*, p. 148).

331 On the moral function of comedy see Bergson, *op. cit.*, pp. 201, 202, and Dugas, *op. cit.*, pp. 149–159.

332 The reference is to an article, "Ridicule and Truth" in the *Cornhill Magazine*, 1877, pp. 580–95. Lessing's plea, in his *Hamburg. Dramaturgie* (Stücke 28 and 29), on behalf of a corrective virtue in comedy owed something, I suspect, to the reading of Shaftesbury and the other English writers.

333 *Ethics*, Bk. x., 6.

334 *Sartor Resartus, loc. cit.*

335 *Letters*, vol. ii., p. 302.

336 See what Aristotle says about the witty (εὐτράπελοι, literally, the easy turning, nimble-minded), *Ethics,* Bk. iv., 8.

337 Mr. Radford, in an article on *Falstaff,* in Mr. Birrell's *Obiter dicta* (First Series).

338 *The Journal of Education,* Nov. 1901, p. 687.

339 Traill, *loc. cit.,* p. 147.

340 Mr. Radford, *loc. cit.*